A Different Kind of Sentinel

A Different Kind of Sentinel

The Strange Case of the United States vs FR Drury

Sir E. J. Drury II

℟
Rivendell Books
St. Louis

A Different Kind of Sentinel

Grateful acknowledgment is made to the following persons
for permission to reprint excerpts from their works:

THE WILDING OF AMERICA: MONEY, MAYHEM, AND THE NEW AMERICAN DREAM (4th Ed.), Charles Derber, Worth, COPYRIGHT © 2007 by Charles Derber

BLOWIN' IN THE WIND, Bob Dylan, COPYRIGHT © 1962 by Warner Bros. Music, Copyright renewed 1990 by Special Rider Music

HIGHWAY 61 REVISITED, Bob Dylan, COPYRIGHT © 1965 by Warner Bros. Music, Copyright renewed 1993 by Special Rider Music

MAGGIE'S FARM, Bob Dylan, COPYRIGHT © 1965 by Warner Bros. Music, Copyright renewed 1993 by Special Rider Music

GATES OF EDEN, Bob Dylan, COPYRIGHT © 1965 by Warner Bros. Music, Copyright renewed 1993 by Special Rider Music

BOB DYLAN'S 115TH DREAM, Bob Dylan, COPYRIGHT © 1965 by Warner Bros. Music, Copyright renewed 1993 by Special Rider Music

A HARD RAIN'S A-GONNA FALL, Bob Dylan, COPYRIGHT © 1963, by Warner Bros. Music, Copyright renewed 1991 by Special Rider Music

ALL RIGHTS RESERVED. INTERNATIONAL COPYRIGHT SECURED.
REPRINTED BY PERMISSION.

Published in the United States of America
By RIVENDELL BOOKS
PO Box 29348, St. Louis, MO 63126-0348

ALL RIGHTS RESERVED. FIFTH EDITION.
COPYRIGHT © 2016 by E. J. Drury II
Cover art by Carlo Crivelli
No part of this book may be reproduced or transmitted in any form or by any means, electronic or mechanical, including photocopying, recording, or by any information storage and retrieval system, without permission in writing from the author.

LIBRARY OF CONGRESS CONTROL NUMBER: 2007939447
ISBN: 978-0-9797023-5-8

To my two fathers,
Who knew war
And were destroyed by it,
As well as my two sons,
Arin and Jesse,
That they may never know war.

Contents

Preface ix

Part I: Awakening From the Big Sleep
1. A Story Unfolds 1
2. United States vs FR Drury 7
3. An Unwilling Fate 16

Part II: The Search For Soul
4. An Instinctive Response 37
5. A Voice in the Wilderness 56
6. A Test of Wills 75
7. Yankee Station 95
8. R & R .121
9. A Real Tour de Force 178
10. Paradise Lost 207
11. Paradise Regained 237

Notes 266
Images 267
Index 268

Preface

Having survived the war in Vietnam, without physical injury to himself, Sir E. J. Drury II *"had nonetheless incurred the deeper wounds of a house divided against itself."* As a child, had not he experienced his real father's schizophrenia and, later, his stepfather's alcoholism as war related, he may very well have written a different kind of story than *A Different Kind of Sentinel*.

For Sir E. J. gives to the imagination what Carl Jung gave to the world—via *Active Imagination* and the *Transcendent Function*—a reality *"that is just as accessible to one's faculties as the material world."*

From the first page of the book to the last, does the author slip so seamlessly from one world to the next, as if there were truly no distinction between the two. While standing, for example, in front of a mirror, one day, he sees an image of his soul, a woman *"standing opposite"* him in the mirror. Alarmed at first, he steps *"back from the mirror only to find himself being inexorably drawn back into her world through the smile on her face."* In the end, is he *"left standing in front of the mirror, smiling at an image of himself dressed as a white knight."*

And therein lies the whole story in a nutshell. For this remarkable story is as much about the author as it is about the soul and their eventual reunion. While he fears the white knight, she loves the White Knight *"above all else."* Where he longs to be free of his indenture to the beast, she longs to be free of her imprisonment in nature. *"I am the way,"* she boldly proclaims when he finally admits he is lost. And though the two suffer the same agonizing pain of separation from each other and their respective worlds, both seek the one person they are meant to become.

As a sailor then, does he reluctantly set off in search of she who must be obeyed if he is to overcome the beast that burdens him and the rest of humanity with self-destruction or destruction of the self.

"Whatever you do," is he forewarned by a fellow shipmate, "don't let them rob you of the most precious gift you have, your humanity, for the wraiths will claw away at it until all that remains is the shadow of what was once you." So must he, at all costs, resist the temptation of his fathers before him, *"to live out the visions of others rather than the one with which he had been entrusted at birth,"* a vision that eventually pits him against the Navy as he comes to a fuller understanding of the true meaning of military service.

Filled with many insights into the workings of the soul and the trinity, human sexuality and creativity, war and the beastly side of human nature, the book is intended for those intrepid souls who will venture to open its pages in search of what might free them from the clutches of the beast that threatens to destroy us all before we destroy our selves—the beast's only mode of operation.

October 17, 2015   Sir E. J. Drury II

Acknowledgments

To one of the holiest spirits I know, my wife, Valerie, do I owe the greatest gratitude, first, for giving me the room to write this book, and second, for providing me with such a fine example of the liaison between my self and my imagination. To Marty, Harold, Greg and Red, wherever they may be, am I forever indebted for their friendship when I needed it most. And I thank Jim Douglass for having introduced me to Walter and Betty Johnson, my lawyer Brook Hart—the party most responsible for planting the idea in my head to write this book—and all the other members of the Hawaii Resistance circa 1968, who helped me through those trying times with their love and support, both in body and in spirit. To my longtime friends Steve Maassen and Nancy Derton, as well as Cindy Fehmel and the other members of the LTD Tuesday night writer's group, am I grateful for their words of encouragement, when I felt nothing but rejection, and constructive criticism, which gave this book its final form. My hat goes off, too, to all those who had to work with me as I suffered through the vagaries of the melancholy mood that'd descend upon me as I wrestled with the creative spirit within, over the contents of the book. My heart goes out, as well, to my parents for the story of my life. And last but not least, I'd like to thank the Father, Son, and Holy Spirit—the party most responsible for the book—for the experiences of a lifetime and the courage to share them with you, the reader of this madcap escapade through the mind of one really crazy dude.

Part I

Awakening From the Big Sleep

1
A Story Unfolds

Towards the end of the summer of 1985, after having poured the foundation for our new home in the country, I was rudely awakened one night by an ominous dream—an all too familiar one in which the life I have been leading comes to an abrupt end. As I stand there, on the precipice of utter darkness, I am struck by the brilliance of the light that seems to emanate from deep within the dark side of my being.

"What are you going to do now?" Asks the source of this great light, in a voice that permeates my whole being.

Immediately, I wake up feeling as if I'm being called to do something else with my life. What, I don't find out until later that fall when I permanently injure my back on the job. No longer able to pursue my present livelihood as a carpenter, I begin the search for what I'm going to do with my life now.

When my old high school counselor suggests, in a dream, that I go into the electrical field instead of pursuing my latest whim to become a writer, I enroll in a training program for electricians at a local vocational school. Shortly thereafter, I begin to feel as if I've been led astray when, in yet another dream, I run into my own potential as a writer in the form of my dead brother, Scott.

Shocked, I ask him, "What the hell are you doing here?"

He replies, "I'm a writer."

"You're no writer," I contest.

"You're no carpenter either," he yells back as he disappears.

So did I awaken to the new direction my life seemed headed.

At the time, reality for me was a wife and a four-year-old son to support, besides a house note and other bills to pay. Confronted by the ever-worsening condition of my back and bank account as well, was I forced to see the folly in my choice to pursue a career as an electrician. Reluctantly, did I seek out the only work I could find—given my background in construction—as a building inspector.

A year at this job only seemed to bring me greater dissatisfaction, for building inspection simply did not meet my deeper emotional needs.

Left wondering if any job in today's market could meet my needs, I am dropped off, in a dream, on some deserted island in the South Pacific where I am confronted, one day, while musing over the possibility of returning to school—should I ever get out of this mess in one piece—by that same permeating voice.

"Why do you refuse to write?" It asks me.

Astonished, I wake up more convinced than ever that I should be writing instead of what I'm doing. Still I resist for some reason.

"Why are you so afraid to write?" Asks this same voice in yet another dream, later that fall.

Obviously, some fear was keeping me from writing then. Was it a lack of confidence in myself? Or was it a fear of where the writing might lead me?

Stymied for the time being, I stewed over the matter until the following summer when dissatisfaction with my job reached an all time high. With no other recourse, I finally turned to writing as I begin to keep a journal.

My first entry is a dream I have that night, in which I find my self scrambling to get away from the huge hound into whose backyard I have strayed. Having roused its master as well, in the ensuing commotion, I duck behind a car parked nearby, only to be confronted by the same truth that has been dogging me for some time now. Since the truth no longer poses such a threat, I finally get up enough nerve to stand up and introduce my self to the lady of the house before she exposes me for what I really am.

"Hi! I'm a sick writer," I proclaim as I cough up the half-digested body of a red and white frog, less the head and limbs, to prove it.

Alarmed by such behavior, she darts off to fetch the resident monk. Because she has finally taken an interest in someone outside herself, she is healed, along the way, of an infirmity that has afflicted her for many years.

I too dart off, but in the opposite direction. Ducking inside the door of a nearby blacksmith's shop, I find its smithy hard at work, pounding out a long slender piece of red-hot steel on his anvil. As my attention focuses elsewhere, I spy the woman and the monk standing opposite me near the rear of the shop. Having obviously set off all kinds of alarm bells within the monk as our eyes met, I finally wake up to what it is about me that he finds so alarming.

Alarmed by my inability to see what condition my condition is in, I wander off, one afternoon shortly thereafter, into an imaginary meadow where I catch sight of the most beautiful white horse, I have ever seen. As I pursue this fantasy further, I find my self flying across the meadow on the back of the white horse. I'm in heaven. Exhausted, I flop off the back of the horse to catch my breath. As it saunters off, I lay down in the grass to rest. When I spy the horse again, I see, riding upon its back, a white knight who strikes such fear into my heart, I am effectively jettisoned from this visual experience before I can get a closer look at him.

When, three days later, I find myself alone again, I manage to slip back into the vision where I'd left it. This time, I'm not so afraid of the white knight when I see him, for I realize that he and I are somehow connected. Called to appear before a very old man whose form, with the exception of his head, remains hidden from me, like the Wizard of Oz, within a thick swirling mass of wind and cloud, I am overcome by an incredible fear as I look beyond the long white hair and beard blowing wildly about the angry features of his face.

"Humble yourself before the Lord," commands that same permeating voice ere I can flee.

With that, I fall face down to the floor where I feel the Old Man's presence pass before me, over me and through me in one breath.

"Who are you?" I ask out of a need to hear it from the horse's own mouth.

"I Am Who Am." He responds in a way that only seems to further fuel the fear filling my frame.

"What do you want with me?" I inquire as my curiosity finally gets the best of me.

"As I have need of a good knight," He replies, "I have called you into my service."

"But Sir," I respond, "I am not a knight; besides, I would be of little use to One so powerful as You."

Having touched me upon the shoulder with the point of a red-hot sword, fresh from the forge, He says to me as the fire He has ignited within my heart consumes me, "I dub thee Sir Eodor, Knight Exemplar. Rise! And go forth as thy heart shall lead thee."

Rising to the occasion, I ask Him, "How am I to serve Thee, O Mighty One?"

Left standing beside that gallant white steed of mine in the guise of the white knight, with nigh a thought in mind, I hop onto the horse and gallop back into the darkness of my past. As I race back through the years, to an even darker period of my life, I realize that the blacksmith and the Old Man are the same person, like the white knight and me. Looking down at my side, I see that I have no sword, which concerns me at first, for what's a knight without a sword. Through a break in the clouds, I see an island below that reminds me, a lot, of the island of Oahu. As I enter that period of my life when I was in the Navy, some twenty or more years ago, I realize that I am to use my pen as a sword.

As the events of this story continue to unfold, I find my self back onboard my old ship, the USS Davidson, where I hear a voice that looms louder and louder, calling out my name. And as I'm pulled into this particular moment from my past, the fall of 1968—November 7 to be exact—I realize the master-at-arms is calling me.

"Drury!" He yells out. "Haven't you heard me callin' you?"

"Huh?" I reply as if I've just been awakened from a deep sleep.

"Come on!" He groans. "Or you'll be late."

I grab my hat lying before me on the table, a hat I have shaped into a square in mockery of the traditionally circular-fashioned hat worn by the enlisted man. As I begin to stare at my hat, to turn it round and round in my hands, I'm drawn elsewhere, deep within my being where I run into the monk again.

"Do not fear," he tells me, "for I will not harm you. I am an image of wisdom as you see it, one that veils my true form but suits you for now. I have come to you as your master, for you are to be my pupil. Ask of me whatever you wish to know of wisdom, and I will show you, with the exception of the future, which is not mine to reveal. For I can only help you understand the events in your life as they unfold.

"You have entered the realm of the Kingdom of God where you will encounter various forms to assist you on the journey on which you are about to embark—forms that are spiritual in nature and incapable of hurting you. For even you, as you stand here, do so only in the form of a spirit that, unlike the body, cannot be harmed.

"In the womb prior to your birth," he tells me before I can verbalize the questions that come pouring into my head, "you were programmed with everything you would need to know about the Kingdom of God and the life awaiting you. Despite your mother's efforts to spare you the pain Adam and Eve experienced at the moment of their expulsion from the garden, you were so traumatized by your descent from the womb, or fall from grace, that you forgot the way back. So were you born into the world without a clue as to how to access the information with which you had been programmed, until you reached the age of puberty and received a key to the Kingdom.

"Thus do you see the nature of the first birth and the need for the second. The second birth is that which Jesus alludes to in His conversation with Nicodemus, 'Truly, I say to you, unless one is born anew, he cannot see the Kingdom of God.' Jn. 3:3.

"To experience the second birth, you must leave behind the world as you know it, and enter the womb of your imagination. You must be willing to relive the trauma of the first birth—to endure the pain of becoming aware of Who You Really Are—to enjoy the fruits of this birth. But more importantly, you must overcome the fear you have of finding out who this person is, that lives and grows within you, like an only begotten son."

"Damn it, Drury! Let's go!" Yells the master-at-arms down through the hatch, causing the monk in me to vanish.

Startled back into the compartment space on the ship, I put on my hat and grab my statement—the script ghostwritten for the Old Man who needed my hand just as much as I needed His eloquent words of wisdom. Because I worried about what to say to other people, I had to plan every word I was going to say ahead of time—I needed a script; He needed a writer.

As I leave the compartment, I stop to take one last look into the mirror. As I laugh at the ill-fitting clothes on my body, which remind me of a monkey's suit instead of a uniform, I conclude that the service does not suit me well.

Then, in a flashback, I see the woman who had sought out the monk in me, standing opposite me in the mirror. Alarmed at first, I step back from the mirror, only to find my self being inexorably drawn back into her world through the smile on her face. Having just received the only affirmation a well-drawn conclusion needs, I reach out to her in the only way I know—with sword in hand. In my inability to give any more reality to her than this, am I left standing alone in front of the mirror, smiling at an image of my self dressed as the white knight.

Spinning around, I charge up the ladder and race down the passageway in a last-ditch effort to catch up with the master-at-arms before this last bit of reality, onto which I cling, ducks through a hatch on the starboard side of the ship and disappears without me. Coming up on his heels, I follow him at a brisk pace aft to the fantail where, in quick succession, he smartly salutes the flag and the officer of the deck before proceeding down the gangplank. As I leave the ship, I give them both a halfhearted salute that resembles more the greeting of some lady than it does a military salute. For today, I'm on my way to meet Lady Liberty—to seek a discharge from the Navy.

As I walk beside the master-at-arms to the administrative building, I hear the voice of the monk inside my head giving me some last minute instructions.

"When you are brought before the authorities," he tells me, "do not worry about how to defend yourself or what to say, for I will show you all that you need to tell them.

"Above all," continues the monk, "you must write. You don't need to understand everything, right now. You must have faith in the process of writing, for the story will reveal the knowledge you seek. You must enter the story and forget about analyzing it, as it will analyze itself, in due time. Since the answers that you seek, lay hidden deep within you, within the various parts of you that you will encounter, you must not be afraid to talk to them or hear them out. No matter how crude their ideas may seem, take what they give you, and let the oyster in you shape the grit into a pearl of great price."

"How do I know," I interrupt, "that you are not some cruel hoax or misleading figment of my imagination?"

He laughs. "You do not know now; but you will know by the time you have completed this story. Trust me."

"Why should I?" Asks this recalcitrant self of mine.

"Because," he replies, "you have your soul to free and heaven to gain. Write! You must write," he repeats as his voice fades away.

"Write," I mutter to myself.

"That's right," comes back the echo of his voice from somewhere across the great void that still separated me from who I really am.

With that, I laugh aloud, thus evoking the strangest look from the master-at-arms as we enter the ADMIN building.

2

United States vs FR Drury

Inside, I fall prey to another fantasy, as my thoughts drift back to the first time I wondered why the Lord of Darkness had fought so hard to keep me in the dark about this island of mine. If left alone long enough, I would invariably get sucked into the fight as the forces of darkness rose up against me to inundate me with their lies. So would I lose sight of who I really am until I reemerged from this latest flood of images with some heretofore-unrecognized truth about myself. Unchallenged, I would never have taken the plunge into this two-dimensional, holographic world of his to free my soul from her imprisonment in nature. Nor would I have ever gotten to the bottom of the matter of the United States versus Fireman Recruit Drury.

"You are late," booms a voice from out across the threshold of consciousness, as I step forth from the looking-glass world of my soul to greet the only defense I have, a legal adviser of my own ilk willing to take on Uncle Sam's lieutenants for the sake of the soul alone.

"Have you rewritten your statement?" He asks as I enter the courtroom to be judged, this time around, on the grounds of my own being instead of theirs.

"I have," I respond with a big grin, "to more accurately reflect what has taken place inside me over the past two years."

"Good," he replies.

With that, in bursts the recorder—or lawyer for the Navy—like a steam engine from the judge's chamber. As the five officers, who will decide my fate, file past him like empty boxcars, to take up their predisposed positions on this lonesome freight, he commands the real E. J. Drury to stand up.

Not until the only ear on the whole train, the court reporter in the caboose, has set up to record all this gibberish, am I told to be seated by the senior member of the board, a throwback to prehistoric times named Fitzgibbons.

As he swings from one limb to another in my mind's eye, like some great tailless ape does he convene the hearing.

SENIOR MEMBER: *This hearing will come to order. This hearing convened in the General Court Martial Room of the Commandant, Fourteenth Naval District, U.S. Naval Station, Pearl Harbor, Hawaii, in accordance with the Commanding Officer, USS Goldsborough DDG-20, appointing order serial 603 dated 4 November 1968. The appointed members of the board are all present.*
The board convened at 0927 hours, 7 November 1968.
Fireman Recruit Drury is the respondent in this hearing and shall be referred to as such throughout these proceedings.
Mr. Brook Hart will represent the respondent.

As this great ape swung past the court reporter to introduce us all to the recorder, another tailless ape of less rank, named Gleason, I fell victim to my own thoughts about my defense.

An attorney admitted to practice before the Bar of New York and Hawaii, this young and impeccably dressed upstart had been retained by the Hawaii Resistance to defend me, one among a growing clientele of young revolutionaries refusing to cooperate with either the military or the draft. Even though he had not evolved that far, he adamantly defended those who like myself had. For he still believed that the legal system protected the rights of those who oppose all military service, or at least afforded redress when these rights were trampled upon by the old evolutionary order. Because he believed that the law could change the attitudes of these Neanderthals, that courtroom drama could transform their hearts, he was forever encouraging me to operate within the framework of the law.

But I had problems with his approach. For I had found that two very different levels of law exist in life, and that these two are often at odds with each other, because the one had been fashioned by imperfect hands, the other by God, to show us how to act as human beings, should we ever get there. So does the higher law, in its watered-down state, struggle to get out from underneath this contamination by the darker side of human nature. Like the pieces of an island submerged below the surface of the water does the higher law remain hidden behind the man-made law, in the shadows of human ignorance until some individual dives deep enough below the surface to retrieve it.

Most people, who live on the surface, tend to move in the direction of the man-made law, against the individual caught up in the undercurrent created by the higher law. Because these people lead surface lives, they believe only what they see on the surface. They disbelieve the higher law when the individual brings it to the surface. Those who look at reality, with the eyes and mentality of the surface only, are quick to denounce the higher law as preposterous. Clinging to the man-made law, they try to discredit the individual, to punish him or to eliminate him by imprisonment or execution. They display a low level of tolerance for the individual who stands upto the current on the surface, for they don't want to see their own darkness.

So do those who are guilty of the real crime, the transgression of the hidden but perfect higher law, find the individual who obeys the higher law guilty of an obvious crime, the transgression of an imperfect man-made law. The individual is then made to pay a great price for his transgression, by the people on the surface who, at first, appear to go scot-free in the face of their transgression but, in the end, pay an even greater price than the individual does.

As I begin to wonder what effect, if any, I will have on these Neanderthals today, I am pulled back into this charade by way of an inquiry from the leader of this pack of tailless apes.

SENIOR MEMBER: *Are there any questions as to the proceedings of the board concerning the rights of the respondent?*

MR. HART: *No questions, other than I understand that we have the right to ask certain questions of the members of the board to determine whether they may or may not have a predetermined opinion about what should be done with the respondent in this case.*

SENIOR MEMBER: *Yes, that's right. Do you wish to question any members of the board concerning their qualifications?*

MR. HART: *Yes, I would.*

Questions by Counsel:
Q. *Mr. Fitzgibbons, how long have you been in the Navy?*
A. *Eleven and a half years, sir.*
Q. *Have you ever served on an administrative board before?*
A. *Yes, I have.*
Q. *Could you estimate how many?*
A. *Two.*
Q. *Have you ever served on a court-martial board?*
A. *Yes, I have.*
Q. *Would you estimate how many?*
A. *About twenty.*
Q. *Now, have you ever had any occasion, in the course of your eleven and a half years of service, to have contact with any naval personnel who opposed military service?*

A. No, sir.

Q. Do you have any prior knowledge as to the regulations pertaining to the processing of such an individual?

A. Nothing specific, only the general background which every naval officer, you might say, should have.

Q. Could you describe briefly for me, what that background is?

A. While I am aware that there are procedures recently revised by the Department of Defense, to afford any member of the naval service the right to refuse military service if he understands the true meaning of military service, and that there are certain formal procedures that should be followed in these cases, I am not familiar with the details.

Q. Now, Mr. Fitzgibbons, do you have any personal feelings about a man who would refuse to kill those he has been ordered to kill?

A. No, sir.

Q. If the evidence were to show that Drury has refused to take part in the killing of other human beings as a fact, which was his reason for having been involved in certain matters, you would have no prior opinion of his refusal to kill on another's command?

A. No, sir. If I may point out, as far as any individual refusing to take part in the killing of other human beings, I stand firm in my own personal opinion that every individual has the right to refuse. As far as a prior notion, I have no preconceived notion one way or the other. I think I will have to analyze the facts and the arguments as they come up, before I am sure of what I am talking about.

Q. Now, do you know what ship Mr. Drury served on?

A. I am aware that he was transferred to the USS Goldsborough from the Davidson, but I know little else of his previous record or length of service on the Davidson.

Q. Do you know anybody on the Davidson?

A. Not personally—no, sir.

In like manner were the other members of the board grilled. Having neither seen nor heard nor spoken anything that might prejudice themselves against the Daniel, who did so vociferously object to their way of life, did all but the last of these great tailless apes step forth, unscathed, from the fiery furnace into which they had been cast by that Nebuchadnezzar lawyer of mine. For it seemed that the last of this breed of warmongering apes had actually had contact with someone on my old ship, the USS Davidson. But he too failed to cough up anything more significant than this half-digested tidbit, as he finished testifying in the same monkey-see, monkey-do fashion of those who had testified before him.

MR. HART: *I have no further questions; and I have no challenges for cause.*
SENIOR MEMBER: *Does the recorder wish to challenge any of the members of the board for cause?*
RECORDER: *The recorder does not.*
SENIOR MEMBER: *The recorder may now present his case.*
RECORDER: *Gentlemen of the board, FR Drury is before us today because of his repeated violations of military law. I would like to submit to you a brief concerning his conduct during the past two years; and I would like to introduce these exhibits now. They are contained in the green folders in front of you.*

As they all pawed over the papers in front of them, with the hairy hands of the hideous Hyde that resided within the shallow graves of everyone of these Jekylls in disguise, I winced at the mere mention that I am entitled to wear the National Defense Service Medal, the Vietnam Service Medal with bronze star, and the Republic of Vietnam Campaign Bar for my contribution to the war in Vietnam. However, I got a little boost in self-esteem when I learned that I'd been assigned, according to the recorder, a 2.6 out of a possible 4.0 for military performance, appearance, and adaptability, and a mere 1.0 for military behavior, because I had disobeyed orders and had flaunted all authority. Unbeknownst to me at the time, I was only trying to tell them, by my behavior, that I wanted no part in the war being waged against the people of Vietnam. In fact, I felt downright proud of myself as he read off the long list of NJPs, Nonjudicial Punishments or Captain's Masts, and court-martials to which I had been subjected for my noncooperation, as it further bolstered how far I was willing to go to limit my participation in something as abhorrent to me as the war in Vietnam.

My bubble was pricked when this Hyde lit into my clinical records with the relish of a raptor on his face, the signal for which the leader of this vulturous pack of meat-eating apes seemed to have been waiting.

SENIOR MEMBER: *Before you proceed, the board would like to look over these psychological evaluations so that we may properly consider them in the context of the chronology of events in this case. If the recorder will stand by, we will familiarize ourselves with the contents of these documents; and if we have any questions, we will ask them before we proceed any further.*

I was concerned about how the board would view these psychological evaluations of me, how much weight each member would give these reports. I disliked the senior member's eagerness to focus on them before I had the chance to proffer their contents. I felt violated by these men, who appeared much too eager to claw away at the worst secrets of my soul, like vultures over a carcass, in search of the heart of this case, as determined by experts.

On the one hand, the evaluations seemed to reveal too much—the secret torments of my soul—the problem I had with accepting my sexuality and with adjusting not only to military life but also to life in general. On the other hand, the reports actually exposed very little, only the symptoms—the tip of the iceberg, as it were, of the far more serious sickness of being dangerously out of touch with my soul.

In the report, dated 19 February 1968, the psychiatrist who had interviewed me accused me of being *"an immature young man who is chronically rebelling against society, and who has no insight into his provocativeness."* He claimed, *"I provoked the environment into retaliating against me as a way to explain my depression, that my depression had deeper roots than my current problems, and that my behavior helped me to look on current problems as an explanation for my difficulties rather than to look into myself and my past."* He diagnosed me as a schizoid and emotionally unstable personality with passive aggressive tendencies.

I was troubled by his observations. From the very beginning of my term of enlistment, I sensed that I had made a terrible mistake, and that I had to do whatever to get out of the Navy. Only later, did I learn the identity of my provocateur as my soul with her unwavering opposition to military service and war in general.

As I stumbled along under the weight of my own cross, overtime I found that I could lighten my load if only I would succumb to the urgings of my soul, to rise up against the Navy and the war in Vietnam instead of her and this house of mine, divided as it were against its self. Only then, would I experience the inner peace and joy so lacking in my life when I broke down and cooperated with the Navy, or pursued my own course of action, or caved into the desires of my animal nature. Such behavior generally left me feeling so unstable—or emotionally unattached to what the Navy wanted me to do—and depressed, that I often bit back at my captor to relieve my anguish.

In the last psychological evaluation, I underwent on 27 September 1968, another psychiatrist wrote: *"This man still manifests emotional instability and a great deal of passive-aggressive rebellion to authority figures, in his opposition to military service. In explaining his position, he speaks in grandiose generalities, often in conflict with one another, and shows much confusion and stretching of facts to conform to his own philosophical system. I find no evidence of any true religious or moral opposition to his participation in the killing of other human beings, but feel that his assertions are based upon his previous diagnosis of emotional instability and passive aggression. That diagnosis is still valid. I recommend, as was recommended before, that this man be considered for administrative separation for unsuitability, on the basis of his established psychiatric diagnosis."*

In the same breath that these wolves in sheep's clothing had accused me of having no insight into myself, they as much as admitted to their lack of insight into the problems of human sexuality and war. When they claimed I stretched the facts to conform to my own philosophical system, they admitted to their own stretching of the truth, which they saw as grandiose generalities in conflict with their own perceptions of reality. Diagnoses, such as schizoid or emotionally unstable or passive aggressive, only showed their split from soul in the choice to pursue a military career—literally exposed the instability of their own position, built on the sands of half-truths and lies—and exhibited their own passive aggressive tendencies to denigrate me and my opposition to military service and war in general. After all, they're the ones who had sown the seeds of my rebellion. Clearly, these so-called doctors of the soul were not out to help me as much as they were out to hinder me. They couldn't help me, for not one of them had anything more positive to offer than the lifeless responses of the dead men who, in pioneering the field of psychology, had barely touched upon the true nature of the soul. Having never entered their own beings to search for the truth of themselves, they feared and attacked the truth instead.

The onus was on me now, to venture where they dared not tread, to stumble through the darkest recesses of my being, in search of the hidden pieces to the puzzling problems of my existence, that I might convey a more complete picture of myself to the members of the board, and explain to them the events of the past two years of my life.

SENIOR MEMBER: *Very well, let us continue.*
RECORDER: *Gentlemen, you are here to decide, on the basis of the information before you, and of the information that Drury will submit, if Drury should be retained in the U. S. Navy or discharged, and if so, what type of discharge he should receive. You are not here to decide how or why Drury violated the UCMJ, nor are you here to decide if he was right in doing so. You are not here to pass judgment on his reasons nor on his convictions. But you must reach the decision, retention or discharge. Now perhaps Drury or his counsel will present witnesses testifying to the sincerity of Drury's character, or try to justify his misbehavior. This is not the question here.*

Gentlemen, if Drury were being tried in a court of law this may be proper in extenuation or mitigation. The offense has been committed—the guilt has already been decided—and there is no use arguing the point. We must presume that Drury knew full well when he committed these offenses that he did so in violation of the very Code under which we all live and work. He also knew that for these acts or omissions he would be punished. Whether or not Drury had reason to commit these offenses has no bearing whatsoever on this board's decision. The facts are clear.

There is no issue clouding them. Drury knew full well what he was doing; and now the piper has to be paid.

SENIOR MEMBER: *Does counsel for the respondent wish to make a statement?*

MR. HART: *Yes, I do. Quite respectfully, I would disagree with the statement made to the board by the recorder. By way of agreement, I would say that Drury has been the subject of judicial proceedings throughout his career in the Navy. However, our only consideration here is whether or not Drury is to be retained in the Navy, not whether he has been convicted or not. What is relevant are the circumstances surrounding these violations. If they are not relevant, we can all pack up and go home. For if it were not relevant that these circumstances be brought to you, there would be no point in having this proceeding.*

Drury's position is not that he is here to justify what he did. You may find there are some things he was charged here with, for which he was ultimately acquitted. You will also find there are circumstances you will want to seriously consider in your determination of what you are going to want to do with him.

You have two choices before you, retention or discharge. If it is the latter, you have a number of other choices. And those choices go to the type of discharge he will receive. For the type of discharge, which one receives from the military, stays with him for the rest of his life. The reason for that is that certain types of discharge operate as a kind of punishment in civilian life. It affects the nature of a job he might hold, the attitude of those who may deal with him. It affects the possibility of his going back to school. All of these are important. Now, if you do decide for a discharge, first you have to determine what kind of discharge. And there are going to be mainly two tests. One of them is probably quite apparent to you, and that is the nature of this man's psychological evaluations, as evidenced by the reports of the doctors you have before you. As board members, you will consider, in your own good faith, whether that evidence should be taken under consideration in your determination of the type of discharge this man should receive. On the other hand, I think the evidence will show that Mr. Drury is a sincere and trustworthy person, and that his actions can be characterized only as immature in the case of some of the acts. So what kind of discharge is proper, that this man should have to carry with him through his adult life—a dishonorable or an undesirable discharge?

Perhaps you might consider a general discharge under other than honorable conditions, or a general discharge under honorable conditions. Here is a man who has been in the brig; he has done extra duty and been busted. He is not here to pay the piper as Mr. Gleason suggested earlier. You are here to determine the type of discharge with which he will have to go out into civilian life, to make his way...

...At this time, counsel for the respondent would like to call FR Drury to the stand. The respondent wishes to testify in his own behalf—to read a statement,

which he has composed for the board, respond to direct questioning with respect to his conduct in the Navy, and to be available for what, I hope, will be a thorough and extensive examination by both the recorder and the members of the board.

The more I thought about it, the more I realized that this hearing was about the transgressions of these men as well—their transgressions of soul or blasphemes of the Holy Spirit that will never be forgiven—their transgressions of the laws of the jungle that were written in our hearts, long ago, forbidding us to kill any member of our own species. And the deeper I dove, the more I realized how much this hearing was about judgment too—how those, who would judge me today, will indeed judge themselves in the end—how those who have failed to evolve, emotionally, beyond the level of a warmongering animal, will judge their own humanity.

3

An Unwilling Fate

RECORDER: *Raise your right hand. Do you swear to tell the truth, the whole truth and nothing but the truth, so help you God?*
RESPONDENT: *I do.*
RECORDER: *You may be seated.*
MR. HART: *FR Drury, you are the respondent here today, are you not?*
RESPONDENT: *Yes, I am.*
MR. HART: *And you desire to make a sworn statement to this board?*
RESPONDENT: *Yes, I do.*
MR. HART: *Before I ask you to read your statement to the board, I am going to ask you a few preliminary questions. When did you go on active duty?*
RESPONDENT: *I came on active duty 5 February 1967.*
MR. HART: *Preceding your entry into the Navy, what circumstances in your life led up to your coming on active duty?*
RESPONDENT: *My entry into the Navy was a bit unusual. It all began one evening while my family and I were seated at the dining room table for dinner. [Actually, it all began when the monk in me started showing me flashbacks of my past, this time from his point of view.] As I recall, my stepdad had just broken the usual mealtime silence with a cough, then a sputter as he almost choked to death on his own words before he could spit them out. You see, besides being a heavy smoker, my stepdad was also an ailing alcoholic. Seldom sober by dinnertime, he had limited his abuse, in the past, to angry verbal outbursts that had gone unchallenged out of our fear of his physical prowess. Only recently, as the disease progressed, had he begun to display random acts of physical violence. On one such occasion, in front of guests at the dinner table, had he backhanded my mother across the mouth after she had said something that had upset him. So had we, as a matter of*

self-preservation, learned to keep our mouths shut, or if accosted, to measure carefully our responses.

"Your mother and I have been talking," he began, which generally meant that he had done the talking, my mother the listening. "We have decided to send you to the Naval Academy for your college education," inflicted he the wound that never heals. "We feel the academy will provide you with the finest education money can buy, only at the expense of the federal government instead of your mother and me," gloated he who had so hoped to spare me his pain. "I have already contacted our congressman, Tom Curtis, for the appointment..."

In the anguish of my own soul, I grew deaf to whatever else he had to say, for I knew my fate had been sealed. Talking to him about what I might want was futile. In the past, whenever I had requested to speak to him concerning some matter of importance to me, he had simply put me off until he had gotten so drunk, he could barely talk, much less listen to me, without passing out. Nor could I turn to my mother who, long ago, had already betrayed my trust in her by siding with my stepfather, in domestic quarrels, instead of me when I was right. Nor could I count on my brothers or my sister who, in retaliation for something I had done to one of them, might blurt out to my stepfather my best-kept secrets. You see, my stepfather was such a tyrant that I didn't want to infuriate him, in any way, by letting him know that I might be opposed to his plans for me.

In his eyes, he could do no wrong, even though he was often dead wrong in the eyes of the rest of us. In fact, he frequently boasted that he and Christ were the only perfect people ever created. He was unapproachable, totally unwilling to listen to the viewpoint of another, or to allow us to touch him with expressions of physical affection. And except for bedroom encounters with my mother, he showed very little affection towards us. As an ex-serviceman, he identified more with the macho image of the marines he had fought beside in the South Pacific during World War II, than he did with the image of the Navy corpsman he had actually been. He continually bragged about how strong he was—how he could crush our skulls with one hand, if he wanted to. He even boasted that he could kill a man with his bare hands, which had already squeezed life from the young men he faced in combat during WWII. As evidence, he kept in the garage a box filled with the bloody uniform and flag, glasses and several gold teeth of one of his victims, a dead Japanese soldier. Periodically, he even threatened to kill mom if she ever tried to leave him. He instilled in us fear and contempt for him, rather than love and respect. In his inability to accept me as I was, he strove to make me into something he wanted me to be, something he had failed to attain for himself but now sought vicariously through me.

On the other hand, he did possess a few, more admirable qualities, even though his tyranny tainted these too. Having always provided us with what little food and clothing we needed, and a roof over our heads, he once told me that was all he had to do when I confronted him about how little time he spent with us. For he seemed to have a better relationship with the neighborhood toughs—parodies of the youth he never outgrew—than he did with us. Having bought what few friends he did have, he failed to buy his way into our hearts with all of his bravado. Instead, he scared us off. He was so totally incapable of relating to us in any other way but this macho-man style of his, that it was difficult for us as children to see the tenderness, my mother saw in him, beneath all the callousness of the mask he had donned, so long ago, as a child in the service of his country.

While he was quite enamored by the images of the manhood he had acquired in the military, they also haunted him. Many a night was he awakened in his torment by the images of combat from his past, and forced to relive them in his dreams. In his sleep, he would shout out the vivid detail and horror of his experiences, until Mom roused him from his nightmare. Obviously, he was tormented during the day too, by these haunting memories, as evidenced by the incredible amount of alcohol he consumed, to numb the terrible pain they must have caused him. Alas, he suffered a life of quiet desperation and utter loneliness.

In her fear of him, my mom conceded to his tyranny. Having gone back to work to escape the worsening situation at home, as well as to empower what little sense of herself she had left, for a while, she engaged in drinking with him at the tavern, to the point of becoming inebriated. Embittered by the lack of a relationship with him on any other terms than his own, she scapegoated her frustration onto her children, those weaker than herself. She not only failed to protect us from his tyranny, but also committed the almost unpardonable sin of going over to his side, against her own flesh and blood.

What did we do? We escaped into those areas of our lives where we found some sense of well-being and empowerment. Scott and I propelled ourselves to the tops of our respective classes, with straight A's. For a while, I was tied for first, then second, at the top of my class. While my sister proceeded to win many honors in sports, my youngest brother excelled as an automobile mechanic. Essentially, we all escaped from the pain of relationships, to the painlessness of work.

Only, I found little in the pursuit of intellectual excellence to ease the pain that had crept into my life because of the continual emotional abuse and betrayal I experienced at home. Instead, I found more pain creeping into my life as I distanced myself from adverse conditions at home, the rest of my family and friends. And with the onset of puberty, I experienced a greater increase in the amount of hurt I was feeling when I started abusing my self as well.

With a tremendous feeling of guilt now hanging from my neck like a great millstone, I fell into that maddening rift between body and mind, from which no one could help me escape. By asking me to make a more concerted effort to avoid this occasion with sin, the priests I saw in the confessional only increased my sense of guilt, as will power alone was no match for the unholy desires that had taken possession of my body. Even the psychiatrist, I was sent to, offered little comfort. In the only response, he made during the brief session I had with him, he merely said, "You'll work it out." When I related the matter to my old high school counselor in the form of a tale in which I had been responsible for the drowning death and disappearance of a little girl, she too was unable to unravel the mystery of my situation. Even God, Whom I prayed to unceasingly concerning this thorn in my side, afforded me little relief than a glimmer of hope that the solution did indeed lie hidden out there, somewhere within the quagmire of my life.

For now, I had no idea what direction my life should take. I feared everyone and every situation over which I had no control. I no longer knew how to relate to people or enjoy myself, or how to play with others, which left my life feeling dry and empty, like a wasteland. I felt as if I had gotten lost in a howling desert, in search of the oasis in which I might find the life-giving waters to quench the terrible thirst that self-indulgence could never satisfy.

At the same time, I found my classes no longer satisfied this gnawing passion either. Because they offered nothing in the way of bringing the fire that raged within me under control, I quit going to some of them during my last year in high school. Instead, I spent time in the library reading only those books to which I had been drawn, for some unknown reason.

Then, one day, it happened. From one such book, Einstein's Theory of Relativity, I discovered a whole new perspective on life, that the true nature of reality lies within our grasp of space and time. I learned that another reality much closer to the truth lies hidden behind what we merely perceive with our eyes as reality, that all of man's perceptions of the world around him, in other words, are relative to the eye of the beholder. Radicalized by this latest insight, I decided to take a new tack on life, to confront what is held to be self-evident when such evidence proved to contradict the truth of my being, that I might lift from my shoulders the meaninglessness that weighed them down.

I began by confronting my English teacher. Of the small faction of dissatisfied students, I was the only one to confront her as we had all planned to do. Where she had us memorizing passage after passage of Shakespeare, in preparation for our entrance into college, the following year, I believed that honing up on our writing skills would better prepare us for what lay ahead. While the old southern spinster argued from her many years of experience as an English teacher, I stood behind my gut feeling as to what would help me succeed. The upshot of it all was that I flat out refused to memorize another line of Shakespeare, forcing the incorrigible old maid to drop my grades, so that I fell in rank to third place out of 356 students by the time I graduated.

Then I began to confront myself around my isolationism, now seeing it as part of the self-destructive pattern that helped to perpetuate the conflicts ripping me apart. While I struggled to rekindle relationships with old friends, I attempted to make new ones as well. Because I never quite fit in with any one group—the brains, the jocks, or the John Does—I remained troubled throughout high school by my apparent inability to relate well with others.

In retrospect, I am not so sure the problem I had, in trying to find someone to bare my soul to, was just my own. At first, I wondered if I had somehow acquired my fathers' inability to relate well with others. Then I wondered if my troubles with real relationship were not a part of some greater problem of the people in my social milieu, who seemed to have difficulty relating to each other on any other level than a superficial one. And since no one ever talked about the real problems affecting his or her life, I felt as if I was the only one drowning in his own personal pain and suffering.

That's when I became interested in women; for I saw in them something I desired, but could not put my finger on, yet. Was I seeking that one special relationship with whoever would bear my soul? Or was I looking for a better relationship with my soul? I wasn't sure, because one was just as painful an experience as the other was.

I'll never forget when one of Cupid's arrows pierced my heart with a crush for Bunny Early....

RECORDER: *I fail to see the significance of this line of testimony.*
MR. HART: *If the board will bear with the testimony of the respondent, its members will get a psychological portrait of this young man, one yet untouched by the opinions or prejudices of psychiatric experts, with which to form their own conclusions about his character.*
SENIOR MEMBER: *Very well, you may proceed.*

RESPONDENT: Except in my own mind, a relationship between us never materialized because I could never summon up the courage, as a junior in high school, to ask out a senior. Anyway, she graduated that year and left school, which effectively ended any chance I had at making a stab at a romantic relationship with her.

The following spring, I fell madly in love again, this time with a classmate named Cheri Nichols. Even though we dated occasionally, I still had trouble communicating with her. I was either too self-conscious of my misperceived inability to relate well with others, or too preoccupied with keeping the lid on my sexual feelings. I tried to befriend her, but failed miserably, as if she weren't meant for me. At the time, I could not see beyond my own muddled confusion, clearly enough to perceive the true nature of the relationship. Instead, I clung onto it as if my life depended upon her.

One night, when I came home late from a date with her, I remember my stepdad, in a drunken stupor, accusing me of "screwing around with that Nichols' girl again". I was deeply hurt by his insinuation because it was so untrue in reality, and yet uncannily true on the level of my imagination, as I recalled struggling, with great difficulty, to control my desires to have sex with her. In spite of how I felt, I had been challenged by my fear of disobeying the sixth commandment, and of getting her pregnant, to maintain a chaste relationship with her. I needed to find out if there was anymore to what I was feeling for her than pure sexual desire. For the time being, I was madly in love with her.

Because I felt so separated from her, whether I was with her or not, I hurt terribly inside. Filled with this pain of separation from others, I felt like an island entirely unto itself. As I struggled in vain to distance myself from my sexual feelings, I longed for the carefree and painless days of the childhood nature had taken away from me in puberty. If my present life was a taste of adulthood, then I did not want to grow up. I did not like hurting all the time, or having so little control over myself.

As the school year ended, I was accepted at the academy. While I wasn't that excited about my appointment, I acquiesced for lack of anything better to do. Besides, I had become a big attraction as the only student from my high school, at the time, to have garnered an appointment to the U. S. Naval Academy. I thrived on the attention, which seemed to ease somewhat, the pain of separation I felt. By the end of June 1965, I found myself unhappily alone again, on a Greyhound bus bound for Annapolis, Maryland.

Only, I found the trip to be a very unsettling one. When, after an hour or two out of St. Louis, the clouds of a dark and somber mood overtook me, I grew afraid of the psychic storm brewing within me. As a vicious whirlwind of self-abuse swept over me, I watched it destroy what little serenity the countryside had afforded me as the bus zigzagged its way eastward. While my true nature rose up in angry opposition to the direction my life had taken, I was overcome by the irrational fear that I might have inherited the tendency for my real father's schizophrenia.

You see, my real father had been hospitalized when I was about three years old, after he had grown increasingly incapable of functioning in everyday life, and had so withdrawn from the world around him. In fact, his personality had disintegrated to such an extent, he could no longer take care of himself, hold down a job or communicate with his family and friends coherently. As his responses to the daily demands of life grew increasingly more violent, he was eventually taken away by the police, and incarcerated in the VA hospital at Jefferson Barracks, until I was almost eleven years old.

Around the time my mother divorced him and married my stepfather, he was released to the custody of his mother, who began to demand visitation rights for him, with his children. Having had very little contact with him since his incarceration, we looked forward to periodic visits with him until grandma and my Uncle Irvin started talking about taking us away from my mother, and placing us in the custody of my real father. On one such occasion, they even claimed to have hired a lawyer to get us back. Well, Dad was certainly in no condition to take on the responsibility of raising three young children. Why, he could barely stay coherent, an hour or two into our visit with him, much less hold down a job to support us. Nor was my grandmother any better off as she, who was aged and physically ailing, lived on the disability pension my father received from the Veterans Administration. Alarmed by such unrealistic plans, I insisted that they take us home, immediately; or I would call a cab. Once home, I refused to ever go back over to see my dad, for no one was going to take me away from my mother.

Now, nine years later, as I sat staring out the window of a bus, I worried that I might be losing my own sanity. I felt so utterly incapable of controlling myself, that I wondered how long I could endure the pain of the ever-widening rift between the visible life of an accomplished student and the hidden one of a hound always on the prowl. Was I doomed to fall through this crack into some frightful fantasy world, never to return, like my real father before me? Or was I condemned to straddle this bottomless pit as Dr. Jekyll/Mr. Hyde, until I was consumed with the evil of Hyde and had to be destroyed?

I blamed my obsession with self-gratification as the source of my unhappiness. I didn't want to abuse myself and yet I did, as this irresistible persistent impulse welled up from deep within this split in my personality, like hot magma from a volcanic rift in the earth. I had no idea of the origin of this impulse, other than some vague notion that it was caused by an incredible buildup of tension from deep within, to create a new life for myself. Afterward, guilt and the fear of eternal damnation always drove me humiliatingly back to the confessional for absolution. While I felt better spiritually, I now craved the satisfaction it had stirred up but ultimately failed to fulfill. By the time I was able to quell the impulse, I found myself battling the rapid rise in tension again.

In the cold war that ensued between the animal passions of my lower nature and the higher aspirations of the intellect, I erected a psychological barrier, or Berlin Wall of sorts, at the waist to stem the foul flow of fiendishness from that vast sea of unconsciousness to the south. As the wilder side of my nature rose up from across these waters—in an endless cycle of storms that easily penetrated the civilized veneer behind which I hid—to inflame the passion of my body for union with soul, I could do nothing to stop it. From time to time, then, would I be forced to go with the flow wherever it might take me.

While I struggled to keep my head above water at the swearing-in, on my first day at the academy, I was seized by a strong undercurrent from which the only way I could extricate myself, without drowning, was to act immediately upon the image that had just presented itself to me as I was being sucked down into the netherworld. With my body's repudiation of the oath to defend the United States of America under any pretext, I quickly found my self standing on dry land with the other guys, only this time, on a very different level of reality. Having looked to the horizons of my imagination for a way out of this desert, I saw nothing but an endless stretch of searing heat and sand, as I trudged off with the others in search of my fate.

As the sands of time swirled about me, it wasn't long before I found myself in a whirl of trouble. To keep myself from choking on all the sand that was being shoved down my throat by the upperclassmen who hovered over me, like dust devils that refused to budge, I had only to live out the image that had presented itself to me as an oasis from this desert storm. And so did I begin to passively resist the memorization and recitation, on command, of the most absurd trivia from a silly little book called Reef Points, which every plebe was required to carry around in his belt, at all times.

In response to Nature's call to mimic her, as she made a mockery of their version of reality, I quickly moved onto other things, like mischievously marching out of step and intentionally holding my piece askew during reviews. Because her revues were so much more entertaining, I had a hard time wiping the smile off my face, or erasing the mirth from my heart, upon command, which only seemed to infuriate them even more. In having assumed the role of a satyr, I found great joy in satirizing their theatrical productions—the sort of joy Paul speaks of in the epistles when Peter and he were mistreated for their Satyagraha, or passive resistance of the old evolutionary order.

Not until later that fall, did I wake up to the truth when the vehicle, that had been driving my imagination wild, crossed over the line, in a class on ethics, and crashed, head-on, into the bandwagon onto which the others had hopped out of ignorance. Having finally broken through the barrier that separates this world from the next, I about died when I realized I could never order a subordinate to do what I could never do, to ruthlessly take the life of another human being for my own. Thus, did I awaken from this near-death experience aware, for the first time, that I did not belong here.

Obviously distressed by the categorical imperative that had just risen from the dead, was I sent to see the psychiatrist in residence. I began by telling him how much trouble I was having, trying to control my desires for union with soul on the physical plane. I was startled when he asked me why I was afraid to tell him I no longer wished to attend the academy. I laughed—his words were so freeing. I didn't know I could leave like that, whereupon he terminated the interview with a written recommendation that I be released from the academy as soon as possible. Though it seemed as if I were throwing away a wonderful opportunity, I knew, in my heart of hearts, that I had made the right choice, for the inner peace I experienced as I left his office, was difficult to deny.

In the weeks that followed, I had to overcome a greater hurdle, attempts by the members of my family to dissuade me from leaving the academy. As one upperclassman after another filed into my room to congratulate me on having made the decision to leave, I was told one woeful tale after another of how they had caved into pressure from their families to stick it out, a choice they had later grown to regret. To avoid falling into the same trap, I knew I had to leave before I reached that point of no return, to the road yet untraveled but meant for me.

In response to an explanatory note, I had sent home to my folks after having briefly talked with them by phone, my stepfather wrote:

Dear Butch,

I received your letter today and must admit that some of it makes little sense. You state that you must prove to yourself and to us that you are a man and that you can overcome obstacles if you come out. That's a wonderful attitude and for some unknown reason I want to believe you. All, I'm trying to make you see, is what you are throwing away. You will no doubt be inducted into the army, which will disrupt your education—Although the present policy is to exempt college students, if you are fortunate enough to be one, I feel it is going to be changed. The general public is getting disgusted with unwashed rabble-rousers on campuses, and will soon demand a change. Public opinion can do more to influence a policy than anything I can think of—With what you would learn at the academy, you could pick a firm to go to work.

I guess I had better stop trying to convince you, for your own welfare, that you should stay there. No matter what your decision is, you will be unable to attend school in 1965-66 if you come out; so you may as well get at least one year of school. At the end of the year, if you still feel that you have had it, at least you will be in a better position to make it on your own. And even if you are unable to transfer your service credits, you will have knowledge that cannot be taken from you.

No amount of preaching can change your mind if there is no desire to see the other side. You are trying to convince me, and I you.

Take care and keep your nose clean.

Dad

In another letter from my stepdad, I learned that my commanding officer had been in contact with him concerning my request to leave the academy. But I saw through the insidiousness of this ploy, to stall for time, with the hope that I might change my mind. And so did I continue to press my CO for release.

When he informed me that I could not be discharged from the Navy, I grew quite dismayed. Even though I had declined to take the oath, I had unwittingly signed enlistment papers, the very same day—I was in the Navy whether I liked it or not. I was given the choice to serve four years of active duty, beginning immediately, or six years of inactive duty in the reserves, with two years of active duty to serve sometime before the end of my enlistment. I chose the latter, as I needed the time to figure out what I wanted to do with my life before I had to commit to doing something I did not want.

On 4 November, was I released from the Academy to the inactive reserves. While my records were in transit to Bainbridge, Maryland, via official channels, I was en route to St. Louis on what turned out to be a much more peaceful ride than had been the case on the way to Annapolis. In spite of feeling some anxiety about my immediate future and this reserve business, I felt hopeful.

Besides, I was just glad to be back home again, until I found out from my sister that conditions there had improved at the expense of my brother, Scott. Having come home drunk, late one evening that October, my stepfather had gotten into an argument with Scott, who had recently begun to rebel against some of the abuse he had been quietly enduring, all these years. As tempers flared, my stepdad jumped my brother and knocked him to the floor. With both hands around my brother's neck, he then tried to strangle Scott as he banged my brother's head, repeatedly, against the floor. My sister saved my brother's life when she whopped my stepfather on the head with a cast-iron skillet, and knocked him out. After she and Mom had pulled his unconscious body off Scott, my brother rose slowly to the call of freedom, grabbed some of his clothes, in the ensuing confusion, and ran away to a friend's house nearby, never to return home to live.

While I missed my brother, things were not quite the same with him gone. Fortunately, for the rest of us, Mom seemed to express less of the frustration she had heaped primarily upon his shoulders when he was still at home. My stepfather too, seemed to be in a much more amiable and sober mood. For my brother's banishment from home appeared to have had a cleansing effect upon the whole household, as if whatever had poisoned life around here, in the past, had been expunged with my brother as the scapegoat.

Having taken a part-time job selling men's clothing, I started looking for a more challenging position, which materialized that December, in an almost irrefutable offer from Monsanto Chemical Company. Upon applying for the job, I was interviewed by the personnel director, and given the grand tour of my prospective work area. Afterward, I began to experience some vague apprehension I brushed aside, for the time being, in my excitement over the possibility of having procured the job. Within a day or two of the interview, I received that much-coveted letter from the personnel director, confirming my worst fears, that I had the job if I wanted it.

By then, my apprehensions about the company had mushroomed into such a strong feeling of resistance to taking the job, that I did not know what to do. Overnight had I grown suspicious of the possible side effects the chemicals, I would be using, might have on other people, the environment, or myself. As I grew leery of the great wealth I would help Monsanto generate through my participation in the research and development of new chemical products, at the expense of Mother Nature and her children, I challenged the rebellious spirit that had filled my head with such alien thoughts. Under no circumstance was I to accept the position, did she inform me. In my inability to explain this sudden change of heart with regard to my taking the job, I simply neglected to contact the personnel director at Monsanto, thus letting the position go.

With the arrival of the Christmas holidays, I ran into a few of my old high school buddies, who were not in the least bit surprised when they learned of my resignation from the academy, for I had been too much of a rebel in high school, according to them, to have warranted my going there, in the first place. So did I learn something about myself, my friends had known all along.

Around this time too, I ran into Cheri, with whom I had continued to correspond while she attended Southeast Missouri State in Cape Girardeau, a town about 125 miles south of St. Louis. Seeing her again, for the first time since last June, only rekindled the old flames of desire I had felt for her in high school. Without a driver's license or a car, I spent less time with her than I had wanted to, before she returned to school after the holidays.

Having lost my job as the Christmas season ended, I grew increasingly distraught over what I should be doing with my life, which meant that I just had to see Cheri again. While my folks were at work, I taught myself to drive the old 1953 Dodge, my stepfather had abandoned to the backyard for a newer automobile. Then I took the car, without their permission, and drove it to Cape where I had to abandon it after I blew a rod.

To make matters worse, I was devastated when I found her in the arms of another guy. To add insult to injury, she then had the nerve to invite me to a party that evening, with her and her new beau, before she conveniently dismissed herself from this very uncomfortable situation and returned to her room. Like a fool, I went. Feeling sorry for myself and hurt by her, I started drinking until I blacked out. Afterward, I learned from her new beau, as he stuck my head under a shower in the men's dorm, to sober me up, that I had quite crudely told her off. Badly shaken by the whole affair, had she run from the party sobbing, to my satisfaction, all the way back to her room. As I stepped from the shower towards the end of our little discussion about Cheri, I was surprised to find that we both had agreed to dump her. Angry over the way she had mistreated me, I returned to her dorm to finish what I had started earlier, only to be hauled off to jail, for the night, after her dorm mother had called the police.

Released the following morning, with no charges having been filed against me, I phoned my stepdad to tell him about the car, which he had almost reported as a stolen vehicle, when he realized I was gone too—and quite possibly with the car. He told me that I would have to take a bus back to St. Louis, as he was going to have the car repaired in Cape and driven back home by one of his buddies. When I found another job, I was to reimburse him for the cost of the repairs, which only amounted to about $200. Much to my surprise, then, he dropped the matter and never mentioned it again.

To top that off, he went out and found his prodigal son a job, if I wanted it, working as an oiler on a towboat called the Ann King. Apparently, he had learned about the position through one of his drinking buddies, Ed Dlubec, who just happened to be one of the engineers on the boat. I was to start immediately, at $780 a month, and to work in increments of thirty days on—in twelve-hour shifts—and thirty days off. My responsibilities were to keep the engine room spotless and to report any unusual oil leaks.

I decided to take the job, as I really had nothing else to turn to. Even the rebellious spirit within me seemed to acquiesce for the time being, sensing that I needed to do something to help build my self-esteem. Nevertheless, I knew in my heart that this job would never satisfy the aching longing for my life's aspiration, which continued to so frustratingly elude my grasp. For now, I was as excited about the chance to work on a riverboat as I imagined Mark Twain had been, in his youth.

The only problem I had with the job was what I should do with all the time I had on my hands. Whenever I tried to read the same stuff that had been crammed down my throat in high school, I could barely get through it without falling asleep. That worried me since I was planning to return to college in the fall. The old academic pursuits of my high school days no longer seemed to hold my interest like the discussions I would get into with Gene, another one of the boat's engineers, around such highly emotional issues as the civil rights movement.

Here was real life happening, history unfolding, right before my eyes. I was inspired by those blacks who had laid their lives on the line in nonviolent protests against the tyranny of white America. At the same time, I was abhorred by the violent responses of the members of my own race to black protest, and by the hateful attitudes of these very same people towards black people in general. Like most of these prejudiced white people, Gene would begin his tirade against blacks by putting down their tactics, which I thought were rather ingenious. How else were the powerless to overcome the tyranny of the rich and powerful except by willingly subjecting themselves to its ruthless attacks, like the sacrificial lamb, to expose the true nature of its abusive power to the scrutiny of public opinion, which alone has the willpower to transform such abuse into justice. "If they want their freedom," Gene would say, almost paraphrasing my stepfather's own words, "then let's round 'em up and ship 'em all back to Africa where they belong. There, they can run around in the bush like a bunch of wild animals." Because his words hurt me as well, I quickly developed the courage to confront such prejudice whenever it raised its ugly head. Moreover, I found that these confrontations actually added meaning to my life, where lately, so much meaninglessness did abound.

That winter, when the Ann King went into dry dock at Woodriver, Illinois, I remained onboard to assist in the overhaul of her engines. In reality, I fluctuated between the role of an errand boy and that of a janitor. And in the loneliness of the evenings after work, I would occasionally play the part of a penitent pilgrim in search of a confessor because I had abused my self again.

I could not handle time alone, as I would invariably wind up caving into my obsession for union with my own body. For I wanted nothing more than to play with my self as any respectable author, in those days, would his main character. Restricted to the anatomical intrusions into my life by the limitations of my imagination, did I long for the intimacy of a relationship with the author of my being. "Who are you?" I demanded to know. As I stood in the quiet of my room, I detected nothing but the rapidly rising fear that Peter must have felt when he began to sink beneath the waves as he walked across the water. I greatly feared this sinking feeling into the crazy world of the imagination or passions of the body, where I'd be forced to live like Hyde instead.

Or, if I was lucky, I could escape this sinking feeling by fleeing into the cold, night air for a long walk down the highway, in an attempt to either chill or exhaust Hyde's passion for union with my body. One night, I coaxed two of my buddies to drive up from St. Louis to take me out, which usually meant drinking. Unable to drink in moderation, I drank so much, they had to help me back to my room onboard the boat before they could return to St. Louis.

The next morning, Ed Dlubec read me the riot act. "I am not going to put up with another drunken oiler on this boat," he insisted. No matter how hard I tried to convince him, I was not like the other two oilers, or that the previous night's escapade was merely an infrequent fling with friends, he would not believe me. Instead, he worked my ass off until we pulled out of dry dock, later that month.

When I got back home, my stepfather too, lit into me about all of my supposedly drunken escapades into Woodriver. Drunk as usual, he was totally incapable of listening to reason, and therefore completely unwilling to hear my side of the story. He made me mad.

"You have a lot of nerve calling me a little drunk," I blurted out, "for someone like yourself who comes home, night after night, drunk as hell, only to guzzle down more booze and make life miserable for the rest of us. Just look at you! Why, you can't even stand up straight without holding onto the table, you're so goddamn drunk. You nauseate me with your despicable conjectures and arrogant self-righteousness. You're the goddamned drunk around here, not me."

"Why, you little bastard! If I get my hands on you, I'll kill you," he slobbered as I maintained a safe distance from him, on the other side of the dining room table. "Ya coward!" He snarled as I continued to elude his grasp. "Get out of my house you ungrateful son of a bitch! Get out!" He drooled as he pointed to the door.

"I would gladly go," I boasted, "if you would let me get my bags."

"Joe, please don't do this to me," Mom pleaded, as she anxiously positioned herself between us and afforded me the opportunity to easily slip by, grab my bags, and hightail it out the front door.

"I'll even hold the door open for the little bastard," he drooled.

"I wouldn't want to stay in this hellhole any longer than I have to," I shouted back as I disappeared out the front door.

"Get out of my way, woman!" He bellowed as he pushed her aside and started for the door.

"Don't you hurt him, Joe!" She commanded.

"Butch, please come back!" She begged of me, to no avail, as I headed up the sidewalk. "Don't leave me like this."

"Joe, please stop this foolishness!" She pleaded with him.

"Let 'm go," he scoffed. "He'll be back when he realizes how good he had it. He'll come crawling back like he did from the Naval Academy and Cape Girardeau, with his tail between his legs."

He pissed me off. "I'll never come back," I shouted as I walked up the driveway.

"Butch!" Mom screamed. "Please don't leave me."

But I had already disappeared into the darkness up the street. When I heard the front door slam shut and saw the floodlights go out, I sneaked past our house and down the street, to the home of my best friend, Dave. For long ago, I had received an open invitation from his parents, Claude and Marie, to come and stay with them if conditions at my house ever got bad enough that I had to leave. When they saw me standing at their front door with my bags, I did not have to say a word, for they knew. I was immediately taken in and made to feel right at home, as I began to tell them what had happened. And there I stayed until I left for the university later that fall.

I benefited immensely from the experience of more normal family relationships, especially the one of a mother and father who really cared enough about me to translate their love into actions that built self-esteem rather than destroyed it. While Marie found part-time work for me, during the first month I was off the boat, Claude found me an old 1953 Chevy for a hundred dollars. Not only did he work on the car with me to make her street worthy, but he also cosigned for the insurance so that I could get a cheaper rate. [Later, my sister helped me to obtain a driver's license after I drove her down to get hers.] That summer, they even took me on vacation with them, down to Lake Taneycomo in southwestern Missouri. Essentially, they treated me as if I were one of their own children. They provided me with the safe haven, I so badly needed, to begin the long process of healing the deep wounds that afflicted me around relationship to others.

In spite of the consistency of their love, I continued to be plagued by my obsession for union with my own body, as if parental love could no longer satisfy my emotional needs. No matter how hard I tried, I was totally incapable of containing the contents of this Pandora's Box, which had been unleashed on me at puberty. As this unruly tendency of mine forced me from the paradise of my youth, into the desert of my life, to seek my fate, I realized that this oasis was not the vessel, I sought to contain it.

That July, when I returned to work on the riverboat, I was smitten again with love as I caught sight of Mary O'Daniels, the newly hired assistant cook. As the budding friendship that ensued quickly blossomed into a romantic relationship, I found I could talk to her about anything except the thorny problem I had with accepting my own sexual feelings. Because it looked as if we were made for each other, we were the talk of the crew, the Ann King's romance of the year.

The separation from her that followed was inevitable, as our days onboard the towboat together were numbered. As the pain of being separated from her became almost unbearable, in my misery I would pine away for those infrequent times when we could be together again. And as if to make matters worse, both of us had arranged, prior to our meeting, to attend college in the fall in towns over a hundred miles apart. As I went off to the University of Missouri at Rolla to pursue a degree in engineering, she headed for Cape Girardeau in pursuit of a degree in what she knew not, from Southeast Missouri State.

Once again, I set myself up for failure by taking the wrong road. I just couldn't stay away from Mary for very long and still maintain adequate interest in my studies. Besides, my rebellious spirit, who was up to her old tricks again, rose quickly in defiance of my choice to go back to school to take up engineering. The psychic typhoon of very strong feelings, frenzied confusion and resulting bouts of self-abuse and excessive drinking was so unrelenting, I felt as if I were going to lose my mind, or what little grip I had on reality.

And Mary's sudden decision, to cool the relationship, only increased the fury of the tempest raging within me. Unbeknownst to me at the time, she had grown increasingly fearful of the instability I was exhibiting, and suspicious of the exclusive relationship I seemed in such a hurry to force upon her. Even though she still wanted to be friends with me, she insisted she did not love me. Because of the love I felt for her, I insisted that I could continue to see her only if she was open to the possibility of a romantic relationship. While she finally agreed to be more open to love, she insisted her openness in no way meant she was ready for marriage. Fearful of losing her, the only meaning in my life at the time, I reluctantly agreed to date her more as a friend than as a lover. Obviously, I was not ready for marriage either, as I desperately needed to find more meaning to my life than her.

Instead of buckling down, I wound up getting into trouble when, on Halloween night, I got sucked into a panty raid, which, with the coveted prize of a pair of panties in hand, turned into an ugly mob that went on a destructive rampage through downtown Rolla. Later identified as one of the rioters, who had smashed in storefront windows with brickbats, I was asked to leave the university to avoid expulsion and the mark it would leave on my record. Unable to pay for the damage I had done or to face Claude and Marie, after all they had done for me, I approached my mother for the money and a temporary place to stay until I got back on my feet. After she reluctantly relented to help me, I returned home and began to look for another job.

Out of desperation, I decided to drive up to Chicago to inquire about a research position at Argonne National Laboratories. This bubble burst in my face too, when I blew a rod in my car about fifteen miles out of St. Louis. Forced to return home, I instead accepted a position my stepdad had once again found through one of his drinking buddies. As a lab technician, was I to start work at National Lead's paint pigment plant along the Mississippi River in south St. Louis.

This time around, my rebellious spirit seemed to stir little psychic wind; instead, she repeatedly threw up into my face the horrible specter of human and environmental degradation that surrounded the plant. For the air outside was so noxious, my throat and eyes would burn as I made my way to the lab from my car. What the plant did not pour into the river, it spewed out into the atmosphere in clouds of lead oxides and sulfur dioxide, which chemically combined with the moisture that evaporated from the river to produce tiny droplets of sulfuric acid. While the resulting cloud of acid, which hung in the air over the surrounding area, ate holes in the nylons of our secretaries, it slowly etched the paint off the homes and cars of the people who lived in the neighborhood. To make matters worse, within the first month after I started, my stepdad's buddy, the one who had gotten me the job, died from white lead poisoning of his lungs. Rather than stir up some violent internal storm, my rebellious spirit simply resorted to filling me with resentment for what I was doing, as if to say, "See, this is not the way."

Then, one day, a gentle breeze arose in my psyche and stirred me to consult my old high school counselor concerning my latest vocational crisis. When she tested me, I was surprised to learn my vocational interests were most characteristic of those of an author-journalist or artist. Because I had never exhibited any creative potential, or shown any interest in either writing or art, we dismissed such occupational endeavors as unrealistic. As we continued down the list of the most likely vocational possibilities for me, according to the test, I was quick to reject her suggestion to pursue a career in chemistry or engineering, only because my body seemed to have already overwhelmingly rejected these choices. That left me with the choice of a career as either an architect or a mathematician, neither of which really turned me on. And what especially concerned me was the low score I had received in specialization, which essentially meant I would find the advanced study or narrow focus of a college education to be too stifling. "My God! What am I to do?" I asked myself, out of desperation, as I left her office completely bewildered.

As I grew increasingly more despondent over ever finding a way out of this job, into a more meaningful one, I began to binge drink to forget about my woes. Shortly thereafter, I was confronted by my old drinking buddies who, it seems, had grown weary of saving my ass every time I got drunk. As they told me one tale after another of the trouble I had caused them when I was drunk, I refused to believe them, at first, and accused them of lying. In the heat of the confrontation that ensued, it slowly dawned on me that they were telling the truth. I never remembered any of the sordid details, because I had blacked out, from consuming too much alcohol. Shocked by what my friends had told me, I actually quit drinking, for the time being, and out of fear that I might become an alcoholic like my stepfather, never got drunk again.

Right before Christmas that year, I received a present from my draft board, a notice reclassifying me 1-A, and ordering me to report for induction into the army. When I asked the clerk at my draft board how I could be inducted into the army as a member of the Naval Reserves, I was informed that the Naval Reserve Center had reported me as delinquent. According to the personnel officer at the center, my records had temporarily gotten misplaced, somewhere in the shuffle between St. Louis and Bainbridge, Maryland. When my records did finally surface, I never received any new orders or notification that I had been delinquent in my duty to the Navy, even though my draft board had received such notice. To avoid induction into the army, I was called up for two years of active duty in the Navy, and ordered to report to Treasure Island, San Francisco, California, on 5 February 1967.

Like Jonah, I felt defeated, as if every effort to go my own way had been thwarted by the wrath, my very nature had conjured up. Having infuriated almost every aspect of myself that I possibly could, I was thrown overboard, in over my head, to either sink or swim. As I sank beneath the surface of the sea of life, I was swallowed by a great gray whale, the US Navy, only to be regurgitated on some unknown shore, to do my duty for God and my country.

Maybe the Navy could awaken me from the Big Sleep, God had cast over the original being before separating it into man and woman. Maybe the Navy could reunite me with my soul.

Part II

The Search For Soul

4

An Instinctive Response

As I await further counsel as to where to go from here, I finally get the cue from my lawyer to consult the script that now lay before me like an open book.

MR. HART: *I would like you to read your statement to the board.*

RESPONDENT: Today, I am being considered for an administrative discharge based solely upon my judicial record since I went on active duty. While it is true that I have defied every aspect of military life, I only did so in response to an interior call urging me "not" to participate in this way of life in any manner whatsoever. Like a dumb ass, I had recognized neither the taskmaster nor my motives until I discovered my rightful place in life as the missing link—that hypothetical intermediate evolutionary form between god and beast, in which the two came together, as never before, into one harmonious whole. Thus, do I now feel compelled to bare my soul, so that you might see us for who we truly are.

In the beginning, I found comfort in being in the Navy, especially while I was stationed at Treasure Island. In having turned my life over to a higher power, I let go of all the frustration I had been experiencing as I tried to figure out what I wanted to do with my life. I felt encouraged by all of the testing I was undergoing, both physically and mentally, ere the Navy determined a way of life for me. "Maybe I would find something here I had overlooked in civilian life," I thought to myself.

Even though fate had forced me back into the Navy, I felt as if I'd been given another chance to find my way before I lost it forever. Tethered to the womb of this Great Gray Mother for all my needs, by a two-year commitment to my country, I longed for the birth of my real Self. Thus, did I resign myself to a fate pregnant with that one hope.

To ease the pain of this difficult pregnancy and the suffering of a forced separation from Mary, I sought out the companionship of other guys of my own ilk. As I reached out, one day shortly thereafter, to shake the hand of an unlikely dude from Colorado, I was deeply touched by the encounter. The instant I touched his hand, I felt as if my heart had been pierced by a tiny point of truth, some hidden aspect of my personality that had manifested itself to me in his demeanor. Out of the painful vacuum in my life then, came the answer to a prayer in the form of Elrie Van Slagle.

For it was Van, as he liked to be called, who unwittingly gave to me exactly what I needed in my life at the time, help to grow in relationship not only to others but also to myself. So adept was he at relating to others, that I was like putty in his hands. Gently manipulating me with the skill of a true craftsman, he pulled forth from me feelings, I never knew I had, as he listened not only to what I said but also to what I did not say. Because he neither condoned nor condemned my feelings, he helped me to rescue them from the eternal damnation of dissociation. In his generosity, Van helped me to feel better about myself, as if what I had to say really did matter.

Never before had I experienced such a freeing response to my feelings—the good, the bad, and the ugly. I had grown so accustomed to having my feelings trampled on and castigated by my parents, that I continued the same pattern of putting them down as a learned response. And so did I lose the ability to evaluate my life. As I entangled myself in one web after another of failed attempts to intellectually escape real life, I lost my way in the anguish of my own bleeding heart where I had condemned genuine feeling and my true Self to the miserable existence, I was living until the day Elrie came along.

Because feeling exhibited itself, so irradicably, across such a broad spectrum, from the loftiest to the vilest of feelings, I was still too afraid to let genuine feeling out, other than in small measured doses. In the past, I had felt so helpless in protecting myself from the seemingly endless cycle of passionate eruptions, which took control of me against my will, that I never learned to trust this unpredictable and seething volcano of feelings within me. How often had I tried, in earnest, to reason with this irrational side of me, to no avail. O, how I longed to communicate with this other will that sought so passionately to enter my life. Alas, I lacked the knowledge of a means of communicating with the other member of my body, or so I thought at the time.

Then, one day, as I was struggling to discern what I had been feeling, I experienced a sudden burst of insight into the difference between feelings and emotions, which I had confused, all these years, as the same. In a flash, I realized feelings are actually thoughts from the heart rather than from the head, while emotions are the packets of energy that surround feelings like a dark cloud, and move them into consciousness. I saw how emotions, the body's first line of defense, alerted me somatically, that is, in the language of the body, to any penetrations of consciousness by feeling. Where feeling's arrows of truth struck my body, I saw emotion quickly surround the wound and immediately surrender the intruding feeling to consciousness as pure thought. As I incorporated the words of this thought into my life, I saw the wound miraculously heal without a scar.

Instantly, I understood how feeling had been trying to help me sort through the limitless possibilities of life, to determine which, if any of the countless thoughts and ideas I had, were real. Contrary to what I had previously thought, I realized feeling had indeed been working for rather than against me, as I fled from one pursuit to another in search of the way intended for me.

I saw how feeling had access to a primordial wisdom of instinctive truth that allowed it to get quickly to the heart of a matter while the intellect tarried around with any number of meaningless thoughts. When feeling evaluated a situation for me, I knew immediately, in my heart of hearts, what I must do, even though I might not yet have formulated the reasons why.

Because of my inability to see through feeling's emotional disguise, I had damned feeling to an emotional hell that inflamed my body with the desire to penetrate the womb of my imagination, to release the feelings imprisoned there. I had damned up the natural flow of thought from my heart—this lava of new life—to such an extent that my feelings had no other avenue of escape than having sex with my self. In my failure to embrace my feelings, I suffered the chronic pain of a wound that never healed—a split in my personality that greatly inhibited my ability to communicate with others.

Because feeling had always appeared cloaked in a cloud of emotion, I had incorrectly seen feeling not only as the emotion itself but also as some manifestation of the primitive side of my personality that I needed to bring under the control of my will. How quickly, I realized that the will was incapable of controlling these instinctive responses whenever they rose up before my eyes masquerading as genuine feeling. I was apparently being asked, according to the laws of nature, to respond to life one way or the other, with either the raw emotions of an unconscious animal or the genuine feeling of an enlightened human being. In other words, I was being forced by natural law to follow the dictates of a much greater will than my own or face certain ruin. Thus did I learn obedience to a higher law by suffering through the tyrannous reign of instinct over my life—particularly my body.

In the past when willpower failed me, as it often did, I simply caved into the raw emotional responses of my animal nature. Unable to see through the thick clouds of stormy emotions that induced me to behave like an animal, I pissed away untold opportunities to hear out my feelings. Or, if by chance, I caught the content of a feeling that had somehow slipped through my defenses, I dismissed this message as unbelievable, for I had absolutely no faith in these serpentine emotions of mine. Or, if I had the faith, then I generally lacked the courage to overcome the fear and the inertia of expressing the feeling, in spite of the incredible strength of the emotional energy surrounding it.

Though feeling, with its concomitant emotional energy, whether positive or negative, arose purely for the sake of increasing my awareness, I often put down its ingenuous efforts, due to my fear of enlightenment. Only later, did I realize I actually feared some dark evil, I was sure, lurked within these foul clouds of hot volcanic emotions that spewed forth from my being with such animalistic passion.

As a disquieting mood or cloud of vague feelings and emotions settled in on me, one day shortly thereafter, like the dense fog that had moved in over the Bay area, I experienced a dampening of the warm friendly feelings which had blossomed within me for Van, during my brief stay with him here, at Treasure Island. I sensed a change coming, which could affect our relationship, as the thought of us having to go our separate ways pierced my heart, for I had grown quite fond of the dude. Sure enough, as the fog lifted that afternoon, I received the ill-fated news from Van.

"Guess what, ya lucky stiff!" He shouted rather disappointedly as he came sauntering up to me. "You're goin' to Hawaii."

"You're kiddin'!" I shouted. "Are you goin' too?"

"Nah!" He replied, "I'm bein' shipped off to some place in the Philippines called Subic Bay. I got orders for a tender, the Dixie. You got orders for a destroyer escort, the Davidson, out of Pearl Harbor."

"I had a premonition," I interjected, "we would be separated."

"Yeah," he replied, "I had a feelin' we would too. Son of a gun, ole buddy! I'm sure gonna miss ya."

"Yeah," I added, "I'm gonna miss you too, Elrie."

As he shook my hand for what seemed like a long time, I let this larger than life aspect of myself look into my eyes, only so long, before my gaze dropped to the ground so he couldn't see my pain.

"Well," he said, "I have a feelin' we'll be runnin' into each other, somewhere out there in the great South Pacific."

"Yeah, maybe so," I muttered. "I wish you would've got orders for Hawaii though. We would've had a blast over there together."

"Yeah," he added, "we could've...." So did we saunter off together, dreaming aloud and reminiscing about the good times we'd had at TI.

In the background, where bits and pieces of the conversations of those with whom we passed in close proximity faded in and out of my range of hearing, I overheard expressions of concern that not only distracted me from Van but also pricked my interest for obvious reasons.

"I hope I don't get sent to Nam," I heard one sailor say.

"Why, I haven't seen this many reserves reportin' for active duty in years," commented another.

"Yeah, somethin's goin' on over there, they ain't tellin' us," added yet another.

"It's a war, man! Our guys are gettin' killed over there! That's what the fuck's goin' on," interjected some sarcastic dude standing nearby.

"Yeah, one of my buddies came home last month, in a box," said the last guy I could hear.

"I sure am glad we ain't gonna see any combat," added Van.

"Yeah," I muttered, as I wandered back down into myself trying to find the chord that had been struck by all this talk of war and people getting killed. Since I had never experienced a war firsthand, or had the opportunity to explore my feelings about war, I wasn't sure why I had been so deeply disturbed by such talk.

I knew only that I was already too preoccupied with fighting a war within myself, to get involved in an external conflict that did not concern me. How could I solve other peoples' problems if I could not resolve my own? So I quickly dropped the subject of war as being way beyond my comprehension. For I felt it was a matter best left to the experts who, in their irrefutable wisdom and knowledge of war, were so much better equipped to think about it than I was.

As I wondered if it wasn't a little too late for me to be entertaining second thoughts about my decision to reenter the Navy, I was somewhat surprised by my willingness to even give feeling this opportunity to express her views. In the past, I would have simply ignored her until she went into another one of her rages, to get my attention. With Elrie's help, I had grown not only to trust her point of view but also to depend on her periodic evaluations, to help me sort through the rapidly changing circumstances in my life. Obviously, I needed her help to get a better handle on where I was to go from here.

So did I, after parting company with Van, depart from Treasure Island somewhat perplexed by the appearance of the notion that feeling is a feminine quality. Once my plane was in the air, I grew increasingly concerned about my references to feeling as she or her, as if, within my body, there dwelled another person or woman who embodied all of my feelings. While I shuddered at such a schizophrenic thought, I had the feeling that such references to feeling, as she or her, were quite natural for young men my age who tended to erroneously associate feeling with women only.

I easily debunked that myth, for I was a man with lots of feeling. Only, I didn't like the way I felt, the constant ache inside my heart, which I had mistakenly attributed, at the time, to the great distance that separated me from Mary. Having felt, at such times, as if I were standing outside my body terribly removed from what I was really feeling, I realized my pain had more to do with the distance that separated me from my soul than it had with my separation from Mary, as the latter reality merely reflected the former truth. Now I understood why I had so much more feeling for Mary than I had for what I wanted to do with my life, for Mary had captured the image of my soul.

With such limited access to my soul's designs for me, I felt as if all I ever knew for certain was what I did not want to do. For instance, I knew I did not want to come back into the Navy, but I felt as if I had no other choice, since I lacked the awareness of any alternative. Like Van, I had no real desire to see combat, for I shuddered at the thought of having to kill another human being with my own hands. Although I could never actually kill another human being, I wasn't sure what I would do in a battle where I would be under pressure to kill. I knew only that I wanted to avoid being placed into such a position, if at all possible.

On the other hand, I did feel drawn to serve the citizens of this country in some way. I was so disappointed when I learned that I was to serve as a deckhand onboard a ship, for I'd had such high hopes of receiving a more emotionally satisfying assignment, in spite of my low rank and lack of training. Why, I felt as if I had been betrayed by the process at Treasure Island, as I pondered two safe but boring years before the mast, cleaning compartment spaces and heads, shining brass, painting over and over what didn't need to be painted, standing watches and occasionally playing war games with imaginary enemies. I really wanted to serve my country, but only in a more tangibly humanitarian way.

Because I had gotten so wrapped up in my self, over the past few years, I needed to find an occupation which would draw me out of myself—completely absorbing my creative energies and utilizing my abilities to the fullest. Otherwise, I would just end up getting bored, that is, providing fertile ground for yet another uprising by the underground resistance within me. How quickly I realized there was nothing for me onboard this ship—no job that even came close to attracting my interest or meeting the needs of my soul.

Instead, I began to feel as if I really didn't belong here. Besides, I wasn't too fond of having to live at such close quarters with so many other young men who were as abusive of sex and alcohol as these guys were. In view of my abuse of alcohol in the past and current struggle with my own sexuality, I certainly did not need this kind of peer pressure, to help me get a better handle on my life.

As I had no inkling of what had caused such bitterness and moral depravity to infect them, I was stunned by the obscene diatribes with which these guys so obsessively attacked not only each other but also the Navy. In fact, I was so stunned I never forgot my first real taste of life onboard the biggest little destroyer in all the South Pacific.

As I awakened to the shrill sound of the boatswain mate's whistle, that first morning, and the call of reveille over the loudspeaker, I continued to lie in my bunk while my eyes adjusted to the bright lights of the compartment. Then, I heard this gravelly, nasally voice growl, "Get the fuck outta them racks, ya fuckin' cunts. What the fuck ya think this is, the fuckin' beach!" Immediately, I hit the deck, only to see a weasely little ole first class petty officer working his way around the compartment, prodding late stragglers to get out of their bunks.

He reminded me of my stepfather, a rough, James Cagney type, tough guy, except that he had the ugliest weather-beaten prune face, I had ever seen, and wore a pair of wire rimmed glasses down on the end of his nose, which he pushed back up when he tilted his head back to get a closer look at you.

"Who're you?" He growled as he approached me.

"My name's Drury, sir," I replied rather sheepishly.

"Dury, huh," he grunted as he looked me over, with a scornful smile on his face.

"Yes sir," I responded, feeling as intimidated by his demeanor as I had in the past by my stepfather's.

Chuckling to himself as he shook his head in disbelief, he turned to get a glimpse of the look on the face of his tagalong, a slightly taller, potbellied and round-faced second class petty officer—with rosy red cheeks and a Walter Brennan limp—who appeared to hold a similar view of me. They both had a way of making me feel rather small.

In fact, I felt as if there were something wrong with me, till I heard someone behind me say in a low reassuring voice, "Don't let 'em git to ya like that. They treat us all like scum. That's just the way they are, the lousy sons of bitches."

As they continued to make their rounds, I could still hear his voice booming throughout the compartment, "Get the fuck outta that rack, ya fuckin' pussy. Hey, ya fuckin' faggot, get outta there. I ain't your fuckin' mother, ya fuckin' rack-rat." So on they went until everyone had been rousted from his bunk.

When I turned to see who had consoled me, a tall lanky fella with dark hair and a baby face greeted me. "Hi, my name's Rulli," he said with a western Great Lakes coastal accent.

"Hi, mine's Drury," I replied as we shook hands heartily.

"Don't mind the motherfuckers," he said with a sneer. "The fuckin' lifers have been in the Navy so long, they got fucked up in the head. Now all they know is how to fuck with yours. But they ain't gonna fuck up ole Rulli's head, cause I ain't gonna let 'em. And don't you let 'em fuck up your head either, Drury, cause the motherfuckers will sure try."

"Fuck 'em! Fuck all the motherfuckers! And fuck the goddamn Navy too!" Blurted out some dude standing nearby.

RECORDER: *Objection. I find this line of testimony to be completely irrelevant to the proceedings here.*

SENIOR MEMBER: *The objection is noted. However, because this is his statement, he will be allowed to continue until he finishes it.*

You may continue.

RESPONDENT: I laughed aloud, out of nervousness more than anything else, as I wasn't quite sure how to take all of this.

Then, from across the compartment came the curse of yet another embittered sailor. "Yeah, fuck the goddamn Navy! Fuck all the motherfuckin' lifers that fuck with your head!" He cried out.

"Aw, fuck you Moss," I heard another yell back, "you're already so goddamned fucked up in the head you don't even know what the fuck's goin' on anymore."

"Fuck you, motherfucker," shouted back this ugly, round-faced lad who looked like Dracula with his deep dark angry eyes and small canine teeth that stuck out—only because the others were in various stages of decay—from the fleshy rotund body, he carried around with the dignity of a southern gentleman and the accent to match.

As he walked over to where I was standing, staring at me intently, the whole time, with those piercing devilish eyes of his, he cried out in jest, "Well, if it ain't a fuckin' boot! What's your name boot?"

"Drury," I replied.

"Dury, huh," he snarled. "We got a new boot," he shouted off to the side as if to let everyone else down in the compartment space know who I was. Locking in on me with the glare of a Bela Lugosi, he wasted no time in verbally sinking his teeth into me. "What the fuck ya lookin' at boot?" Bellowed this uncouth lug.

"Nothin'," I responded as I backed up to avoid the spray of his spit and a breath that reeked of booze.

"You callin' me nothin', boot?" He hollered in my face.

Just then, Rulli stepped between us. "Leave 'm alone, Moss."

"Fuck you, Rulli!" Snapped back Moss, with a snicker. "I was just havin' fun with the new boot," he added as he backed off. "I meant no harm. I'm still fucked up from all the pussy I got last night. Why, I ate so much goddamn pussy, last night, I'm still pullin' the fuckin' cunt's hair outta my teeth."

"You eat pussy, boot?" He inquired of me as he traipsed off to his locker to change his clothes.

"You don't know what good pussy is, Moss," countered some short chubby fella standing close by.

"Fuck you, motherfucker!" Moss yelled back.

"Fuck yo mamma," yelled a Mexican-American sailor named Martinez.

"Fuck you, ya motherfuckin' faggot," shouted a somewhat agitated Moss. "What the fuck ya think this is, a fuckin' gang rape?"

And so did this repugnant process of natural selection, the survival of the grossest, evolve while I finished dressing, only to end in a dead heat. Like the billy over a herd of wild goats, had the leader of the pack arrived on the scene, that morning, only to find a number of his young charges dawdling in their night's repose instead of hopping to the business of the day. Perturbed by the lackadaisical attitude of these young billies, he had not only roused them from their languor but also stirred up their ire for the Navy. As these surly young billies turned out to butt heads with each other rather than the Navy, the real source of their frustration, they concocted the crudest, most vulgar one-liners, deliberately designed to incite each other to the lusty and depraved behavior of a herd of wild goats.

Although this crude intercourse reflected a goat-like aspect of man's animal history, such behavior now fell well outside the bounds of human instinct. Whereas a goat is unable to act any other way but instinctively, that is, as it is programmed to behave, due to a lack of free will, man is free to act contrary to his recently acquired nature, like an animal if he chooses. In doing so, he breaks the laws of Nature as they currently stand. Instead of acting instinctively, these guys were acting compulsively, out of instinct that has run amok. For their crude behavior signaled a very dangerous condition, a complete loss of soul, the object of instinct's desires.

As I sat down to breakfast, I was bombarded from almost every direction by more of the same base conversation. I felt as if nothing around me were real, as if it were all some sort of cruel hoax. I even rubbed my eyes at one point, halfway expecting to awaken from this bad dream. Although I felt like screaming, I couldn't, for I felt as if my soul had been violated, only without a clear understanding of what had taken place. Because of the way in which these guys fucked with Mother Nature, to satisfy their own hedonistic whims, I felt as if they were the very motherfuckers, they called each other.

For the first time in my life, did I experience a clear distinction between my self and my soul, as I felt her feelings. Thus did I begin to feel as if this body of mine were divided against itself, just like home. As I stood there on the edge, overlooking the great abyss that separated me from her, my present way of life from the one intended for me, I could see neither her nor the other side.

Overcome by a sudden urge to jump into the abyss, I panicked. As I teetered on the edge, I heard someone ask, "Are you all right?"

As the din of conversation on the mess decks came rushing back within range of my hearing, I spied a third class boatswain's mate, staring down at me from where he stood on the other side of the table.

"Yeah, I'm fine," I said as I tried to regain my composure, "just fine." But I wasn't all right, for I still felt very uneasy.

"Are you finished eating?" He asked.

"Yeah, as a matter of fact I am," I replied.

"Good," he responded. "I want to show you around the ship before quarters."

Still feeling somewhat shaken, I got up, discarded my tray, and followed him down the passageway, oblivious, at first, of anything but my feelings. In the struggle to collect my wits about my self, long enough to hear what he was trying to tell me as he pointed out the locations of the various offices and shops onboard the ship, I was gradually distracted from these noisome feelings by the impressive layout of this labyrinthine maze of steel passageways and hidden spaces.

Having popped through a forward hatch onto the bow of the ship, I immediately encountered a guard with a .45 strapped to his side, pacing back and forth across the deck, oblivious of the shrill sound that pierced the air like the screaming of a woman in distress. "This is ASROC," I heard my guide say above the ever increasing intensity of the screaming in my ears, "a torpedo launcher with nuclear capabilities..." At that point, I could no longer hear what he was saying, as the screaming in my ears had drowned out his voice. Obviously distressed, I cupped my hands over my ears to drown out the screaming.

"Are you all right?" My guide asked again.

"I don't know," I replied. "That shrill sound is hurting my ears."

"Didn't you hear it?" I asked as I looked into two of the most bewildered faces, I had ever seen.

"No," my guide said, as he looked to the guard for another perspective on the matter.

"Well, I definitely heard a high pitched scream that grew louder and louder as you spoke, whether you-all heard it or not," I insisted.

"I didn't hear any high pitched scream. Did you?" My guide asked the guard.

"No, I didn't," replied the guard.

"Forget it," I said out of frustration. "I must have heard something far off. It's nothing. Go on—I'm all right."

But I wasn't all right, for I definitely heard what had sounded to me like a woman screaming out at the top of her lungs. And I hadn't just imagined it either, because I heard the screaming again as I rounded the ASROC launcher, on the heels of my guide, to see one of the ship's five-inch gun mounts. This time, I tried not to make such a big deal out of it. Instead, I simply rubbed my finger in my ear to determine whether the screaming was actually coming from my head or from some outside source. Besides, I didn't want to give him the impression, I had heard the screaming again, when he obviously had not.

As I tried to collect my wits about my self, I wondered about the origins of this screaming. At first, I'd had the sense that it came from a great distance outside my body. However, as the screaming increased in intensity, I had felt as if someone were standing right next to me screaming in my ear. Besides, I'd heard the screaming, with the same intensity, whether I plugged my ear with my finger or not. Since the others had not heard it, I reluctantly concluded the screaming had come from within my head, as a product of my imagination, I supposed, even though it had sounded so real to me.

With that, I later realized the screaming had actually been the crying out of my feelings in horror of the weaponry that had sprung into view. In my fascination with appearances, I had been momentarily lulled away from the reality that such weapons are, after all, instruments of death and destruction. In fact, I recalled that the screaming had actually begun to subside as I paid more attention to it. I wondered then, if she had not screamed at me, just to get my attention.

The whole experience left me with more questions than it did answers. Who was this other within me, that she could manipulate reality in such a way as to get me to hear screams, no one else heard? Why should I be so horrified by the sight of a weapon, which otherwise meant absolutely nothing to me? Why had I been the only one who had heard her screaming? As these questions popped into my head, I dared not repeat them, for fear of learning the truth.

What is real, I wondered, only that which I can see and physically touch? In this instance, I had only the validation of my own feelings and sense of hearing, but nothing tangible. Did that make this experience any less real? Or is there an intangible side to reality that is just as accessible to my faculties as the material world? If so, why had I never encountered it before? Or was I going crazy, simply imagining all of this? Yet my feelings insisted that I was neither cracking up nor imagining what I had just heard.

Instead, she informed me that I had heard what others had not, only because I'd been sensitive to her feelings, open to her pain—which I had experienced as my own—and willing to listen to another point of view.

Are there two sides to reality then, the physical and the metaphysical? If so, is one any more real than the other? If not, why had I gotten so bogged down with just the physical side of reality?

While I knew little about my mother, that is, the physical side of my nature, I knew even less about my real father or metaphysical side of my being. I knew only that these two sides of my nature had been divorced from each other for some time now. As a child, I had been deprived of any relationship with either my real father, who had been taken away from me at a very early age by schizophrenia, or my stepfather, who turned his life over to alcohol instead of me at an age when I most needed a father. As a result, I lost my mother also, to all the disappointment, frustration and bitterness of another dismally failing relationship. For the first time, I saw my difficulties with both the physical and the metaphysical aspects of my nature as an extension of not only my parents' personal shortcomings but more importantly of their dismal failure to have ever learned to relate to each other in any more meaningful a way than through their own sexuality.

Having reached the age of personal responsibility for myself, I suddenly inherited all the unresolved conflicts of my parents. Overnight, I grew just as incapable of relating with others, particularly the opposite sex, as my stepfather had, my mother. When my mother rejected his sexual entreaties, out of the very real fear she might not survive another pregnancy, and upon medical advice to avoid another pregnancy, at all costs, because of the complications she had experienced during the birth of my youngest brother, I began to experience great difficulty in accepting my own sexual feelings. And when my stepdad failed to accept the challenge to find another outlet for his creative energies by turning instead, to the spirits of alcohol to drown out his pain, I too lost my way, that is, I lost touch with the metaphysical side of my nature.

Since the physical and the metaphysical were no longer in proper relationship to each other, I started drinking and abusing the other member of my body. When confronted about my drinking, thank God, I had the fortitude to quit. Only, I wasn't able to quit the other as easily, as the solution to this problem eluded my grasp yet.

The problem became so acute, only because I had never been taught by my fathers, or by the religion of my fathers, how to communicate with the metaphysical side of my nature. O, I had learned how to ask God for things, as if the Almighty were some genie who could grant my every wish. But I was never taught how to listen or what to listen for. In other words, I had never learned how God communicated with me.

Were the screams I heard, a last ditch effort by the inhabitants of the metaphysical realm to reach me? If so, who were they? What did they want? And did I really want to know? I did and I did not, because I feared getting caught up in some metaphysical mumbo jumbo that would ultimately lead to my own self-destruction.

As time wore on, I tried to forget about the screaming in my head, to no avail, since it corresponded with the pain that continually racked my heart. Whenever I felt a flare-up of pain, I also experienced a greater intensity of screaming in my head. With time, I found, in those brief moments when I could accept my pain, the screaming in my head actually subsided. In letting go of my pain, I experienced the release of feeling's arrows, which then penetrated my thickheadedness as pure thought instead of frenzied screaming. Thus did I learn to verbalize some of the anguish of my situation.

An Instinctive Response

For I felt as if I were in prison serving time for a crime I had not committed. I felt as if I had been pressed into service to do dull, routine tasks, day after day, to keep me down, to dull my thinking, to tire me out, and to isolate me from the others—from realizing I was not alone in my feelings. In fact, I saw the whole regimen as a deliberate attempt by the authorities to slowly wear down any rebelliousness of spirit with tedium.

I began to understand Rulli's admonition to fight any attempt by the lifers to "fuck up my head," for their real intention was to break my spirit, just as theirs had been broken by lifers before them. Only, I was not about to let that happen to me.

What I saw, in Moss and many of the others, were men with broken spirits, hollow men who had sold their souls to the Great Gray Mother for a mere pittance—the intoxicating drink, they sought to ease their pain, and the favors of her prostitutes, to satisfy their compulsion for union with soul. As the Great Gray Bitch sucked the very marrow of life from them through the wanton dissipation of themselves in booze and sex, they quickly faded away into the shadows of the very men whom, in the past, they had only reflected in the dirt but had never dared to embody before now.

I saw, too, how the spirits of both my fathers had been broken before me. When my real father unwittingly traded his soul to the Great Gray Bitch, she broke him in two, stole his mind, and carried it off to the metaphysical realm where he roams in madness, to this very day, unconsciously trying to find his way out. In the case of my stepfather, who had offered his body to her as cannon fodder, in an earnest attempt to die to himself, she snatched up his soul instead, and imprisoned it in a bottle with the spirits of alcohol, who eventually granted him his wish. Though they both found soul in my mother, such solace came as too little, too late, to stave off the fate they had inadvertently bought from the Great Gray Mother with their souls.

So had I inherited from them this tendency to cash in on the same terrible fate. Having given the Great Gray Bitch my body but not my soul, I still had a chance to change my fate before it was signed, sealed and delivered to me in an even more despicable form. I was not about to live and die as half a man, or some soulless beast, as had both of my fathers before me.

Thus did I come to realize the Navy was about destroying my manhood, squashing my femininity, and imprisoning my soul in the bestiality of an animal. How could I attain full human stature when the sanctuary priests of the Great Gray Bitch, or lifers as they were called, put down, at every turn, genuine feeling, the more feminine qualities of my nature, and women in general. If I displayed any feeling other than grabbing a shipmate's ass or goosing him, I was ridiculed or blackballed as a *"fuckin' pussy, a cunt or a faggot"*. As an unmarried nonbeliever in extramarital sex, I was suspected of having homosexual leanings whenever I displayed the gentleness of soul. And Lord help me if I dared to shed a tear.

In many ways, I was just like them. For I generally showed as little feeling towards anyone outside my self as they did, only because I was still too much into the habit of putting down my feelings—a pattern of behavior I had acquired from my stepfather who, in turn, had acquired it from the temple priests of the Great Gray Bitch. Like the others, I too suffered the same psychosomatic consequence, the awful pain that accompanied our persistent abuse of the other member of our bodies. Only, when they were driven to indulge the temple prostitutes, I felt compelled to indulge my self.

I was just as incapable of accepting my sexual feelings, as they were theirs. Where they sought acceptance in the arms of a prostitute, I fled to the confessional for absolution from my guilt—to ease the burden of my pain. Where they sought to escape their pain in the forgetfulness of an alcoholic stupor, I wallowed in mine, day and night, in one attempt after another to find the underlying cause of it. And where they discarded the responsibility for their pain onto the outcasts of society, I held tenaciously onto mine, fearful of letting it go.

For oddly enough, I needed my pain as much as this crutch needed me, as I had the distinct feeling Nature was driving me to lose my self in some yet unknown task. If only I could let go of my self, long enough to taste how it felt to forget about oneself, I believed I would actually find my Self. In imbibing the spirits of alcohol, I had sought the spirit of such an experience. Because my actions were self-serving, that is, unfulfilling, I drank excessively, ever seeking to find the state of mind that could ultimately free me from the pain of my Self. Instead of losing my self to the Spirit crying out within me, I lost my self to the spirits of alcohol, which then blacked out my pain and brought to life the soulless Hyde, hiding behind Nature's desire for unity with spirit.

Compelled to release the incredible tension that had built up between Mother Nature and Father Spirit as a result of their long separation from each other, I gradually realized that I could not accept any ole way of life that fate, or the Great Gray Bitch, threw at me. Only the real thing could ever cool my obsession for union with soul.

Thus did I begin to feel as if service to my country was more of a disservice to my Self. Burdened with the small-mindedness and petty tyranny of lost souls, I found nothing here that even remotely appeared to build character. Instead, I felt as if I were being used by a bunch of self-serving old cronies—whitened sepulchers who had dressed themselves up in priestly garb, pretending to be servants of the people.

Only, this supposed service of the people was, in reality, all a big lie, a monstrous cover-up for servicing the self instead—an orgy meant to whip its participants into a frenzy for that ultimate orgy, the blood bath of battle. It was the reenactment of an age-old drama or myth in which an offended Olympian Goddess stirs the passions of her defenders, in a rite of intoxicating drink and sexual orgy, to avenge her honor—that she might retain her hold on the minds of those who needed her as much as she needed them to keep such bloody rituals from dying out.

Sensing that this way of life was not meant for me or anyone else, for that matter, I wanted off this ship of fools, or rite of passage to hell. Instead, I was taken out to sea.

Shortly after arriving onboard the Davidson, did I get my sea legs, or first real taste of life at sea, which turned out to be a little more hectic than life in port because of the added burden of having to stand four hour watches after a day's work. While most of the crew hated going out to sea, I loved it. In my awe of the incredible vastness and the magnificent beauty of the deep blue waters that surrounded Hawaii, I had somehow stumbled upon the balm of Gilead. In the pall that overcame most of the crew, like the endless sands of a desert, I discovered an oasis, a bit of heaven on earth. In other words, I experienced God for the first time since coming onboard the ship.

To remove myself from the hold the ship had on me, I had only to go up topside and plop down on a mooring head, just aft of the bow along the port side. There, was I shielded from the salt sea spray—which rained down on me as the ship sliced through the surface of the sea—by an umbrella of steel that stretched across the bow like a castle wall. In the sights and sounds of the churning waters below, would I lose my self, until someone disturbed me from my contemplation to relieve the watch.

As a watchman of another sort, how quickly was I rotated, one night shortly thereafter, from one position to another, ever closer to where the Captain slouched in an elevated swivel seat on the starboard side of the bridge, with his feet propped up, while the rest of us humiliatingly acquiesced to his majesty's every command. By the time I had reached the helm, I'd had about enough of this charade, and started responding to his commands with an obviously defiant tone of voice. For I hated standing there, quietly in my place while he chitchatted with the officer of the deck who, in my eyes, deserved no more respect than the lowest man present, that is, than I did.

"Who did this gaunt weasely-looking old man think he was anyway—God?" I inquired of myself.

Instantly, I knew in my heart of hearts that he was not man enough to take charge of my life, for I sought someone much wiser than this old fool to guide me. Warned by my soul not to yield to such hollow displays of worldly power, I was told to stand tall for what I truly believed. Having inherited the timidity and indecisiveness of my mother, I would need the strong will of my stepfather to combat the obstinacy of this old man.

"It seems," proclaimed the old man as we locked horns for one last time, "the new seaman is in need of a haircut."

As he smiled after having almost gotten the better of me, I stepped back, for a moment, to collect my wits about my self. Determined to unseat the old goat, I returned the smile with the assurance, it would take more to subdue this Samson than a haircut, which sent him scurrying below—as I had the last laugh—for the cover of his own lair.

With the fall of this dark knight, I eventually rotated up topside to stand watch under a magnificent dome of stars. As the winds of time sped past me, I imagined my self standing on the earth many thousands of years ago, looking up into the same dome of stars. With that, I realized the stars had moved with the passage of time, and that I had changed too, for I was now a hairy, naked cave man. Instead of walking upon the earth, I found my self literally traversing the ridges of my brain back in time. For under the dome of my own skull now shined brightly the stars of a prehistoric night sky.

Just then, I encountered a large group of Neanderthals. As they stood there staring at me, amazed at how different I looked, I realized that I was the next evolutionary link in the development of mankind. Ere they could grab me, I was snatched back to the ship by my relief.

That night, I lay awake pondering over this unusual reverie. Were my shipmates, the Neanderthals I had encountered in this fantasy? Was I actually carrying, within my own despicable body, the next stage of human development? If so, what was it? Since I really had no answers to such far-reaching questions, I simply stored the reverie away, to savor bits and pieces of it as the aroma of its subtle meanings arose from the ground of my being.

Having stirred up more than I had initially intended, I awoke the following morning to what I had hoped to be a leisurely breakfast. When the call went out over the loudspeaker for all hands to report to general quarters, I found my self, instead, rushing around to get to my battle station for my first real taste of war games since coming onboard the ship. No sooner had I plopped my self down inside the five-inch gun mount to which I had been assigned for GQ, than I succumbed to a frightfully dissociative mood. Rendered barely functional by the feeling side of my personality, as she dissociated herself from me, I could hardly hear what the others were saying to each other, in the resulting void.

At that point, I was abruptly pulled back from the void and temporarily reunited with what I was painfully feeling, when a third class gunner's mate questioned me. "You don't like the Navy, do ya Dury?"

"No, I don't," I replied rather feebly as the sights and sounds of the present moment came crashing back into my awareness.

With that, the gun mount began to swivel about, jerking back and forth with a whining sound, before it settled upon a particular position. The cannon too, was raised and then lowered into position for firing. In quick succession, were several rounds fired at the Navy's firing range, a small island called Kahoolawe.

While the gun mount recoiled around the deafening sound of each round, I found myself getting sick from the combination of the smell of gunpowder, the gyrations of the gun mount and the ship's bobbing up and down like a cork, as it stood dead in the water. With that, did I slip back into my stupor to escape the intolerableness of the moment—the intensity of the screaming in my head, and pain in my chest. How long I remained mentally and emotionally blacked out, I do not know since I didn't come to, until sometime later, down in the compartment. What had transpired in the interim, I could not recall at the time.

Only now do I recollect having had a fantasy in which I washed up onto the shore of some strange island as the sole survivor of a shipwreck. How long I lay there passed out upon the beach, I do not know. At some point, I vaguely remember feeling the soft hand of a woman caressing my face. But I could not see her, for I was unable to open my eyes, which had swollen shut as a result of their overexposure to salt water. When I did finally manage to open my eyes, I found my self standing down in the compartment, looking into the mirror that hung there. And at first, I could've sworn I saw no reflection of my self in the mirror. In fact, I was shocked when I actually felt an urge to walk back into the mirror, or through the looking glass, so to speak. At that point, I saw my reflection and began to hear the sounds of the other guys milling about the compartment.

Only, I had come back filled with all kinds of emotion surrounding my participation in this evil affair. Why, I had been so repulsed by the firing of this big gun that at one point I felt like vomiting. Badly shaken by the whole affair—for my unwitting participation in some unnameable crime against the laws of nature—I knew one thing only, I never wanted to participate in such an exercise again, which suited my soul just fine since I never did figure out what I had done wrong.

As Fate would have her way, thereafter I reported to the mess decks for GQ. I'm sure my overseers had decided I would have been a liability to the crew of the gun mount, given my schizophrenic response to it.

About this time, too, word began to filter down through the crew about a West Pac cruise, during which we might pull liberty in the ports of such notable places as Japan, South Korea, Taiwan, Thailand, Hong Kong, the Philippines and Australia. There was talk of more money, hazardous duty pay on the gun line or at Yankee Station off the coast of Vietnam. But the bulk of the conversation gravitated down around all the "free pussy" to be had overseas. Such comments as "I can already feel my cock gettin' hard, just thinkin' about all that pussy," could be heard in all quarters of the ship. Not a word came from their mouths regarding Vietnam.

I knew very little about Vietnam, except that US troops were being deployed there to halt the spread of Communism. While I had no qualms with this goal on the surface, underneath, I simmered in a pot of emotional uncertainty that seemed to contradict this a priori assertion. At the time, I was unable to pinpoint any specific feeling, other than a certain uneasiness I experienced around just how far I could go with regard to taking part in the killing of other human beings.

By now, my discomfort with the Navy had grown to such an extent that I began to wonder what my body, in its infinite wisdom, was trying to tell me. As the underground resistance to my participation in the Navy spread throughout my body, the more I felt like a stubborn mule that refused to budge no matter how much I cajoled or prodded it, than I did the human being that had gotten it into this mess. O, how I wished I could see what it saw in its earthy wisdom. Alas, I seemed hopelessly trapped in an inescapable morass or nightmare from which not even I could free my own ass.

Although the mule has received a bum rap as being a dumb animal or "dumb ass", like the jackass who sired it, more often than not it takes after its mother, the mare who gave birth to it, in the way it generally behaves. However, if it senses a command would shove it beyond the boundaries of appropriate behavior for a mule, it will quickly revert to behaving like an ass. Seeing such orders as a lie to be resisted with every wily trick at its disposal, thus will it play dumb, ignore the command or refuse to budge, choosing instead to sit down on its haunches and bray at our stupidity, while we—with our superior intellect—stumble off into the very nightmares our more asinine instincts refuse to go.

Thus did I assume a more mulish role onboard the ship by playing dumb, ignoring commands or pretending to misunderstand such orders. In fact, the closer I came to imitating my ancestral father, the ass, the more poorly did I perform my work, to the point that someone else had to redo it. O, how my mule rejoiced in having finally found a friend who saw through the white lie of the temple priests. Why, even my soul found consolation in my joining the underground resistance that had welled up within me.

Though I could neither see nor touch him, I still felt the real presence of this mule somewhere deep inside me. I just knew he was right about the white lie of the temple priests, for I experienced joy in my heart and peace of mind when we rode together, or acted in unison. Whenever I followed the dictates of the mule rather than of the Navy, I experienced mirth of soul, a laughing at the absurdity of the Navy and my self. Thus did I find genuine happiness in following my own mulish instincts.

An Instinctive Response

Whenever I caved into the demands of the lifers and tried to lead an exemplary seaman's life, I would grow increasingly agitated. As soon as I returned to my mulish escapades, I found happiness again. Subjected to a form of behavior modification by my mule, I quickly learned to pay closer attention to his wily ways. Like the mule then, I could see that this life was not for me, that it was out of bounds for me—against my truest instincts. Only, I could not see any further than the end of my nose or the instinctive reactions of a dumb ass, for unlike my mother, or the more marish part of me, I was incapable, at the time, of verbalizing what I felt.

It felt terrible knowing that I was acting against my truest instincts by being in the Navy. Who would've thought that participation in the Navy was against the nature of a human being? What was I to do with such a realization? And how much longer could I continue to act like an ass without getting into serious trouble with the Navy? Obviously, I had to find some way out of this nightmare before I got sucked into doing something, I would later regret.

5
A Voice in the Wilderness

Since each division was required to supply the mess decks with a new man every three months, I was the logical choice when the time came for First Division to send a replacement. Besides being low man on the totem pole, I proved to be such a vexation to the lifers in First Division, they no doubt welcomed the opportunity to get rid of me. So off to the mess decks, I went.

Greatly disappointed, I would much rather have stayed where I was. At least with the lifers in First Division, I knew how far I could push my rebelliousness without blatantly overstepping the rules and regulations of the UCMJ. By playing ignorant and purposely fouling up whatever I touched, I had been relegated to the innocuous task of cleaning the head. Even this job I performed so poorly that, presumably, the lifers decided to transfer me up to the mess decks, to see if they could break my rebellious spirit by subjecting me to an even more onerous task. Thus would I have to start all over again, in testing out a new set of guys, to see just how far I could push my noncooperation without being written up.

Besides, I had finally found someone, in the person of Rulli, with whom I could go on liberty and have a good time without getting drunk or laid, but only when he wasn't hell-bent on "gettin' liquored up enough, to go down on the strip to get some of that nasty ole pussy," as he used to say.

For Rulli was a simple kind of guy who expressed little feeling except around sex and his hate for the Navy, which was very profound. In fact, he blamed the Navy for having made him into a "fuckin' animal". "There are times," he would say, "when I feel like goin' out and fuckin' every bitch in sight, or else gettin' good and goddamn drunk, or kickin' ass just for the hell of it. I never felt like that before I came into the Navy. I'm tellin' ya Dury, the Navy fucks with your mind in a way that turns ya into a fuckin' animal."

Although I empathized with Rulli's problems around sex and his dislike for the Navy, I would talk to him only about my feelings regarding the latter. For in my shame, I could never talk to him about my obsession for union with soul. Whenever he brought up the subject then, I merely listened to what he had to say in hopes of picking up anything that might help me understand this insatiable drive.

About all I ever gleaned from these sessions was some vague notion that both problems were inextricably bound together. At first, I couldn't imagine how the two were even remotely related. Then the connection dawned on me one day when I imagined I was back at the Academy, bemoaning my plight. Having walked out into a courtyard between dormitories, I shouted out in a loud tone of voice, "I wish I could get the fuck out of this hole". Only, instead of hearing an echo of what I had just said, I heard "and that hole too," meaning the female genitalia. That's when it dawned on me that I had symbolically plugged my libido into the wrong hole when I joined the Navy. Because I continued to put my energies into the wrong place, I was being driven by instinct to seek that outlet into which I could rightly plug my libido.

"What the hell am I to do?" I shouted back in angry frustration.

"Hey, Dury!" I heard Rulli yell out as he tugged away at my arm. "Who the fuck ya talkin' to?"

I laughed. "O, I was just thinking out loud, that's all," I replied.

"Well, you sure looked awful serious," added Rulli.

"Yeah," I replied, "I sometimes get a little too carried away by my own thoughts."

"I thought maybe you were trippin' out on me," he replied.

I laughed again. "Nah," I refuted. "I was so deep in thought when you startled me, I don't even remember what the hell I was thinking about."

For some strange reason, I started thinking about Van. I really missed him. I missed having someone who would not only listen to me as I bared my soul, but also help me sort through some of what I was feeling. Instead, I found myself playing Van's role as I listened to Rulli vent his feelings, for he seemed to have just as strong a need to be heard as I did. But I also needed to learn how to listen—how to let go of my self long enough to hear what someone else had to say.

As I turned away from the mirror down in the compartment space, Rulli handed me a letter from Van, into which I tore. There I found the lucky stiff had been made a yeoman on the Dixie. Having stated, much to my consolation, that he missed me, he ended this brief letter by asking how Mary was doing and if I had heard from her recently.

Well I hadn't heard from her since I had arrived onboard the ship, three or four weeks ago, until I found a letter from her lying on my bunk, later that afternoon. As my heart leapt within my chest, I grabbed the letter and tore into it.

Dear Butch,

Sounds as if you don't think too much of the Navy. I think it is because of all the rules and regulations. You haven't had many restrictions put on you in a long time. It's going to take a lot of getting used to. The only thing you can do is to make the best of it. Otherwise, you will go crazy. You are never going to be completely satisfied with the job you are doing—that is human nature. Make the time you have to spend in the Navy, one you will never forget. Remember, life is what you make of it. Whatever job you are doing, do it well, even if you do not like it. You have no choice. Remember, it is only temporary.

Love,
Mary

Now I felt totally misunderstood. While I sometimes doubted my sanity, I certainly did not want to become some socially accepted, schizophrenic beast like Moss. For I saw the rules and regulations, all the pomp and plume of the military, as a facade shrewdly constructed long ago to hide the true nature of this beast from the consciousness of the public. With the beast so well concealed, how could I ever get Mary to see military service as the bloody poison which transforms the young Jekylls of this country into hideous Hydes, so that they, who were once men, can kill without feeling, consciousness of the soul or a conscience. How could I convey to her what has happened to the Mosses of this country? How could I tell her about the Hyde who lurked within my own body and periodically dragged me down to hell? Lastly, how could I ever convince her, it is the discipline of the soul rather than of the military that ultimately transforms the beast?

Even the mess decks had its share of seedy rogues, of whom the worst was a little wiry, dark complected guy named Bechtol who cussed incessantly in that same gruff gravelly voice. Just watching him cook was enough to make me sick. Having wiped the sweat from his brow, he would often fling it into the food he was preparing. Or whenever he cleared his throat or blew his nose, he would occasionally spit the phlegm or blow the snot onto the grill and mix it into the food he was frying. Once he even beat off on a raw steak, which he then threw onto the grill to be cooked and served to the crew, along with the others. In my opinion, the dude was crazy, and yet he was greatly admired by those around him for his audacity.

For my part, I absolutely refused to eat whenever he cooked. How else was I to make the best of such memorable experiences? If I reported him, who would believe me? It would be his word against that of a fuck-up. How could I ever make the best out of anything in this hellhole?

At home, I didn't mind washing dishes for my mother, even though my stepfather had disallowed any son of his to perform women's work when he was around.

However, I hated washing my way through the seemingly endless train of crusty ole aluminum pots and pans that quickly piled up and surrounded me after each meal on the mess decks.

Alone and isolated, I grew despondent. I didn't care if the Navy broke my spirit. I hated the pain this spirit caused me. I hated the tension it created in my life, between what is in the flesh and what is not, and the way it drove me to release this tension. I hated this spirit—I hated it.

Yet, I found myself falling in love with the very same spirit. "How could this be?" I wondered. "How could I fall in love with what I could not see?" Yet, the feelings I was experiencing were unmistakably clear. After all, had not I fallen in love with Mary, for the very same reason, the love of some spirit I could not see? Who was this spirit, which so skillfully eluded my grasp? Why did I feel such a compulsion to unite with it—with what I did not yet know?

Overcome by an incredible hunger for self-knowledge, I wanted to know everything there was to know about myself. As tears welled up in my eyes, I felt excited about the prospect of getting to know myself from head to toe. I looked forward to this new relationship with my Self, like a newfound love. Impatient, I wanted the relationship to develop more quickly than it was, for I'd been overcome by an insatiable desire to learn the true nature of this spirit.

"How amazing is this spirit!" I thought. "Where just a moment ago, I felt depressed and even expressed hate for this spirit, I now felt hope." What I had to be hopeful about, I knew not until I walked out onto the mess decks, in response to an inner urge to do so.

Turning, I caught sight of this dude standing there, with his dungaree pants cut into ribbons from the knees down. Shocked, I approached him. "What happened to your pants?" I asked with a slight snicker.

"I cut them up," he arrogantly replied, "to protest the deplorable condition in which my clothes repeatedly come back to me from the ship's laundry—chewed up, torn, wrinkled and often unwashed."

I laughed.

"It's not a laughing matter," he bemoaned with raised brows and a wrinkled forehead.

"I know," I replied with a chuckle. "Many of my own clothes have gotten lost in the laundry. In fact, I am down to my last pair of dungarees, and do not have the money to buy another pair."

"You see!" He added. "I'm sick and tired of it all."

"But what do you hope to accomplish by parading around like this?" I asked.

"Well," he exclaimed, "I may not accomplish a goddamn thing, other than the ventilation of a little steam. And that's okay. After having failed to elicit a response from the goddamn lifers on this ship, by going through their silly-ass chain of command, I'll guarantee you one thing, that my appearance will raise more than a few eyebrows before the day is done. I'll get a response, all right, from the lousy sons of bitches, before I take these rags off. You'll see!" He boasted as he turned and marched off the mess decks, muttering to himself.

"Who is that guy?" I asked someone sitting at a table nearby.

"His name's Wulf; he's a signalman," came the reply.

He impressed the hell out of me, for here was an individual who not only thought for himself but also acted upon his thoughts with volition and courage. He was like a breath of fresh air to the lamp of hope barely flickering within me, due to the moral vacuum, the rest of the crew had created. In fact, he raised the expectation that I might find a like-minded friend in this hellhole, after all.

Later that evening, I found him up on the Signal Bridge where, with a fixed gaze, he stood wrapped in thought. Startled by the sound of my approach, he turned and smiled halfheartedly as if he were not too pleased to see me. "Hi," he finally said, with raised brows and a wrinkled forehead, facial features he characteristically used to display an arrogant self-assuredness.

"I hope I'm not disturbing you," I replied.

"If you were, I would have asked you to leave," he said. "As it is, I feel the need for some good company and a bit of stimulating conversation."

Struck by not only his honesty but also his impeccable dress, a freshly pressed set of tailor-made dungarees, I asked him, "Did you get in trouble today?"

"Nah," he answered. "I'm too short. With less than a week to go on this godforsaken can, they (meaning the lifers) can't touch me."

I was saddened by the news that he would be leaving so soon. Even though he wasn't as warm and vibrant as Van, I nonetheless took an immediate liking to him, for I experienced this rebellious intellectual from Boston, Massachusetts, as a godsend. Envious of his impending discharge, I wished I were in his shoes instead.

"For four long years," he continued, "I have struggled against becoming an animal like the rest of these bastards. Next week when I walk off this ship for the last time, I will have prevailed."

"I know the feeling," I interjected.

"From the first day of my enlistment," he rejoined, "they drummed the idea into my head that I had joined this outfit for one reason only: to fight for my country. But they lied to me, for I ended up spending four long years fighting to save my ass from them.

"Don't believe a word of what the lying vultures say, for they prey upon human flesh, with talons made of lies. Resist the temptation to become one of them. And whatever you do, don't let them rob you of the most precious gift you have, your humanity, for the wraiths will claw away at it until all that remains is the shadow of what was once you."

"What do you mean?" I asked out of the very real fear that such a thing could happen to me.

"For four long years," he went on to say, "they tried to convince me this way of life is a necessary evil. They almost succeeded until I went to Vietnam, supposedly, to stop the spread of Communism, and saw the truth for myself.

"It appears, they suffer some grand delusion that we are the good guys who are going to save the rest of the world from bad guys like the Communists. They misled me, for a while, with this white lie of theirs, until I discovered they were only protecting their delusion—some fantasy called the American dream, which has become a real nightmare for many throughout the world.

"For the real fight is not out there, over in Vietnam, it is in here, within ourselves. It is the struggle with our own delusions, the lies we live by, especially the one which has us so convinced that what we need is more of what is out there in Nature."

"I don't understand," I interjected.

"Since time immemorial," he went on, "have we fallen for this lie, that our future lies hidden within our material progress. Yet, in our pursuit of this delusion, we have only succeeded in impoverishing the earth and its people. Thus have we created a bipolar world, consisting of the haves and the have-nots, who have further polarized themselves over the issue of materialism, by squaring off on either side of an iron curtain, into two heavily armed, ideologically opposed camps or isms.

"As I chipped away at all the hype and hysteria surrounding communism, I began to see it as a rather ambitious attempt by the have-nots to right the wrongs of capitalism, which has only succeeded in impoverishing the many for the benefit of a few. However, in their struggle to purge from the masses the sins of capitalism—its rugged individualism, greed and failed trickle-down economics—the communists have only succeeded in creating a totalitarian nightmare instead of a utopia. As this nightmare invaded the collective consciousness of the world, it struck fear into the heart of the American dreamer and created mass hysteria. For this Red scare threatened to take everything from the American dreamer, to redistribute the wealth, he had misappropriated, more equitably among its rightful inheritors, the have-nots of the world.

"That's when I saw the nightmare and the dream as two sides of the same coin, for both of them have resorted, in the past, to propaganda, economic ideology and guns, to force their inhumane ways of life on the rest of us, the guilty bystanders caught up in this Mexican standoff. Whether we choose heads or tails, we lose—the many are impoverished for the benefit of a few—for a single coin was given to us long ago, to benefit not only the individual but also the collective.

"Only when the individual and the collective realize their indebtedness to each other, will we tear down the iron curtain that so divides our collective psyche. As the collective must put everything, it possesses, into the development of the individual, so must the individual give back to the collective, all it has given him. Only then, will we truly be free.

"Only then, will we realize that our future lies not out there in our own self-centered materialism, but on the other side of the iron curtain within the collective unconsciousness of our beings. Only then, will we see the iron curtain as the veil of matter that has so blurred our vision—our materialism as the wall that has so divided us. Only then, will we take the next great step and cross the threshold to embrace our humanity, a life given to us for the sake of each other, as exemplified in simple living and the right use of the material goods of this world."

"I see," I muttered as he paused for a moment, to get some assurance from me that I understood what he had just shared with me.

"What we sorely need," he continued to preach from his soapbox on the bridge, "is an amalgam of communism and capitalism around the issue of materialism, a single coin that combines the best of all three. What we'll get, I'm afraid, is the appearance of a winner and a loser. In that case, we'll all lose. Though communism may recede into the shadows of our collective imaginations, like a tyrannosaur, the truth of its ideals will rise again as the disparity between the haves and the have-nots worsens under capitalism, that other dinosaur, which may not pass on until it has devoured everything and transformed this Eden into a living hell.

"So don't be fooled into believing the real battle is outside your body between one delusion and another, for the real war wages on deep within you, even now as I speak. That's where the outcome will be decided. The real enemy is not out there; he is in here, for we are our own worst enemy."

As he fell silent, I grew uneasy. What could I add to such an eloquent discourse? Besides feeling intimidated by his intellectual acumen, I was embarrassed that I had never given such thought to my situation. How could I? I was too wrapped up in my self, to have time to think about anything or anyone else. Could I ever break free from this chain of circular thinking and instinctive behavior, which devoured me like a snake its own tail? I certainly was being challenged by this very perceptive young man to do so.

While my feelings validated the truth of his perceptions, I wondered how he had acquired such knowledge. "Where did you get this information?" I asked, wondering if he hadn't gotten it from a book that I might also read.

After what seemed like a long time, he finally responded, "Even though I have gone along with their program, over the past four years, I've been haunted by a vague sense that I am missing something. Only, I haven't a clue of what it is. For hours, I have racked my brain, and have come up with little else than the insight, I just shared with you, which leaves me feeling as if I am still missing something."

"Indeed, you are!" I blurted out.

Astonished, he asked in reply, "What do you mean?"

"I mean this," I responded, "that you haven't paid enough attention to your feelings. You have given your situation entirely too much thought on a head level. As a result, you have missed half the equation. You have fallen into the same snare I have in the past, namely, circular thinking.

"With the thought processes of the head, you can only develop and organize what you see. With feeling, or thoughts from the heart, you are exposed to what you do not see, to an entirely new way of looking at what you thought you saw.

"As feeling helps you grope through the darkness of your own ignorance, she not only raises your level of consciousness, but also gradually reveals the way you must go, which lies hidden out there in Nature, as you say. For feeling is a completely different way of thinking. While thinking is like walking through a room with your eyes open, feeling is like walking through that same room, only with your eyes closed. It's like putting your trust in the hand of another as she leads the way.

"To help you find the way, she separates the wheat from the chaff, that is, she gives insight into what your senses have gathered. For her vision, she demands not only blind faith, the letting go of cherished concepts, but also blind obedience, the embodying of insight, for she needs a body in which these seeds can take root and bear fruit.

"So must the head and the heart become as one. For as a body thinks, so does it act. Whereas the head needs the heart to give order to its chaos, the heart needs the head to give direction to its intentions. While the thoughts of the heart must eventually become those of the head, in turn, the head must willingly act upon or give body to the thoughts of the heart. Only then, does a body find peace and harmony with itself."

Thus were our individual horizons broadened that night as we soaked up the perspectives of each other as the parched earth, a good rain. What poured forth from my mouth surprised me as much as what had spilled out of Wulf's, for I had actually found something to talk about besides my obsession for union with my body. Maybe my world was beginning to expand beyond itself, after all.

The last few days he remained onboard the ship, I clung to him like a pesky little fly. I was so needy for a like-minded friend, I couldn't help myself. As I buzzed about his head, I picked his brain for any tiny morsel that might help me to survive in this wasteland of dead heads after he was gone.

Besides, the lifers razzed him mercilessly. "You'll be back," they said mockingly, "to ship over."

"Fuck you!" He barked back. "Just because you couldn't make it on the outside, doesn't mean I can't—ya low-life motherfuckers."

He would never ship over, and they knew that. They were jealous of him—that he was an individual with an agenda of his own, for they would never see the likes of him again.

While I was happy for him, I felt sad at the same time, for his departure certainly left a big hole in my life. I was hurt, even more, when in his hurriedness to get off the ship, he left without saying a word to me. Nor did I ever hear from him again.

To make matters worse, a day or so later, I received a very disheartening letter from Mary. I had begun to wonder about her after her letters had grown fewer in number and farther apart, which wouldn't have bothered me so much if she hadn't been the only consistent relationship in my life, at the time. Shipwrecked and marooned on an island with a bunch of savages, I saw her as the one last hope, I had, of keeping myself connected to my humanity. When mail call came and went with nigh a word from her, I hurt. Although school most assuredly kept her busy, I still expected her to let me know, occasionally, how she was doing or that she was at least thinking of me.

She began her letter by telling me how sick she had gotten. As her health continued to decline, she decided to go home. There, she developed a lump on her throat. Frightened, she went to see a doctor who, upon diagnosing it as a toxic goiter, put her on thyroid medication and a tranquilizer. Forced to quit school, she claimed all the worry and excitement over her condition had prevented her from writing any sooner. She then went on to say:

"Butch, I want you to know you mean a great deal to me. I care about what happens to you, what you do. As I recall the good times we've had, I want to thank you for all of them. But I'm afraid you look at them a lot differently than I do. I've said this before and I mean it—you are a very good friend and I will always want to keep your friendship. I don't want anything to happen to our friendship, or should I say my friendship with you, because you feel so differently about me. I regard you as one of my best friends, and that's all.

"You said you love me and maybe you do. I can't say what you're feeling, I can only tell you what I feel, that I feel only a very strong need for you as a friend. If I've given you the impression my feelings for you are the same as those you hold for me, I'm sorry. I never meant to do that. And if what I've said has offended you in any way, I am deeply hurt. If you love me, then I have hurt you too. I'm sorry.

"I hated having to say this to you, but I believe it had to be said. I can only hope that you will understand what I'm trying to tell you. I did not write this letter to hurt you, for I would rather die than hurt you. However, it was not fair to you, to go

on believing I love you too. I can only say I care very much about what happens to you. You will never know how much you have given me. But Butch, I cannot return the same feelings you have for me. I can only say I hope this letter does not affect our friendship. Remember, I do care about you, more than you will ever know.

"From now on my letters will be far apart because the doctor wants me to do nothing that will excite me. I will write as often as I can. Butch, please read this letter carefully and try to understand what I'm saying. I never was very good at expressing my feelings on paper.

Love,
Mary

I was devastated. While she had never verbally expressed her love for me, that message had certainly been conveyed in her physical responses to me. As I read and reread her letter, between the lines, I spotted an immature love, one in which she wanted to enjoy the luxury of a romantic relationship with no strings attached. Well I wasn't going to stand for it. And I told her as much in a letter, I fired off to her, later that evening.

I couldn't continue with the relationship as just a friend, unless she was more open to the love that was there. For we were more than good friends, we were also romantically involved with each other, and had been for some time, whether she wanted to admit it or not. I wasn't asking her to marry me when I expressed the love I felt for her, if that's what was scaring her off, for I was no more ready to marry than she was. While I courted her with marriage in the back of my mind, at this point, I knew only that I loved her very much.

Or was I only fooling myself? Was I guilty of romanticizing a friendship—of refusing to accept the true nature of the relationship? Or was she backing off from me again because of the instability I was exhibiting, only this time, with the Navy? Obviously, I was no more open to a mere friendship than she was, to courtship. Yet, because the relationship held up before our eyes some unknown potential, neither one of us was willing to let go of it. Had we fallen for each other then, before either one of us was ready for love? Is that what she was really trying to tell me in her letter? While I wouldn't know for sure until I heard from her again, I couldn't help wondering.

While I had certainly reached a low point in my life, I had no inkling of how I could escape this black hole. Caught up in the vortex of this hell, I cried out in anguish one night, "O God, please help me, for I am at my wits end. I must get out of here before this place destroys me. Please show me the way."

Just then, I saw a way out. I will refuse to eat until the Navy discharges me. "What a great idea!" I said to my self. "Since I won't be hurting anyone, what can they do to me? They can't make me eat if I don't want to. What are they going do with an emaciated sailor? Force me to eat. I'm afraid not, for I refuse to eat another bite until they promise to discharge me from the Navy."

From that moment on, I took in nothing by mouth except liquids. Before each meal, I drank a large glass of juice to quell the pangs of hunger my body suffered while I served food on the mess line. In between meals, I drank enough water to keep me hydrated as I continued to sweat it out in the galley.

The first week of my fast was the hardest. With food in front of my face and in my hands throughout most of the day, the temptation to eat was always there. To resist such habits as nibbling in between meals, or testing the food being prepared, or licking my fingers, took considerable effort. Even more difficult was spitting out the morsel of food I would unwittingly stick into my mouth as I worked.

I found solace, however, in the most unlikely place, my body. As my mule carried me on its back across this barren desert, in the most striking fantasy, I saw the bubble of each temptation to eat burst in front of my eyes like a mirage. Instead, was I transported to a small oasis that jutted up from the floor of the desert like a mount of olive trees. Dismounting, I entered the garden to pray. While those around me slept, I sweated blood. Several times, I arose to arouse them, to no avail. As I continued to pray, I asked God to let this cup pass if it be His will, for evil men waited outside this garden to do me harm.

As an angry crew forced its way onto the mess decks, in reality, was I pulled from my fantasy, to help serve them their dinner, which in their eyes, had been unduly delayed. With the opening of the mess decks for a slightly delayed evening meal, I lost my way in this desert of dead heads. Separated from my mule, I crawled back into my fantasy, across the hot desert sands on my hands and knees, in search of a way out as I plunked down spoonful after spoonful of food onto the trays of these wild angry boors.

Due to unforeseen circumstances, I was eventually transferred off the mess decks. Although I had continued to bathe and put on clean underclothes daily, it had been a month since I last changed my pants. Because I had no other pants to wear, I couldn't throw them into the laundry when they got dirty. To protest my predicament, I simply allowed them to get so filthy and foul smelling, that even I could barely stand to wear them. Therefore, I was not too surprised when I began to hear snide remarks from some of the lifers as they passed through the mess line. Nor was I any more surprised when one of my detractors finally blew up that Sunday. Fortunately, I had made the mistake of serving him while standing over the pan with my fly wide open. In the ensuing furor he raised with the chief of the mess crew, over the unsanitary condition of my dress, I was relieved of my duties and sent back down to First Division.

As I pondered over this small victory, I learned a very important lesson, that a man can stand up for what he believes and prevail, in spite of the most incredible odds against his ever doing so, but only if he stands for the truth.

Here I was, taking on the Navy, based on some foggy notion that I should free myself from this indenture to butchering other human beings in some Southeast Asian slaughterhouse. Although humans sometimes got their way with animals, I wasn't too sure I would get mine, in this instance. Nonetheless, with this small success as a feather in my cap, I was sure going to try.

About the twentieth day of my fast, I woke up feeling light-headed and weak. Not until my heart started fluttering rapidly, as I stood up to get dressed, did I get scared. Scurrying up to the mess decks, I gulped down a glass of fruit juice, with the hope it would alleviate these symptoms. Instead, I experienced an increase in the magnitude of the symptoms as I returned to the compartment. Growing ever more fearful of what was happening to me, I hurried over to my bunk to lie down. As long as I lay there, I felt all right. Whenever I tried to get back up, I found that the symptoms quickly returned. Like a woman in labor, I knew the time had arrived for me to let someone know about my fast before I really hurt myself. So I lay there until my PO, who had just stumbled upon me as he was making his rounds, ordered me to report up topside for work.

"I can't go," I replied.

"Why not?" He demanded to know.

"I'm not feeling very well, today," I answered.

Spinning around, he flew up the ladder, only to return as quickly as he had disappeared. "Report to sick bay, immediately," he barked.

As he left, I slipped from my rack and scurried over to the fountain, to get a drink of water. Feeling somewhat revived, I hurried up the ladder. By now, I was much more concerned with what I was going to tell the Corpsman than I was with any of the symptoms of my fast. With the shot of adrenaline, my body had given me as it revved itself up for the uncertainties of my next encounter, I easily made my way back to sick bay without getting dizzy.

Inside stood the Corpsman with his back turned towards the door. So engrossed was he in his work, that he didn't even hear me. While I stood there in the doorway, ever so quietly, waiting for him to recognize me, he fiddled around with some bottles in a cabinet on the bulkhead behind his desk. He was a stout young man, whose dress struck me as rather odd, only because he wore his pants so high up and tight around his waist, they looked to be several sizes too small for him. Responding to a vague sense of someone else's presence, he eventually turned his head around to see if indeed, anyone had invaded his space while he had been so preoccupied.

"Well, what do you want?" He asked, as he nudged his thick, dark-rimmed glasses back up on his nose.

"I'm not feeling very well today," I replied rather sheepishly.

"What's the matter with you?" He asked in a tone of voice that left me feeling rather suspect.

"Ever since I got up this morning," I began, "I have felt terribly weak and light-headed, as if I am going to pass out if I don't lie back down on my bunk. Whenever I try to get back up or exert myself in any way, my heart immediately goes into this fluttering mode, that is, it begins to beat very rapidly."

"Sit down here," he commanded as he grabbed his stethoscope and took my blood pressure. After listening to my heartbeat, he dropped the stethoscope down onto my abdomen to get a sounding of my bowels. Snatching the stethoscope from his ears, he asked, "When was the last time you had a bowel movement?"

As my body grew taut with anxiety, I broke out into a cold sweat. "About three weeks ago," I responded with some hesitation.

"Three weeks ago!" He exclaimed.

At a loss for words, I simply remained silent.

"Have you been eating all this time?" He asked.

"No, sir, I haven't eaten a thing for almost three weeks," I responded feebly.

"Are you constipated?" He inquired.

"No, sir," I replied.

"Then, why haven't you been eating?" Asked a puzzled Corpsman.

"Because I don't want to eat anymore," I replied.

Scratching his head, he asked, "And why don't you want to eat?"

"I just don't want to eat anymore?" I repeated.

Completely bewildered by my response, he rubbed his hand back and forth through his thick black stubbly hair. "Excuse me," he said, as he jumped up and darted out the door.

Sitting on the edge of my seat, I wished it were over. Now that my fast was out in the open, I felt relieved, but not for very long. As I wondered what was going to happen next, I was overcome with anxiety.

Just then, the Corpsman popped back into sick bay. "Come with me," he commanded. "Your division officer, Lt. Smyth, would like to see you in his stateroom."

Nervous as hell, I sprang to my feet and followed him down this passageway, to a ladder that led upto officer's country. While the Corpsman and my Division Officer conferred briefly, I stood outside his stateroom.

With that, the door popped open.

"Come in, Mr. Drury," commanded the Corpsman. As I entered, he introduced me to the Lieutenant.

"You may go," said the Lieutenant to the Corpsman as he left the room.

"Have a seat, Mr. Drury," said the Lieutenant after a brief interlude in which he sat behind his desk looking me over while I stood there at attention, with my eyes transfixed on a spot over his head, on the bulkhead behind him.

As I sat down, I was struck by how much he resembled a television character from my youth—a puppet named Howdy Doody. That the Lieutenant had a smaller head and wore glasses was all that differentiated him from his caricature.

"The Corpsman tells me you don't want to eat anymore. Is that true, Mr. Drury?" He finally asked.

Looking him straight in the eye, I smiled nervously. "The Corpsman has told you the truth. I don't want to eat anymore," I replied.

Completely taken aback by my candor, he broke into a monologue, in an attempt to regain control of the situation.

"Now, Mr. Drury," he began, "you and I both know that we must eat in order to survive. Isn't that correct?"

As I struggled to gain control over my fear of speaking from the heart, I regurgitated a biblical quote in response, *"Man does not live on bread alone,* Sir, *but on every word that comes from the mouth of God."* Mt. 4:4

Now I was just as surprised by my response as he was. Though the words had flown way over his head, I was struck by how instinctively they had gushed forth from my mouth. As we both struggled during this very brief interlude, to comprehend what the hell I was trying to say, I experienced some vague notion that man does not live by images alone, like an animal, but on the meaning of those images instead.

Ignoring the quote, again he asked me, "Can you tell me, Mr. Drury, in your own words, this time, why you no longer wish to eat?"

Because I had not given much thought to what I would tell them when they found out about my fast, I didn't know what to say. How could I tell him I just wanted out of the Navy?

To buy myself more time in which to collect my thoughts, I simply repeated my initial statement, *"Man does not live on bread alone, but on every word that comes from the mouth of God."* Mt. 4:4

"Come now, Mr. Drury," he replied, "I find it hard to believe that you have quit eating for God's sake. There must be some reason why you have chosen to hurt yourself in this manner. Now what is it?"

Having sat in silence while I waited for my next cue, I finally blurted out, "I didn't know what else to do. I was so disappointed by the Navy's failure to satisfy the insatiable longing for self-fulfillment that has afflicted me since puberty, I could not bear the additional pain of the remorse I felt after having made the irreversible choice to go on active duty. Or so I thought, until the day I decided to starve myself, to dramatize how the Navy is starving me, that is, depriving me of the means to fulfill myself. I had to do something to stop the endless bouts of self-abuse I fall prey to whenever I am held captive, like an animal in a cage, and made to do the bidding of a taskmaster as unsuited for the job of managing my soul as the Navy is."

As soon as he heard the "s" word, he honed in on it like a vulture on a fly, as if the real reason for my fast were hidden in some dark dirty little secret surrounding my sexuality. "Have you ever desired sex or had sex with anyone onboard this ship?" He asked.

Momentarily left feeling quite bewildered by what I thought was the most bizarre question I had ever been asked, I finally responded, "No, I can't say that I have ever desired to have sex with anyone onboard the ship. I do have a girl friend back home in St. Louis, whom I love very much and dream about marrying some day. Occasionally, I have fantasies of having sex with her. As far as having sex with another guy, why, I've never heard of such a thing! I can't even imagine how that would work. I assure you, Lt. Smith, that my problem with self-abuse has nothing to do with anyone else onboard this ship but me. I just can't seem to find out where I fit in."

"Mr. Drury, I fail to see anything in what you have said that would warrant taking such a drastic step as your refusing to eat," he concluded.

"I feel sorry for you, Sir," I rejoined, "that you are so oblivious to the pain and suffering you inflict upon the souls under your command. You have my sympathies, Sir, for in choosing to live blindly, you can't even see beyond the bread you eat."

It became clear to me that we were not talking to each other, on the same wavelength. At that point, I wasn't too sure, where the hell I was coming from either. Normally, I didn't talk like this, especially to a lieutenant. Besides, I wasn't sure that I saw much beyond the bread I used to eat, for I felt as if someone else had put those words into my mouth.

In an attempt to regain control over the situation, the Lieutenant resorted to his power as a superior officer. "Mr. Drury," he snapped back, "I order you to eat."

Chuckling to myself, I shook my head in disbelief. Then looking him in the eye, I responded, "Sir, neither you nor the whole damn Navy can make me eat if I don't want to. What makes you think you can order me to eat?"

"Do you know the consequences, Mr. Drury, for refusing the direct order of a superior officer?" He asked.

"No, I'm afraid I don't, Sir," I answered.

"A court-martial," he replied with a grin when he saw me squirm in my seat. "And brig time," he added. Having succeeded in stirring up a great deal of fear within me, he again ordered me to eat.

"You can't make me eat," I insisted as I struggled, desperately, to stay on top of the fear that, by now, had my whole body trembling.

"You leave me no choice, Mr. Drury, but to refer the matter to the Executive Officer," he snapped. "Come with me," he commanded as he sprang from his seat and hurried out the door, only to disappear through another down the passageway.

Left standing outside the XO's stateroom, I felt a bit like Jesus, who had been shuffled from one authority to the next, in much the same manner, as each one realized he had no authority over He Who Is. In that one brief moment, I felt as if I were in contact with some incredibly powerful force, I perceived to be the force of truth. Because I didn't know this truth, I could not hold onto it for very long. As its intoxicating grip on me faded, I was summoned by the Lieutenant and, with all due haste, officially introduced to the XO.

"Mr. Drury, Sir," smartly snapped the Lieutenant.

"Thank you, Mr. Smyth," snapped the XO. "You may go now."

"Have a seat, Mr. Drury," the XO said in a rather annoyed tone of voice as the door slammed shut behind the Lieutenant.

"What's this, I hear, about your refusing to eat?" He asked.

"I don't want to eat anymore," I managed to squeak out as I struggled to control the trembling of my body with fear.

"Poppycock!" He shouted in my face. "You will eat, Mr. Drury, because I order you to eat. Do you understand?"

"No Sir, I don't," I replied rather indignantly.

Failing to elicit an obedient response from me, he decided to take a different tack. "Do you know, Mr. Drury," he began, "that by refusing to eat, you are willfully destroying government property?"

Puzzled, I asked, "How's that, Sir?"

"When you enlisted in the Navy," he replied, "you signed your life over to the government of the United States to be used as it sees fit. In effect, you became government property. Whatever befalls you befalls the property of the government of the United States. So you see, Mr. Drury, you could be charged with the willful destruction of government property if, in the continuation of this ridiculous fast of yours, you harm yourself in any way."

Irked by his insistence that I was government property, I responded rather coldly, "I see." For I wanted so badly to tell him I was not some soulless piece of meat, the Navy could order around like a zombie, but bit my lip instead.

Having threatened to write me up if I did not eat, he again ordered me to eat.

Once again, I refused.

"Then you leave me no choice," he concluded as he rose from his chair and hurried out the door.

After what seemed like an eternity, the door to the stateroom flew open. In walked an older looking officer whom I had never seen before. A hefty though fleshy gentleman, he introduced himself as the ship's Chaplain.

"What's your name, son?" He asked reassuringly.

"Drury, Sir," I responded as I wondered what tack he would take.

"Mr. Drury, I understand from the Executive Officer, LCDR Merwin, that you refuse to eat. Is that correct?" He asked.

"Yes Sir, it is," I replied in a bit more relaxed, though slightly guarded manner.

As I shifted the weight of my body in the chair, he continued, "I am sure you have a good reason for not wanting to eat, but that is not why I have come to talk with you. I have come as a man of the cloth who is very concerned about the welfare of a particular seaman on this ship. You see, Mr. Drury, you do not realize the physical harm you are inflicting upon yourself as you continue to deny your body the nutrients it needs to function properly."

"When was the last time you had anything to eat?" He asked.

"About three weeks ago," I answered.

"Have you been drinking plenty of fluids?" He inquired further.

"Yes Sir," I replied. "I've been drinking a glass of fruit juice at meal times, and lots of water in between."

"And it has been three weeks, you say, since you last ate solid food of any kind?" He asked again.

"Yes Sir," I replied.

As the expression on his face filled with alarm, I was again overcome with fear.

"You know, Mr. Drury," he went on to say, "the body can survive for awhile without food, as it feeds off the reserves it has stored up for leaner times. If this deprivation persists, the body will eventually deplete these reserves. When that happens, it will begin to feed on its own muscle tissue and organs, causing irreversible damage. As your body literally eats itself up, you will suffer an agonizingly slow and painful death.

"I offer you this perspective," he concluded, "with the hope that you may realize, before it is too late, the great harm you will be inflicting upon your body, should you decide to continue with your fast."

As he fell silent, I grew fearful of what harm I might already have caused my body. I felt confused. When I began this fast, I certainly never had any intention of harming my body or causing my own death. Thus did I take the appearance of the symptoms of my fast as a sign that maybe I was pushing this whole thing, a bit too far.

As I stewed over the matter, I wondered what would happen if I caved into them and broke my fast. Would I be discharged anyway? Regardless of whether I was or not, I certainly could not continue on, without eating. Besides, I could never bear the thought that I had caused my body to suffer irreparable damage, just because I had wanted out of the Navy. At least, I felt my actions had let them know I was having a difficult time adjusting to the Navy. Or had I simply convinced them I was only half-crazy? As my feelings came to a head, I realized that I must eat, no matter what they thought.

"I'll eat," I finally said with some reluctance.

"Good!" He exclaimed. "I think you have made a wise decision."

While I felt good about the decision to eat again, I experienced a certain sadness too. I felt a bit like Jesus who, as a young lad, had wandered off from his parent's side to begin His Father's work before it was time. Though I wasn't ready yet, I sensed the hour was fast approaching when I would again be called upon, by God, to stand tall.

As the Chaplain patted me on the back, he dismissed me. "You may go below now," he said.

As soon as I had reached the compartment, the Corpsman showed up and insisted on escorting me up to the mess decks to eat. "Since the mess line had already shut down for the morning, I didn't want you to have to wait until lunch before you got something to eat," he explained.

"That's fine," I said as I turned, without hesitating, to follow him up the ladder.

As soon as we arrived on the mess decks, he approached one of the cooks. "Give him whatever he wants," he instructed the cook, "for this boy is mighty hungry." After I filled my tray and sat down to eat, he stuck around for a while, to make sure that I ate, which of course, I did with great relish.

That evening, as I lay on my bunk, I felt an urge to go up topside to be alone. I had just approached the ladder leading out of the compartment, when a voice rang out, loud and clear, from somewhere within me. "You must find out why you want out of the Navy," it commanded.

Why, I was elated the other side had finally spoken to me, after all these years, in plain English rather than through the usual mode of difficult-to-decipher dreams and fantasies. Like a crazy man, I ran up topside, laughing and crying, and continued to do so, even after I had plopped down on my favorite perch. I felt as if my pursuit of a discharge from the Navy had just been endorsed by the highest authority in existence, the very source of truth itself. Now, I had only to find the real reason why I wanted out of the Navy so badly.

For now, I just wanted to sit and savor the sweetness of the moment. While I sat there, wishing and hoping the voice would speak to me again, I recalled a similar night, many years ago, when I lay down in the grass and dared the heavens to make contact with me. Then, as now, I heard nigh a word. Instead, I sat wondering why the voice had not just told me the reason. And I wondered why it still chose to remain so aloof, especially after having made this initial contact, for I wanted so badly to see the owner of the voice. Alas, I was again disappointed by sleep as it began to rob me of the ability to stay awake any longer. Exhausted, I stumbled off to my bunk where, after undressing and climbing into it, I fell fast asleep.

6

A Test of Wills

That night I had a dream in which I found my self wrestling with a prostitute who kept insisting that I give into her. All night long did I struggle, in and out of sleep, to resist her entreaties. Just before dawn, I gave into her in a moment of weakness. Immediately, I woke up.

Deeply troubled by the dream, I lay awake for what seemed like a long time. Upset with myself for having given into my sexual desires, I sincerely hoped the dream was not a portent of how I would be conducting myself in real life at some point in the near future. Haunted by an inability to control my obsession for union with soul, I eventually cajoled myself back to sleep with the thought that, until I found a suitable mate, maybe wet dreams were the only outlet I had, to protect me from sexual promiscuity.

As I fell back to dreaming again, I beheld a white knight riding toward me on the back of an incredibly beautiful white horse. Overcome by a tremendous fear of what I was seeing, I woke up wondering what I had been so afraid of. In my drowsiness, I managed to unearth some vague notion that the white knight and I were the same person, before I fell back to sleep.

This time, as I slipped back into the dream, I was not so afraid of the white knight when I ran into him again. Much to my consternation, I was informed by him that I must serve She Who Must Be Obeyed if I wished to free my self from the spell of the Great Gray Whore. Startled by this revelation, I woke up.

Unable to fall back to sleep, I got up, dressed myself and moseyed up topside to my favorite perch to begin the painful process of trying to catch a glimpse into the meaning of these god-awful dreams. Not until I had let go of the thoughts that had so concerned me through the night, long enough to hear those of my heart, did I realize the mistake I'd made. Having told the Temple Priest, under psychological duress, that I would eat again, I essentially gave my self back to the Navy. In other words, before I had received instructions from the author of this narrative to find the real reason why I wanted out of the Navy, I fell victim to servicing one of the prostitutes of the Great Gray Whore again—to putting my energies back into a way of life that was not meant for me. Even though I had been enthralled by the incredible power, I had briefly commanded in my new role as the white knight, I grew fearful of the price I might have to pay to play such an obscure part. Out of fear, I relinquished this new role, and fell back into an unconscious state of being. By emotionally distancing my self from the white knight, I effectively rid myself of the fear of stepping into his shoes before I was ready. To my consternation, was I informed that I could serve only one mistress, either She Who Must Be Obeyed or her shadow, the Great Gray Whore.

Through these dreams did I reclaim, from that vast sea of unconsciousness, which surrounds us all like the great oceans of the earth, some important pieces of the island that makes up one's consciousness. As I tried to put these pieces to the puzzle of myself into place, I realized my rebellious spirit and this She Who Must Be Obeyed were somehow connected. At the same time, I found nothing in Her unusual name that shed any light on Her real identity. While the white knight remained the biggest mystery of all, I just knew he embodied the reason why I wanted out of the Navy so badly. Unable to crack the shell surrounding the truth of these images, I began to feel some regret over having ended my fast so soon, and wondered if more would have been revealed to me had I not agreed to eat again.

As I continued to listen to my feelings, I felt as if I were stuck on the threshold of a dream, only because I did not know how to enter it. For I was beginning to feel as if the Great Gray Whore had a hold on me which She Who Must Be Obeyed and the white knight were trying to help me break. While the Great Gray Whore drove me to act instinctively, like a wild animal, She and the white knight were trying to show me the way out, the doorway to my humanity. Only, I just couldn't get my self to take that first step—that big of a leap in faith. I was too afraid to walk into the unknown without having some idea of where I was going. Like Thomas, I had to see before I could believe. I had to find out what was driving me to act this way. I had to find out if the spell, instinct had on me, could indeed be broken as I was being led to believe by the white knight. Lastly, I had to find a way to free myself from the torment of this Neanderthal existence.

It wasn't until later on that morning that I saw the door inch open, ever so slightly. Having been sent to the shipyard dispensary, I figured they (meaning the Navy) wanted to examine me, that is, my body, to see if I was physically upto making a Westpac cruise after my fast. Little did I know that they only wanted to examine my head, as I was actually being sent there to see a psychologist.

A Test of Wills

MR. HART: *What was the date of this first psychiatric evaluation?*
RESPONDENT: *About mid-April, I would say.*
MR. HART: *About the 15th of April 1967, would you say?*
RESPONDENT: *Yes, about the 15th of April.*

While I sat inside the dispensary, awaiting my debut with a Navy psychologist, I wondered if my real father had been sent here for psychiatric evaluations when he too began to display bizarre behavior, in response to the beast that had been unleashed with the bombing of Pearl Harbor. I wondered if he, too, had been bombarded by the same barrage of fantasies that I had experienced, to help me make sense of what I had seen. Just then, I realized what a tragic mistake he had made when he stumbled upon that great abyss, which separates this world from the next. For it was in his inability to make any sense of either world that I saw him clasp his ears as the frenzied screaming of his soul filled his head like the song of a Siren, and drove him over the edge of the abyss to his destruction below. As these perceptions about my real father shot through my head, I shivered at the thought that I had stood on the same brink of insanity, he had stumbled over.

Having gone into the interview hoping to find some answers, I instead left empty-handed. While the psychologist only seemed to be interested in probing into my past and the history of my family, I was eager to talk to him about the problems I'd had with accepting my new role as a sexual being and a sailor in the Navy, at the same time. For I saw, within me, the struggle to give birth to a whole new way of life, the past as well as the present were impeding. Because he had not the foresight to look beyond the dirt in my past, I never gained any insight from him into the troubles of the present. Nor was I ever allowed to see this evaluation until today.

MR. HART: *I believe this particular psychological evaluation appears as page thirteen of the clinical record.*
RESPONDENT: *Yes, dated 14 April 1967, it reads as follows:*

This 20-year-old, single SA/USN with two years active service was referred by the Naval Shipyard Dispensary for evaluation of a possible schizoid personality. The subject presents a problem with self-gratification, which he regards as unholy. Also, he reports a rather vague problem with adjusting to the shipboard environment.

Mental status examination reveals a well-developed, clean cut, blond-haired young man who relates to the examiner in a self-effacing fashion. He is not demonstrably anxious, but does convey the impression of being overly ashamed of himself. Flow of speech is smooth and thought content is focused on his obsession with self-gratification. His guilt feelings regarding this behavior have persisted despite professional reassurance regarding the normality of this behavior. He describes distant relationships with his peers, indicating he has never formed long lasting or deep-seated interpersonal relationships. He denies any conflict with authority figures. He has experienced some recent impairment of sleep and appetite. His thinking is at all times clear, coherent and goal directed. He is capable of spontaneity and appropriate emotional expressiveness. There is no evidence of loosened associations, delusions or hallucinations. Intelligence is estimated in the high average to superior range; and judgment is considered essentially intact.

A brief review of background history reveals distant relationships with peers and lack of persistence in reaching goals. The patient's natural father reportedly suffers from schizophrenia and has been hospitalized since the patient was three years old. The patient's stepfather is described as an alcoholic who never established a meaningful relationship with the patient. The patient's mother worked frequently and he has no warm feelings about her. He reports several episodes of stealing minor objects as a child. He progressed through high school making excellent grades and graduating at the age of 18. He briefly attended the Naval Academy, making excellent grades, but dropped out for vague, unspecified reasons. He attended another college but dropped out for similar reasons. He held several jobs briefly but terminated his employment following impulsive trips out of town. On one such occasion, he was apprehended outside a girl's dormitory. He has dated only occasionally, usually upon the initiative of the girl, and presently feels uncomfortable in the presence of women.

Impression: *No psychiatric diagnosis is indicated at this time. There is evidence of a schizoid personality makeup with some depressive features.*

Comments & recommendations: *The subject is considered capable of remaining on active duty. There is evidence, however, of an underlying instability that may require periodic reevaluation and supportive therapy in the future.*

Signed L. Bonney LTJG MSC USNR
Clinical Psychologist

SENIOR MEMBER: *In this psychiatric evaluation of you, the clinical psychologist clearly indicated, at one point, that you had presented no evidence of ever having had any delusions or loosened associations. During the course of your interview then, did you not discuss with him any of the very vivid visual and auditory fantasies you had presented here earlier in your testimony before this board?*

RESPONDENT: *No Sir, I did not. It never occurred to me, he would be interested in my fantasies. Only recently, as I have begun to unearth the enormous wealth of wisdom warehoused within these fantasies of mine, have I taken a greater interest in them. And judging from the contents of his evaluation, I would say the Navy had actually been more interested in seeing that I was capable of remaining on active duty than it had been in looking into any ability I possessed at the time, for discerning the direction of my life.*

Besides, I feared being misdiagnosed as a schizophrenic, like my real father. For I wasn't crazy, I just didn't fit into this way of life, which is exactly what these fantasies were trying to tell me. In fact, I had even been forewarned by my soul that until I understood them more clearly, I should not throw these pearls of wisdom out to be trampled upon by swine, that is, by literal interpretations that simply were not true. What I needed, but did not get, was help in unearthing the truth rather than in suppressing it with misinformation.

Around this time, I bought some civilian clothes so that I could go down to Waikiki Beach in the evenings, and blend in with the rest of the tourists. For the sake of my humanity, I needed to get away from that menagerie of animals back onboard the ship, as much as possible, to avoid reverting back to the bush. Having bought a pair of swimming trunks and a large beach towel with a woman in a bathing suit printed on the front, I wound up spending most of my time down on the beach pining away for better days while I basked in the sun, swam or body-surfed the small tidal waves that constantly licked the shore. Exhausted, I would often fall fast asleep on my beach towel until dusk, when I would awaken to a nearly deserted beach. After slipping into my shirt and the tennis shoes I'd bought, I would comb my hair before beginning my long lonely jaunts down the beach. Somewhere along the way, I would stop to buy a little food and drink, or whatever I could afford, to tide me over until morning, when I could fill up for free back onboard the ship. Occasionally, I might even meet a casual acquaintance but most often roamed about alone, wishing Mary could be at my side with her hand in mine, for I used to think that would be heaven.

Alas, heaven seemed to be some vast dream that I could only skirt, at best, like the ocean. With the exception of an occasional glimpse through the hole made by a dream or a fantasy, heaven kept itself ever so well concealed behind an invisible barrier of images, specifically designed for just such a task. Only on rare occasions, would it deem me worthy enough to be transported up through this barrier, via some phantasmagoric beam of images, to catch a glimpse of this world from its perspective. Even rarer were the occasions upon which it might reveal to me the meaning of such phantasms.

As heaven contained me, so did I contain heaven. Only I did not yet know how to keep my self from getting carried away with some of the images that came and went through heaven's door, at their own behest. For I could stand up to only those myths I knew well enough to let pass without getting emotionally caught up as a passenger on the train of images that would fly past me. Otherwise, would I get sucked into taking part in the dream or fantasy either in real life or within my imagination. In the latter instance, I had the distinct advantage of seeing the myth before I acted, which gave me some leeway, depending upon my knowledge of the myth, to decide whether I wanted to hop onboard this train of images or not. I was free to choose only when I saw through the myth, a formidable barrier which protects the truth from an unworthy intruder by disguising it in images that appear meaningless to the untrained eye. After all, was not I made in the image of a God Whose likeness remained hidden from me?

Then one day, upon the gentle breath of a sigh from Fate, Herself, were a number of new mates wafted onboard to fill the vacancies created by those who had transferred off the ship since the last Westpac cruise. Not only were these new shipmates reservists like myself, but they were also still very much alive with the warmth and the feeling of their own humanity. They were a welcome sight for sore eyes, for out of this small cadre of replacements, there arose four in particular with whom I quickly developed friendships that would last until we were all eventually discharged.

The first person I met was Greg, the only one of the four to have been plunked down into First Division with me. Hailing from the greater Los Angeles area, he was the gregarious magnet that initially drew us all together. In build, he reminded me of a lanky turtle without its shell, for from out of his rounded shoulders protruded a long skinny neck on top of which sat a head he always held cocked slightly forward and off to one side. He stood his ground, though, against the taunts he incurred around his slow, deliberate movements and somewhat effeminate mannerisms. Gifted with an ability to draw, he rose above the herd mentality of his tormentors by drawing satirical caricatures of them. He hated the Navy, with its inane work and disgustingly low level of life. To escape the pain of it all, he regularly smoked marijuana and, on occasion, dropped acid with another shipmate named Dink.

Shortly after I had met Greg, he introduced me to Harold, a rabbity-looking fella from Collinsville, Illinois, a small rural community about twenty miles northeast of my hometown of St. Louis, Missouri. Of slight build, Harold was a very warm and gentle person who approached others with a certain degree of caution. With his nose twitching as he sniffed out the situation, would he inch his way into the conversation at hand. Until then, he either nibbled on one of his fingers or puffed on a cigarette, like a novice smoker. Seldom did he ever look anyone in the eye with his big watery brown eyes, for his gaze appeared fixed elsewhere on some distant worry that continually nagged at him from somewhere within himself. Because of this preoccupation of his, Harold was a hard person to get to know. Generally speaking, he had little to say and often left me wondering if he had even heard what I had said. Very rarely did Harold have an unkind word to say about anyone, even the lifers. Unlike Greg and me, his dislike of the Navy had been tempered by the somewhat more satisfying position, he held as a clerk typist in the ship's office. Besides, he had a wife and a newborn baby back home to think about. For he had apparently gotten her pregnant before they were married—before he was even ready to assume that much responsibility in his life.

The next person, I met, was Marty who actually introduced himself to us as he overheard three like-minded souls talking to each other in the mess line, one day. A wild and high-spirited stallion, Marty would soon prove much more difficult to keep corralled than either a boxed turtle or a caged rabbit. For, he would go on to become one of the most outspoken members of the crew beside myself. While he could never accept such a position for himself, he deeply respected the stand I had taken against the Navy. Standing by me until the end, he was the only member of the crew who unabashedly gave me his full moral support.

From a tough working class neighborhood in Baltimore, Maryland, Marty never cowered from speaking his mind and challenging the other members of the crew. Like Rulli, he hated the Navy with a passion, especially the animal-like behavior of the lifers and their stooges. A hard worker, he always followed orders, in spite of the abuse of authority he suffered at the hands of some of the lifers, for expressing his views. Even though Marty stood up for what he believed, he always acted within the confines of the law, he felt bound to obey. As an electrician's mate did he short-circuit many a lie, the lifers lived by. An answer to a prayer, Marty was more than a like-minded companion, for he was another voice in the desert.

Rick or Red, as he was more commonly called because of his flaming red hair, ran into us much later. From Kansas City, Missouri, he replaced the position Wulf had vacated as a signalman. Like a fox, Red was a very secretive person who kept to himself, for the most part, by hiding out in various holds around the ship to read or listen to music when he was off duty. And like Wulf, he was always impeccably dressed. Tainted with the same degree of arrogance, he came across as being a tad better than the rest of us commoners. A slight little guy, he was the only one I never really got to know very well.

And even though I didn't know it at the time, I was the missing link, that hypothetical intermediate between the myth of man and his animal ancestry. Indeed, I was the next great step in the evolution of mankind, which so many of us unconsciously long to see and yet bitterly detest when we do finally stumble upon it. While I hadn't found the way yet, I was closer than I imagined.

In my satisfaction with having found a few like-minded friends, I stepped back from the edge of the abyss, to seek out the one who could show me the way to safely reach the bottom without acting like an animal or going insane. Thus did my search for She Who Must Be Obeyed begin as our flotilla steamed out of Pearl Harbor on 18 April 1967, to rendezvous with the Japanese and South Korean Navies for joint maneuvers or war games, as they were commonly called.

Having arrived at our destination somewhere off the coast of South Korea, about a week or so later, we encountered more than just our allies, as we almost literally ran into a Russian Naval vessel. With the coming about of our ship, to avoid a collision with the Russian vessel, was I slammed up against the bulkhead in the passageway where I had been assigned to work. Out of the flurry of crewmen that descended upon the passageway from both directions, did I hear someone ask, "What the hell's goin' on?"

"We damn near hit a Russian ship," came the reply.

In a panic, I dropped what I was doing and raced up topside to see what was going on. Off the stern of the ship, I saw two Russian Naval vessels coming about, to head us off. Sure enough, within moments, it seemed as if we were going to collide into one of them again. Only this time, we reached the crash point first, forcing the Russian vessel to come about, to avoid hitting us.

At one point, I went down below to retrieve my camera, to get some pictures of the Russian ships whenever we maneuvered close enough to get a good shot. As I continued to watch the game, the two of us were playing, I saw the Russians as the kid on the block who had not been invited over to play. Miffed at having been excluded from our games, he then goaded us into playing a dangerous game of chicken. Intimidated at first, we decided that what this turkey needed was a dose of its own medicine. After getting in a few good licks, we finally drove the Russian kid back to the horizon, where he hung around for awhile to watch us play our precious little war games.

Shortly thereafter, we were granted shore leave into some small port along the coast of South Korea, accessible only by launch. Since I had to stand watch that evening, I could not go ashore. But that didn't stop those whose noses had sniffed out some free pussy. Hooting and hollering like a pack of wolves hot on the trail of a stray pack of females, they all but stumbled over each other as they grabbed their gonads and scurried over the side into the launches that sped them off to the lairs of their precious little whores.

That same evening before the next watch, I ran into Rulli up topside. As we approached each other, I sensed that something was not quite right with him, for he looked terribly jaundiced. "What the hell's the matter with you?" I asked, halting ere I got too close to him.

Smiling, he replied, "I've got hepatitis."

"No kiddin'!" I exclaimed. "How the hell did you get that?"

"I don't know," he answered.

"Are you contagious?" I inquired further.

"Only if I spit, piss, or shit on you," he responded with a chuckle.

"Maybe I'll keep my distance," I said. "I wondered what had happened to you when I hadn't seen you around for awhile."

"Yeah," he began, "I've been stuck in sick bay ever since they found out what I got. I'm bein' quarantined until they transfer me off the ship."

"When's that?" I asked.

"As soon as we pull into Yokosuka," he answered.

"You lucky stiff!" I exclaimed. "I mean you're lucky to be gettin' off the ship, not that you got hepatitis."

Again, he smiled. "I know what you mean," he said.

"Hey," I hastily added, "I'm gonna miss you."

"Yeah," he concluded, "I'll miss you too, Dury. But I sure as hell ain't gonna miss this fuckin' can or any of the motherfuckin' lifers on it."

"Listen, Dury," he continued, "I gotta get back down below fore the Corpsman finds out I'm up here. Havin' been cooped up down there for a week now, I needed a little fresh air, if you know what I mean."

"Yeah, sure," I replied. "You take care of yourself now."

"And I hope you get over this thing soon," I added.

"Are they gonna put you in the hospital in Yokosuka?" I asked.

"Nah," he replied. "They're gonna ship me back to the States."

"You lucky dog!" I exclaimed.

"Yeah, ain't I real lucky now," he muttered as he turned to walk below, with that wry little smile of his on his face.

I was shocked. Poor Rulli! I felt sorry for him. At the same time, I almost wished I were in his shoes, except for the hepatitis. I would not have wanted that for anything, even if it did mean getting off the ship. At one point, I almost wished he had spit on me, as he had so often in the past whenever he got up in my face to speak to me. I had stood off from him for that very reason. The more I thought about it, the more I had to find the real reason why I wanted off this ship so badly.

For the most part, I had given up thinking about why I wanted out of the Navy, since the reason seemed so far removed from my awareness yet. Why, I had even temporarily suspended my noncooperation. After all the confrontation I had experienced around my fast, I needed a break.

As Fate would have Her way, I was not destined to enjoy any pleasure cruise, for She was determined to stir up the waters of life, enough to keep me at odds with the Navy. Unable to circumvent my fate for very long, I began to see why this entity had earned the name She Who Must Be Obeyed. Obviously, I was being shown how to conduct myself in this situation, even though I had no real reason for acting this way. I knew only that I should resist the Navy with my whole mind, whole heart and whole body, for the Navy had not the capacity to captivate either my mind or my heart, both of which remained free to roam at will. So did I, as the two learned to work together to free my body from the stranglehold the Navy had on it, get into trouble, the next day.

Upon learning, right before lunch, that I was scheduled to stand the afternoon watch, I hurried up to the mess decks, only to find a long line. So I grabbed an orange, to tide me over until dinner, and raced up to the bridge where I was ordered to relieve the starboard lookout. Once up topside, I was informed by the last watch to keep a sharp lookout for any torpedoes—dummies, that is, of course—headed our way, for we were involved in an antisubmarine warfare exercise with the other ships in the fleet. Having donned the microphone and headset, I quickly scanned the surface of the water with my binoculars. However, I saw nothing that even remotely resembled a torpedo. Instead, I felt as if it were going to be just another one of those long boring watches, I had grown so used to standing by now.

How quickly I found my self sitting out in the middle of the ocean in a rowboat or daydream, without any means to propel it. At that point, I heard a young girl scream, from out across the water, for help as she struggled to keep her head above water. Without thinking, I leapt out of the boat and ran across the surface of the water to save her. Having pulled her from the water, I carried her in my arms, back to the boat. As I stepped into the boat, it dawned on me that I had just walked on water. Astounded, I put her down in the boat.

"Are you all right?" I asked as I sat down across from her.

"Yes," she replied. "I will be fine as soon as I catch my breath."

"What're you doin' out here, by yourself, in the middle of nowhere?" I asked.

"I've been waiting for you to save me," she replied.

"I don't understand," I declared. "Who are you, anyway?"

"I'm the little girl you left to drown some years ago," she answered haughtily. "Don't you remember? You told your high school counselor about me."

"Why, that was just a story I made up," I responded, "to help me explain what I was feelin' at the time."

"No," she screamed. "It really happened—you left me to drown, choosing instead, to go off and play with your self."

Momentarily struck speechless by the truth of her words, I wondered how what had started out as make-believe could end up being so real.

"May I have a bite of your orange?" She asked after a long pause during which neither one of us had said a word.

"What orange?" I muttered, for I still couldn't believe this was really happening.

"The orange you have in your pocket," she replied.

"Of course!" I exclaimed as I grabbed the orange and started to peel it. "How did you know I had an orange?"

"I've been waiting for you to peel it," she replied with a smile.

As I did so, I tossed the peelings over the side, completely unaware that in reality I was bombarding the Captain and the Officer of the Deck with them.

With that, I heard the Captain scream, "Why hasn't the starboard lookout reported the torpedo approaching the Davidson off the starboard bow? I want that man relieved of his watch, immediately, goddamn it!"

I looked at the little girl in the boat, as she smiled at me with the most sympathetic look on her face. "You set me up for this, didn't you?" I demanded to know before she vanished.

As the rowboat sank beneath the surface of the water, I realized she had just torpedoed me again. If these were the sort of tricks, the little sprite was going to play on me, no wonder I had been so reluctant to rescue her in the past.

Having been relieved of my duties, I was sent below, never to stand another watch while I remained in First Division. Even I had to laugh as variations of the story, about how I had hit the old man in the head with orange peelings, filtered back down to me through the crew. Lest I get a swelled head over the matter, I was put on report for having been derelict in the performance of my duties while on watch. Why, just the thought alone, of a Captain's Mast, had a very sobering effect on me as I wondered how the Captain could objectively preside over a hearing around an incident in which he had also been involved. How could he deliver a fair and impartial verdict? Just because he had seen the torpedo before I had, did that mean I had been derelict in the performance of my duties? Or had he written me up because I had accidentally hit him in the head with orange peelings? Again, did that mean I had not been paying attention to what I was supposed to be doing? What if my attention had been focused in a different quadrant, as it was, from that in which the torpedo first appeared? Would that have meant I had been negligent in any way? Or was it because he had been personally offended by my failure to conform to his expectations of me, that he wrote me up? Obviously, a bruised ego was hardly sufficient evidence to prove my guilt, unless he, whom I had so offended, also happened to be the Captain, my appointed judge and jury in this instance.

Was I guilty of having been derelict in the performance of my duties? In deed I was, for had not I left my soul to drown in a sea of unconscious behavior? Having performed a minor miracle by staying on top of all this instinctive behavior, I had yet to rescue her from the clutches of the Great Gray Mother of Instinct. In other words, I had yet to find my way in either world. Because the way I should go remained so unclear to me at the time, I could not hold onto it for very long, without its vanishing from my grasp. I had a choice, either I played with my self, that is, I played along with the Navy's program for me or I played, once again, with my old imaginary or real—depending on how one viewed the matter—childhood playmate, my soul. Whereas I had made the right choice when I rescued her from the sea in the metaphysical realm, at the same time, I had offended the Great Gray Whore on the physical plane. In deed, was I beginning to see how difficult it is to serve two masters.

By means of a simple torpedo had my soul brought home to me not only the threat of death and destruction, but also the promise of new life. In her own way, had she forced me to rise above my feelings of powerlessness, to stand tall against the raw power of Nature. In other words, she had tricked me into momentarily embracing a completely new approach to life, one in which I could indeed walk on water or at least overcome the severe limitations of a purely instinctive existence.

Before my Captain's Mast, I pulled two days of shore leave in Japan. While the conversation for many of the crew gravitated down around sampling some of the finest pussy to be found anywhere on the Asian Continent, I looked forward to stepping out into the first foreign country I had ever visited. I was disappointed, though, when I found out that both Marty and Greg had pulled duty for the weekend. Only later, did I learn why Harold had declined to go ashore with me, for he had evidently sent most of his meager pay back home to his wife for child support. So did I go ashore alone.

Having just been paid, I decided to spend the first day rummaging through the Navy Exchange in Yokosuka where I had heard that I could find some good bargains. While I struggled to work up the courage to venture out into the countryside by myself, I went looking for gifts to give to my mother and Mary. With so much to choose from, I opted to buy my mother a beautiful set of china and a set of silverware, to boot. For Mary, I bought a Japanese doll adorned in the traditional dress of a woman living in the Japan of yesteryear. After seeing to it, that these gifts had been wrapped and shipped off, I realized how much I needed to do something for myself too. With that, I finally made up my mind to go sightseeing in Tokyo on the morrow.

That evening, word reached us warning of a possible demonstration in the morning, in front of the main gate to the shipyards at Yokosuka. Ever since the bombing of Hiroshima and Nagasaki, have a growing number of Japanese adamantly opposed port of entry to any foreign vessel suspected of carrying nuclear weapons. Because the whereabouts of our nuclear arsenal was such a carefully guarded secret known to only a select few in the fleet, they had no way of ascertaining whether we were actually carrying nuclear warheads on the tips of our torpedoes or not. For some reason, though, the demonstrators drew upon my sympathies, so much so, that had I been more aware of my own position on nuclear weapons, I might have joined them.

Bright and early the next morning, did I arise and, after a hearty breakfast, slip off to the train station in Yokosuka where I purchased a round trip ticket to Tokyo. Nowhere along the way did I encounter any demonstrators, which left me feeling a little ambivalent. While I really wanted to take this trip into Tokyo, I would like to have seen the demonstration, more so.

So much taller was I, than the local inhabitants were, that I felt like Gulliver, walking amongst the Lilliputians. Besides, I had to laugh at the din of completely incomprehensible cackling that rose to greet my ears. Though I spoke not a word of Japanese, I had little trouble purchasing a ticket for Tokyo.

Once on the train, I was amazed at the speed with which it zoomed through the countryside, stopping just long enough to allow passengers to get on and off it. And I wondered why we did not have in place such a modern and efficient means of transportation in St. Louis. I certainly would have had it easier, traveling from South County, where I lived, to see Mary at her parents place in North County.

What little I saw of the countryside from the window of the train was simply gorgeous. However, the lush beauty of the precipitous foothills that surrounded the quaint little villages, nestled snugly into every nook and cranny along the line, quickly gave way to a flattened terrain, monotonously dressed in the urban sprawl of a more modern Tokyo.

When it came time for me to disembark from the train, I felt as if I were stepping into some fantasy without the slightest clue of what was going to happen next. For I had found no unfolding tale here to guide me, until I stumbled upon the most unusual park I had ever seen, one completely surrounded by a massive stone wall, like the fief of some medieval warlord. Upon entering the grounds, through one of its large open gates, I wound up roaming about this dreamlike world for hours, taking pictures of its perfectly manicured gardens, groves of cherry trees in full bloom, and quaint old Japanese structures. I was never more impressed by anything I saw in Tokyo than by this singular glimpse into Japan's past, for Tokyo was like any other large city in the States, choked with its monuments to commercialism, like an overcrowded cemetery.

Having worked up quite an appetite, I flagged down a cabdriver who seemed to understand as well as speak a little English. When I asked him to take me to a good albeit reasonably priced restaurant, we sped off through a maze of narrow and windy, alley-like side streets as if he were trying to catch up with the other entrants in the Grand Prix after having made an unexpected pit stop. And every time we sped past another oncoming vehicle traveling at the same high rate of speed, I about had a heart attack. Not realizing what I had gotten myself into, I thought for sure, my fate was sealed, as I imagined a head-on collision with every hot rod that zoomed past us. Still in a near state of shock, by the time this roller coaster ride ended, I was miraculously left standing in one piece, on the sidewalk in front of a building that looked like any other small ethnic, neighborhood restaurant back in the States.

Having regained my wits about myself, I entered the restaurant and sat down. Shortly thereafter, an elderly Japanese woman handed me a menu that, much to my surprise, was written in English. Looking forward to a good sampling of Japanese cuisine, I soon discovered that I was about to enjoy a good old-fashioned American meal. After feasting on a sumptuous steak dinner, I graciously thanked my modest hostess for such an excellent meal, whereupon I quickly found myself back out on the street again.

Before long, I stumbled upon some unusual looking buildings, which immediately grabbed my attention, but no more than did the tug at the back of my jumper. "Excuse, please," said this tiny voice as I turned to greet a young Japanese woman with a smile on her face that almost extended from one ear to the other.

"Hello," she said.

Caught off guard by her boldness, I finally managed to say, "Hi," in response.

"I study English at university. You understand?" She asked.

"Yes," I answered. "I understand you perfectly. Can you understand me? Or am I speaking too fast for you?" I asked as I recalled my own inability to grasp every word of Spanish spoken to me during the course of a conversation, I'd had with my Spanish teacher in high school, after two years of exposure to the language.

"Yes, I understand," she replied. "I study English, many years now. In Japan, English is student requirement in early grades."

"My name is Jun," she added with a smile that seemed to invite me in, without any hesitation, and make me feel right at home.

"Mine's Butch," I replied.

"Butch," she repeated. "You mind, I practice English with you?"

"Not at all," I answered. "I would enjoy your company, for I've been roaming about the city since early morning, clueless as to where I've been or where I'm going. In return, maybe you can show me Tokyo."

She laughed. "I show you Tokyo, practice English," she added.

"I student," she continued. "I study home economics at university. I in second year. And you—how long you visit Tokyo?"

"Only today," I responded, "as my ship departs for Vietnam in the morning."

"Vietnam," she repeated as her brow furrowed and her gaze grew distant. How quickly did her wonderful smile return to her face as she came back from wherever she had wondered off.

While not a very pretty woman, she was attractive in her own way, especially when she smiled, since her whole face would just beam with a warmth and genuineness that was really quite touching. A short fleshy gal, she reminded me, a lot, of Mary. Alas, she was not Mary.

"I wish I had met you earlier in the day," I finally said. "You could've taken me on a personally guided tour of the city."

She laughed. "You come back to Tokyo?" She asked.

"Probably not," I replied.

With a look of disappointment on her face, did she smile.

Changing the subject, I asked her about the unusual park I had stumbled upon earlier in the day.

As I gave her a description of the park, to help her determine where I had been, she blurted out, "You visit Emperor's Palace."

I laughed. "And here I thought it was a park," I interjected. "I wondered why you-all would have gone to the trouble of building such a massive wall around a park. I should've known better."

"Emperor's Palace," she explained, "open to public, two weeks, this time of year, no other time. Understand?"

"Yes," I replied.

"You lucky to see," she added.

"And what're these unusual buildings?" I asked.

"They buildings from World's Fair," she answered.

Noticing the sun had set, she told me she had to return to her dorm. "Have curfew," she said with a look that begged for understanding.

Disappointed, I asked if I could take her picture, to which she readily agreed.

In return, she asked me for my address, which I gave her.

"I write you, on ship," she told me. "You write back?"

"Yes," I responded with a smile.

"Good-bye," she said. "I enjoy visit very much. Look forward, hear from you. Good luck!"

"Bye now," I said.

As I watched her disappear into a throng of pedestrians, I was tempted to go after her but hesitated, only because I did not know what I wanted from her, sex or friendship. In my confusion, I wondered if somewhere behind my desires for sex was hidden the much deeper need for relationship, a longing for a saner, more humane and civilized way of life. By the time I realized my mistake, I had already let this angel slip away, as heaven's door slammed shut in my face. For the first time, did I encounter a resistance within myself to returning to the ship, that is, to going back down to hell.

I was so overwhelmed by my own existential pain that, to this day, I can recall little else about the trip back to Yokosuka. O, how I did long for a way out of the nightmare that haunted me, both day and night. O, how I ached for the physical presence of Mary, as if she embodied the way out. In fact, I was hurting so badly, at one point, I wanted to stand up and scream. But I restrained myself until I reached Yokosuka, where I could no longer contain the rage brewing within me.

Like a branch on a huge sycamore tree, did I extend a clenched fist into the dark night that overshadowed my soul. In a Herculean effort to free myself from the chains that fettered me to the earth, I cursed the day I was born. I cursed my parents for having pulled me down from the heavens into this wretched life. And I cursed God for having allowed this travesty to take place. I hated my parents not only for what they had done, but also for the life they had squandered away. I hated them. "I hate you," I finally screamed out into the night sky with a clenched fist.

Like the bursting of a long awaited thundershower upon parched earth, did I break down and cry. "Forgive them God," I sputtered, "for they know not what they have done."

As I caught sight of the ship, out of the corner of my eye, I flew into yet another rage. With a clenched fist, I reached out, only this time to condemn the crew of the ship. "I hate you," I screamed out in between fits of sobbing. "I hate all of you lousy bastards." But in my heart of hearts, I knew I did not hate them, for they too knew not what they had done. Only, I found it harder to forgive them since I, who was like them in so many ways, would ultimately have to forgive myself.

Sobbing uncontrollably, as I stumbled along, I beat my chest with a clenched fist. "Ah," I screamed out. "I hate you. I hate this body. I hate this life."

As this psychic storm brought relief to my desolateness, I found myself standing in the middle of the shipyard, laughing, of all things, while I finished crying, for I had just grasped the true meaning of forgiveness. In releasing my hatred for my parents and the crew of the ship, I had released my own hatred of myself. In the past, I had failed to see that what I hated in them, I actually hated about myself, for I was mistreating myself in the same manner they mistreated themselves and others, only in ways yet barely visible to me. Since none of us knew what we were really doing to ourselves or to each other, I had to forgive them for their trespasses against me if I was to find forgiveness for my trespasses. In letting go of the hatred that had clenched my fist, I freed forgiveness from not only my hand but from heaven's as well, for what is loosed on earth shall be loosed in heaven. More importantly, I freed myself from the chain of hatred that binds us to instinctively taking an eye for an eye in a heinous repetition of history from one generation to the next.

Like a drunken man who has come to his senses, did I slip onboard the ship, hardly noticed, and slither down the ladder to my compartment. Instead of lying down, I decided to stay up and write Mary a letter. Only this time, after recounting the events of my trip into Tokyo, including my encounter with Jun, I purposely left off telling her, as usual, how much I loved her. Thus did I deal with the other chain that bound me to the earth like the roots of a huge sycamore tree.

After we had pulled out of Yokosuka, later that morning, I was ordered to report, in dress whites, to the Captain's stateroom for a Captain's Mast. As I entered the Captain's stateroom on the heels of the master-at-arms, I found the XO and a yeoman from the ship's office already standing by. I was ordered to snap to attention, as the Captain burst into the room, in his usual hurried manner.

Having snatched my records from the yeoman, the XO proceeded to read aloud the charge against me. "Mr. Drury, you have been charged with having violated Article 92 of the Uniform Code of Military Justice, specifically the section which deals with dereliction in the performance of duties, in that while standing watch onboard the USS Davidson at 1230 hours, 13 May 1967, you did fail to report the approach of an oncoming torpedo during a fleet exercise. How do you plead, guilty or not guilty?" He asked.

"Not guilty," I proclaimed as I struggled like a lowly worm to free myself from the hook that had gotten under the Captain's skin. While the Captain showed signs of squirming around my plea, I was not let off the hook that easily.

"Because you have pled not guilty," interjected the XO, "you have the right, Mr. Drury, to testify in your behalf or to remain silent. You may request the appearance, before this mast, of any witness whose testimony you believe to be pertinent to your case. If you choose to present no evidence, that fact may not be used against you as an admission of guilt. If there is any evidence you wish to present, you must do so at this time. Let me remind you, that whatever you say may also be used as evidence against you."

"Do you understand, Mr. Drury?" He asked.

"Yes, I do," I replied.

"Do you have anything to say in your defense?" He asked.

As I agonized over how I could tell the Captain he is not my master, I balked. If I told him the truth, my words would only be used against me. How could I convince him that my failure to see the torpedo, as he had seen it, had literally saved the life of my soul? How could I show him that he was guilty of the greater offense here? While I had only offended a mere mortal, I saw his participation in the exercise as an offense against the very soul of mankind, the Great Spirit She Who Must Be Obeyed.

"I have nothing to say at this time," I finally capitulated.

While the Captain had been noticeably unnerved by the tone of my response, as evidenced by his fidgeting before he pronounced me guilty, he nonetheless sentenced me to 30 days of extra duty. Why, the words had hardly left his mouth before he scurried out the door, satisfied that he had dealt with this thorn in his side. Little did he know this irritant was in the early stages of developing into the pearl of great price.

Visibly shaken by the whole affair, I was dismissed and sent below. Even though I was still unwilling to simply fall into step, I was sure glad it was all over, for now. As shy as I was, I hated the encounters into which my soul forced me. And since I had no idea of just how miserable these guys could make my life, I greatly feared the price I might have to pay for any further action on my part. Unaware of the price that had already been exacted from me, for my participation in the Navy, thus far, I would buckle under, for now, or at least until my soul forced me into yet another close encounter with the Navy.

As I was changing my clothes and winding down, the master-at-arms approached me. "Mr. Drury," he commanded, "you are to report to me on the mess decks every evening at 1800 hours, for the next thirty days, to perform extra duty."

"Do you understand?" He asked.

"Yes," I reluctantly replied.

"How long do I have to work each night?" I asked.

"Two hours," he curtly replied.

Even though two hours of extra duty for that long a period seemed a little excessive to me, I did not say a word.

"If you have no further questions, I will see you up on the mess decks at 1800 hours," he concluded.

Over the next thirty days, I was made to perform the most inane work imaginable, tasks strictly meant to be punitive. Many an evening was I forced to scrub oily decks down in the bilges, on my hands and knees, with an old brush and can of scouring powder. Worse yet, was I made to climb atop and clean around the boilers, where the temperature often exceeded 110 degrees. Nonetheless, I worked hard at doing just enough to make it look as if I'd done something.

One night, as I worked down in the bilges, scrubbing a deck with soap and water, a third class petty officer nicknamed Shorty sneaked up behind me and, for whatever reason, reared back and kicked me in the rear end, sending me reeling across the deck where I landed flat on my face.

Rolling over onto my side, I looked him right in the eye and smiled. "I'm sorry you feel that way," I said, whereupon he spun around and disappeared through the hatch.

That night, I touched Shorty in much the same way St. Paul had been touched by the suffering of the early Christians. In other words, I awakened Shorty to his own feelings, from which he fled out of fear. As a result, I earned his respect, the respect a wild animal has for fire, once it has been illuminated by the light of its own feelings.

Nor did I ever report him. Given my reputation onboard the ship, I figured nobody would ever believe me. Besides, in my naiveté, it never occurred to me that I could have had him written up for manhandling a subordinate. However, I did find great satisfaction in just knowing that, from that moment on, I commanded his respect as a human being.

Only later, did I learn from a First Class Boilerman who, out of the kindness of his heart, had permitted me to stand with him, for a moment, to cool off in front of a fresh air intake port, that he had been instructed to give me the hottest and nastiest work he could find.

I shook my head and smiled. "Thanks for tellin' me," I shouted over the roar of the boilers. "And thanks for lettin' me cool off."

He just looked at me and smiled.

Not long afterwards, was I ordered, one day, to report to the XO's stateroom. With some anxiety, did I proceed to his stateroom, for I had been on good behavior, of late, or so I thought.

"Come in," responded the XO to the knock on his door.

"Mr. Drury, Sir," I reported upon entering his stateroom.

"Have a seat, Mr. Drury," he said.

"I have a statement," he continued, "I want you to read. Once you have read it, I want you to sign it right above your name, exactly as your name appears, to acknowledge that you have read the statement and understand what it says."

Looking down at the piece of paper he had handed me, I saw two small paragraphs, each dated 23 May 1967, which read as follows:

You are hereby advised that because of the nature of your conduct onboard ship, you are being considered for discharge from the Navy for reasons of unsuitability, in accordance with BUPERS Manual, Article C-10310.

P. L. Merwin, LCDR USN, Executive Officer
By direction of the Commanding Officer

I acknowledge that I have been counseled and advised that any further irregular behavior on my part may cause my discharge from the Navy for reasons of unsuitability, in accordance with BUPERS Manual, Article C-10310.

Witnessed: E. J. Drury, SA
P. L. Merwin, LCDR USN

When I had finished reading the statement, I looked up at him.

"Do you understand what you have just read?" He asked.

"I do," I replied.

"Then sign it, right here above your name," he commanded, whereupon I signed the statement just as he had instructed.

MR. HART: *The statement you signed, is that page 13-5 of the records introduced here, earlier today, by the Recorder?*
RESPONDENT: *Yes, sir.*
MR. HART: *All right, go ahead.*

After the XO had signed his name beneath both paragraphs, he dismissed me.

I grew wild with excitement over the possibility of being discharged if my behavior did not change. Why, I felt as if the Navy had just given me the cue to misbehave. For lack of better insight into myself, I could not have agreed with the Navy more, that I was totally unsuited for this way of life.

7

Yankee Station

As the ship steamed relentlessly southward at full speed ahead, the mood of the crew grew conspicuously more somber. Forced to let go of the frenzied and orgiastic pleasures of a Dionysian holiday in Japan, they unwillingly surrendered themselves to the more Apollonian way of life found onboard the ship. Incapable of seeing beyond a purely emotional response to their situation, they quickly succumbed, one after another, to the vagaries of a melancholy mood.

How easily were they seduced by this invisible body of nebulous feelings and deep dark emotions as it descended upon them with the caprice of an Olympian god. Instead of wrestling with this god, as Jacob had, they fell prey to all of its emotional bluster. In their inability to free their feelings from the emotional pall that overshadowed their souls like a dark night, they failed to expose the naked truth of the god that lay hidden within the mood.

Having not yet succumbed to the mood that had descended upon the rest of the crew like the plague, I was struck by the magnitude of its power when the ship pulled within sight of the coast of Vietnam. While I stood in awe of the dark foreboding clouds which now hugged the earth and stirred the passions of her murky green waters into a squall, I sensed a great evil lurked about this land—that no good could come from our being here. "You do not belong here," I heard my soul scream out in the shrill voice of a Siren. Immediately, I saw her words as the truth that lay hidden at the very core of the mood that had finally swept over us all.

Badly shaken by this revelation, I turned aside, only to find Greg and Harold standing there. "We do not belong here," I prophetically proclaimed.

The two of them just looked at me and smiled, as if to say that while they both agreed with my assessment of this external sign, they were at a complete loss as to what to do about it.

In the silence that overcame me as I refixed my gaze upon the stark panorama, which had unfolded before my eyes, I recalled some vague passage from the Gospel of Luke (12:54-57): *"When you see a cloud rising in the west, you say immediately that rain is coming—and so it does. When the wind blows up from the south, you say it is going to be hot—and so it is. You hypocrites! If you can interpret the portents of earth and sky, why can't you interpret the present time? Tell me, why don't you judge for yourselves what is just?"*

"So this's Yankee Station," I muttered to myself as we all laughed to assuage our fear of the dreadful truth this silence had stirred up from the depths of our beings.

Yankee Station essentially consisted of patrolling the waters off the coast of Vietnam in semi-alert, battle-station mode, whereby we remained on the lookout for enemy vessels both above and below the surface of the water, around the clock. Since the North had a virtually nonexistent naval fleet, our task was greatly simplified. As we maneuvered up and down the coast at varying distances from land, our greatest threat came from kamikaze sampans loaded with explosives, or from artillery set up in the jungles along the coast to keep our ships with their big guns at bay. For the most part, we remained far enough out at sea, that I seldom saw land.

Otherwise, I found life onboard the ship so boring, that one day I was moved to paint what I was feeling after having been assigned to paint some pipes that ran up an exterior bulkhead along the starboard side of the hangar bay. Since these pipes had already been prepped, that is, chipped and primed with red lead by other hands in my division, I needed only to apply the final coat of battleship gray. Because a fresh coat of paint could easily be ruined before it dried, by the spray that continually bathed the ship with salt water as it glided across the open sea, I was given a can of paint, which contained agents to hasten the drying and hardening of the paint. As I approached the pipes to begin painting, I was unexpectedly accosted by my soul.

"What are you doing?" She asked me.

"What does it look like I'm doing?" I replied rather rudely, for I was still a little upset with her over the incident around the torpedo.

"You know," I added, "not only did you make a fool out of me, but you also got me into a lot of trouble, I did not appreciate."

"I was only thinking of you," she replied.

"Thinking of me!" I exclaimed. "If that's what you think of me, then I don't need your help."

"You never heed my warnings," she insisted.

"Warnings!" I exclaimed. "What warnings?"

"I have told you," she continued, "that you do not belong here. Yet you ignore me."

"What do you want me to do, walk on water?" I asked her. "Obviously, if I had found the way out, I would've taken it."

"I am the way," she proclaimed.

I laughed. "If you are the way, it's no wonder I'm still stuck here," I concluded. "Why, I can't even see you!"

"You are so unimaginative," she replied. "When I opened the door for you back in Tokyo, you simply slammed it shut in my face."

"And who do you think handed you forgiveness when you reached out for it back in Yokosuka?" She asked.

"Then why don't you just tell me what to do?" I scoffed.

"You don't listen!" She replied. "You don't pay attention to your imagination."

"What imagination?" I grumbled.

"Who do you think is talking to you?" She asked. "Is it not a product of your imagination?"

"I don't know," I screamed out in anguish. "I don't know who the hell you are."

"Why don't you try letting go of your self, for just a moment," she hastily added, "and instead, try painting me."

"Paint you!" I exclaimed. "How ridiculous! I have already told you, I can't see you. So how the hell do you expect me to paint you?"

"I know you can't see me, but don't worry about that for now," she said. "I will stand right here in front of you as you slap paint on my form."

"This's insane," I replied. "What do you think my superiors are gonna say when they see me wavin' a paint brush around in midair?"

"They won't know the difference," she responded. "I will stand right here in front of the pipes you are supposed to paint. They will just see you painting the pipes."

"I don't know about this," I said. "This all sounds so silly."

"Come on," she prodded me.

When I waved a brush full of paint in her direction, to dismiss her, I was amazed by what I saw—gray paint actually adhering to a form that had previously been invisible to me. Giddy with excitement, I began to hastily fling paint in the direction of the pipes, and smear it around with my brush. While she giggled and goaded me on, I worked like a madman to cover her invisible form with enough paint so that I could see her. In fact, I had gotten so engrossed in painting her, that I was oblivious of the crowd that had gathered behind me, back towards the fantail, to watch as I continued to fling paint at my invisible canvas with the agility of an abstract artist. Instead of building up paint on a canvas, in reality, I was building up layer upon layer of paint on the pipes until they looked like the trunks of some gnarled old tree. Just as I caught sight of the gray form of a woman standing naked before me, I heard a gravelly nasally voice shout out, "That's enough, Dury."

After taking one last look at her, I spun around, right smack dab into the face of an angry First Class Boatswain's Mate.

"You did it," my soul whispered in my ear as she vanished. "You visualized me."

"O, I am so proud of you. I knew you could do it if only you used your imagination," I heard her say as her voice gave way to the groans of the boatswain's mate.

"Not bad for a novice, eh?" Responded I to his great displeasure.

"Go on down below and pass out laundry," he snarled.

Staring at me as if I were nuts, did they all quickly step aside to let me pass. Not a one of them said a word to me as I went below.

For days afterwards, I was so excited, I could care less what the Navy did with me. Having finally been relegated to the position of a compartment cleaner suited me just fine, for I was certainly beginning to feel more pressure from within to contribute as little of myself as possible to the war effort in Vietnam, regardless of the consequences.

Having visualized my soul for the first time, I wanted nothing more than to see her again. How quickly I learned she was not some genie I could simply conjure up at will. For now, I would have to settle for the very gray but lasting impression she had left on my mind.

While she was no prima donna, I nonetheless found her to be very attractive. Somewhat shorter than I am, she had long, flowing hair and a rather unspectacular face. But what really struck me about her shapely form were her breasts, for she had undoubtedly been endowed with the most beautiful breasts I had ever seen. Why, even I was astounded that I possessed such an animated image of a woman within my psyche.

At this point, I still wasn't too sure, just what to believe. While these experiences led me to believe, on the one hand, that certain aspects of my life, that is, those pertaining to the Navy, were a part of some grand illusion, on the other hand, I wondered if I wasn't the one who in reality was suffering the delusion, especially after that last encounter I'd had with my soul. As I struggled to gain some perspective on this last experience, it became clear to me that the path to sanity led not into the insanity of the collective or mutual destruction of ourselves in war, but rather into the insanity of my own delusions—the myths that were driving me to act as I had.

As I unconsciously searched that unruly body of mine for some way to objectify the truth, I wound up painting a picture of a woman, albeit a very gray one, who presumably portrayed my soul. Finally, I had found someone with whom I could communicate—who actually knew me better than I knew myself. Where in the past I had been unable to put any trust in this gray area of my life, in this close encounter, I took a great leap in faith. When I saw her standing there, I knew in my heart of hearts that I had found the one who could show me the way. And by visualizing her, I gave her a life of her own. In admitting to her existence, I finally admitted her into my life.

Before I would see her again, I was offered an opportunity, I could not refuse, the chance to leave First Division. To my utter disbelief, I was approached, one day, by a chief named Neely who asked me if I would like to transfer over to "R" Division to work as a shipfitter, the Navy's version of a sheet metal worker/plumber.

"What would I be required to do as a shipfitter?" I asked him.

"Until you have completed your apprenticeship," he replied, "you will be required to assist the other, more experienced shipfitters in making minor repairs to the ship, wherever they are needed. You will also be required to stand sounding and security watches, which consist of taking measurements of the depth of the water that normally accumulates in the bilges at key points around the ship, to see if those particular areas need to be pumped out or not. While on watch, you will be expected to report your findings to the officer-in-charge on the bridge, every hour on the hour. Other than that, you may be asked, on occasion, to help clean your own compartment, the passageway outside the shop or the head we share with First Division.

"Well, what do you think?" He asked. "Would you like to become a shipfitter?"

"Yes, I would," I said without thinking, for I wanted so badly to do something constructive for a change.

"Good!" He exclaimed. "I'll see what I can do to get you transferred. I think you will find your tasks as a shipfitter, a bit more satisfying than those you have been asked to perform in First Division."

Left standing in a quandary over whether or not I should have accepted this offer, I began to have serious doubts about the reality of these encounters with my soul. As I looked back upon the last stunt she had pulled on me, I wondered if maybe I wasn't getting a little too carried away with all of this imaginary stuff, and if instead I was getting sucked into some schizophrenic nightmare by a Siren I had inadvertently helped to create. Then too, I wondered if maybe I ought to be ignoring her and all of her nonsensical little tricks, rather than allowing her to hornswoggle me as she has in the past.

The more I thought about it, the more I wanted to forget about her and get back to living some semblance of a normal life. Why should I let some imaginary little sprite, which no one else can see, ruin my life. I had to be strong; I had to stand up to her and stave off the tendency, I had inherited from my father, to be driven mad. I had to pull myself together before it was too late. And I could do that with a fresh start in another division on the ship.

Early the next day was I transferred out of First Division with little more fanfare than the handful of well-wishers who had gathered around, as I was leaving. Escorted by a very amiable, though loquacious shipfitter named Aubrey, was I shown to my new quarters where initially I experienced an even colder reception. Figuring that my reputation had preceded me, I looked every single one of those who glared at me as I passed, right in the eye, to let them know that I was not about to be intimidated by their shortsightedness. Left in the lurch by Aubrey, who had been called to the bridge, I simply proceeded to stow my gear in my new locker. Only after I had heard the familiar voice of a friend call out to me from somewhere across the compartment, did I let go of the apprehension I had begun to feel around ever having transferred over here, in the first place.

"Hey, Dury!" Exclaimed Marty as I spun around to greet him. "Welcome to 'R' Division."

"Thanks," I responded with a nervous smile. "For a minute there, I wasn't too sure if I was welcome or not."

Just then, another shipfitter came up and introduced himself. "Hi," he said. "My name's Romesburg."

"Mine's Drury," I replied as I turned to shake his hand.

Romesburg had a fleshy white, round face accented by a very small mouth and a little bit of hair above his lip, which he claimed as a mustache. Unkempt in his appearance, he was one of those friendly, albeit foulmouthed characters who moved at about the same speed as a sloth. And seldom was he ever seen without either a lit or an unlit cigarette dangling from the corner of his mouth.

"I'm one of the guys you'll be workin' with," he added.

"Do you like workin' as a shipfitter?" I asked him.

"It's all right," he responded. "While it's still the fuckin' Navy, it sure beats the hell out of workin' as a fuckin' boatswain's mate."

"That's for damn sure," interjected Aubrey, who had just returned from the bridge. "It ain't nothin' like First Division where they treat you like a fuckin' animal. Here, you'll be treated like a human being."

Plump in build, Aubrey reminded me of a cartoon character named Porky Pig. Why, he even had the same penchant for stuttering as this caricature of him. Only Aubrey had a tendency to get on my nerves with his incessant babbling about the most mundane concerns of day-to-day life—an aspect of himself that had already manifested itself when he escorted me to my new quarters.

"Have you met Shorty yet?" Asked Aubrey as Shorty tried to slip by unnoticed.

When a very embarrassed Shorty turned to greet me, I made the comment that we had run into each other not too long ago down in the bilges, whereupon Shorty promptly excused himself again.

While his nickname was obviously a takeoff on his diminutive stature, Shorty was nonetheless a very powerfully built young roustabout who carried a terrible chip on his shoulder. For he had a way of badgering hapless souls into fighting him so that he could beat the hell out of them instead of himself. A very moody person, he kept to himself for the most part, or at least until he again felt the need to spar with the unseen evil he saw in the faces of his victims, but which really lay hidden behind his own facade.

In Shorty's place, there appeared another shipfitter affectionately nicknamed Sleepy. Because Sleepy habitually used marijuana to help him cope with the otherwise unbearable pain that being in the Navy caused him to experience, he always looked as if he were about to fall asleep. With his long lanky limbs, reddish brown hair and slow deliberate movements, he reminded me of an orangutan, which had to take this drug to ease the pain that wracked its body as it struggled in vain to adjust to captivity.

While Sleepy and I were introducing ourselves to each other, I noticed a first class petty officer nudging his way through the small crowd of shipfitters and curiosity seekers that had gathered around me.

With a look of apprehension on his face, he hesitated before introducing himself. "Hi," he said. "I'm Joe, your new boss."

"Welcome to the shipfitters," he added rather hastily, as if he had not really meant it.

Like the wise pig in the tale of "The Three Little Pigs," Joe had chosen a career in the Navy as a shelter against the wiles of a civilian economy that would otherwise have devoured him. As an added safeguard against job insecurity, he quickly earned the love and respect of his men by treating them exactly as he would want to be treated if he were in their shoes. Because Joe sensed, right away, that I was different, he felt a little ambivalent about having to take me in under his roof.

"After you get your gear stowed away, come on back to the shop; and I'll show ya around," he concluded in a rather rapid manner of speaking that was quite characteristic of him.

"Okay," I responded with the uncertainty of one who fully expected that, at any moment, the real Joe would leap out from behind this facade and pounce on me like the big bad wolf or that weasel of a first class petty officer back in First Division.

"You'll like it in 'R' Division," said Marty as he left to go to work.

"Maybe so," I replied, "maybe so."

Even though the shipfitters went out of their way to make me feel like one of them, I could never rid myself of the feeling that I didn't belong here. In spite of all the camaraderie, I could never stoop to their level, either in horseplay, which generally consisted of grabbing another guy's ass and goosing him, or in conversation, which invariably dealt with getting laid, drunk or high. Obviously, I was the only one who felt there was more to life than these rudimentary pleasures.

Because I was low man on the totem pole, I again got stuck with cleaning our compartment, which I wouldn't have minded if my body had been a little more cooperative. Unchallenged, I quickly became the breeding ground for discontent, which simmered for only so long before it gathered enough steam to force its way into my life as a full-blown underground movement to resist the Navy. Unable to find a more positive direction for my creative energies, was I driven to rebel against the limitations the Navy placed upon my soul.

Unfortunately, I got to play shipfitter for only about a week or so, before I was sent back up to the mess decks to serve three months for "R" Division, whose turn it was to send someone. Under great protest did I go, only to find friends like Greg and Dink among the new faces that greeted me up there. With a little gentle persuasion from them, I decided to give it my best shot, in spite of how unfair it seemed that I had to go back upto the mess decks so soon after having already served two months up there for First Division.

How quickly did Fate reenter my life, this time around, by using a third class boilerman named Farris, who had just been assigned to the mess decks as our new petty officer, for She wasted no time in creating friction between this petty tyrant and me, the ship's rebel without a cause. In Her usual manner, did She convince a few of the more enterprising among us to get our work done early, so that we could gather up topside to expand upon a fantasy that had recently gripped us all. Having originally filled our heads with mutiny—with the idea of seizing control of the ship, letting the old guard off in boats, and then setting sail for Australia—She skillfully steered subsequent conversations around to other possibilities such as a general strike, to shut down the ship, so that it could not fulfill its mission in Vietnam. At the same time that She was spurring us on to resist the Navy in some realistic way, She roused Her Nemesis, the Great Gray Whore, into convincing a few of the old guard—those cocks who still remained faithful to the Old Gray Bitch—that the morale of the crew was seriously being undermined by these clandestine meetings. To force us into giving body to our fantasies, Fate allowed Her nemesis to take possession of Farris and drive him to decree that we could no longer leave the mess decks to fraternize with other members of the crew, without his permission. She let the Old Gray Bitch convince him that order amongst us plebes could only be maintained so long as we were kept busy enough to inhibit reflection upon our present condition, and were prevented from sharing our feelings with other like-minded souls.

Although this fellowship was short lived, I nonetheless found great consolation in the affirmation I received from them, for the views I held. Seeing others, for the first time, under the spell of the same fantasy that plagued me—namely this underground resistance to the war in Vietnam—helped me to realize that I wasn't crazy, after all. With participants from every division on the ship, I felt energized by the potential for action that lay within our grasp.

In the face of similar decrees in other divisions throughout the ship, and with the exception of a few stalwarts like Marty and me, I saw this fellowship quickly disintegrate. In the end, I—like so many of the others—grew fearful of the consequences we would suffer if we acted against the Navy. Unwilling to lay my life on the line, by joining the underground resistance, I simply stood aside and watched it fester beneath the surface, until it gained enough momentum to push me over the threshold between fantasy and reality—to openly rebel.

As Fate would have Her way, it was not long before I was pushed over the threshold by another aspect of Her, Nature. Feeling the urgency to defecate, one day, I slipped off the mess decks to use the head after I had tried in vain to find Farris who, by the way, had wandered off to fraternize with some of his cronies. Since the head was only about fifteen feet off the mess decks, I didn't think Farris would mind if I stepped out to use it without his permission. On the way back, I ran into Marty in the passageway and stopped to talk to him. As soon as I spied Farris out of the corner of my eye, I knew by the look on his face that I was dead meat.

Like a vulture, he swooped down on me, screeching, "You're on report."

"What for?" I asked.

"For disobeying a direct order," he squawked, "and for leaving your appointed place of duty without my permission."

"I had to take a shit, Farris," I tried to explain to him. "And when I couldn't find you anywhere on the mess decks..."

It was useless trying to explain anything to him, for he was totally unreasonable. "You're on report," he kept screaming into my face, over 'n' over. "You're on report."

"I'll tell you one goddamn thing, Farris," I finally interjected. "I have never once had to ask anyone on this ship for permission to take a shit, unless I was on watch. And I'll be damned if I'm going start now."

Immediately, he spun around and raced off across the mess decks, only to disappear down the forward passageway.

"The guy's a fuckin' animal!" Exclaimed Marty.

"Nah," I replied. "He's just afraid; that's all. Like the rest of them, he's afraid of the tide of resistance that has risen up from amongst us plebes, and threatens to sweep over the ship like a tidal wave.

"Don't ya see it, Marty?" I asked him. "There's a spirit arising all over this ship to stir up opposition to what we are being asked to do in Vietnam. Haven't you felt it rising up inside of you like magma in a volcano that has long been dead?"

"If you mean the hate I feel for the Navy and for fuckin' lifers like Farris, yeah, I've felt it," replied Marty, "eatin' away at my insides till I'm ready to fuckin' explode."

"Can't you see, Marty?" I exclaimed. "Filling you with hate for the Navy is soul's way of letting you know she cannot tolerate the life you are leading. Having shown you what she doesn't like in your life, she has also given you some indication of the direction she would like to see it move.

"Don't you recall how alive we all felt as we shared with each other our fantasies, the rebellious ideas our souls had awakened in us? Don't you see how listless we've all gotten since they cracked down on us with their decrees? Don't you ever feel like just reaching out and grabbing hold of the life that would relieve the ache inside your heart and set you free?

"Don't you see what we do to ourselves, Marty? When the soul draws us to her, with tantalizing fantasies, we quite naturally stop what we are doing, and go to her. But let her demand commitment from us, and we drop her, like a hot potato, for some whore or unbefitting way of life that neither satisfies our desires nor fulfills our needs.

"Why? Why do we reject one set of fantasies as unrealistic and accept another as real? Why don't we decide for ourselves what is real?

"Don't you see, it's because we're afraid? Because their fantasy's overshadowed the hearts and minds of men for so long, we've grown up fearing the power they have over our lives, what they can do to us if we disobey them.

"While the havoc wreaked upon our souls, by our unwitting participation in their crimes against the rest of humanity, is far greater than the damage they could ever inflict upon our bodies for our noncooperation, we kowtow to their god—to the cyclops who resides within the great pyramid on the almighty dollar. At a young age, are we taught that it is our sacred duty, when called upon, to sacrifice our lives to the incarnations of this god, in the bloody rituals that seem to arise with every new threat to their opulent way of life. Through one of the biggest pyramid schemes in history, the American Dream, have we been sucked into believing that we too can become immortal like them, but only if we buy into their scheme and turn our lives over to them to be used as they see fit. Thus are we bilked out of a truly fulfilling way of life.

"As our broken lives and dead bodies become the bricks and mortar with which they continue to build this colossal monument to their god, the question arises, do we really want to spend the rest of our lives struggling, fighting and dying, just to help make some lousy bastard back home filthy rich? Or do we want to espouse a new fantasy, one based upon truth and justice for all?

"Don't you see how much they fear us? How afraid they are of what we are saying. How afraid they are of the rebellious tone of our voices. How afraid they are of our reluctance to carry out their every command. How afraid they are of the truth that keeps oozing out of us no matter what they do to us.

"And so I ask, who has more to fear? I daresay, they do."

"I don't know about that," exclaimed Marty before he excused himself to go back to work. "They still have the upper hand, you know."

"Only because we let them have it," I yelled back as he disappeared down the passageway.

As I walked back to the mess decks, wrapped in my own thoughts, I realized I had betrayed my soul when I agreed to become a shipfitter. And I wondered if she would forgive me for having listened to my doubts instead. Obviously, I had needed the confirmation of other real flesh and blood beings, of what I was feeling, before I could go on any further in my relationship to her.

Several days later, I was again written up for the same crime. Unable to find Farris, I scooted down to the head when I needed to, but only after I had told the other guys on the mess decks where I was going. Upon returning to the mess decks after one such jaunt, I was informed by Farris, who had just returned, that I was on report again.

Shortly thereafter, the ship pulled off Yankee Station to steam about the South China Sea for several days. Exhausted, I went up topside after dinner one evening to be alone for a while. As I stepped out onto the deck, I was astounded by the spectacle of nature that greeted me. Except for the V-shaped wake that extended out from the stern of the ship in two perfectly straight lines, all the way to the horizon, the water was dead calm. With the exception of the slight breeze created by the movement of the ship through the water, so too was the air. There were definitely no other signs of life around, neither fish nor fowl. While the hazy sky burned with the orange glow of a dying ember, like a great mirror, did the murky waters below reflect this final act of the day so perfectly that, except for the sheen on the water, heaven and earth appeared as one.

As I plopped down onto my usual perch to watch the passing of such a glorious day, I was drawn to retrace the steps I had taken to get there, as if I were on the verge of discovering something new about myself. I had the strangest feeling, as I reached for the door, this was not the one I had opened earlier. For a moment, I hesitated before I finally pushed the door open. Having stepped off into that twilight zone between wakefulness and sleep, I lost sight of my self until I came to, sometime later.

Where I had been, I could not recall. Had I fallen asleep? While I didn't think I had, I wasn't sure I hadn't either. I was sure of one thing only, that I had finally come back to where I belonged, for I had never before experienced such total peace of mind.

Wherever I had been, for the time being, I felt at one with myself. I felt as if I had finally come back to my senses. As tears welled up in my eyes, I recalled what had happened to me when I went out—I had unexpectedly gotten back in touch with my feelings.

As I sat pondering over my next move, I was pricked by the painful thought that I should have nothing to do with the Navy. Like an expectant mother, I had no conception of the form in which this child would appear when it was born. I knew only that I was a long way off from giving birth to the new life taking shape within me. Because I wanted it to happen now, I was pricked with the pain that I sometimes felt when I did not get my way.

Even though I still did not know what to do with my feelings towards the Navy, I knew that I could no longer simply ignore them either. Because the soul eventually requires a little action from the body, I had no choice but to do what she asked of me if I wanted to keep myself out of the arms of some whore. Only, I did not want to have to endure any suffering in the process. Little did I know that labor pain is a prerequisite for the birth of truth. In spite of the great pain I normally felt because of the severe limitations the Navy placed upon my soul, I found great joy in those moments when she was free to act. In my struggle to find a way out of this maze, I felt as if I were being subjected to a course in behavior modification, to see if I could be prodded into following the orders of a much greater will than my own, that of either She Who Must Be Obeyed or the Great Gray Whore. While I certainly preferred the joy my soul gave me to the pain the Navy inflicted upon her, I had never realized that new life was taking shape within me, until now. Thus did I resign myself to the task of meeting the needs of this new life whenever my soul prevailed upon me to do so.

Having finally accepted responsibility for this unwanted pregnancy, I went below to hit the sack.

Later, the following morning, after our ship had rendezvoused with a tender to take on stores of food and fuel, I wandered down below only to find, much to my surprise, a letter from Mary lying on my bunk.

"I was so happy and relieved," she wrote, *"to receive the letter and package you sent me. To show you how greedy I am, when I get a package, I usually rip into it first, then read the letter. This time, I grabbed your letter first—to find out how you are doing—to see if you are all right. When I had not heard from you by the first of the month, I began to worry. I about died when I read the opening line of your letter—'Golly, by now I imagine you are thinking I have run off with some cute little Japanese gal and forgotten all about you....' For it said exactly what I was thinking. Even though I do not like to think about things like that, as hard as I tried, I couldn't help thinking about the Japanese student you had encountered. I must have thought of a hundred different reasons why I had not heard from you. (Jealous thing, aren't*

I?) Then I thought, 'what good is this doing me? I should not be thinking about you and your Japanese guide, but where you are and if you are all right.' You know, this is the first time I have ever opened a letter before a package.

"After I read your letter, I ripped into the box. Butch, the doll is so beautiful! I have never seen anything like it. I just felt like crying when I held it in my hands. I felt very close to you, as if I had only to turn around and there you would be, with that little grin you have on your face when you give me something. Butch, it is so beautiful! Thank you very much. You don't know how much it means to me.

"I was also glad to receive the pictures. They really turned out good. I bought a small album for them. In your many travels, I would appreciate it if you would send me a few pictures from time to time. That way I can see where you have been. Besides, when you come home, you can look at them and reminisce. That will be nice, don't you think?

"Anyway, I am sending you a picture, I don't think you have ever seen. It is called 'my thinker'. I took some pictures back when you and I were still on the Ann King, together. When I get them developed, I will send it to you.

"Before I go, I have got to tell you about the time the Ann King went Hawaiian. When I woke up one afternoon after a short nap, I put on the muumuu you had sent me. When Sarah saw it, she went wild. We rushed back to our room to get some plastic orchids to put in our hair. Then she put on a real bright colored shift. In the end, we came out looking like two good imitation Hawaiians. While we all got a few good laughs out of it, everyone really liked the muumuu.

"As soon as the pictures get back, I'll send 'em to you. I hope they turn out okay.

"I had better stop now and get to bed, as it is getting late.

"Please remember to take care of yourself. You are in my prayers and always in my thoughts."

Love always,
Mary

While it certainly was a great letter, I could not help feeling terribly hurt by the circumstances that currently kept us apart. As tears welled up in my eyes, I longed to be in the warm hold of her love and mine, in place of the doll I had sent her. Alas, I was separated from my soul by a great void, for I still did not know where to find her. Was she hiding out within my fickle friend Mary after all, as the jealous lover? Or was I just barking up the wrong tree again?

After taking on stores, we returned to the doldrums of Yankee Station where for kicks one night, Marty and I attended our first ship-over spiel. Our recruiter, a first class petty officer named Kraft, bore such a close resemblance to a mouse, I was not too surprised when Marty told me he often went by the nickname of

Mouse rather than his real name. As an unofficial solicitor for the Great Gray Whore, Mouse nibbled away at what was left of a man's soul, with enticements that gnawed on him to extend his enlistment. For every year of service he solicited from a man, Mouse received a handsome bonus from the Great Gray Whore. A crafty little dude, Mouse got caught in his own trap, the night he tried to solicit Marty, who had been sent there, on a mission from God, to expose this scam.

"First, I would like to talk to you-all about the benefits of a career in the Navy," Kraft began, at which point Marty and I burst out laughing.

"Benefits!" Marty exclaimed. "How the fuck you can stand there, Kraft, and tell me that years of fuckin' with other people's lives are going to do anything for me but fuckin' guarantee me a place in hell, really burns my ass."

"What do you mean?" Kraft asked Marty as I swiveled in my seat laughing at how seriously Kraft was taking Marty. Kraft should never have indulged him, for there was no stopping Marty, once he got started badmouthing the Navy.

"You know damn well what I mean, Kraft," replied Marty. "Why, it was fuckin' parasites like you who promised me a place in paradise if I joined the fuckin' Navy. Only, you fuckers never told me I would have to go sloggin' through hell to get there. Here I am, stuck on some godforsaken can, ridin' herd with a bunch of fuckin' wild animals, for some would-be cattle baron back up in Washington, who got a wild hair up his ass, to sell us out to some Southeast Asian slaughterhouse, fearful of losin' its ass in a hostile takeover bid by some gook tycoon, named Ho Chi Minh. Unable to comply with the wishes of my heart, am I forced now, by low life motherfuckers like you, to do what runs contrary to my true nature. That is not paradise by any stretch of the imagination, Kraft. That's fuckin' hell.

"Until I experienced your version of paradise, a Westpac cruise with plenty of booze and pussy galore, I never understood why the fuck anyone in his right mind would want to make a career out of the fuckin' Navy. Seein' how your own goddamn dicks drove you to seek out the one fuckin' whore who could give you what you have always wanted, I knew why fuckers like you chose to stay in the goddamn Navy."

"Where else," interjected Kraft, "could you get a job that'd guarantee you an income and free health care for the rest of your life, give you free room and board, or send you to school for nothing but a few years of service to your country?"

"Ya know, Kraft," Marty replied, "you have been lyin' to us peons for so goddamn long, you have got your self believin' your own fuckin' lies. You ain't servin' the people of this country; you're servin' your own fuckin' goddamn dick. Pussy is your god, and you would do anything for it. You ain't fightin' for freedom, or for the people of this country, or for any of the other bullshit reasons, you've concocted. You're fightin' to maintain your own fuckin' way of life, the right to live like a fuckin' animal. You're fightin' to protect the last place on earth where fuckers like you can unleash their animal natures to prey upon the rest of us without fear of punishment. And because there ain't no other place in a civilized society for fuckin' animals like you, but prison, you stay in this fuckin' zoo where you are protected by the culture, loved and revered by all but a few stalwarts like me and Dury, who have chosen to remain true to their own souls.

"Why, you ain't nothin' but a fuckin' goddamn pimp for the Navy, Kraft. When this fuckin' bitch grabbed you by the dick, you fell for her like every other dick she has sucked the life out of, before you. By turnin' your life over to her, you have helped her become one of the greatest goddamn whores that have ever lived.

"But a bitch like her cannot remain a whore for very long without fuckin' Johnnies like you and me. While she may have me by the balls, right now, she ain't never gonna get hold of my dick, like she did yours, Kraft, for the fuckin' bitch has already caused me enough goddamn pain to last the rest of my life. She ain't never gonna trick this Johnnie again, cause this Johnnie is gonna be marchin' to the beat of his own goddamn drum when it comes time for him to go marchin' home."

As those who had gathered around Marty and me broke out laughing and cheering, Kraft shook his head in disgust. "I feel sorry for you," he muttered as he turned in righteous indignation to hightail it off the mess decks before he was run out of town as a charlatan.

"I feel sorry for you," Marty yelled back, "for you're the one who's fuckin' sick, Kraft, not me."

I was shocked. Never had I heard Marty speak with such conviction concerning perceptions, which only yesterday he had refuted when they came from my mouth. In reality, I was more surprised by his translation of my ideas than I was by his sudden turnabout. For the first time in my life, I realized that I mattered—that my perceptions had just as great an impact on the lives of other people as they had upon my life.

Later that evening, as I sat up topside at my usual perch before retiring, I was startled from contemplation of the day's events by Marty's appearance.

"Dury," shouted Marty in a tone of voice that alarmed me.

"What's the matter?" I inquired, for he looked as if he had just seen a ghost.

"He's plannin' to kill you, Dury!" Exclaimed Marty.

"Who's plannin' to kill me?" I asked.

"Kraft," he answered. "He thinks you were behind the fiasco down on the mess decks earlier this evening. He is so convinced you poisoned my mind and then turned me loose to make a fool out of him in front of everyone."

"He has made a fool out of himself," I exclaimed, "by choosing to live like an animal. He just didn't like the way you pointed that out to him, that's all.

"So he thinks I set him up, does he," I mused, a bit perturbed by his insinuation, for the whole thing had really been quite spontaneous.

"Yeah," replied Marty, with a sarcastic little chuckle.

"And then," Marty continued, "when he plunked $50 down onto the table and offered it to whoever would push you overboard, I thought I had heard everything until he called those who were standin' there, all cowards because no one had taken 'm up on his offer. He shut up real quick when they asked him why he didn't wanna do it himself."

"Why, that Judas priest!" I exclaimed. "Who the hell does he think he is, anyway? Why, no one in his right mind would kill another person for a measly fifty bucks!"

"They killed Jesus for less," rebutted Marty.

"Yeah, but thirty pieces of silver was a lot of money back then," I added. "Fifty dollars, today, is nothin'."

"I don't know, Dury," rejoined Marty. "I wouldn't put anything past the motherfuckers. Look at how they cheat on their wives. Seein' how you sit up here by yourself, night after night, why, any one of them could sneak up behind you and push you overboard before you knew what hit you. In this part of the world, life is so cheap that fifty bucks could buy some crazy motherfucker a lot of pussy."

Unwilling to believe that anyone in his right mind could stoop so low, I concluded that Kraft had merely let off a little steam. "Look at how you act when you get mad at one of them," I finally said. "You go off on the poor son of a buck, ranting and raving about how you will kill the motherfucker when you get your hands on him. But you don't ever physically grab hold of him and wring his neck, as you said you would when you were still angry. Instead, you imagine what you will do, in order to vent your anger in much the same way you observed Kraft venting his."

"Only, I don't plunk money down on the table and ask someone else to do my dirty work," rejoined Marty. "I'm tellin' you, Dury, you could've heard a pin drop when Kraft told them you were a threat that had to be reckoned with, if they did not want to see your rebelliousness spread around the ship, like some fuckin' infectious disease."

"Why, I'm impressed," I exclaimed.

"Don't you see, Dury," Marty insisted, "the motherfuckers mean business. If you piss enough of them off, they're gonna do you in, for they don't give a fuck about anyone else but their own fuckin' asses."

"I don't know, Marty," I replied. "I still can't believe they would go that far. After all, this is the twentieth century, you know."

"You can believe what you want, Dury," Marty persisted, "cause that don't mean a goddamn thing to these medieval motherfuckers. You would have to have been there, Dury, to get a sense of what I'm tryin' to tell you. And I'm tellin' you, you better watch your step, cause the motherfuckers are out to nail your ass, whether you fuckin' believe me or not."

"I have a hard time looking at Kraft's conversation any differently than the ones we had around mutiny," I rebutted. "While there was a lot of talk about mutinying, we never did, cause that was not our real intention—just as I don't believe Kraft really intends to have me killed. I see his actions as the reaction of his animal nature to being cornered by his own human nature, which he sees as belonging to me rather than himself. Unable to reconcile these two aspects of himself, he has decided to go after his humanity before it takes away the double life he has been leading as an animal, for he has yet to learn that domestication is really the only way out of the Jekyll/Hyde dilemma."

"Listen, Dury," insisted Marty. "While all that may be true, you have forgotten one thing—the motherfuckers don't know how to do anything else but live out their fuckin' fantasies on other people. Why, they would just as soon push you overboard as to have to think about it. You've got to realize, Dury, that you are dealin' with a bunch of fuckin' wild animals, who will turn on you, the minute you think you have tamed them."

"It is written, Marty, that *'the wolf shall live with the lamb, the leopard shall lie down with the kid, the calf and the lion and the fatling together, and a little child shall lead them. The cow and the bear shall graze, their young shall lie down together, and the lion shall eat straw like the ox. The nursing child shall play over the hole of the asp, and the weaned child shall put its hand on the adder's den. They will not hurt or destroy on all of my holy mountain; for the earth will be full of the knowledge of the Lord as the waters cover the sea.'* Is. 11:6-9. The picture painted here, Marty, by the prophet, is one depicting the end of evolution, for it is within man that these miraculous changes will take place."

"You're impossible, Dury," exclaimed Marty as we both looked at each other and smiled.

"Thanks for warning me," I finally conceded, whereupon we both broke out laughing hysterically.

"I don't know what I would do without you, Marty," I confessed after we had stopped laughing.

"I know one thing for sure," Marty concluded. "If I don't hit the sack soon, I ain't gonna feel like gettin' up in the morning."

Having bid him goodnight, I went below, assured that harm was less likely to befall me as long as I had friends like Marty, watching out for me. And look after me, he certainly did. He made sure that I never sat up topside by myself. I was deeply touched by such care and concern. In response to a growing need for solitude, I was not always as cooperative with this unsolicited, secret service protection as I could have been.

Ever since I had opened the door to that twilight zone between wakefulness and sleep, I found my self continually being drawn back into my own interior with the curiosity of a little kid, to explore new and uncharted territory. Having parked my ass atop my usual perch, I would find my self riding my mule across a barren stretch of sand from which the waters had only recently receded. Looking back, I could still see the ship, mired in sand and deserted by all but my self.

As the supplies in her hold dwindled with each passing day, I ventured out into this harsh and desolate wasteland, farther and farther, in search of food for thought and the waters of life. However, I would only let my mule go so far, since I feared losing touch with this last bit of reality onto which I still clung. In fact, I unwittingly held such a tight rein on my mule, I succeeded in doing nothing more than going in circles around my present position. After all, how could I put my trust in an animal nature that has so often led me astray? Deserted by every aspect of myself but my animal nature, was I forced to rely on my own ass—to trust my instincts. Unaware that I had let loose of the tight grip, I had held on the reins, I finally got up off my ass, one day, to go off in search of soul, no matter where my ass might lead me.

Unable to keep up with my own ass, the instinct that seemed to be leading me ever more deeply into the hinterland of my being, I realized that I had lost sight of my guide. In a panic, I raced off in the direction in which its barely visible footprints seemed to lead. When they too disappeared beneath the blowing and shifting sands of time, I fell flat on my face. Exhausted, I rolled over on my back and swirled off into unconsciousness where I lay until I caught wind of a gentle breeze blowing about my face.

Opening my eyes, I caught sight of a dove fluttering its wings in midair just above my head. Certain that I was still under the spell of some dream, I closed my eyes to rub the sleep from them, whereupon the dove disappeared. Looking out over the length of my body, I thought I saw the dove again, this time fluttering at my feet where it simply vanished as I blinked my eyes. The third time around, I spotted the dove fluttering in midair at my left side just above my heart where instead of disappearing again, it suddenly transformed itself into the image of my soul, right before my very eyes.

"Come with me," she begged with a smile I could hardly refuse.

How quickly did I find my self standing knee deep in a sea of grass that thrashed about wildly, in response to the strong gusts of wind that came and went like the breath of some mighty being. Never before had I seen such a wind, which could buffet my body and, in the same breath, blow right through me as if there were nothing to me. Never before had I been permitted to see the world around me with such clarity, for a great light penetrated everything. No longer did I, or anything else for that matter, cast a shadow. Never before had I encountered such all-encompassing unity.

As my vision refocused on the forest surrounding this magical meadow, I quickly honed in on a lone tree, the only one bold enough to wear an evening gown in broad daylight—to sport her true colors before it was time. Why, I was so completely captivated by the radiant splendor of her gown, the exquisite blend of yellow, orange, and red in the leaves of her dress, I could not take my eyes off her.

Whatever I so earnestly sought out there in nature suddenly manifested itself in the form of a young woman of Mediterranean descent. Dressed in a simple gown, the style women wore around the time of Christ, she held in her bosom a stone tablet that was divided into two pages like the face of an open book, and upon which were written, in some ancient middle-eastern script, Ten Commandments.

As soon as I realized the significance of the stone tablet, I found my self standing beside an image of my soul in an enormous cavern filled with every religious symbol in the world.

"Do you see anything else that strikes your fancy?" She asked.

"No, I don't." I replied as she reached out to open a door that had not been there before.

"You know," she added, "you are a very interesting person."

"Really!" I exclaimed, quite surprised by what I had just encountered within my own being.

With that, she closed the door and disappeared within.

In my ecstasy, I realize that I have just awakened to the dwelling place of the Holy Trinity. Immediately, I recall a line from the Gospel of John (14:23): *"Those who love me will be true to my word, and my Father will love them; we will come and make our dwelling place with them."* For the first time in my life, I encounter God, and of all places, within myself. Shocked, I realize that heaven is within the grasp of my own imagination.

As the experience opens, I find my self at odds again with my body. Driven by some asinine instinct to look beyond the dry, uninspiring and lifeless mode of existence my head has chosen to pursue, I trudge off, one day, with the curiosity of my youth, to explore the farthest reaches of my imagination. Looking back, I see that I have gotten mired down in an unsuitable way of life, due primarily to a stubborn refusal on my part to trust any other aspect of myself but my head.

At wit's end, I am forced to delve ever more deeply into my imagination for inspiration. Because I have such a great fear of losing control, I'm willing to go only so far, to keep from getting too carried away by my imagination. Naturally, I only succeed in getting caught up in circular thinking. After all, how can I trust an instinct that has so often, in the past, led me astray. Yet, I am forced to rely on this same instinct or inner urge to play with my self, if ever I wish to find a way out of reliving the fate of my fathers. In the struggle to let go of my self, I finally give my imagination free rein.

As I lose my self in play, I panic. In my inability to let go of the urge to play with my self, I race off after this instinct, only to fall flat on my face when my imagination fails me. Having exhausted every effort on my part to make something happen, I finally let go of my conscious self, long enough to fall into the dreadful darkness that still clouds my mind, where I lay until I catch wind of a new awareness stirring about my head.

Once I engage my imagination, I catch sight of some vague notion fluttering about my head, which at first seems so preposterous, I simply dismiss it. As I come to my senses, I think, "there is no way this crazy notion can be true," whereupon my feelings quickly let me know that what I am about to see is the truth and nothing but the truth so help me God.

As I approach this new awareness, I find my self deeply engaged with the concept that consciousness and the material world are the same. Stirred by the very breath of life within me, I realize that I live in this Spirit, just as She lives in me. And I come to a much fuller understanding of Jesus' words: *"On that day you will know that I am in my Father, and you in me, and I in you,"* (Jn. 14:20) for *"I am the light of the world. Whoever follows me will never walk in darkness but will have the light of life."* (Jn. 8:12) *"Is it not written in your law, 'I have said you are gods'?"* (Jn. 10:34) Again, *"I say, 'you are gods, children of the Most High, all of you'."* (Ps. 82:6) Made in the image and likeness of God, in my ecstasy, I realize that, like Jesus, I Am Who Am.

As I struggle to see through the matter that envelopes all consciousness, I am drawn to the tree of life, an image of God in which the hidden feminine side of the Original Being stands out, like never before. At first, I am so completely captivated by the exquisite beauty of Nature, I cannot yet see her real identity, the feminine side of my nature. Taking a closer look at this image, I see Wisdom, her whom the Creator *"poured out upon all his works, upon all the living according to his gift."* (Sir. 1:9-10) Cloaked in the simple language of her images, I find Christ's words: *"You will live in my love, if you keep my commandments, even as I have kept my Father's commandments, and live in his love. All this I tell you that my joy may be yours and your joy may be complete."* (Jn. 15:10-11) For true wisdom is the ability to apply what one has acquired mentally to the conduct of his own affairs.

Once I realize the significance of the stone tablet, I find a way back to my heart where I encounter the terse words of the prophet Jeremiah: *"I will put my law within them, and I will write it on their hearts. No longer shall they teach one another, or say to each other, 'Know the Lord,' for they shall all know me, from the least of them to the greatest, says the Lord."* (Jer. 31:33-34)

I find that the way back to my heart is through the door, opened by those things in the world that contain a hint of what I do not yet know about myself. As soon as something in the material world strikes a chord in my heart, I am reunited with that part of my soul that has been locked up, out there in nature, far from consciousness. Struck by an arrow of Eros or some feeling for the thing, am I driven to take possession of whatever it is that has eluded my grasp. In my lust or need for instant gratification, I may fall for the very thing itself if it remains too far from consciousness. Or if I am patient, I may stumble upon the naked truth of Wisdom Herself as I play with Her images, for it is in going to Her as a lover of truth, that She whispers their meaning in my ear.

Thus did I come to an understanding of the great need I had to free Wisdom from the clutches of Nature, my soul from a fate worse than hell—the Great Separation of the Original Being. Only, I had to find another way than my own sexuality to bridge the great abyss that separated me from my own femininity. I had to find a way to free the seeds of Consciousness from the womb of Wisdom without losing a single one in wanton dissipation. And I found the way, hidden in the love that lay buried deep within my heart.

Having found the love, I had so earnestly sought, all these years, I felt special, as if someone (that someone being God) really loved me. I felt as if Wisdom were trying to show me the way I should go. Only, I would have to cover a lot of ground before I could even come close to bridging the abysmal gap that stood between Her and my understanding of myself.

While this experience healed some of the division in my life, the one involving Kraft only created more. Why overnight it rent the ship into two factions that held so much animosity towards each other, you would have thought we were at war with ourselves rather than the Viet Cong. With a few reservists on one side and an even larger number of lifers on the other, it created a vast pool of uncommitted souls over which the two sides fought like cats and dogs.

A new breed of men, the reservists differed from the low-life Neanderthals as much as did the Cro-Magnon men of prehistoric times. A more intelligent and sensitive lot, they hated their indentured servitude to a lower form of life, and rued the day they had ever gotten involved in this country's military solution to the problems in Vietnam. However much they indulged in grass, hashish, peyote or acid to escape the hellish conflict within themselves over their participation in this war, they nevertheless remained faithful to the wives and fiancées they had left behind. In spite of their disaffection with the Navy and the war in Vietnam, they still performed their tasks, only to the beat of the rock music to which they constantly subjected themselves, to drown out the screaming of their souls in righteous indignation over their complicity. More often than not were they standing up for what they believed, and at least confronting the low-lifers before they'd agree to carry out those commands that offended their sensibilities in any way. Because I seemed to speak to something hidden deep within their beings, they unconsciously adopted me as the rebel for their cause, the white knight who might free them from themselves.

The lifers, on the other hand, feared this new breed of man who dared to stand up to them and question their authority. Like outcasts, the lifers had flocked to the Great Gray Whore, only because she appeared to give them what this society otherwise withheld from them—a reason for living. Driven to serve the soul of this sick society, these patriots of the Great Gray Whore searched in vain through the brothels of the Far East for her ever-elusive form. In their quest for the Great Prostitute, the genie who could fulfill their every desire, they turned to the Spirits of Alcohol. Instead of releasing the genie bottled up within them, they aroused from his slumber, the ogre who ruled over her, the instinctive beast hidden within us all—Hyde. Because Hyde gave them what they wanted, they grew fond of the horny old devil. Then one day, they ran into their own shadowy perception of the white knight, hiding out within a lowly peon named Drury, and grew fearful; for somewhere in the back pages of their minds, they recalled a tale from the days of old, in which the white knight slays the beast.

In the middle, stood the majority of the crew who, unlike the lifers, still had some semblance of a conscience to which the white knight could appeal. Caught up in this tug-of-war for their souls, they often fell prey to the ways of their animal natures. In their inability to interpret the language of the body, they easily lost their heads when confronted by the rawness of their desires. With their heads in the clouds, and their feet mired down in clay, were they driven to live like the gods, one day, and the beasts of the earth, the next, for this, they believed, was the fate of those who lived in the middle.

While neither lifers nor reservists would have much to do with each other, those who lived in the middle associated freely with the members of both factions. By keeping open the paths of communication between the two sides, they seemed to temper some of the hostility each side felt for the other. For now, they were the glue that tenuously held the crew together.

On the same day (29 June 1967) that we pulled off Yankee Station for a little R & R or rest and relaxation in the southern port of Sasebo, Japan, I was ordered to appear at a Captain's Mast for the offenses I had committed earlier that month. As usual, I got all shook up about having to speak on my behalf. Because I had never been allowed to speak freely in my own home, I had been seriously handicapped by my stepfather. Lacking the ability to express myself when confronted by figures of authority that threatened me in any way, I felt like David having to confront Goliath without a slingshot. Like so many other times in the past, I simply retreated into myself, in search of a safe place to hide.

Only this time, I was confronted by a shadowy figure riding my ass as I ran up over the top of a huge sand dune in the desert of my mind. Startled, I demanded that this ethereal invader of my space reveal his identity to me.

"I am but a shadowy glimpse of who you really are," he whispered as if it were his last dying breath. With that, he slipped from the mule, and fell face first into the sand.

Alarmed, I stepped back from this mirage, which, at that point, was so thin, I could almost see right through it. Moved to resuscitate him, I knelt down in the sand at his side, quickly rolled him over, and began to breathe new life into his vanishing form.

"You must stand tall," he whispered before the whole vision vanished.

At the master-at-arms' behest, I entered the Captain's stateroom where Farris, a yeoman and the ship's new Executive Officer—a LCDR Kihune—had already gathered for this charade. A native of Hawaii, the new XO immediately struck me as being rather pharisaical. Decked out in a precisely pressed and tailor-made set of khakis, he not only chose his words very carefully before he spoke, but also expressed himself in excellent form. At first, I was envious of his ability to speak so well. The more I observed him, the more I found to dislike. For he was so methodical, almost mechanical in his movements, that he impressed me as having been programmed like some computerized robot to move in a particular way upon receipt of certain data from his environment. Even his laughter lacked the full-bodied spontaneity of a good laugh. One hundred percent military, he stirred up within me a deep revulsion for what he had become—the embodiment of the perfect executive, law enforcement officer for the state. As a High Priest for the Great Gray Whore, he was the antithesis of the very Spirit for which I'd been asked to stand tall. While we stood there psyching each other out, I felt his repugnance for me, whereupon he promptly withdrew his gaze to fidget with himself instead.

Unwilling to let a pawn beat him at his own game, he approached me with the idea of trying to put me down in some way. "What's this?" He demanded to know as he pointed to the hair I had recently started to legally cultivate on my upper lip.

"Why, it's a mustache, Sir," I replied, "and a darn good looking one at that—don't you think?"

"I see, Mr. Drury, that you and I have a very different perspective on life," he concluded with a wry little smile on his face. "And if I may make a suggestion to you, don't let your feelings get in the way of your obligations, for I will personally see that you pay dearly for any transgressions in which your feelings embroil you."

"Touché," I muttered to myself as he resumed his previous position. Inside, I shuddered at the thought of what he could do to me.

"Stand tall," whispered the shadowy depths of my being.

As the Captain entered the room, I picked up my shoulders and raised my head, not so much for him, as for my shadow. "O Captain, my Captain," I heard my self exclaim from somewhere deep within me.

"O courage, my life," I heard this wispy shadow of me reply.

Just then, the XO began to read the charges against me. "Mr. Drury, you are charged here, today, with having violated Article 86 of the UCMJ, after failing to go at the time prescribed to your appointed place of duty on 13 June 1967—with having violated Article 92 of the UCMJ, after failing to obey a lawful order on 13 June 1967—and with having violated Article 86 of the UCMJ, after failing to go at the time prescribed to your appointed place of duty on 17 June 1967. How do you wish to plead, guilty or not guilty?"

Within the confines of my mind, I bent down to scratch around in the sand for a suitable response. When I found the words written in the sand, I stood up to face my accusers who, by then, had succumbed to fidgeting with themselves. "Not guilty," I proclaimed, whereupon the XO promptly proceeded to read me my rights.

As soon as he had finished, he asked Farris to step forward. "Mr. Farris," he commanded, "in your own words, would you briefly relate to the Captain the events that took place on the 13th and 17th of June, 1967, which then led you to place Drury on report."

"Well, Sir," began Farris in a sheepish tone of voice that was quite uncharacteristic of him, "I had been havin' a little trouble with Dury and some of the other men down on the mess decks, leavin' their duty stations before their work was done. So I gave 'em all a direct order, not to leave the mess decks without my permission.

"On the morning of the thirteenth, I had given Dury several tasks to perform before I left the mess decks to take care of unfinished business up in supply. I had actually given 'm more than he could possibly complete before I got back. When I returned, I found Dury fraternizin' with another shipmate in the passageway aft of the mess decks. Immediately, I informed 'm that he was on report for disobeyin' the order, forbiddin' 'm to leave the mess decks without my permission, and for leavin' his appointed place of duty.

"On the 17th, I again found Dury fraternizin' with another shipmate, this time down in the head. Rather than say anything to him that might ruffle his feathers, I went off to get another report chit to write 'm up for leavin' the mess decks again without my permission."

"Thank you, Mr. Farris," interjected the XO at that point.

Confident he held the winning hand this time around, he then asked me if I wished to make a statement in my own defense.

Within my imagination, I bent down to sift through the shifting sands for the words to defend myself. As the words issued forth from the ground of my being, I spoke thus: "In the past, I have experienced considerable difficulty in trying to locate Farris—he so needlessly spends that much of his time off the mess decks. I don't know about you-all, but when Mother Nature calls, I have to go. Besides, I think you would be hard pressed to find anyone onboard the ship, who has ever had to ask his superior if he could defecate, before he went, unless, of course, he was standing watch. When I couldn't find Farris, I simply told my coworkers where I was headed. On the way back, I stopped, unfortunately, just outside the door to the mess decks to chat briefly with a fellow shipmate. At the time, I did not think that I was doing anything wrong until I saw Farris swoop down upon me, like a bird of prey, screeching out, over and over, that I was on report. To this day, I still do not feel that I did anything wrong."

By the time I had finished speaking, I noticed they were all fidgeting with themselves, from the Captain on down to Farris. I was tickled that they had been touched by what I'd had to say, for in my naiveté, I actually believed the spirit of love would win out over the letter of the law, this time around. Boy, was I sadly disillusioned when the Captain announced his verdict, that I was guilty of passively resisting their efforts to control that part of my nature over which not even I have any control. As a punishment for my terrible crime, I was busted to a recruit and given 20 days of extra duty.

Dismissed by the XO, I went back down to my locker where I was surrounded by those anxious to hear the outcome of my Captain's mast. While I had not expected the Captain to find me guilty, I was just as surprised as they were, that he had busted me to a recruit. Because I had stepped over the line into that gray area of life, which lies hidden somewhere between obedience and disobedience of the law, I saw this whole affair as a last ditch effort by the Captain to reassert his authority where he had none. In rising above the law, I no longer felt bound by all of its inadequacies. Instead, I found freedom and fulfillment. While I could certainly have used the extra pay, I never missed the rank I lost that day; nor did I ever seek to regain it.

Forced to let go of yet another aspect of the life onto which I clung, for fear of falling through the void it had created in my life, did I draw ever so close to understanding one of the most puzzling pieces of my life, the urge to stand tall as a beacon to all. Rather than falling headlong into the Great Abyss as many of my shipmates had, I felt urged to hold my head high as I stepped into the infernal pit to shed light on whatever remained bound to the beast that inhabited its dank, dirty corridors. Alas, I was not quite ready for so bold an undertaking.

Having never been initiated into the underground resistance, until this Captain's mast, I lacked any training in the ways of the underworld. Why, I barely understood the language, much less how to access this world or go about doing anything once I got there. I knew only that it seemed to stir with the slightest ripple, I made at the surface, whereupon I would start receiving images of its perception of what was taking place on the surface. I always had a choice in the matter, I did either what I saw or what I was meant to do. If I failed to do the latter, for whatever reason, then I no longer had a choice in the matter—I would be forced to do the former unless my will remained sufficiently strong to withstand its enticing images while I tried to figure out which way I should go. Because the images were so highly charged with the energy to pull Consciousness down from the heavens, in brilliant flashes of insight, I had little time to dally here, lest I be struck by the energy contained within the images, to act them out before I found out what I was meant to do. How quickly did I learn that She Who Must Be Obeyed always got her man, one way or the other, through either his gonads or his heart.

In other words, just as I had to defecate, so did I have to stand tall to spit out the truth. One way or another, I had to sow the seeds of Consciousness out there in Nature. If I did not want to spend the rest of my life wrestling with the other member of my body, in one hellish bout after another, then I had only to stand out from the body of mankind, like a great lighthouse, so that all men might one day come to see the truth hidden within them.

8
R & R

After having been at sea for well over a month, I looked forward to getting off this bobbing cork and stepping onto solid ground again, no matter if it was foreign soil. Fortunate enough to have pulled two days of liberty, I made sure that I was among the second wave of sailors to go ashore when the ship pulled into Sasebo, the following morning. To avoid getting trampled by the sudden release from their cages, of those animals barely able to contain the seminal fluid dribbling from their sexual appendages, I waited until the first wave had crested before I gently rolled onto shore with Greg and Harold to do a little sightseeing and shopping. Laughing and carrying on like a gaggle of giddy girls as we browsed through one shop after another in search of knickknacks and that special something to buy our sweethearts or wives back home, I ended up buying Mary a patch displaying the cartoon character, Snoopy, riding on a surfboard. With the words "Vietnam Cruise" printed in large letters over his head, and the year 1967 stamped in an even smaller script underneath the wave that'd risen up to overtake him, I was reminded of my own dogged pursuit of the truth in my one-man crusade against the Navy and the war in Vietnam, but only briefly. I was not about to let anything destroy the few precious moments I got to spend outside the belly of the great gray whale.

As quickly as my attention had been captured by these few stray thoughts, was it captivated by the sound of the rock 'n' roll music that had broken through as this lonesome freight came screeching to a halt at Greg's insistence.

"That sounds like the Beatles!" Exclaimed Greg, amateur musician and avid Beatles' fan that he was. As we drew closer to the source of the music, a record shop up the street, he surmised that we were hearing, for the first time, songs from a new album they had released while we had been at sea, cut off from any news of what had been happening around the rest of the world.

Once we were inside the shop, Greg quickly solved the mystery as he honed in on the new album like a homing pigeon, and snatched it up in his claws. "Fancy this," he exclaimed, "finding the Beatles' latest album in Japan, of all places." As soon as we had all had a good laugh, he turned around and bought it.

On the way back to the ship, we made another stop, this time at my insistence, for I really wanted to buy something more than the silly little patch, I had gotten Mary, to let her know how much I loved her.

"Look!" I exclaimed as I emerged from a small shop to the acclaim of Greg and Harold as I held high the silk blouse I had bought Mary.

"Say," I blurted out as they took off without me, "if we want to eat supper back onboard the ship, we'd better get going. Besides, I can't be late for my date with the master-at-arms; or my ass'll be grass."

While the work was still very menial, I noticed a slight change in my taskmasters. As they got to know me, I was no longer given the meanest and nastiest work they could muster up. When they stuck around to keep an eye on me, which was very seldom, I would engage them in a bit of conversation. I found that even those, who still treated me so callously, had a heart I could touch if they let me. For the most part, I was left alone, unsupervised, to do however much I felt like doing, so long as I put in two hours of my time.

Active Imagination

Later that evening, after having completed my extra duty and taken a shower, I ran into Greg and company up topside as they sat around a portable record player, listening to his new album. Exhausted, I plopped down on the deck and leaned back against a bulkhead where, at the inducement of the music, I wandered off into that twilit world, the others seemed unable to penetrate without smoking marijuana. There, I found my self trying to fill the crack in my nature that had preoccupied my mind for so many years. Only, I was shocked when I saw my self trying to fill the crack with the other member of my body. At the same time, I realized it didn't matter how I felt about this image. Though I knew it would have been morally reprehensible for me to have acted in the manner proposed, I sensed there was something still psychologically correct about such dark, dirty images.

"What am I to do?" Asked I of the more civilized aspects of my nature who, in their ongoing feud with the uncivilized parts of me, had never won a single round in the debate over this question, and then wondered why I had thrown out their unworkable old solutions, along with those of the beastly neighbors beneath them.

Having been encouraged to imagine my way out, did I slip into that region of the brain where I could venture without having to act like a beast, one day, and a god, the next. Though, I wasn't too sure I had found the place until the voices in my head had dropped me off there, in their own picturesque way.

"The uncivilized run around like chickens with their heads chopped off," gave I some thought to the unthinkable side of nature. "They worry me with the half-baked ideas they concoct and force down the throats of unsuspecting souls like me, as if their solutions were the only way to go. And they wonder why I don't ever take them very seriously."

So off I went to fill the hole these images invariably left behind whenever I slipped into this region of the brain to find the words to express myself in a more civilized manner.

Having closed the door to my heart, had my soul, in the meantime, slipped down to my gut like a sinking feeling. Once there, she hoped to turn me on to another way out, one in which she was no longer the object of my fathers' lust or their fathers' before them, something that had been denied my mother who, like my fathers before me, had never given her the freedom she now sought in me.

As I turned to face the music of my own dreams, I slipped, unnoticed, through the gate my soul had provided at her expense. Inside, I ran smack dab into an incredibly massive and seemingly impenetrable wall of stone, the likes of which I had never seen before. Standing back for a moment to take in the full measure of the barrier I had constructed between my self and my imagination with the help of all those who had ever passed this way, I caught sight of an invisible opening in the wall, a black hole through which only the undaunted passed. Overcoming my dismay over the shadow of a noose that hung on the wall above the opening just beyond my reach, I stepped off into the black hole where I encountered the spirits of what had long ago been condemned by the Church of the Living Dead and strangled to death by the Wraiths of the State. As the spirits swarmed and slithered about me like venomous snakes, I knew the lies, which enveloped the truth of these spirits in such vile forms, could do me no harm. Allowed to pass unharmed, was I greeted by the Great Necromancer, the one whom men have called the Adversary ever since he tricked them out of Paradise. While the Trickster stood there smiling at me with the conceited assurance that the likes of me would never see through the magic of an erect phallus, I watched as his form slowly gave way to the very pillar of my being, on top of which sat a pearl, the size of a large grapefruit. Immediately, I recognized it as the Pearl of Great Price, a symbol of the individual, which, at birth, God had ordained me to become. Moreover, I saw it as the only way in which I could ever hope to withstand the lure of the Great Magician to act instinctively. Lacking any awareness of this individual, I lost sight of the apparition as it slowly gave way to the illuminating light of a fire that burned brighter and brighter, the closer I got to it.

In response to the wailful sound that emanated from somewhere deep within my being, it dawned on me how badly I was in need of a mentor, at this point in my life. Having honed in on the beating of my heart, I quickly found my self staring into the flames of the fire that burned therein. Looking up, for just a moment, I spied, through the flames, the form of an old Indian seated opposite me on the ground in front of the fire.

Immediately, did he start talking to me about the images that had popped into my head, giving new meaning to them. For, he certainly seemed to know more about them than I did—the reason I had been drawn to him, in the first place.

"You have chosen wisely, my son," he went on to say, "for seldom has one, so young, ever slipped past the Magician and the wall of illusion that surrounds him without falling prey to his magic. If you want to see the face of God, you will have to remove the Magician's mask from your face. Made in the image and likeness of God, you will have to tear down the facade behind which you hide, if you want to see yourself as you really are—for the only mask you can safely wear, without being destroyed by it, is the one God specifically fashioned for you alone.

"In looking to the void—the space created by the emotional departure of your soul from the illusory way of life you inherited from your parents—for the help you will need as you attempt to find this mask, you have, once again, chosen wisely, my son. In your fear, however, of letting go of the life the Navy has imposed upon you, to embrace that of your own soul, you have gotten bogged down in this limbo or gray area between heaven and hell. For, you have yet to learn the lesson of the void, that everything you seek is all right here within you."

As I slid deeper into the void, I could hear people laughing. Evidently, I had stretched their imaginations too far. Yet, I wondered if they really weren't laughing at themselves in response to my having struck a chord, deep within their hearts.

Older and much wiser in this fantasy, I find my self speaking to a small gathering about the wonderful relationship my soul and I have enjoyed down through the years, for they had never cultivated as close a relationship with their souls as I had with mine. I wondered, though, if she would still be sending me such revelations when I reached the age of sixty-four. Or would I find that she had already locked the door through which I had always returned to the land of the living, and thrown away the key instead. To such a far-reaching question, did I hear the voices in my head insist they knew not the answer. As I continued to reminisce over our long walk together, through the garden of life, I had just begun to tell my audience how I could never have asked for more when I heard the voices in my head say that they wanted no more than to see my self retire to the back pages of my mind. As I journeyed back to the places in nature where she had hidden herself in the game she used to play, to see if I could find her, I realized that life was much too short to piddle away on the unthinkable. Having been sentenced to two years before the mast for the sins of my generation and those long past, had I found the answer to my dilemma in the person of my own soul.

"Remember, my son," admonished the old Indian from afar, "when darkness descends upon you, seek the fire that burns within your heart, for it is written that nothing, neither the Magician nor his Wraiths, can separate you from my love."

Instead of finding the fire that burned within, I somehow ignited a small brush fire at my genitals, which threatened to burn out of control if I didn't do something quick. Panicking, I only succeeded in fanning the flames that swiftly consumed me.

"Let go!" Commanded the old Indian from across the void.

"Let go of what?" I demanded to know.

"Let go of the illusion that holds on to you as tightly as you hold on to it," he replied.

"I don't know how to do that," I shouted back.

"You must stand emotionally aloof from the illusion until it begins to dissipate of its own accord," he responded, "for it is nothing without your participation. Your imagination will then show you the way to go."

"It's not working," I cried out, after I had tried to close my eyes to the illusion instead of trying to disentangle my emotions from it.

"O ye of little faith," he muttered. "Look around you."

Opening my eyes, I watched with amazement as the last of the fire died out, for I had inadvertently allowed the old Indian to distract me from the fire of my desires, long enough to keep me from fueling it with my emotions. The more I let go of the illusion and refocused my attention elsewhere, the faster the whole scene changed of its own accord, exactly as he had said it would. With the climax of yet another daydream, did I find my self seated at a table in a small European-style cafe, opposite my soul who had just ordered tea for the two of us from a waiter whom I immediately recognized as the old Indian.

As I cringed with embarrassment over my handling of this last affair, she laughed. "I see you have already met my father," she concluded.

"Good morning," said the old Indian.

For lack of anything better to say, I wished him the same.

With that, did I find my self walking alone, down some dark, deserted street in that gray, twilit world within, where the light of consciousness is eclipsed by our ignorance of who we really are. By the time I had walked several blocks, it dawned on me that I was headed for work at a place where I neither belonged nor desired to work any longer. Sickened by the mere thought of having to work another day in this hellhole, I had just turned around to head back home, when I decided to go roaming about this ghostly world instead.

As I ventured down avenues seldom traveled by the likes of me, I stumbled upon a great rift in my personality, between self and soul, which had been handed down to me through a line of ancestors that went back to the beginning, when the Original Being was split in two for the sake of consciousness. Peering over the side into the historic depths of this great rift, I watched as this crack spewed forth a magician whose magical powers were second to none but those of the Creator. Immediately I recognized the magician as the Great Necromancer whom I had encountered earlier. As it became clearer to me how much his very existence depended on this rift, I realized he was the one who had driven the soul underground and set up the self as a puppet dictator.

Having grown up oblivious to the wants and needs of my soul, with the onset of puberty had I fallen headfirst into this rift, where I wandered in darkness until Fate, the mother of soul, forced me to choose between her daughter and my self. Having been enlisted by the Navy to go off and free the soul of this country, Miss Liberty, from the clutches of the evil magician, Ho Chi Minh, little did I know I had been duped, along with thousands of other young men, into fighting for one of Uncle Sam's alter egos, a puppet dictator in South Vietnam. Thus was I cast to play the part of a fool in this human tragedy or adaptation of a divine drama in which I was to simultaneously star as the real hero.

As my mind went wandering off with the sounds of the voices in my head, like a hound that had just picked up the scent of a fox, I was deeply touched by my soul's response.

"Why do you flirt with every skirt that passes, when you have me, the envy of every man who has ever lived?" She begged to know. "Am I not enough for you—that you have to go looking elsewhere? Why do you insist on looking for the solution to the Jekyll/Hyde dilemma in the faces of these beauties, when mine alone reflects the beauty of the life you seek? How can I convince you that I am the one meant for you?"

"It would help if you had a real body," I replied.

"O, but I do," she exclaimed.

"Then where is it?" I demanded to know.

"Why, it's right here in front of you," she answered with that cute little smile of hers, "for I occupy the same body you do."

"Very funny," I muttered.

"It's really not very funny at all," she retorted. "As it stands, neither one of us has any control over this body of ours."

"What do you mean?" I asked with some concern.

"I mean this," she responded quite frankly, "our body is in the possession of the evil Magician."

Rendered speechless, I gulped down the last bit of tea in my cup and looked out the window of the cafe, at the people racing up and down the streets like a bunch of wild nocturnal animals that have just been aroused from another day of sleep, to prowl about the growing darkness in search of what they will need to survive another day in a world, they have never quite reconciled with their deepest aspirations.

"I am glad you have brought me here," I finally said, "for someone needs to wake up to an understanding of the time in which we're living, before it's too late and we have destroyed ourselves."

"How many have been freed from the Magician's spell?" I asked.

"Very few," she answered rather grimly.

"Then we had better get started," I concluded, "if we want to increase that number by one more."

"You really mean it?" She asked as tears welled up in her eyes.

"What's the matter?" I asked. "Did I say something wrong?"

"No," she sputtered. "It's just that I have had to wait so long, without really knowing if you would ever commit yourself to the task of helping me reclaim our body from the Magician. Now that you have come to my aid, you come as a broken young man in need of much mending because of the wound that was inflicted upon you, long ago, and still festers deep within you. And I have to tell you, just as I have told myself over the years, to be patient, for it is going to take a long time to gain the strength you will need to withstand the Magician. I am sorry. So you may as well sit tight and enjoy the rest of what my father has prepared for you, as it is almost over."

The moment I realized it was "me" time to die, I found my self lying there half-dead. While I stood there, staring at my self, along with those who had come out to see such sport, I watched the face of this puppet slowly give way to that of the Magician's. "Was this the mask about which the old Indian had warned me?" I wondered.

Only later, when I saw Uncle Sam lose the only whore I had ever experienced, would I come to a better understanding of the hole this mask had left behind. Having fallen into an urge to play with my self, had I succumbed to this dream when one of my shipmates mentioned something about all the holes in the DMZ, something I had never given any consideration until I realized just how many whores it would take to placate Uncle Sam's appetite for more.

As the murky waters of unconsciousness swept over me, I watched the evil Magician take control of my body. For the first time, I saw how he used my weakness for self-love to transform me into one of his puppets. Abandoned by my real father at an early age, I was deeply wounded by this loss of love. While my mother poured most of her energy into work, to feed, clothe and shelter three young children, I unwittingly turned to the Magician, in my inability to find love for self anywhere else. Again was I deeply wounded when my stepfather abandoned me for booze. In my insatiable hunger for love, I got hooked, instead, on the ultimate form of self-love. In my search for the one high that would satisfy this ever growing appetite of mine for real love, I fell for the other member of my body. Not until I moved beyond my self, one day, in response to the loving call of the evil Magician's fraternal twin, my mentor, the old Indian, was I filled with the love I had not received as a child. For, I was being asked to love this instinctive brother of mine, until the other member of my body revealed all of its dark, dirty little secrets, which meant I would have to give my mentor more say over my life if I was to resist the seductive pull of his evil twin to act instinctively. To keep my head above water, was I turned onto resisting the urge to fight the image of the Magician that'd been projected onto Ho Chi Minh when Uncle Sam looked to this mirror, in his inability to see through the holes in the mask he was wearing.

"How accountable is one for these holes in his personality if he cannot see them?" I wondered, ere the answer leapt from the pages of the Old Testament in the words of the Lord to the Prophet Ezekiel: *"Mortal, I have made you a sentinel for the house of Israel; whenever you hear a word from my mouth, you shall give them warning from me. If I say to the wicked, 'You shall surely die,' and you give them no warning, or speak to warn the wicked from their wicked ways, in order to save their lives, they shall die for their iniquity; but their blood I will require at your hand. But if you warn the wicked, and they do not turn from their wickedness, or from their wicked ways, they shall die for their iniquity; but you shall have saved your life. Again, if the righteous turn from their righteousness and commit iniquity, and I lay a stumbling block before them, they shall die; because you have not warned them, they shall die for their sin, and the righteous deeds they have done shall not be remembered; but their blood I will require at your hand. If you warn the righteous not to sin, and they do not sin, they shall surely live, because they took warning; and you will have saved your life."* Ezek. 3:17-21.

Because I had been late for the beginning of the show, I was allowed to sit through a repeat performance. Before I finally got the message, I quite often had to be subjected to the same experiences, over and over.

Having barely made it through the initiation process, that is, the trial by fire, was I inducted into this small band of resisters on 24 June 1967, in a serious attempt to harmonize the various aspects of myself into one voice. Of late, I had found my self speaking in harmony with the one voice that has power over the multitude of voices that arise, like demons, at the slightest provocation, from black holes in our personalities, to spread their lies. With the realization that so many of us become personifications of these false voices, I saw this collaboration with my soul and my mentor as an important step toward warding off any takeover attempts by my own personal demons, for I dreaded the thought of ever becoming a permanent puppet, or worse yet, a wraith or shadow of the Magician. Unlike so many of my shipmates, I sought the one true identity that would bring together the renegade forces within me and bind their rebellious cackle into one voice forever. Because I had never seen a living example of an individual who had found his true identity, as they seemed to come and go with the times, I had no way of visualizing what such a person looked like on the inside, other than through this image of a band playing and singing together in perfect harmony.

Having sat on my duff as an observer through many of these encounters, or at best, having unwittingly participated in them, I suddenly found my self up on stage, with the others, as a full participant in the process of trying to bring my earthly existence into harmony with heaven's goal for me. With the approval of my own audience, did I reluctantly step forward to share my thoughts with them.

I used to get upset with my soul when she took off for parts unknown, without me, for I would invariably be driven by my own sexual desires to seek her out within the very hole into which she had disappeared, unbeknownst to me. Then it dawned on me, one day, that she was the crack I had tried to penetrate in an earlier fantasy, the very hole itself through which I must pass to free consciousness from the clutches of Mother Nature. Regardless of how she disguised the truth, I saw my soul as the Spirit who animated both the real world and its black hole, the imagination from which all reality had long ago been stripped, to create consciousness. With the realization that reality is a three-dimensional projection of the Original Being frozen in time—an illusion, in other words, of our real identities, scattered about us like the pieces of some great, yet unsolved jigsaw puzzle—I saw instinct as one side of the electromagnetic force that drove us to penetrate the holes within our consciousness, and love as the flip side of the same coin, drawing us instead to those images that would help us fill in these gaps. Thus, did I become aware of my need for others, both real and imaginary.

Through the images to which I had been drawn, of late, did I come to see my soul as an intermediary between the physical world and the world of the imagination, as an allusion to the truth, in other words, for she had an uncanny way of showing me what remained invisible yet to the naked eye. If I limited myself to using just the light of day in the examination of the events in my life that had struck some chord in me, I saw only those images that came into focus out in front of my eyes. On the other hand, if I looked at these same events with the illuminating light of the imagination, I saw a different set of images come into focus behind my eyes. Since neither view alone gave me a very accurate picture of reality, I decided to take my soul up on the suggestion she seemed to be offering me via these images. In allowing the light of day to reunite itself with its long lost and seemingly more incoherent mate, the illuminating light that radiated from her eyes, I saw the most exquisite images, which, in spite of their intangibility, revealed a kaleidoscopic picture of reality that transcended all duality. In my struggle to grasp hold of one of these fleeting glimpses into Paradise, I got sucked into the spiritual vacuum that still separated me from the truth. Grabbing hold of the magic lamp I had found there, within my imagination, I started rubbing it with my hand as fast as I could. In a sudden burst of ecstasy that gripped my whole being, I saw brilliant streams of white light spew forth from the opening in the lamp and quickly fill the void in a dense sea of lava. Having finally released the seeds of consciousness imprisoned within the lamp of my imagination, I found my self swimming in a virtual sea of ideas. As my mind raced with a jillion other ideas toward some unspecified goal, I easily outdistanced my competitors with the nascent idea that I embodied. In my inability to see where I was going, I ran smack dab into the realization that the ultimate act of love is the creation of consciousness. Left standing in front of a mirror, staring at an image of my soul, I realized she was the illusion behind which the truth is hidden from all but those who dare to walk back through the looking glass of their own eyes to see the world from her point of view.

Though I had begun to see some improvement in the status of my interior life, especially since I had gotten reacquainted with my soul, I grew quite upset with those who had taught me in school, down through the years, for having filled my head with everything but the knowledge that would have given me peace of mind. In my anger, had I pulled back into my shell, like a turtle, to protect myself from further harm. In the hull of this crude boat, had I suffered great deprivation at my own hand. Having gotten hopelessly lost upon the high seas of life, had I drifted about, until that fateful day when I rescued my soul from the sea of abuse to which I had abandoned her.

On that note, I found my self back at the entrance to my imagination, that black hole from which the truth came forth, to put an end to my wandering about the real world in search of what I knew not.

"Good night," I said to all my friends, both real and imaginary, as I got up to go below and hit the sack for the night.

"Good night," responded a chorus of voices that literally spanned both worlds.

"Congratulations my son," I heard the old Indian say as I dozed off to sleep. "You have just passed through your first mental breakdown, and with flying colors, I might add," whereupon I tumbled headfirst down the rabbit's hole, into the next adventure that awaited me in the dreamworld, that life which flows on, both within and without, with little regard for such boundaries.

As I woke up, the following morning, I recalled having dreamt I had spent the night holed up in my study where the Dr. Jekyll in me had retreated in an experimental effort to humanize the more beastly side of my nature before our bad chemistry transformed me again, into Hyde. With the inundation of the world, as I knew it, under a sea of lava that neither burned nor destroyed, I realized that mental breakdowns were nothing more than harmless eruptions of unconscious material into one's awareness. Driven by this primordial soup to give conscious form to itself, had I gained a small measure of freedom from Hyde, with the knowledge that was strained from this soup as it passed through the semipermeable walls of my study, to strike a happy medium between the better side of me and the beast within.

Overwhelmed by the tension to create a new life for myself, I woke up exhausted, as if my main drive in life had been broken down into its component parts, during the night, and had been reconstructed with a new program in mind—to resist the Navy at all cost—for with the exception of the dark side of me, I had nothing left to give the Navy. Since my energies belonged to neither my self nor the Navy, but rather to my soul, to the extent that I let her use them in her struggle to resist the war in Vietnam, I gained that much more strength to resist the seductive pull of the evil Magician to act instinctively. Thus was I awakened to the path I must take if I wished to gain mastery over my self and its penchant for playing with the other member of my body.

"What you need," interjected a third-class boilerman who had recently befriended me, "is a good hot sauna and a massage to set your mind at ease."

"Yeah, right!" I exclaimed.

"You would be a fool," he insisted, "not to take advantage of the bathhouses in Sasebo, for they are among some of the finest in the world."

"Humph," I muttered as he piqued my interest with a more detailed description of what to expect once I got there.

Upon arriving, I would be whisked off to a room containing two tubs of hot water, in which to bathe and then rinse myself before entering the sauna to sweat out the toxins that were supposedly making me feel so sluggish. After that, I would be shown the shower to wash away any poisons my body might have released in the sauna. Directed to lie down on a table, I would then be given a massage guaranteed to release any residual tension that might still be bogging me down.

"If you've never had one," he added, "you don't know what you're missin'."

Since he had never given me any reason to doubt him, like a fool did I follow him to the bathhouse where I was treated just as he had described, back onboard the ship. However, when it came time for the massage, I experienced some reservations about the attendants, who were apparently all females. I grew even more apprehensive when my masseuse yanked away the towel that had been covering my privates, and with a smile, threw it to the floor. As soon as she began to rub my upper thighs in a seductive manner, I knew right away what kind of massage she intended to give me. And when the guy on the table next door to me jumped up from behind the curtain that separated us and went running off after his masseuse with an erection, I grabbed her hand and motioned for her to stop, whereupon she immediately backed off.

"You, good man," she said, bowing low as she excused herself.

Well, I never got dressed so fast in all my life, as I did that day. Angry with Crosby for having deliberately misled me, I was even more upset with myself for having been so naive. And before I was tempted to change my mind, I hightailed it out of the place as fast as my legs could carry me. For had my masseuse grabbed hold of my sexual appendage and started fondling it, I'm not sure what I would have done. As much as I desired to have sex, I was damn lucky to have gotten out of the place with my virginity still intact.

Outside, I stopped short of running into the ship's Captain as he was getting into a black sedan with the high-class whore he had just rented from the same massage parlor. Immediately, I felt as if I were going to pass out. Instead, I passed into a gray twilit world in which the sun had been eclipsed by some huge black smudge. As the Captain's car eased past me, I was horrified by the look on his face, for it had been transformed into Hyde's. With the passage of his black sedan, was I left standing, once again, on the sunny side of life. Badly shaken, I scurried back to the safety of the ship.

Instead of commending me for having passed my first real trial by fire, the old Indian reprimanded me for having acted so foolishly. "Had you sought our counsel before you acted," chided he from somewhere across the void, "you would never have strayed so close to the edge of the Great Abyss, that vast sea of unconscious behavior, which separates your world from mine."

Before I could get a word in edgewise, he proceeded to lambaste me: "Prior to your gallivanting off like an ass, and endangering your soul so egregiously, you never once gave this latest fiasco of yours a second thought. Why? Because your ability to think has been relegated to the odious task of tormenting the hell out of you with unfounded thoughts about yourself—which have helped to shape this shadowy specter—you abandoned this endeavor as useless, even though it was only trying to get you back in touch with your feelings. In your inability to see through the disguise of this sick shadowy specter, you inadvertently banished the guardian of your soul, Pure Thought, to the wastelands of your mind. Until you free him from the interminable beating, he suffers at the hands of the opinionated old witch who has taken possession of your mother imago, you will likewise be driven to beat off the advances of this spirit whenever he rises up, disguised as the other member of your body, to release his thoughts. In your condemnation of them, you break the chain of thought that would normally link you with your feelings, to create consciousness. Therefore, you must learn to attune yourself to only those thoughts which truly reflect your feelings if, in the future, you wish to avoid falling prey to the evil of an asinine choice, that is, one marked by an inexcusable failure to exercise intelligence and sound judgment."

"I do not know this witch you speak of," I interjected.

"You know her all too well," replied my mentor, "as the only mother to have donned one of the magician's masks when she failed to conjure up genuine love from the cauldron of life. Cut off from her feelings by the thoughtless spirit that had overtaken your stepfather, she lashed out at you and your brother with the bitter tongue of her own unhappiness. Whenever she saw the spirit of truth rise from either one of you to challenge her, she condemned it as the thoughtless spirit that had overtaken your stepfather, for that is how she perceived it through the eyes of the witch. By her own example, did she unwittingly teach you to beat off the advances of the spirit of truth whenever the thoughtless spirit raised its ugly head to release unsettling thoughts. Once you acquired the habit of restricting the free flow of thought from your psyche, you lost the ability to think for yourself, as these damned-up thoughts began to spill over into the physical realm to find expression."

"To free yourself from her spell," concluded the old Indian, "you must learn to love all your feelings, from the least to the most vile, for hidden within their ugly forms lie truths that still defy consciousness. Until you have hatched the truth yet hidden in such raw form, brood over these feelings without judgment. Make the incestuous return to the womb of your imagination when the need for creating consciousness arises. Follow the chain of thought, the Spirit of Pure Thought feeds you as he unravels the string of images your soul has left behind, to help you find your way through the dark spots in your life. When you have found the truth at the other end of the tunnel of vision, you will certainly know it, for a sudden swell of feeling will greet you as the tension, which has built up in you to create consciousness, is released. And as you lie there, with her in your arms, you will say to yourself, 'Ah! So this is She Who Must Be Obeyed!'"

What could I say, for I knew he was right. "I'm sorry," I finally admitted, "for not having used my head when I should have."

"On the other hand," he exclaimed, "considering what you have had to work with, maybe I have been a bit too hard on you."

With that, he embraced me.

As tears welled up in my eyes, I hugged him back.

"You must be ever vigilant, my son," he added as he disappeared from my grasp, "as the forces of darkness are cunning."

Like the apostles at the transfiguration of Christ, I wanted to hold onto these precious moments, which came and went as quickly as those in reality. In other words, whenever I caught sight of the extraordinary within the ordinary, I wanted to immortalize what was already immortal, for such is the nature of truth. I wanted only to hold onto that part of my life that would not slip through my fingers like sand, at the end of my time on earth, for such is the nature of immortality. Since I did not yet have a firm grasp of my own truth, I could not hold onto my immortality for very long, for such is the nature of a fleeting awareness.

Later that evening, when I ran into Crosby, I accosted him for having made such a fool out of me. "You tricked me," I protested angrily.

"What do you mean?" He asked with a snicker.

"You know damn well what I mean," I insisted. "You knew this massage parlor was nothing more than a whorehouse, from the very beginning. Yet, you deliberately set me up. Why?"

"Why, I thought a little pussy would do you some good," he replied.

"You're wrong," I declared, "cause I don't believe in free love."

"Here I thought I was doin' you a favor," he responded. "Since this is your first West Pac cruise, I figured you didn't know how to go about gettin' laid in a foreign country."

"Your problem, Crosby, is that you don't think, period," I retorted.

"That's a hell of a way to treat a guy for helpin' you get your first piece of ass," he responded sarcastically.

"For your information," I boasted, "I didn't get laid. As soon as I saw what was going on, I got the hell out of there before I caved into such craven behavior, which is what you should have done too."

"And miss out on some of the finest pussy in the world!" He exclaimed. "You must be puttin' me on!"

On that note, I realized there was no reasoning with him. At a loss for words, I simply shook my head and smiled. "I don't know about you," I muttered as I turned to leave.

"Likewise," he bewilderingly retorted, for I had the sense that he really believed he had only been trying to help me.

"You see, my son," counseled the old Indian from across the void, "the truth is cloaked in many layers of imagery. To get to the bottom of this imagery, one must penetrate the tunnel of vision with his sights set on the truth hidden within the images, Wisdom throws down for him like discarded articles of clothing. This tunnel is fraught with many pitfalls into which the unwary can easily slip and fall if he misinterprets any of the images he encounters along the way."

"What is this tunnel of vision of which you speak?" I asked.

"It is the path you took," he replied, "when you walked through the black hole or pupil in the looking glass or eye of your being, to seek the viewpoint of the Council, that point of truth upon which its four seemingly disparate members converge like the faces of a pyramid. While Pure Thought struggles to give rational form to the mass of confusing sensations that have arisen, soul runs with his ideas as she leaps into the unknown, to feel her way around in the dark, on the hunch she might find, lurking about my form, the insight we have all been struggling to raise to a conscious level."

"How can you get someone, like Crosby, to remove the speck from his own eye?" I begged to know.

"You can never point out a man's demons to him," he warned me, "for they will only gang up on you and try to outwit you. Rather you must reveal to him the myth that has him under its spell, and stretch his imagination back through the tunnel of vision, to give him the opportunity to see the truth for himself, if he so chooses. However, you must first remove this splinter from your own eye to acquire the myth or antidote with which to inoculate him if he wishes to be healed of his affliction. While this myth contains tremendous power to heal, you will also find it to be a great stumbling block to the truth, as many will choose to hold onto its affliction rather than let go of its appeal."

Fearing the exposure of my demons, I left off asking him any more questions and hoped like hell he had nothing more to say to me. Since there seemed to be a limit to the amount of truth I could handle at any one time, I could stand to be around my mentor for only so long before I needed to get away from him for a while. Besides, I found it hard being around someone, even if he was imaginary, who had the answers, whether I liked them or not, to all my questions. Yet, I found myself continually being drawn back to him for the insight into my life that I still so desperately needed.

While I valued these encounters for the truth that they revealed, I was concerned about spending so much of my time playing with imaginary friends in imaginary places. Having tapped into an inexhaustible supply of energy for making consciousness, I generally left these encounters feeling renewed by them. Nonetheless, I was having a hard time letting go of a fantasy life that offered me so much more than the meaningless existence I was being forced to lead on the outside.

The following morning, I found myself back out at sea. As my mind wandered off, after some stray thought about Mary, it occurred to me that I had been driven ashore, back in Sasebo, by my own desire to make love to Mary.

"It is not she you desire," uttered my soul from afar. "Rather it is I, whose image you have only recently come to see in her, after whom you really lust."

Immediately, I broke out laughing.

"You laugh because you know I have spoken the truth," she insisted.

"While that may be true," I responded, "I am also laughing because of all the feeling you have just expressed. I never realized, until now, how much you care for me," whereupon I caught sight of her, long enough, to see her blush before she disappeared.

With that, I felt a twinge of pain, a tug on my heartstrings in the direction she had disappeared. From that moment on, I no longer knew with any certainty, which one I really loved, Mary or this image of my soul. Having been smitten by both the physical and the spiritual aspects of love, how could I let go of either one?

Yet, I was terrified of both, for love appeared to be such a harsh and dreadful thing. Unprepared for the sudden eruption of creative energy that had shattered my life as a child, was I driven from paradise by my own sexuality. In other words, had I lost control of myself upon having been given the responsibility for it. Because I had never been shown how to make contact with She Who Ruled Over Instinct, I was being driven to have intercourse with her, one way or the other, to reproduce a being made not only in the likeness of God, but in Her image as well.

Later that evening, I sat down to write Mary a letter, with the intention of telling her about the difficulties I have had in dealing with my own sexuality. Afraid that she might think less of me if I told her the truth, I avoided telling her outright that I abused my self. Instead, I alluded to it, telling her only that I occasionally lost control of myself whenever the desire for union with soul arose from its brief slumbers to satisfy its voracious appetite for whatever was missing from my life. I apologized, too, for not having been more affectionate with her. Fearing that these affections might lead to intercourse, I had intentionally held back. To make up for this lack of affection, I showered her with gifts as tokens of my love for her. And because I loved her deeply, I held back from taking advantage of her or anyone else for that matter, to satisfy my need for union with soul on the physical plane. Alone, I simply had no self-control.

Around this time, I received some information about taking a correspondence course in response to a hankering I'd had to do something a little more constructive with all the time I had on my hands. Drawn to a course in creative writing, I opted for a refresher course in English, out of a lack of confidence in my ability to write. I was so disappointed when I received the materials for the course, that I never started it. Obviously, I had not found what I had been looking for.

In a second letter, I fired off to Mary before I received any response to the last one I had sent her, I hinted around, again without coming out and telling her specifically what I'd done, that I had been getting into trouble with the Navy, for I had need of her perspective, whether I agreed with it or not. How else was I to find out if we were compatible enough to marry. Unless she was open to the new direction, my life seemed to be headed, I saw no future in our relationship. On the other hand, maybe I needed the reality check she offered.

While the mail came and went by helicopter, on a regular basis, I still experienced long delays in hearing from her, for I would often mail off two or three letters before I would hear from her. Since she was the only source of real life I had outside myself, I pined away for any word from her and clung onto her letters for dear life. In my need for instant gratification, I experienced an intolerable ache inside my heart when I had not heard from her any sooner than I did. I read her letters over and over in search of the love, I so desperately needed but could not see in the blindness of my own self-centeredness. O, how I longed to hear her tell the beast within that she loved him. Not until the early part of August, did I receive that long awaited response to my letters.

Dear Butch,

I was glad to receive your letter today. While I had every intention of answering the last one, I got sick again—nothing serious, just a small relapse into what had happened to me last March. I had gotten to feeling down in the dumps before I realized there was something wrong with me, for I just didn't feel like doing anything but laying around and sleeping all the time. Now that I am back on my feet, I feel my old healthy and completely lucky Irish self.

I want to thank you for the wonderful gifts you sent me. Having received both packages on the same day, I felt as if I were celebrating Christmas and my birthday at the same time. Butch, the blouse is beautiful! I have gotten so many compliments on it. The Peanut's books came at just the right time. I was feeling so down because I was sick again, they really helped to bring me out of it. The Snoopy mug occupies a place of honor on my desk at work, right beside my adding machine. I did just as you had suggested with the Snoopy patch and sewed it on the flap of the jumper you had sent me. It really looks sharp. Thank you very much. You don't know how much you are spoiling me. But I love every minute of it.

Butch, I was upset when I read about what you are doing. You once told me you would move the world for me, if ever I asked you. I don't want the world moved; I only want the Navy moved. I know you don't like the Navy. You are only going to be in there for a short time; why not make that time count. I was so happy to read that you are going to take a correspondence course. That is one thing about you, Butch, you cannot let yourself have idle time on your hands; you have to keep yourself busy. You have to show the Navy what you are made of, what you can do. If you can't do it for yourself, then do it for me. Give the remainder of your time in the Navy everything you have, for you have so much potential that can't be kept inside but must be given to others as God intended. And it's up to you to find a way to give it to them. While the others may act like animals, that's no reason for you to go along with the wave. You must walk out ahead of it to get where you are going. Butch, you have so much going for you, if only you would put it to good use. I know you can do it, because you have done it before. That is why I have never stopped being proud of you. And I know that your taking this course will only make me feel even prouder. I hope it will keep your mind occupied, and challenge you to think real hard. Though I am no longer in school, I still like to see others studying hard, so long as it is not me sweating it out over a new course. Aren't I awful?

Guess I had better sign off before I go off on any more tangents. I know you will be glad of that.

Remember you are in my thoughts and always in my prayers.

Love,

Mary

PS. Just to set the record straight, I met you on July 23, 1966. See, I don't forget dates very easily—important ones, that is.

Mary was right—I had to find a way to share the fruit of the womb of my imagination with the rest of the world. Because I had never shared with her many of the particulars surrounding the new life taking shape within me, for fear of sounding half crazy, she had no way of knowing how hell-bent on resisting the Navy was my soul. For she had been misled into believing it was the Navy, rather than the Resistance, into which I should be pouring my energies. Yet she had sure struck a chord when she suggested that I move the Navy for her instead of the world—that I get out in front of the swell of unconsciousness, which had arisen from so many of my fellow countrymen, and threatened to inundate us all in a tidal wave of beastliness if no one dared to stand up to it.

Having gotten myself into a whale of a predicament when I joined the Navy, I was still no closer to finding the real reason why I wanted out, than I had been back in April when the one voice first imposed this thorny task upon me. Since then, about all I had come to know for sure, was that I did not belong here, which apparently was not enough of a reason by itself, to qualify me as being unsuitable for further military service. Otherwise, I would have been discharged by now.

Besides having let go of trying to find this seemingly evermore elusive reason, I had grown weary of trying to get out of the Navy under any pretense, for it seemed as if the new Executive Officer had a different strategy in mind—to make it as difficult as possible for me to get an administrative discharge. I wondered, too, if I had not made a strategic error when I decided, without consulting my soul, to transfer to the shipfitters instead of staying put in First Division. Had I continued to act crazy, would I have received the discharge that I coveted? But I wasn't crazy. Or was I? Had I finally slipped off the deep end, into the insanity of the great abyss when I broke down, according to my mentor, a week or two ago? Or like Peter Pan, had I returned to never-never land out of a stubborn refusal to grow up and accept the responsibilities of real life? Was I acting like a child then, because I had not gotten my way? Or was I acting more like one who had lost his way, and knew not where else to turn but to those long forgotten friends of his childhood imagination? Had I let on, too much, how badly I wanted out of the Navy? Or had I just not found a logical reason yet, for the way I was acting? Obviously, I had run into this brick wall, for no other reason than to provide the stumbling block that would force me to dig a little deeper for the truth.

"Do you see now, what I can do for you," stressed my shadow, the importance he played in helping me come to a better understanding of my life.

"I do," I replied, on the heels of a slight blush and the realization of just how much I really did need his help.

"Tell me then," I begged of him, "why are you so much more transparent than any of the other images I have encountered thus far?"

"As both gate and gatekeeper to the vast and unexplored reaches of your own inner space—the void that separates the gates of heaven from the jaws of hell—I allow free passage to any thought form, whether good or evil, who wishes to enter your life," he replied. "Like any shadow, I simply reflect what still remains hidden from consciousness."

"Is that why I am so afraid of you?" I asked, as I grew increasingly more apprehensive of the anxiety that had overtaken my body, which had begun shaking so violently, I could barely control my own movements.

"The fear, you are experiencing, is really that of your demons, who are deathly afraid they are about to be exposed," he replied.

As my head went into a spin, and my heart pounded away at the bars of my chest in wild gyrations, I slumped to my knees, gasping for air, for his words had gotten stuck in my throat. In one violent convulsion after another, did I vomit up three, large and gray, leathery-skinned demons who just stood there looking at my wretched self, with their fiery red eyes, before diving back down through my shadow to seek out the darkest depths of the void in which to hide. With that, I broke out crying and laughing hysterically, whereupon my shadow stooped down and gently helped me to my feet.

"My God!" I gasped. "I had no idea that such hideous creatures as these even existed, much less dwelt within me."

"And still do," piped up my shadow. "You have only visualized what you have yet to exorcise from yourself. Until they slip up and reveal their stooges, or those parts of your personality that do their dirty work, they will remain too formidable a foe for you to overcome yet. Now that you have become a threat to their existence, they will do everything in their power to keep you from exposing the truth hidden within them from even themselves. In other words, they are, in all likelihood, going to deal you a real fit before it is all over."

Still shaking, I sat down on my usual perch up topside, in an effort to regain my composure. As my thoughts wandered out over the surface of the water, I came to an understanding of what my soul had meant when she told me our body was in the possession of the evil Magician. "I'm possessed," I cried out of the feelings of humiliation and defeat that had overtaken me.

"Come now, my lad!" Exclaimed my shadow. "You must get hold of yourself, for all is not as bad as it seems. Why, you have been given a great gift in the ability to see your demons, or that part of your animal nature that still has you in its grip. While you may now see this knowledge as more of a burden than a boon, you will one day be called upon to share it with the rest of the world, for like Jonah, you have been confined to this instinctive existence, to force you to find the way out."

"If you know the way, why don't you show me?" I beseeched him.

"I know no more than what the Council has deciphered thus far," he replied.

"Well I guess that leaves us all in the dark," I quipped.

"Not quite," he rebutted. "For we are continually being fed images that shed light on the way you must go. Until recently, I have not been at liberty to discuss with you our latest translation—into thought—of some of the material we had received from your senses awhile back. If you are up to it, I would like to share with you those thoughts that speak to the qualms you are having with your participation in the war in Vietnam."

"Are you game?" He asked.

"Sure! Why not!" I exclaimed. "Like any true glutton for punishment, I want more, as long as it's not too painful. Only, I'm not sure I could handle coughing up any more demons," whereupon he assured me that was not what he had in mind.

"If you don't know it yet," he began, "you will soon find out that war is hell. Unless you deal with me on a personal level, that is, integrate me into your life, you will be forced to fight me on a transpersonal level in the faces of the Viet Cong, for the Beast has been unleashed."

"What beast?" I asked out of the alarm, he had just sounded to alert me to the very real dangers that lay ahead.

"Why, that part of Nature which still defies Consciousness," he answered.

"I don't understand," I exclaimed.

"You see," he replied, "each human being is given, at birth, a little piece of the dark side of Nature, or hell as you-all call it, from which to free the truth he will need to get back into paradise. Until he frees the truth yet hidden within the animal side of his nature, it will haunt him like a specter. This worthiest of opponents will act as a thorn in his side, and thwart his every effort to live out any other truth than the one meant for him. And he will be unable to resist such behavior because the laws of Nature must be obeyed, one way or the other, as either an unconscious animal or a conscious human being.

"Like the fissile material in a nuclear reactor, the energy to live out this truth lies dormant in you until you reach the age of puberty, at which time the One Who Rules Over All releases control of it to you through your rod. If you lose control of your rod, by using your libidinal energy for any other purpose than that intended, you risk releasing this creative energy in the form of that beast which had best expressed this truth, no matter how crudely, before you came along. If enough of your countrymen lose control of this energy, so that critical mass is reached, a chain reaction of great destructive power is set in motion, above which only the individual can rise, until those who have contributed to this war regain their senses and banish the beast back to the wildest parts of their imaginations.

"The time is approaching," he concluded, "when you will be forced to enter my domain to match wits with the forces of darkness, unless you prefer killing images of real people versus those of your imagination."

"To be perfectly honest," I interjected, "I really don't want to kill anyone, real or imaginary."

"You no longer have a choice," he replied. "Either you destroy the image, which tells you it is okay to take the life of another human being when sanctioned by the State, or this image will destroy you, as surely as it destroyed your stepfather when it robbed him of the very manhood he had taken from his opponents in battle."

"Why must I destroy this image?" I asked. "Surely there must be some other way to deal with it."

"Because you have allowed this image to acquire a life of its own," he responded, "this Frankenstein will never give it back to you, until you take it from him."

"Until you remove this parasitic growth from your own eye," he continued, "you will never see how to remove the corresponding speck from your neighbor's eye, for war is really about the killing of your own demons as you see them outside yourself in the hapless neighbor upon whom you have cast such dark shadowy aspersions. In the ensuing struggle to take your neighbor's life before he takes yours, you fight not so much to protect your life as you do to protect the lives of those demons who have taken over some part of you. He who has overcome his own demons has no need to take his neighbor's life, nor defend his own, because it is already in the hands of the One Voice. And so are you tricked, by the projection of your shadow onto a neighbor, into believing you have slain your demons, in the slaying of that neighbor, when in reality you have only given your demons a little more control over your life."

"What are demons, anyway?" I asked him.

"They are extremely complex thought forms," he responded, "which tend to develop around those parts of your personality that remain too far from consciousness, to exercise any control over them. They represent all of the raw, pent-up emotional energy in you that has not the foggiest notion of what its true purpose in life is. As images of those parts of you, which still defy consciousness, they provide the antagonism needed to spur you onto bringing these hidden traits to light, that you might live like a human being rather than some brute."

"I would rather die first," I insisted, "than live like Hyde."

"Then die you shall—or at least that part of you whose time has come," he forewarned me, "for you are the only one who can penetrate the dark storm, which has been brewing at my gate since first we met. To get to the heart of this dark swirl, you must leave this conversation and enter the world of experience," whereupon he loomed up over me, larger than life, to facilitate my entry into the void.

Once again, did I encounter the spirits of what my parents had long ago condemned to a fate worse than hell. As the vile spirits swarmed and slithered about me like venomous snakes, I realized that they represented the thoughts and feelings my inner mother had condemned, down through the years. Numbed by the pain of it all, did I stand by and watch as my stepfather attempted to strangle them in the image of my brother, Scott, but failed. As the hair stood up on the back of my neck, I grew larger than life. Only this time, was I transformed into a great gray wolf instead of Hyde. Sniffing the air, I quickly picked up the scent of the old witch as she lurked about in darkness, to escape the fury that had been unleashed upon her. With saliva streaming from my mouth in torrents, I lunged for her throat. Grasping hold of her neck with my powerful jaws, I shook her until she resisted no more. Letting out a howl of remorse, I stooped to lick her face clean of the mask that had enveloped her true beauty. On her last dying breath, I heard my mother say, "I am sorry, my son, for having offended thee." As I wept bitter tears, I washed her body clean of any sign of ever having been a witch. Just then, I felt a hand brush past my ear as its fingers ran through my hair. Opening my eyes, I beheld my soul lying there at my side.

"I don't understand," I exclaimed, for I too had been transformed back into my regular old self.

"It's all over," she replied. "You have finally overcome this terrible image of your mother. All that matters now, is that you have me."

As our eyes welled up with tears, we embraced each other and breathed a sigh of relief.

"By the way," she blurted out. "Before I forget, I have something for you. Prior to the last skit we put on for you, Shad handed me this talisman to give you. He told me you would know what to do with it."

"Why, it's the handle off some old sword," I exclaimed. "What use could I possibly have for such a relic?"

As I took hold of it with my hand, I was startled by the sudden appearance of a blade of bluish-white light. Dropping it from my hand, like a hot potato, I caused the blade of light to disappear as quickly as it had appeared. Grasping hold of it again, I caused the bluish-white blade to reappear, exactly as it had before. This time, I held onto it. Instantly, I knew my task was not over yet, whereupon my soul smiled at me as she disappeared within the wink of an eye.

Left standing in the middle of some dark deserted street, in that twilight zone between wakefulness and sleep where the secrets of darkness are brought to light, I sensed that my opponent would not come out of hiding until I appeared more vulnerable. Having stuck the sword's handle in my belt, I stood there for some time, turning round and round, looking about, before I finally felt safe enough to let go of the only real defense I had.

"Be not afraid," boomed the One Voice from somewhere across the void, "for I have gone before you and will be with you through it all."

Drawn to this one saloon, I had just raised my hand to open one of its swinging doors, when a drunken sailor came flying out, brushing my shoulder as he stumbled off with the whore he had picked up inside. Immediately, I recognized this shadow of the foe, I had yet to meet, as my stepfather when he was in the Navy. Realizing that my stepfather and I held some nefarious trait in common, I burst in upon an old, rundown and abandoned burlesque house with its seating arranged around the stage, like an indoor amphitheater.

"Hello," I yelled out. "Is anyone here?" Having received no response, I spun around to leave and turned right smack dab into the pockmarked face of this big ole fat man, all dressed in black, who seemed to have popped up out of nowhere.

"Who're you?" I asked, whereupon he pulled out a large butcher knife from behind him and, with a smile, held it up to my face. Scared to death, I took off running as fast as my legs could carry me. Round and round the amphitheater I ran with this madman at my heels. For no matter how hard I tried, I could not shake him.

As the amphitheater grew larger and larger with each round I made, I found my self racing around a structure, the size of a football stadium, complete with those who had come out to see such sport. As the burgeoning crowd chanted, "Kill, Kill, Kill," over and over in a deafening scream, I was overcome with the hopelessness of ever getting out of this place alive. Then, I spotted a small slit in the wall of the amphitheater, through which I knew the Fat Man could never pass. Giving my legs everything I possibly could, I began to outdistance the Fat Man as I made tracks for this narrow gate. Alas, not even I could fit through such a narrow opening. Trapped, I turned to face the Fat Man as the crowd whipped itself into a frenzy for blood, screaming louder and louder, "Kill, Kill, Kill." Just then, I remembered the sword my shadow had given me. Drawing forth this blade of bluish-white light, I drew a gasp from the crowd when I held it up for all to see the Fat Man come crashing down upon it, to his death. Having pierced him through the heart, I let go of the sword, just in time to see the Fat Man slump to the ground with a butcher knife stuck in his chest. Standing there, all drenched in blood, I screamed hysterically as the crowd swooped down on me like an angry mob upon a murderer who has just been caught red-handed. Boy, was I ever relieved when they lit into the Fat Man instead. As they took back those parts of themselves which had kept the Fat Man alive, all these years, I watched them tear the flesh off his carcass, like birds of prey on a fresh kill, until there was nothing left but the gray shadow of a demon, the first of the three I had coughed up.

There were many thoughts and feelings freed from the tyranny of the Fat Man, that day, far too many for me to recount. Cheering wildly, they grabbed hold of me and threw me up over their heads as their liberator. After carrying me back and forth in front of the narrow gate through which I tried to escape, they finally released me, but not before every one of them had come forward and embraced me with the utmost gratitude that I have ever experienced. As I walked back through the narrow gate of my own shadow, I watched them all disappear into the great light at the other end of the tunnel of vision, for I had just freed a very small part of humanity from the demon known as Brute Force.

Waiting for me, in the entryway to my imagination, were my soul, the first to greet me with a big hug and a kiss upon the cheek, my mentor and of course Shad, both of whom, through warm embraces, congratulated me on a job well done.

"If you go away from this experience with anything at all," stated my mentor, "I hope it is with the realization that you may never take the life of another human being, no matter how you feel. For, you have been called by the Highest Authority to destroy the images of your enemies as you see them within yourself rather than in your neighbor."

"Do you not see, my son, how the cycle of violence is passed from one generation to the next!" Exclaimed my mentor. "As you acquired the habit of putting down the lesser self and beating off the advances of the greater Self from your parents, so would you have passed this tendency down to your children, had you not chosen to break the cycle."

"I hope you see now, how this behavior has led to the creation of Hyde," added my shadow.

"For, She must be obeyed, one way or the other," interjected my soul, "as either a beast or a human being."

"What I don't understand," I inquired, "is why I was transformed into a wolf instead of Hyde."

"You see, my son," answered my mentor, "because Hyde perpetuated the cycle of self-abuse, in his addiction to this narcotic, he could never have turned against his supplier."

"Since only the witch knew the words to the incantation that transformed you into such a hideous beast," added my shadow, "as Hyde, you could never have destroyed this lifeline to your existence."

"To get you to attack this predaceous image of your mother," insisted my soul, "we had to draw upon the instinct for survival that you found in the image of the wolf."

"It was all so horrible," I cried out as tears welled up in my eyes. "Once I had been transformed into a wolf, I could think of nothing else but killing my prey, the old witch. As I grew more and more intoxicated with the idea of killing her, I had the sense that it was all right, that I was only taking this life in order to live. I felt as if I was only taking back what rightfully belonged to me, my own personhood. I tore into her flesh, not so much for the revenge, as I did for the food of the gods, that knowledge which comes from the destruction of an old image. Then I was overcome by remorse for having taken the life of an old god."

"Only you never realized," interjected my mentor, "how incomplete was your picture of God until you prepared this false image for interment."

"When Mother Nature finally revealed her true identity," added my shadow, "she apologized for the shoddy treatment you had received from her alter ego, the opinionated old witch that had devoured the image of your mother."

"It was only you," insisted my soul, "who could free us from the devouring image of your mother."

"We have yet to get a handle on the meaning of the sword," interrupted my mentor who, in having read my mind, discerned my next question before I had the chance to spit out the words. "We do know this much, that this pencil of light, of which you are still afraid, has a magical significance to you that reaches beyond even your wildest expectations. While it currently causes you to feel blue, it will eventually allow you to open doors and shed light on the secrets of life. For now, this boon remains hidden within the secret of the butcher's knife."

"As you returned to that familiar setting, where darkness still overshadows the truth," continued my shadow, "you realized that your next opponent would not come out of hiding until you let down your guard, which took considerable effort on your part, considering how guarded you are with the contents of your imagination."

"Knowing this about you," added my soul, "the One Voice tried to alleviate your fears with the reassurance that you were going nowhere He had not already been and would be traversing again with you."

"Why didn't I see Him then?" I asked.

"Like any voice," replied my mentor, "you cannot see it. Unlike the One Voice, you saw Him in the images that presented themselves to you after He spoke."

"In response to the call for enlightenment," continued my shadow, "you delved into the dark pall which has hung over your head, like the Sword of Damocles, since puberty. There were you confronted by your alter ego as it flew out of control in its intoxication with the force of Nature that is released whenever the ego takes what does not belong to it. And for the first time, Dr. Jekyll, you recognized this image of Hyde as your stepfather. With the realization that you had vicariously inherited from your stepfather the same ugly tendency to usurp the sovereignty of the One Voice, you entered the theater of the absurd to seek out this tyrant, in a roundabout way, from among your own rundown and abandoned thoughts and feelings."

"Not knowing what to expect," chimed in my soul, "you reluctantly inquired within, making yourself vulnerable to a confrontation with the force that had so marred your life in the past, it now appeared much more menacing than it really was. So threatened were you by the brutish side of your nature, you tried to run away from it again, to no avail. Round and round your mind you raced in an effort to escape having to confront your own brutality. No matter how hard you tried, you could not rationalize it away, this time."

"As your mind expanded upon a way to get out of this pickle with your self-esteem intact," expounded my mentor, "you wound up on the receiving end where your thoughts about the use of force had gathered to make sport of you. As they reiterated the chant you had been taught in boot camp, to yell out every time you thrust your bayonet into one of them, you were overcome by the hopelessness, they had felt back then, of ever seeing the light of day."

"Then," interjected my shadow, "you spotted the narrow gate—the one seldom chosen only because the gate that leads to damnation is so much wider, the way to it, so much clearer to those who choose it. In running with the idea that the narrower choice consisted of putting some distance between your self and the urge to use brute force, you overlooked the limitations this choice really imposed upon you."

"Feeling trapped," continued my soul, "you turned to face the urge to use brute force as every thought and feeling in your body screamed out to kill the urge before it inflicted you with the wound that never heals—that endless cycle of revenge, of taking an eye for an eye and a tooth for a tooth."

"Just then," interrupted my mentor, "you recalled how during that one brief moment, last spring, while standing alone in Lt. Smith's stateroom, you had experienced the incredibly powerful force of truth, which you were unable to hold onto for very long because you did not know this force well enough to use it as intended."

"Drawing upon this force again," continued my shadow, "you were shocked to see the force of truth come to life at the expense of the urge to use brute force, as if both images represented the same force, only from two very different perspectives—whether you have chosen heads or tails, to act consciously or unconsciously."

"Having gotten to the heart of the matter," added my soul, "you not only relinquished the right to take another man's life, but also broke the spell that had bound you to the demon, Brute Force. Just as your father had chased after you, with a real butcher knife, before he was committed, had you chased after the kid next door with a real knife in hand. Realizing that you could never completely rid yourself of the urge to use Brute Force, you cried out in dismay over the paradoxical nature of the force behind this image."

"Mobbed by your own angry thoughts," interjected my mentor, "for having misjudged your self, you were exonerated of all guilt when it was shown that you had, in deed, acted unconsciously. Unaware of just how much of your personality this primitive urge possessed, you were shown, in a very crude manner, exactly what Jesus meant when He told Nicodemus, *'You must be born from above'.*" (Jn. 3:7)

"When you chose to stand by the truth," added my shadow, "instead of giving in to the urge to use Brute Force, you finally pierced through the instinctive image which had developed around the true nature of this urge, like the amniotic sac around an embryo. Until you realized that you had been giving flesh to a mere shadow of the truth, you could never have participated in the labor and delivery of the first of the three great truths to be borne by you in your lifetime."

"Having gotten your hands bloodied at the crowning moment in the birth of this truth," continued my soul, "you panicked at the thought that something had gone terribly wrong. Boy, were you relieved when you saw the truth intact. As you laid claim to this new image of yourself, like any proud father, in your ecstasy, were you carried aloft, that day, by many strange thoughts and feelings."

"Prior to the birth of this new self-image," concluded my mentor, "you wavered for a moment in the birth canal where all new life hesitates before it is forced from the womb to give flesh to the good intentions it has embraced. Having brought to light more truth than you could deal with, you turned to your faculties through that tiny image of your self reflected in the eye of another, the speck you desire to remove from your neighbor's eye. Thus did you return from this near-death experience to a body no longer dominated by Brute Force."

Instantly, I found my self among the lost souls who manned the ship. As the sights and sounds of life onboard came crashing back into my awareness, I struggled momentarily to get my bearings. As I made my way below to hit the sack, I received my mentor's blessing, "May the force of truth be with you, my son." With that, did I collapse in a heap, until I heard talk, the following morning, of pulling into Bangkok, Thailand.

After what I had been through, I was ready for anything but another close encounter. For, I was damn glad to find my self standing firmly on solid ground again, even if it was the deck of a ship.

In the end, I found the experiences on this side of the dreamworld to be just as intangible as those on the imaginary side were. In either case, I was left with little else than a few perceptions of what had actually transpired. In fact, I was beginning to feel as if life were nothing more than one big dream from which one normally did not awaken until he died. Then, I realized there were those who, like me, woke up from the Big Sleep before it was time to officially leave their cocoons and spread their wings. In other words, I could not believe God had marooned us on this island in the sky without some way to access the invisible bands on the spectrum of consciousness. Thus did I come to see reality as much more than just the visible band of the spectrum.

Two Sides of Reality

The trip to Bangkok turned out to be longer than expected by sea. Due to the geography of the region, the ship was forced to steam south along the coast of Vietnam before taking a slight jog west around the horn of Southeast Asia to enter the long stretch north over the entire length of the Gulf of Siam and up the lower navigable waters of the Chao Phraya River. Unable to go any further by ship, were we forced to drop anchor and take a launch into the city.

The Chao Phraya was just as muddy a river as the mighty ole Mississippi back home. Except for an occasional glance from those thatched huts and stilted shanties, which peeped through the dense foliage that skirted her loins, her banks revealed little else about the children she nurtured. O, how her waters did teem with the hustle and bustle of commerce—with sampans and junks of every size and shape. And like the Mississippi as you traveled north to its source, she took you back to a time when life was simpler, when her children were not as abusive.

As I sat down in the back of the launch, I stumbled upon an image of Mother Nature that sent shivers down my spine, for I had found her badly beaten body lying on the cold stone floor of a fantasy that had been forged in hell. Unable to free her from the chains that fettered her to the floor of this fantasy, I stooped to wipe her badly bruised and battered face, but broke down crying instead. As she extended her hand out to comfort me, of all things, I took hold of her terribly mangled fingers and with great care kissed them.

"Thank you, my son," she painfully uttered with the distortion that had once been her mouth.

"Who has done this to thee, my lady, that I might avenge thee?" I demanded to know.

"Why, the beast you call Brute Force!" She exclaimed.

"That cannot be," I retorted, "for I have seen his demise."

"You have seen the demise of but a shadow of the collective beast," she reiterated with great pain, "which like Cain, doeth yet terrorize those able to withstand the temptation to use brute force.

"To defeat the evil beast, once and for all, you must slay the great dragon with which he doeth sleep." She painstakingly added. "For, nothing is more dangerous than sincere ignorance nor mightier than sincere truth—the double-edged sword set in stone, long ago, to keep it out of unscrupulous hands. In defense of the truth only, may you draw upon its incredible power.

"Heed the counsel of your guardian angel, Michael, the very soul of your being and my daughter, Jinny, and her father, Hewhay, whom you have affectionately adopted as your mentor," she concluded with a sigh too deep for words.

With that, I was startled out of my daydream by a somewhat vexed Greg.

"Come on," he exclaimed. "Let's go."

Dropped off on the edge of one of the city's wealthier boroughs, were we left with a very good, albeit false first impression of Thailand, which, I am sure, had not been the intention of those who had worked out where we would disembark. Once we had reached the end of this avenue of Olympian splendor—a perfectly manicured and tree-lined vista of grandiose villas—we were confronted by the rundown and abandoned quarters of the realm where the general populace lived and slaved their lives away, to fill the coffers of the gods who resided in these ostentatious temples of doom. Upon leaving this vainglorious way of life, were we approached by two young Thai women plying the tools of a trade as old as civilization itself.

"Want good fuck?" One of them asked with an inviting smile.

"Only ten dollars," added the other with the same cute smile.

Caught off guard by their bluntness, Greg and I simply looked at each other and laughed in our embarrassment.

"While we appreciate your interest in us," I finally said, "we're really not interested in what you have to offer."

With that, we darted across the street, just to get away from them.

Boy, were they persistent. "Only five dollars," insisted the gal who had negotiated the last offer, as they raced to catch up with us.

Seeing how quickly they were gaining on us, we increased our gait, with the hope of losing them.

Thinking we were simply playing hard to get, our negotiator offered us a new price of only two dollars. Seeing us break into a trot, she even dropped the price down to a dollar. "Fifty cents," she shouted after us as we took off running down the street at full gallop. Having made her final offer, she gave up on us and turned around with her partner, to ply her trade elsewhere.

Saddened by the whole affair, I was sure the encounter had not been a chance one. Whether or not it was anything more than a harbinger of things to come, I had no way of knowing yet, as the meaning of this troubling affair escaped my grasp.

Next, were we approached by a cab driver who, in broken English, offered to drive us wherever we wanted to go throughout the remainder of the day, for the paltry sum of ten dollars.

"Trust," he pleaded with heartfelt sincerity. "I make you offer, no can refuse—no take American money to end of day. What you say?"

While we weren't sure what to believe after our last experience, Greg and I both agreed that we had nothing to lose since we did not have to pay him until the end of the day.

"Trust," he reiterated with a nod, this time.

"Okay," Greg finally agreed.

With a grin that extended from ear to ear, he rushed to open the door of his cab, and bade us to have a seat. Only after he had gotten into the cab, did he ask us where we wanted to go.

As we struggled to communicate to our cabby, the desire we both shared to purchase a nice gift for that special someone back home, he pointed to the ring on his finger. "Eh?" Inquired our cabby.

"Jewelry!" I responded to the charade our hearts had played on us.

"Yes!" Rejoined Greg. "What an excellent idea!"

With our approval, then, did our cabby take off for parts unknown.

It struck me how much Life is like a game of charades in which we're forced to find the Word hidden within Her images, both real and imaginary, to avoid giving flesh to His nemesis, Instinct. In our inability to interpret the language of the body, are we driven to act instinctively, to live out what we see rather than what we hear. For, we have never been taught how to listen to ourselves or seek the counsel of our own faculties. Lured by the attractiveness of Life's images, we let the multitude, rather than the One Voice, interpret them for us, preferring to live as our animal ancestors have always lived, under the tyranny of Instinct. In our failure to realize that She must be obeyed, one way or the other, are we forced to live out the charade instead of the truth.

As I refocused my attention onto a more visible band of the spectrum of consciousness, I found my self getting out of the cab with Greg, in front of a small jewelry store. Inside, I quickly honed in on a gold ring upon which was mounted a star sapphire. Trying it on my baby finger, I just knew it would fit Mary. When I asked the shopkeeper how much it cost, I balked at first.

"Twenty dollars," he finally said, "no lower."

"That's a bargain," piped up Greg. "You could never buy the same ring at that price back in the States."

"You think not?" I asked hesitatingly.

"I know," added Greg, "for gold is much higher back in the States."

"All right," I muttered as I reached into my pocket for the money. "I'll take it."

"I sure wish I could be there," I rambled on, "to see the expression on her face when she tears into this package and feasts her eyes on a ring—it'll blow her mind."

Greg just smiled as if to say he agreed. Having selected a beautiful gold necklace for his wife, he proceeded to pay for it.

Our next stop was the Buddhist temple frequented by our cab driver and his family. This surprisingly small but simply styled structure, which would otherwise never have struck me as a temple, was not, according to our cabby, a place of worship like a church. This hallowed space, with its larger-than-life, gold-leafed statues of the Buddha, each seated in a lotus position, was dedicated to the members of a single family, their ancestors as well as their heirs, and was maintained by the living. It was a place where one came to experience or become mindful of the Buddha or one's own unactualized Self, in much the same manner Moses had approached the burning bush that protruded from the ground of his being. The place so reminded me of the space where I retreated inwardly to commune with Who I Really Am, that the hair actually stood up on the back of my neck.

Were we temples then, so constructed that each of us reflected the light of the fire which burns within, in ways as broadly similar and yet as uniquely different as were the Buddha and Christ? Was each of us a subtle variation of the truth burning to ignite the images that smolder within us and keep us apart? Had we been brought together here, by our nuances, like the pieces of a great jigsaw puzzle, to get a clearer picture of Who We Really Are?

Unaware yet, of the nuances of truth that were driving me to act like a beast, one day, and a god, the next, I immediately became aware or mindful of the need I had to penetrate the void, which enveloped my mind, to see what that Mind of all minds had in mind for me. Only, I had to expend a lot of energy to escape the gravitational pull of all the earthly cares and concerns that weighed me down. At the point where I moved beyond my self, I entered the tunnel of vision, a wormhole of sorts, which took me within reach of the great light at the other end. Fearful yet, of my own enlightenment, I stepped back into the conversation Greg and I had been having with our cabby. Before the wormhole collapsed, I looked back just in time to see the Buddha wink at me. At that point, I made a motion in favor of leaving the place, but not before I had conned our cab driver into taking a picture of us with my camera. As we stood facing the Buddha on this side of the event horizon, I looked back just in time to see the camera wink at me before the whole incident collapsed in upon itself leaving nothing behind but a black hole. With that, I realized I had just hopped from one singularity to another, only this time, in synchronicity with my psyche.

When, later that afternoon, we visited another shrine, a black finger of stone that jutted forth from a modest outcropping of shrubbery and rock, I had to laugh at my own phallicism or worship of the generative principle, symbolized here by an erect phallus. As I watched a woman approach the altar of this god, and place a wreath of flowers around its neck, I wondered what piece of my own ass I would find if this part of my anatomy could grant me a wish. Unlike the woman in this event, I had no faith in my potential for creating a new life; I could put no trust in a god with a mind of its own. In my inability to heed the One Voice, had I been forced, in the past, to pay homage to a lesser god than a stroke of genius.

In a last-ditch effort to win over our hearts, our cabby took us home, towards dusk, to meet his family. To get there, we had to cross a large expanse of abandoned railroad lines. Apparently, he lived on the other side of the tracks, in a low-lying area not too far from the banks of the Chao Phraya River. As a horde of little kids descended upon us, out of curiosity, our cabby was besieged with questions, he answered rather good-naturedly, till he grew weary of their dogged persistence and shooed them away. By this time, he had gotten us across that dry, old riverbed of ribboned steel that had previously stood in our way. Stepping onto the boardwalk, which served as the streets for this stilted shantytown that stretched out before us as far as we could see, did he lead us onto his humble abode. As we entered this tin-roofed, two-roomed shack with see-through walls of rough-sawed lumber, nailed side by side, one board thick, our cabby proceeded to introduce us to his wife and brother, neither of whom could speak a lick of English.

In stark contrast to the villas we had seen when we first landed, these shanties had no electricity, running water or toilet facilities. Whenever I broached the subject of how they kept their food, cooked or bathed, our cabby claimed he did not know enough English to answer me intelligibly. Barring these little miscommunications, our cabby was unsurprisingly open to telling us of his inability to earn enough as a cab driver to provide his wife with such amenities as furniture, for he could offer us no more than the simple mats upon which he bade us to sit.

Unable to communicate with us in any other way, his brother pulled out a pipe, or piece of bamboo, approximately two inches in diameter and about two feet long, with a small bowl positioned on a very short stem several inches up from the lower end. He then filled the bowl with a dark brown paste, Greg immediately recognized as hashish. As Greg and our cabby burst out laughing at Greg's obvious acceptance of the only refreshment this poor family had to offer its guests, his brother ignited the contents of the bowl and took a long draft off the true opiate of the masses, before offering it to the rest of us.

Declining to indulge, I drifted into a little pipe dream of my own. Confronted by the angelic aspect of my shadow, was I split down the middle as his sword came crashing down upon my head and cleaved me into two apparently identical clones of my original self. Left standing there with a split personality, I quickly found out how different were these two aspects of myself when the religiously right side of me proclaimed, as morally and politically correct, what the left side sought to overthrow as exclusionary. As either side stood there, calling the other a liar and a thief, I could not help thinking how right they both were, for the rich man on the right was just as much a liar and a thief as the one with nothing left to do but rob him of what really belonged to neither one of them. In spite of his great wealth, I realized that the rich man was just as poor in spirit as the one left without much, materially. Beckoned back to reality by our cab driver's announcement that it was time to go, I left this fragment of a fantasy, torn between my own desires for material things and those of the spirit.

Unable to let go of the pain of this unresolved conflict, I kept to myself on the way back to ship. At one point, was I forced to let go of my fragmented condition, long enough to reach an agreement with Greg that we should pay our cabby double the fare he had originally asked of us, besides thanking him for such a wonderful splice of life in Thailand, and wishing him well. Forced to listen to Greg ramble on about the events of the day, was I effectively kept from gaining any further insight into the conflict that continued to rage on, within me, between my right side and what was left of me after the former had taken everything it possibly could from the latter.

Back onboard the ship, I bade Greg good night before I disappeared up topside to find a solution to this thorny conflict. Having grown fearful of the designs of the left, I watched the right arm itself with the might it needed to enforce its brand of law and order. In sympathizing with the left, I began to rebel against some of the rules and regulations the right institutes to keep young rebels like me in place. As I passively resisted the pettiest of its laws, like a common criminal was I treated. However, the right was wrong, proclaimed the Judge Who Rules Over All, for it was using those laws as a pretense to justify the evildoings of its own dark side. Because the left too tended to break those laws that heaven had forbidden mortal man to ever break, I was advised not to oversympathize with the left either. While the right protected the laws of man as they have evolved thus far, the left encouraged further evolution of the law, so that man-made laws might one day reflect those of heaven. Where the law protected the actions of men that failed to mirror those of heaven, the left was commissioned to break the law until either the law or the actions of men conformed to the dictates of heaven. Whereas the criminal element of the left broke the law like an unconscious animal, the conscience of the left disobeyed only those laws that protected an offense of heavenly law. By civilly disobeying such laws, could the left bring to light the unapparent offense of the right, which had previously been blind to the beam in its own eye because of its preoccupation with the speck in the eye of the left.

Now the right had amassed for itself a great fortune, with the help of those who were left, the majority of us, in other words. Through one of the biggest pyramid schemes in history, modern capitalism, the right so impoverished the rest of us, that what was left of us organized itself under the banner of communism, into a force to take back its rightful inheritance or share of the earth's resources. Those of us who prospered under capitalism, that is, who were higher up on the pyramid, disagreed with the goals and tactics of the far left, and sided with the right instead. Thus was man split down the middle into two clones, each claiming to be identical to the image of the original man.

Yet, I found the one to be just as big a liar and thief as the other, for neither one even came close to the image of the original man. Whereas the right tended to look like the good guy, and the left, the bad guy, underneath the deception, they both looked like wolves in sheep's clothing. What the right took from the rest of us through brute economics, the left took away through brute politics. T. Rexes in disguise, the two fed off the rest of us like true carnivores, with brute force. And with plenty of propaganda to go around, they both told us we could have it all if only we would sell our souls to them. Little did they tell us that pyramids are built upon the backs of all those from whom everything has been taken. As the two economically and politically gobbled up the world, with an insatiable appetite for what only the truth could ever satisfy, they threatened each other with extinction. For the two needed to return to the wildest parts of our imaginations—to go the way of all dinosaurs—so that the rest of us might live in peace.

Try as I may, to conjure up an image of the original man, I would invariably see my self running from some church, struggling to hold back the tremendous upwelling of emotion that had besieged me with tears. I recall having the experience on more than one occasion, always after the reading of the post-communion prayer at a mass on a Sunday. Never before had I been warned, in such a manner, that something was about to happen. Had I stirred up something I should not have?

While I waited for the sun to shed some light on the matter, the ship set out for Yankee Station, full steam ahead. As the days dragged on, into one long day from which the nights seemed but a brief respite, we inched our way ever closer to the murderous task we had been sent here to perform. After all, had not we been enlisted by those back home to do their dirty work for them, to butcher other human beings, their women and children? Although we no longer overtly cannibalized each other, we nonetheless gobbled up human flesh at an alarming rate. Consumed by the fire that burned within, had we turned into raptors instead of turning to rapture, that mystical experience in which the spirit is exalted to a knowledge of divine things. So did we return, like any T. Rex in those days, to the killing fields to stalk our prey, that image of the original man we sought with such a voracious appetite.

While in the neighborhood of this Jurassic Park, I encountered one of the largest dinosaurs to have escaped from the imaginations of men, a species of Frankensteinian Behemoth, more commonly known as the aircraft carrier Enterprise. When I learned how many hundreds of thousands of pounds of human flesh the beast had consumed since its conception, and saw the staggering amount of raw materials it had gobbled up, I was astounded. Now I understood why so many, like our cabby and myself, were forced to lead lives of quiet desperation, for we were, after all, the very lifeblood of these beasts without whom they would not exist. I saw how those who believed in the efficacy of such beasts had gotten stuck in the Jurassic period of their development in much the same way the image of the original man had for millions of years. And I realized just how difficult was the task that confronted man, the millions of years of evolution he had to work through, within his own lifetime, to give birth to this image of the original man. Yet, I knew that man had to get through this extremely critical period of his development if he wished to survive the inevitable extinction of this Jurassic image of himself.

The sooner we realize T. Rex is dead and gone forever, the better off we will be. If we are to survive as a species, we must overcome the temptation to gobble up everything that stands in the way of our gaining complete ego control of our destiny. This behavior is so destructive, it causes the mind to lose control of the body, the right hand, control of the left, like a schizophrenic whose ability to reason has been lost to instinct. Stripped of all that is human, the left strikes back in the only way possible when reason gives way to terror, with the ferocity of a caged animal. Naturally, the right sees such behavior as barbaric, and rightfully so, for what remains unconscious is bound to act like a beast if the human aspect of the behavior is denied expression on the physical plane. The more the right represses the left, the more barbaric become the actions of the left. In the deadly game of tit for tat that invariably follows, neither side ever realizes that it is Wisdom, the two must obey, one way or the other, in truth or in beastly fashion. Either we embrace the truth that transcends our differences or we condemn ourselves to living out a hellish existence in which we prey upon each other like dinosaurs, until nigh a one of us is left.

That weekend, as I sat up topside at my usual perch, mulling over the events of the last few days, I turned my attention to the cloud hanging over my head. Looking up at the only dark cloud in the whole sky, I realized that at the same time the sun was shining on my side of the ship, it was raining like hell on the other side. Bearing in mind that our ship is not more than forty or so feet wide, I was struck with awe when I realized the odds against such an event taking place. As those, who had been sitting on the other side, came running round to the sunny side, soaking wet, I had to laugh. Instantly, I understood the meaning of this most singular event as I recalled the words of the One Voice:

"You have heard it said, 'You shall love your countryman and hate your enemy.' But I say to you, love your enemies and pray for those who persecute you, so that you may be children of your Father in heaven; for he makes his sun rise on the evil and on the good, and sends rain on the righteous and on the unrighteous. For if you love only those who love you, what reward do you have? Do not the tax collectors do the same? And if you greet only your brothers and sisters, what more are you doing than everyone else? Do not the Gentiles do the same? Be perfect, therefore, as your heavenly Father is perfect." Mt. 5:43-48.

The real kicker came when I realized I didn't love my own countrymen, for I saw them, rather than the Viet Cong, as the real enemy.

"Do not be alarmed by such sentiments," responded my mentor, "for they are the beginning of true wisdom."

"The real enemy," proclaimed my shadow and guardian angel, Michael, "is found within, not without the realm of one's being."

"You feel enmity towards your countrymen," insisted my soul, Jinny, "because you are still in the process of becoming aware of how the enemy manifests itself within our being."

"For the speck you see in the eyes of your persecutors," reiterated Michael, "is but a reflection of the beam in your own eyes."

"You see, my son," concluded my mentor, "in condemning the actions of your countrymen, you condemn those parts of yourself, of which you are unaware, to living out their existence in the only way left them, in some beastly fashion. Therefore, does it behoove you to embrace your countrymen in a more charitable light—to enter into a more reflective dialogue with the darker aspects of yourself, in much the same way a child engages his detractors in imaginative play.

"You really have no way of knowing what form enlightenment will take," he continued, "until it comes raining down upon you. If you embrace only that which bears some semblance to the truth, what reward do you have? Do not those whose behavior sorely taxes your abilities to deal with them, do the same? And if you accept only that with which you are already familiar, what more are you doing than your fellow countrymen? Do not they do the same? Therefore, must you faithfully reproduce the man God intended you to become."

"Only, I do not know this man," I insisted.

"Nor did the Buddha or Christ," responded my mentor. "It took Christ thirty years to come to a fuller understanding of Who He Really Is. Like the Buddha, it may take you longer to find out Who You Really Are."

"Why?" I asked.

"You have so much more of the evolution of man to work through, than did Christ," he replied.

"What do you mean?" I inquired further.

"For Christ," he began, "Wisdom had been extracted from her imprisonment in nature, in the form of Mary, His mother. Through the union of her image with its likeness in heaven, had she conceived the first fully human being, for man had finally evolved into its prototype, God. In other words, with the birth of Christ, had God created the first image of man ever made in His own likeness."

"But I thought Adam was the first man," I exclaimed.

"Adam was man's first conception of his own masculine self," replied my mentor, "just as Eve was his first conceptualization of the soul or feminine side of himself. Because these concepts split the Original Being in two, that is, into the image and likeness of God, the concept of Who Man Really Is was flawed from the beginning. Thus began the long struggle that culminated in the birth of Christ, to conceive of man's true identity, one made in both the image and likeness of God, rather than in one form or the other."

"Jesus wasn't hermaphroditic, was he?" I asked with incredulity.

"All who have evolved into human form are latent hermaphrodites," answered my mentor. "Is not your body housed by an apparently masculine self and a soul that is, by all appearances, feminine? And is not such a union with your soul what you really fear?"

Until I received affirmation from my feelings, I wasn't too sure, what I believed. Though I sensed the presence of truth in his words, I still found them hard to swallow, for I had always been taught that God is our Father.

"The Original Being is also your Mother," insisted my mentor after having read my thoughts.

"But how can that be?" I begged to know. "Did not Jesus always refer to God as our Father who art in heaven?"

"Was not the Virgin Mary, his mother, filled with the Holy Spirit, the spirit of Wisdom?" He asked in response. "Do you not see Mary as the incarnation of her whom the Father had poured out upon all the living? Why else do you think Christ would have spent the first thirty years of His life with this woman if she were not the embodiment of Wisdom? Do you not see the correspondence between Mary and the Holy Spirit?

"You see, my son," concluded my mentor, "without Wisdom, there would be no stories to tell, for devoid of all meaning, life would simply not exist. Above all else, seek her while yet she may be found, for she is the only mistress who can satisfy you. Turn to her, that you may find your way, for she must be obeyed, one way or the other, as the man she wants you to become or as the beast she so badly wants you to overcome. Free her from the image of Nature in which she has unjustly been imprisoned ever since her alter ego, Eve, gave into an instinctive desire to create consciousness."

With the disappearance of my mentor, was I left behind to suffer the unrelenting stagnation of the doldrums—that part of both the cerebral and southern hemispheres abounding in calms, squalls and light shifting winds. At the same time, I noticed how much closer to the coast of Vietnam we had begun cruising. On one such occasion, I happened to be up topside when an empty freighter came under fire from somewhere within the dense foliage that blanketed the Mekong Delta with sufficient cover for the enemy. With my camera at hand, I managed to shoot several pictures through the lens of a binocular, as the shells exploded in the water off the fantail of the freighter before it had steered clear of enemy fire. Only, I was surprised that our guns had remained silent through the whole affair. Between the sudden flurries of PT boats that would descend upon us and disappear in one squall after another, I stood by and watched as, on one other occasion, our guns honed in on the sampan of some poor, hapless fisherman who, as it turns out, was only trying to pull in his nets before an approaching storm. Shocked, I was quite relieved when our canons were retired to a much more relaxed, albeit still erect position, for this was obviously no kamikaze sampan. Like a woman in heat, did I await the spillage of blood that would temporarily relieve me of the tension to create a new life for myself.

Several days later, while sitting at my usual perch, I spied a swarm of sea snakes slithering about in the water, like maggots on a piece of meat. As my stomach churned with the desire to do more with my life than dream it away, I felt a cold chill run down my spine at the sight of such vile little creatures. While the ship stood near dead in the water of an otherwise relatively calm sea, I was forced to look down upon these venomous white worms as I caught sight of the turmoil churning in my stomach. Only, I did not like what I saw, for I imagined I had fallen overboard—that I was the carrion over which these maggots swarmed. Painfully pricked by the irritating process I had to go through to rise above the raw pent-up emotions of a caged animal, I soon found my self back onboard the ship after I had refused to strike out in like manner. Unharmed, I came back filled with the knowledge that kills instinctive acts, for within their venomous bite lie the very antidote to keep me from going out of my head or acting irrationally when smitten with the desire to bite back. To free the truth from instinct, I had only to suffer the sting of death or let go of the desire to commit the instinctive act with which I had been smitten. In so doing, did I free from the act, the very truth driving it.

"Well done, my son!" Exclaimed my mentor from across the void.

Delighted with the advances I had made in my interior life, I wished I could hear from Mary as often as I heard from my mentor. I was particularly anxious to hear from her, only because I had sent, with the ring I had bought her back in Bangkok, the words to an old Everly Brothers' hit about dreaming one's life away. I had worked through most of the first night at sea, cutting from the magazines that littered the compartment, the largest letters and words or parts thereof, until I had recreated the words to the song and strung them together into one long chain. When, lo and behold, I finally received a letter from her that afternoon, I was truly in heaven.

Dear Butch,

I guess by now you are thoroughly convinced that I am dead and buried. Really, I am still around and kicking. Only, I think the mail has been held up lately. I got your package yesterday, and was so thrilled, I could hardly do anything else but stand around and grin. I got scared just thinking about the ring, because the day before I received your package, I had talked about buying another ring. I had lost my class ring not too long ago. I had worn a ring for so long, it felt funny going without one. Then I received your package, and could have sworn you had read my mind, which, by the way, gave me the creepiest feeling. I am so-o-o glad you bought it for me, cause you have a lot better taste than I do. Why, it is so beautiful, Butch, I could not have asked for anything prettier. Talk about a perfect fit! I don't know how you did it, for it fits as if it were actually made for me. How do you manage to make everything so perfect? All I can say is thank you very much. To show you how much I appreciate all you have done for me, I am going to bake you one of the best tasting fruit cakes you have ever eaten—a cake I only make about once a year because of all the ingredients that go into it, and the length of time it takes to bake it. I know you're going like it.

I guess that's about it for now, other than to tell you, "My Song" is strung across my room. That was such a wonderful way to send the ring, I'd hate to think how long it took you to make it. It was wonderful to receive, too. Thank you.

Take care of yourself now. And remember, I am in there rooting for you. Only, I don't know if that is a help or a hindrance, though I am trying to be helpful.

Love,
Mary

I loved her more than anything else in the world. While her letters were in large part what kept me going, I see now how much they held me back too, as they had a very calming effect on me. For a week or so after I received one, I tended to act out less against the Navy, which only made life with my soul so unbearable that by week's end, I was ready to do just about anything she asked, even if it meant getting into trouble again. In my confusion yet, over the image to which I ultimately owed allegiance, I wavered back and forth between the two, to side with whoever captured what I was feeling. Because of Mary's recurrent relapses into hyperthyroidism, at the mere mention of my getting into trouble with the Navy, I avoided telling her anything of that nature until the following summer when I could no longer toe the line for either her or the Navy.

Second Coming

As word spread that the ship was headed for the Naval Base at Subic Bay—an inlet on the west side of Luzon, euphemistically referred to as Pubic Bay—it quickly roused the lowlifes from their slumber, and sent them serenading about the ship with cocks stiffened in anticipation of all the free pussy that awaited them there. Why, the news stirred up such a hunger within them for an encounter with the other side of the Original Being, their gonads actually ached as the pressure built up behind the wall they had constructed across the entrance to their imaginations, to control the free flow of thought from the void. Where as children, they had willingly traveled back and forth between this world and their imaginations, a summons to the pubic region of their minds was all they understood now. For them, the image of Peter Pan had transformed itself into the goaty god Pan, in a last-ditch effort to get them to respond, as of old, to the beck and call of the God hidden away somewhere within the back pages of their imaginations.

When stripped of her masculine persona—symbolized here by the presence of the military and the huge old Spanish cannon that protruded from her body like a phallus that had been rendered impotent—Subic Bay exhibited all the hidden beauty of the female pudendum. To many, she was the biggest little whorehouse in all the South Pacific. Defiled, long ago, by Spanish troops, she unwittingly fell into a life of prostitution. Unable to resist the lure of easy money, she continued to whore herself out to the troops of the new, up-and-coming young pimp on the block, named Uncle Sam, after he ran her old boss and his rival, El Cid, out of the territory in a big shoot-out during the summer of 1898. Although it would be a long time before she got up enough nerve to send Uncle Sam packing, she used him just as much as he did her, for there was definitely no love lost between the two when they parted company after the eruption of an unresolvable squabble over money.

R & R

As the lowlifes swarmed over the side of the ship, half-cocked like Pan, to seek out and rape the nymphs that hid from them, just beyond the gates to the base, in the vulval town of Olongapo, Marty and I decided to pay a visit to the source of all this trouble, the old Spanish cannon, and navel gaze.

"You know, Marty," I exclaimed, as I looked out over the bay to grasp hold of a thought before it disappeared, "we are just as stupid as the Spanish were."

"How's that?" He asked.

"Just as the Spaniards, who had colonized these islands, fell for the fallacy of the phallus, so have we," I responded. "We haven't learned a thing from the last two hundred years of the history of man's mistakes."

"What do you mean?" He asked again.

"We still believe in using brute force to get what we want," I replied, "whether it is ours to have or not. Like a bunch of wild animals, we get all puffed up and bent out of shape at the slightest provocation of our egos. In our inability to make soul without forcing ourselves upon her, we lose our heads instead of using them."

"I pity the poor bloke who takes a poke at me," interjected Marty, "cause I'll kick the motherfucker's face in."

"You see, Marty," I exclaimed, "that's exactly what I mean. Instead of relying on the force of truth, we immediately turn to brute force. We respond instinctively to the differences that rise up between us, for the sake of consciousness, to protect from death that part of us which needs to die, in the first place. In our stubborn refusal to evolve into full human beings, we hold onto a dead way of life and protect it with the old instinctive responses of our animal ancestors."

"There ain't no motherfucker, I'd ever let push me around," insisted Marty, "I'd die fightin', before I'd let that happen."

"Don't you see, Marty," I persisted, "that's the fallacy—you would die fighting for the wrong cause, to protect a way of life that should've died out long ago, for the dinosaur's way of life, we are currently leading, was doomed long before you or I were ever a consideration.

"And even though you and I don't always see things, eye to eye," I proclaimed, "we are more alike than either one of us is willing to admit. Why else would we have become such good friends, if I were not in you, as you are in me. We have been tossed together like the flip sides of the same coin, that we might learn from each other how much better it is to use our heads than our tails to get across the same point.

"In our disagreement with each other," I concluded, "we could have duked it out. Being the stronger, you could've decked me, kicked me in the face, and left me lying there half-dead. But you didn't. Nor did I raise a hand to strike you. Why? Don't you see, Marty, it's because we are saying the same damn thing, only in a different language. While you were pounding my head into the ground with expressions of brute force, I wriggled free of a like response, only to sneak up behind you with a verbal assault that has sent you into a tailspin. Having taken the wind out of your sails, I have mentally accomplished what you had set out to impose upon me, physically. I have defeated the real enemy who uses the language of the body to confuse us in our inability to translate into words what we are truly feeling."

"You have your beliefs, Dury," refuted Marty, "and I have mine. I believe in usin' brute force when necessary. You can't talk to a fuckin' animal, Dury, when it's in attack mode, cause the dumb fucker ain't gonna understand a word you're sayin'. Beat the same motherfucker over the head, and I guarantee he'll get the picture all right."

"Is that the only way you'll ever understand what I'm trying to tell you?" I fired back in my frustration with his stiff-neckedness.

Having shut him up for the moment, I grew depressed at the thought that even my best friend was a Neanderthal.

"Like a chip off the old block, eh?" Did my shadow remind me.

"Aw, shut up," I shouted back across the void. "I'm getting so goddamn sick and tired of hearing about evolution, that I could puke. Why me? Why am I the only one who ever sees this shit? Huh?"

"I can't hear you," I shouted back after a brief pause in which I received no other response from my shadow than dead silence.

"I'm sorry, Marty," I finally said, "for having taken my frustrations out on you. I'm just a little depressed today, that's all."

"This fuckin' hole's enough to depress anyone," rejoined Marty.

"That's just it, Marty," I exclaimed. "It's not the place. It's you and I who are out of sync. And I feel as if I am the only one who sees that."

"I see it," he proclaimed.

"You see only what you want to see, Marty," I rebutted, "whatever demands little or no change on your part."

"I'm not you, Dury," insisted Marty. "And I never will be."

"You are more like me, Marty," I added, "than you will ever admit. You're just as stubborn as I am. Only, you resist change instead of resisting what refuses to change. You are all talk and no action, Marty. In spite of that, you got spunk—one thing I've always liked about you.

"Boy, am I thirsty," I concluded. "Do you want to get somethin' to drink?"

"Sounds good!" He exclaimed as we headed for the exchange.

"Ya know, Dury," Marty finally admitted, "while I sometimes, really like what you have to say, I have a hard time figurin' out how the hell you'd ever live out some of the shit you come up with."

"Yeah, Marty," I stated quite frankly, "so do I. But I can't live like this either."

With that, we both fell silent until we reached the exchange where we ran into Harold and Greg who seemed to be feeling about as blue as I was. After exchanging a few cursory remarks, we all fell silent as one after another drifted off into his own little world to the tune of some melancholy new Beatles' song that had come up on the jukebox playing across the room.

At some point in the song, I found my self standing in a field of the most luscious strawberries I had ever seen. Wary of the sudden craving that had come over me, to jump in and wallow around in the strawberries, rubbing them all over my naked body as I ate whatever I wanted, I backed off with the realization that *"man does not live"* by images *"alone, but on every word that comes from the mouth of God"*. Mt. 4:4.

Then the magician, who had been standing behind this fantasy, waiting for me to choose, took me down to the kore of my being or source of all fantasy, and placed me before the most voluptuous woman I had ever seen. "If you are a true son of God," he said, "then throw yourself upon her; for it is written,

'You will not die;
For God knows,
That when you partake of this fruit,
Your eyes will be opened,
And you will be like God'." Gen. 3:4-5.

"It is also written," I said to him, "that *'you shall not commit adultery, for anyone who looks at a woman with lust has already committed adultery with her in his heart'.*" Mt. 5:27-28.

Again, the magician took me down to the kore of my being and showed me every sensuous fantasy he could drum up, whereupon he said to me, "All these will I fulfill for you if only you let me trick, er, I mean treat you to the delights of your imagination."

"Away with you, Satan!" I finally insisted. "For it is written,

'Indulge not the fantasies of Instinct
But rather the way of the soul,
For it is she who must be obeyed
If you are to be overcome'."

"In what book is that written?" The magician demanded to know.

"Why, right here on this very page from the story of my life," I pithily replied, whereupon he disappeared, leaving me sitting there with a brief glimpse into the strange workings of my soul.

"Come on, Dury," insisted Marty. "Let's get the fuck outta here, go on back to the ship and listen to some real music," for he had been collecting his favorite songs from among the records of the other members of the crew, and recording them on reel to reel tapes with the recorder/player he had bought back in Yokosuka.

"Okay," I responded rather lackadaisically, for I still had no insight into the cause of the tropical depression that had descended upon me after our arrival in Pubic Bay. Since we both pretty much shared the same taste in music, I figured it might just be what I needed to help me take my mind off my self. Only, I found no more solace in his collection of songs than I had in those coming from the jukebox at the exchange.

Still feeling blue by the following evening, I let Marty con me into going back over to the exchange for a few drinks with Harold and Greg. Seeing how I had gotten caught up in one of those psychic tropical lows with which one can do little else but ride it out, I agreed to go with him, for I knew Marty well enough by now, to realize that he was only trying to cheer me up.

"Boy, are they packing 'em in, tonight," observed Harold the hare as we scurried in and snatched up one of the few remaining tables.

"It's all a part of the fuckin' ritual," added Martin, the cynical talking horse, "in which the dumb-ass motherfuckers come in here to get all juiced up before headin' out into Olongapo to get jizzed up."

"It's the last civilized watering hole, this side of hell," snapped back the missing link from his side of the event horizon.

"I must say," added that gregarious little ole tortoise, Greg, "that I quite agree with you-all—this place certainly does have a way of releasing the animal, normally held bound beneath the surface of our civilized veneer by the fetters of a very shaky humanity."

"Why, I feel as if we've all been sucked down into some big black hole," bemused the missing link.

"I see us all," quipped the tortoise, "as having just escaped from the zoo, masquerading as humans."

"And now I suppose you're gonna tell us," insisted the talking horse, "that we've all come together here, tonight, to celebrate our new found freedom."

"That's right!" Exclaimed the tortoise.

"You-all strike me," observed the hare, "as a bunch of kooks whose imaginations have all run away with your sanity."

"Why have we run to the wild side of our natures?" Asked a curiously revitalized missing link.

"Cause we've been caged up like a bunch of wild animals," snarled the talking horse, "onboard some goddamn ark bound for hell."

"Don't you-all see," inquired the missing link, "how easily we revert to animals when we choose not to live out the dictates of our own souls. Don't you see that she must be obeyed, one way or the other, as some soulless animal or as a full human being."

With that we all fell silent, for in our reverie, we had let down our guard, long enough to allow a predator to sneak into our midst.

"I don't like the way you look, sailor," exclaimed the predator.

"Who, me?" Asked the missing link as it faced its natural predator.

"Yeah, you," bellowed the predator, whereupon we all just looked at each other and chuckled nervously, more to make light of the matter than anything else.

"I don't like that hair on your lip, sailor," insisted this predaceous young cad as he tweaked my mustache.

With that, I leaned back in my chair. "Come on, you guys," I said. "Let's get out of here."

It was too late, for the talking horse had already sprung into action. With a hard right to the predator's jaw, did Marty knock the beast to the floor where he proceeded to kick it in the ribs, several times, before smashing into its face with one of his hooves. All this he did ere I could reign in the horse's ass.

"What the hell are you tryin' to do, Marty, kill 'm?" I screamed into his face.

"Yeah," snarled the beast, Brute Force, from somewhere beneath the civilized veneer that normally held it in check.

By that time, Greg and Harold had also tried to rein in Marty, to no avail.

"Get outta my way ya motherfuckers," demanded Marty.

"The shore patrol's comin', Marty," I yelled, unable to come up with anything else. "They're gonna arrest you, Marty, and haul your ass off to the brig if you don't get the hell out of here."

Hesitating for just a moment, I looked down, with some concern, on the blood-stained face of my predator, as it lay there groaning and writhing in pain, after having received another kick in the ribs from Marty as he turned to hightail it out of the place with the rest of us. Boy, did I lay into Marty as soon as we had all gotten safely back to the ship.

"I don't care what he did to me," I insisted, "you had no right to do what you did back there, as he hadn't laid a finger on you."

"Listen, Dury," rejoined Marty, "the motherfucker was out lookin' for a fight—I only gave him what he wanted."

"No, you didn't," I blasted back. "You destroyed the one chance he'd had, to encounter the rebelliousness of his own soul as triggered by my mustache. Had you allowed us to discuss the matter..."

"Before you had said a word, Dury," rebutted Marty, "he would have smacked you upside the head as I did him. Don't ya see, Dury, I had to hit the motherfucker before he got to you."

Unable to get him to step into my shoes, to see things from my point of view, I retreated to my bunk where, due to sheer exhaustion, I fell fast asleep. That night, I dreamed I had run into a wolf while walking through some dark wooded area of my life. Upon bristling, I was instantly transformed into a wolf too. As we both stood there glaring at each other, with teeth bared and drool dripping from our mouths in anticipation of the blood we might draw, I was overcome by an urge to bow to the swipe he had taken at the whiskers on the right side of my face. Bowing low, I rolled over onto my back to bare my stomach to the other wolf, who immediately switched from an attack mode to one of sniffing my coat. Beholden to him now, I hopped to my feet to follow him. As we walked mile after mile along uncharted paths, I listened to one woeful tale of his life after another. Looking up, at one point, I saw standing before me instead, the belligerent sailor I had encountered back at the exchange. Shocked, I stopped short of confronting him as he morphed again, only this time, into my mentor.

"What's the meaning of this?" I asked as I woke up.

"You have heard that it was said," he went on to say, "'an eye for an eye and a tooth for a tooth.' But I say to you, do not resist an evildoer. But if anyone strikes you on the right cheek, turn the other also; and if anyone wants to sue you and take your coat, give your cloak as well; and if anyone forces you to go one mile, go also the second. Give to everyone who begs from you, and do not refuse anyone who wants to borrow from you." Mt. 5:38-42. With that, he disappeared.

That night I encountered the inclination within man to quarrel with another—whether real or imagined—over matters, which, if allowed to grow weary of begging to be heard, will antagonize the hell out of him. In turning to the instinct to survive, had I taken a nip from the cup of my body's supply of adrenaline. In my intoxication with the powerful effects of this drug on my body as it rushed to my head, urging me to use brute force, I was instantaneously transformed into a beast. In the swipe of a paw, however, was I awakened to wisdom infinitely greater than that of taking *"an eye for an eye and a tooth for a tooth"*. In my refusal to add insult to injury, I turned the other cheek, instead, towards my attacker. Why, I even offered him my coat, which, after one sniff, he flat-out refused, for he merely wanted me to walk that extra mile with him in his shoes. Thus did I learn how to bring out the humanity of an animal in attack mode—the truth yet hidden within the natural man.

When I shared the meaning of the dream with Marty, later that day, he just couldn't let go of the old myth—of what had been tried by him and found to be true—long enough to feel what effect, if any, the new myth'd had on him. Like many of our contemporaries, he distrusted what he had not yet experientially come to know. Nor did he put much stock in his own dreams, in their refusal to yield to his meager investment in them. For Marty wanted only what would ultimately get him through his indenture to the government of the United States, with the least amount of pain. He couldn't see that we only hurt others when we ourselves have been hurt, as had that sailor back at the exchange.

Had he associated me with those angry young men on the outside, who had grown mustaches and long hair, in their refusal to serve in the very military that he unquestionably supported? For, he had definitely sensed that I stood for something so contrary to what he believed, that it brought out the beast in him, the very image in which lay hidden yet the truth that threatened the beast with extinction. To protect the life of the demon that had taken possession of his soul, and with which, according to Mother Nature, I had yet to come to terms, he had to attack me.

"What I don't understand, Marty," I complained when, later that day, I again ran into him, "is why you kicked the guy in the face when he was already, obviously down 'n' out for the count."

"Where I come from, Dury," he replied with a little too much glee in my estimation, "ya hit the other guy first, with everything ya got, to disable the motherfucker so he can't strike back."

"How does it feel," I entreated, "knowing you've maimed another human being, possibly for life?"

"He's a fuckin' animal," insisted Marty. "You saw how the motherfucker acted."

"I also saw how you behaved," I rejoined. "Does that make you an animal too? No. Even though he acted like an animal, it doesn't make him one either. You have dehumanized him to justify your own cruelty towards animals. Only, you would never have treated an animal, the way you treated our predatory friend, the other night. Am I not right?"

"Get off my back, Dury," barked Marty. "You've been ridin' my ass ever since I saved yours, the other night at the exchange."

"Saved my ass!" I exclaimed. "How do you think you saved my ass?"

"Seein' how ya feel about strikin' another person," Marty replied, "I knew you wouldn't have hit that guy back if he had jumped you. I couldn't have watched that happen, without doin' somethin' about it. So I stepped in to keep ya from gettin' your ass kicked."

Touched by his brand of chivalry, I didn't quite know what to say. "Well, I guess that about evens the score," I finally said.

"How's that?" He asked rather good-naturedly.

"After you saved my ass," I replied, "I saved yours from gettin' thrown into the brig."

With that, we both laughed.

"Hey, Dury," exclaimed Marty with the Mexican accent of Poncho.

"Hey, Marty," came back I like Cisco the Kid.

As the two of us laughed again, before parting, I was overcome by the warmest feelings of affection for him, for he was more than a good friend. He was that part of me for which I was still struggling to find a more conscious form of expression. In fact, he had so helped to put me back in touch with my animal roots, where lies true wisdom, that without the horse's ass, I would have probably gotten lost somewhere in the back pages of my mind.

Later that evening, when one of the seamen on watch approached me down in the compartment, to tell me some sailor was waiting for me up on the fantail, I about shit in my pants, for I had pictured this guy to be the same fella Marty had roughed up over at the exchange, the night before. Figuring that he had come looking for us, with the authorities, to put the finger on us, I struggled in vain to find some excuse why I could not go up there to face him. Boy, was I relieved when I saw my old buddy, Elrie Van Slagle, standing up on the fantail instead.

As our eyes met, he rushed over to greet me with that big ole grin of his. "Why, ya ole son of a gun!" He exclaimed. "How ya doin'?"

"Not too bad," I hesitated to say. As the sun in his face peeped through a break in the clouds of the tropical depression that had stalled out over the waters of my own ignorance, waiting to gain the strength, it would need to push some great new awareness into my life, I asked him how he had been doing.

"For an old ranch hand who looks as if he's been put out to pasture instead of sea, I'd say I've done well," he replied as he patted a stomach which had quite noticeably grown beyond its old boundaries, or at least those I had remembered from our days together, back at Treasure Island. "As ya can see, I've put on a few more pounds," he added with a slight chuckle. Actually, he looked a bit like an overstuffed teddy bear.

"Havin' spied your ship as we pulled in," he concluded, "I said to my self, 'We've just got to go over and see our old buddy, E. J., as soon as we've docked, for his ship has finally come home to roost'."

"You sure are a sight for sore eyes," I said as my eyes watered with the joy I felt at ever seeing him again.

Apparently, he had landed a cushy job working as a clerk in supply, after having served a brief stint on the mess decks.

"I haven't been so lucky," I exclaimed. "Right off the bat, I got stuck in First Division as a deckhand when, like you, I was transferred up to the mess decks for three months. As my luck changed, I was transferred to 'R' Division. Only, I haven't had much of a chance to work as a shipfitter either, as I was transferred back up to the mess decks for another three months, shortly thereafter.

"I don't know about you, Elrie," I went on to say. "Ever since I came onboard the Davidson, I have had one hell of a time adjusting to this godforsaken way of life," whereupon his countenance fell quite noticeably. "I mean these guys are real animals, Elrie. You should see how they act when word comes down, we're pullin' into port for two or three days. They go bananas over the prospect of drowning in a sea of free pussy. Why, they carry on as if they were married to this bitch of a way of life—as if West Pac cruises could lead them to the ultimate experience with the one whore who could satisfy their every desire.

"But something deep inside, Elrie, is telling me this whole way of life is wrong—that I shouldn't even be here," I continued. "It's been pushing me to resist this animalistic way of life, with everything I've got, for only recently has it captured enough of my imagination, to win over my body as well. So has my conscience been getting me into trouble with the Navy.

"I feel as if I just woke up to the meaning of my life, after having been asleep for years," I concluded. "For, I have stumbled on a great treasure, Elrie, the wisdom of my own being."

"What's the matter?" I asked in response to the terribly wretched look that had overtaken his face. "Did I say something wrong?"

"I came over here," he confessed, "to see if you'd like to go into Olongapo, to have a few drinks for old time's sake, before gettin' laid," whereupon my face fell to the floor under the weight of my disappointment in him. "Now I see you really aren't interested in such mundane affairs," he continued with great difficulty as I struggled to remove the knife, he had just run clean through my heart. "With this bein' my home port, I couldn't resist the lure of all those beautiful women callin' out to me..."

"...Like the Sirens of Greek mythology," I muttered.

"Yeah, like the Sirens," he reiterated. "Then ya understand..."

"...That you had no one to tie you down to the mast while you listened to their enchanting song," I interjected. "I'm sorry I could not have been there for you."

"Who knows. Maybe I'll run into ya again, somewhere down the road, only under better circumstances," he tried to reassure me as he searched for a way to leave without inflicting anymore pain than our differences already had.

"Yeah sure, Elrie!" I exclaimed halfheartedly, for I would never see him again.

"Well, I gotta go now," he added. "You take care of yourself now. Ya hear?"

"Yeah Elrie, you do the same," I muttered as he disappeared down the side of the ship.

Though I felt like crying, I couldn't because I hurt so badly. Shaken by the fall of Elrie, I fell even deeper into the pit of despair in which I had been wallowing now, for days.

That night, I dreamt I finally stumbled on what I had been looking for, of late. Washed ashore along the coast of some islet in the southern Pacific, I abandoned ship, lest she founder when the treacherous tides, which had marooned her, returned to carry her back down to Davy Jones's locker, where she belonged. As I waded across the narrow inlet between the southernmost legs of an islet with a lunarlike landscape, I was struck by the singular beauty of its only foliage, a tangled, triangular-shaped mass of vines draping a crevice in the cliff at the other end of the inlet. Running as fast as my legs could carry me, I dove into this narrow slit only to find my self traversing the proverbial tunnel of vision. Carried off by the powers of my imagination, was I left standing in the mouth of a huge cavern that opened out upon the splendor of Paradise, a world not unlike our own.

"*Go out and stand on the mountain before the Lord, for the Lord is about to pass by,*" commanded the voice of my soul.

"*Now there was a great wind, so strong it split mountains and broke rocks into pieces before the Lord, but the Lord was not in the wind; and after the wind, an earthquake, but the Lord was not in the earthquake; and after the earthquake, a fire, but the Lord was not in the fire; and after the fire, a sound of sheer silence.*" I Kings 19:11-12.

Overcome with fear, I broke out in a cold sweat as I lay there, struggling to awaken from a deep sleep. Unable to let go of my fear, I found little to comfort me as I rhetorically circumambulated the meaning of the dream. "Had I gone over to the exchange with Marty and the others," I asked my self, "only to see the hint of an encounter with God succumb to a whirlwind of Brute Force? Had I been looking for an experience of God, when I was so badly shaken by the fall of Elrie? Had not I found God in the fire that burned to reunite me with the other side of my nature?" Into the feminine side of my nature, had I lunged as I latched onto what my body had grasped. Having abandoned the foundering, one-sided, masculine point of view to wage an unwinnable war in Vietnam, had I darted off, in search of what I knew not. Lest I get swept away by a treacherous undercurrent or backlash of the feminine side of my nature, as had my real father, some twenty-odd years ago, I wanted to know what my soul had seen, the second the sound of sheer silence resonated with my body. Having stumbled across bits and pieces of the truth, I had not yet found the whole truth, for it was nothing but the truth, so help me God whom I sought. And so did I awaken, if only briefly, from the deep sleep that had been imposed upon me before I entered this world in human form, to free my soul from the clutches of Instinct.

As I wondered why I had been so afraid to see the truth of my being, I realized that I actually feared the death of millions of years of evolution—the final awakening of the body from the Big Sleep. After such a long period of gestation in the womb of Mother Nature, I, like so many of the rest of us, was more than a little apprehensive about leaving the world of Instinct behind, since we had relied on him for so long, that is, until he tricked us out of an unconscious identification with the Original

Being. Only, I was no more in touch with my truest instincts than I was with the truth of my being, for I was just as much at odds with this Spirit as I was with my body. With the total annihilation of the parental imago or, in other words, the complete breakdown of the relationship between my mother and stepfather, I had not only lost touch with the two worlds over which each had been given dominion, but also had lost sight of Who I Really Am. In the end, I had no other role model to turn to, than the Holy Family or Blessed Trinity, for had not Christ been abandoned to the world of Instinct by a Father who had gotten stuck so far back in the annals of history—or pages of the imagination—that Jesus too, had to be raised by a stepfather? O, how I, the poor pauper, did envy the young prince! Yet, in my unwillingness to turn the throne back over to the young prince after he had switched places with me at puberty, and had given me a taste of controlling my destiny, I had grown to fear the Prince of Paupers as much as I had, the Prince of Beasts. In other words, I feared the death my body would have to suffer, if I was to find peace of mind or free myself from Instinct's stranglehold over my body.

As I wrestled in and out of sleep, throughout the remainder of the night, with a dapper young dandy—the dark side of my own masculine sexuality, dressed in black—I found out, just how strong he was, when he damn near pinned my ass—the point at which the wormhole, that had streamed this image, collapsed. Saved by the sound of reveille streaming in, from this side of the event horizon, I woke up wondering about the hold this black rogue had on me, and the synchronicity of this event, or likelihood of it occurring in real life.

When the hour had arrived, in the final round of this particular chapter of my life, I leaned forward, onto the table at which Greg and I sat. "I'm going into Olongapo," I stated, after having concluded that Olongapo was the dark cloud hanging over my head. "I've got to go in there, Greg; otherwise, I'll never resolve whatever it is about the place that has been bugging the hell out of me ever since we pulled into this goddamn hole. I realize I'm asking a lot of you, but I'm asking you as a friend if you'll come with me, in this, my hour of greatest need."

Hesitating momentarily, he looked up and smiled. "Against my better judgment, I'll go with you," he replied.

"All right!" I exclaimed triumphantly, though not without some misgivings, especially after we had all agreed, on our arrival in Subic Bay, to avoid Sodom, and keep out of Gomorrah at all costs. Nor did I hear a peep from my faculties, which remained uncharacteristically silent on the matter. Having made up my mind, I wasn't about to cave into their nagging doubts about what I should or shouldn't do.

"I'll meet you up on the fantail. Okay?" I asked, halfway expecting Greg to renege on his pledge to go with me, thus forcing me to reconsider going into Olongapo, as I would never have done so alone.

Quickly finding ourselves outside the main gate to the base, we were immediately set upon by a swarm of hacks driving jeeps, they had purchased through army surplus, and had converted into jitneys, the locals called jeepneys. Having selected the first driver who approached us, were we deposited—without ever having been asked where we wanted to go—in that part of Olongapo's anatomy, most seamen seemed to gravitate. Instantly, were we besieged by a horde of small children of all ages, some of whom began begging us for pesos while their more enterprising compadres offered us sisters and virgin mothers as "good fucks", like commodities on the floor of the New York Stock Exchange, only for dollars instead of pesos. As they raced to get their hands on one of the handful of coins I had flung into the street, to divert their attention, we ducked around a corner, only to be confronted by a young Philippine tough wielding a butterfly knife.

"Ten dollars, please," he demanded as he pressed the blade into my ribs, and threatened, in broken English, to run me through if I failed to comply.

Pulling out the ten-dollar bill I had stuck in my shirt pocket for convenience sake, I handed it over to him, whereupon he immediately disappeared down the gangway between the two buildings, in front of which we had been left standing, a bit shaken by the whole affair.

"So here we stand like two idiots," bemoaned Greg, "after having been fleeced of more money, in the last ten minutes, than we have spent on ourselves, the entire trip, waiting for it to happen again."

"Are you suggesting," I inquired, "that we return to the ship."

"If not," he replied, "then, at least, we get our butts inside one of these places with some other sailors, for our own safety."

Looking down the street, I wondered who had not lived in this godforsaken town, to keep it from turning into the biggest little whorehouse in all the South Pacific. When I saw a drunken sailor go traipsing into some nondescript place several doors down, I turned to Greg, and said, "There's our cue. Let's go."

Inside, I watched with disgust as this same sailor went from one nubile young prostitute to the next, lifting up their short skirts, and spreading their legs apart, to inspect their twats as they sat motionless on their stools at the bar, like pieces of meat on a counter, until he had selected the cut he wanted. Wary of the sudden craving that had come over me, to jump into this field of strawberries, and wallow around, rubbing them all over my naked body, and eating which ever ones I wanted, I backed off with the realization that man does not live by images alone, *"but on every word that comes from the mouth of God"*. Mt. 4:4. As we hurried out the door, I realized that whatever I so sorely sought, lay hidden within this craving, waiting for me to give it the energy it needed to cross over the threshold of consciousness into my awareness.

Stepping outside, was I swept up in a sudden swell of sailors that slammed into some sleazy dive, swirling with the sound of live music. Suckered inside by a facsimile of the real thing, I found my self seated at one of the many small tables that had been crammed together, out front of a slightly elevated stage, to accommodate an anticipatedly large crowd of spectators. Expecting to see some sort of live musical performance, I was disappointed when the most voluptuous female, I had ever seen, seized the stage to titillate us with a striptease act instead.

"I should've known," I yelled across the table to Greg as the hootin' 'n' hollerin' for "more, more" gave way to a frenzy of hand clapping and foot stomping.

Greg said not a word. Nor did he have to, for the look on his face said it all, that we were stuck here until the show was over. Having selected a table at the far end of the building, he had not foreseen the possibility of our getting so completely cut off from access to the building's only exit, by such an unwieldy crowd.

Having stripped down to her panties and a pair of high heels, our stripper teasingly flung her shoes out into the audience in response to its demand for more. In a move calculated to whip her audience into a real frenzy, she stepped up to the edge of the stage, only to taunt those seated in front by thrusting her pelvis back and forth, just inches from their faces. At the height of their frenzy, did she finally yield her panties to the sailor lucky enough to have snatched this little bouquet from the air as it flew out of her hand, and over the heads of her audience. Standing there, now, stark naked, did she begin to wave her perfumed twat in the face of this one sailor, rubbing her hands up and down her thighs and buttocks as if she were taunting him to take her. Unable to resist such an offer, he leaped up onto the stage and quickly stripped down to nothing, as she continued to erotically rub and wriggle her greased body around in front of him. Then, with a fully erect phallus, he pursued her about the stage in a little chase scene that just drove the others wild. Finally catching hold of her arm, he spun her around and plunged this gargantuan erection into her body, leaving none of it to show. With that, she backed off, and grabbing hold of his hand, ran back stage with her catch.

The show was over. Or so we thought until hordes of scantily clad, nubile young females came swooping down upon us, like nymphs from out of the wood, into a clearing spilling over with young bucks.

"It's time to exit, stage left," Greg hollered above all the confusion.

"Yeah," I shouted back. "Before we're attacked."

With that, I felt a hand grab hold of my gonads and start rubbing them. Shocked, I shoved aside the hand of the sweet young thing standing there, looking longingly into my face. Bound by the laws of my humanity, to seek out her alone who could open my eyes to the true nature of my soul, I realized then, that I could not mate with just any available female. As she turned her head to gaze back into my eyes, after having been snatched from me by another able-bodied seaman, I could see that she was not the one I sought.

"Come on," yelled Greg as he tugged at my arm. "Let's get the hell out of here before you change your mind."

"I don't know about you," he exclaimed, once we had gotten clear of the place, "but I've seen about all I care to see. Let's go back to the ship before you do something you'll later regret."

"Not yet," I shot back after having had my appetite for sex whetted.

"Then I'm going back by myself," he insisted.

"Let's try one more place," I pleaded with him. "Then I promise, I'll go back with you. Besides, I don't think it would be very wise for either one of us to go gallivanting off, without the other. Do you?"

"O, all right," he consented. "I'll go with you, this time. But that's it for me cause I'm heading back to the ship, after this, whether you come with me or not."

"Okay," I added with the hope of ending the discussion on a more conciliatory note.

With that, did I step into my next adventure in that twilit zone between mindfulness and sleep, a quiet little bar with a smattering of small tables at which sat a lone sailor or two, with their drinks at hand. What really drew my attention, though, was the lone woman who stood at the other end of the bar, staring at me as we entered the place, for she had one of the most stoic looking faces I had ever seen on a woman, her age, which I took to be about the mid-twenties, if that. A plain but buxom Jane with long black hair that flowed down over a typically small set of Southeast Asian breasts, she nonetheless struck me as a very attractive woman. Having captured my attention, she locked onto me with a cold stare that sent shivers down my spine. In the manner of a true arachnid, did she hypnotically weave her web of intrigue about me as she slowly strolled over to our table and planted herself on a chair opposite her next intended victim, one hell of a sexually aroused male named E. J. Drury. Looking into her cold black eyes revealed the most hideous creature I had ever seen, that gorgon, the Great Gray Whore herself. At that point, I felt a slight tug at my arm, enough of a prod from Greg to break the spell of this black magic woman.

"Come on," he pleaded with me. "Let's get out of this place before it's too late."

Numbed by the whole experience, I nonetheless managed to push my self away from the table and walk out on her.

"You're an angel in disguise," I unabashedly proclaimed to Greg as we scurried back to the ship.

Had it not been for him, I would surely have fallen, back there. As she cast her hypnotic spell upon me, I could feel my heart turning to stone. Mesmerized by her,

I could do nothing but sit there like a statue, and watch as my heart grew harder and harder, the closer I drew to succumbing to her. In my inability to free my self from the seductive web she had woven around me, I could feel my body growing numb to all I truly felt about such intrigue, till Greg prodded me into getting back in touch with my feelings. Only then, before I toppled over on her, a broken man, was I able to see through the outer shell of her being, to the horrid gorgon that had overtaken her soul. Filled with the desire to live out the moment as a human being rather than an animal, I begged this angel in disguise, in silent prayer, to take me back to the ship, that my humanity might once again shine forth from the core of my being, as a beacon to all.

As the tortoise led the missing link back to ship, I could not help noticing the gradual return of the warmth of my humanity to a heart that had grown colder, the farther south I had pushed. For the first time in my life, had I ventured down below the belt, into the world of Hyde, without having been transformed into the hideous beast beforehand, as the only prerequisite for entry into the animal kingdom. Though it was a very chilling experience, I came through it unscathed, for I had, in the process, liberated from the beast, another small part of my humanity—those qualities of compassion, sympathy and consideration for others, so characteristic of a real human being. No longer was I bound to a purely physical response to those persons in my immediate environment, to which I remained unconsciously identified. Nor was I so hopelessly lost when it came to figuring out how to respond in a much warmer, more civilized manner, to those situations in my life that had previously drawn from me only the cold and ruthless response of an animal. Rather than getting stuck with an inappropriate intellectual or physical response, I was learning to use the images the mind and the body, in their infinite love for each other, continually produced and reproduced for me. For, I needed these images to help me feel my way through the dark, or ignorance of the path I must take if I wished to live in harmony with this triune god.

Only after I had gotten back in touch with what I was truly feeling, did I encounter this wonderful amalgam of the mental and physical aspects of my being. So, I was not too surprised when, at mass the following morning, an emotional storm, as I had never experienced before, came barreling down on me as the priest read from the Gospel of John, after communion. *"Anyone who does not enter the sheepfold by the gate but climbs in by another way is a thief and a marauder"* (Jn. 10:1), for *"I am the gate. Whoever enters by me will be saved, and will come and go out and find pasture."* Jn. 10:9. Having been forewarned of the coming of this event, I struggled, to no avail, to keep from breaking down and bawling my eyes out as I left the Chapel, in search of a secluded spot where I could let it all come out without looking like an idiot. Barely able to see through the torrent of tears, which now poured forth from my eyes, I made my way back up to the top of the hill where sat the old Spanish cannon. Having plopped my self down upon a grassy knoll overlooking the bay, I went into one convulsive fit of crying after another, until there were no more tears to shed. Opening my eyes, and looking up into the sky, I beheld the most wondrous sight I have ever seen, our Lord standing there, in the green pastures of Paradise, with his arms outstretched, as if to say, "This is where your heart doeth lie."

"I love you, my Lord Jesus," blurted out my soul from somewhere across the void.

Then Jesus said, *"To you it has been given to know the secrets of the kingdom of heaven, but to the others it has not been given. With them indeed is fulfilled the prophecy of Isaiah that says:*

'You will indeed listen, but never understand;
And you will look, but never perceive.
For this people's heart has grown dull,
And their ears, hard of hearing;
They have shut their eyes
So they might not look with their eyes,
Understand with their heart,
And turn—
That I might heal them.'

"But blessed are your eyes," he continued, *"for they see, and your ears, for they hear. Truly I tell you, many prophets and righteous people longed to see what you see, but did not see it, and to hear what you hear, but did not hear it."* Mt. 13:11 & 14-17.

Turning, Jesus gave the guardian of my soul, who remained out of sight, a few last minute instructions before disappearing.

Instantly, I understood why the Buddha had winked at me back in Bangkok—to let me know that I was on the right track so long as I continued to turn inward, rather than outward, to seek nirvana. That is why, for me, R & R had come to symbolize the retreating of my self inwardly to reflect upon what I found therein, rather than the resting of my ego in the arms of some whore after she had relaxed my joint, as it meant for so many of the others on the ship. Having learned to slip in and out of the darker recesses of my soul without using the other member of my body, I had finally stumbled upon an image of my humanity that could put the snake to rest. For, I had only to die to the urge to act instinctively, before descending into the hellish depths of the imagination, in spirit, to free from the imagery surrounding such compulsory acts, the truth that then allowed me to rise from this death, with the appropriate human behavior in hand. Unlike the Buddha, I had not only found a suitable image for the Voice of Pure Consciousness, in the Lord Jesus Christ, but had also discovered a place called middle earth, where I could wander in and out without fear of having to act like an animal, one day, and a god, the next.

How long I lay there, wrapped in thought, I don't remember, for I felt so relaxed after having been relieved of the terrible tension that had built up within me, over the past month, I could hardly move. After having been visited by the Lord, in such a glorious manner, I wanted nothing more than to lay there as long as I could, to savor the sweetness of the moment. Realizing that I must soon return to the source of my suffering, as Jesus had when He returned to Jerusalem to face an agonizing death after his own transfiguration, I finally got up and meandered back to the ship before it departed. As I boarded her, I could not help thinking about what the others had missed—the Second Coming of our Lord Jesus Christ—after they had fallen for the old way of relieving the tension to create a new life for themselves.

In all, those who fell at Subic Bay numbered about two hundred. Though they would be given another chance, after receiving the antidote for the gonorrhea they had contracted back in Olongapo, they still lacked any awareness of the real war being waged by Instinct, for the soul of man. Having received their fill of sex and booze, they were prepared to do anything Instinct might demand of them as the ship set sail for the coast of Vietnam, to kill not the real enemy of mankind but rather a facsimile of themselves. Thus were they forced back out to sea with the only sailor equipped with the knowledge to save the soul from drowning in such beastly behavior.

9

A Real Tour de Force

"All aboard," commanded the conductor of a catchy little tune that had popped into my head as the ship steamed out of Subic Bay, full speed ahead. "This way, sir," directed the conductor as I stood there not knowing which way to turn, to the right or to the left, that is, back to the humdrum reality of life onboard the ship or to the imagination for the insight into my life I still so desperately needed.

"All aboard," rang out the voices of my faculties in the almost effortless, musical charade they played to entice me back into the world of the imagination.

At the invitation of the conductor who looked a bit like my old mentor, I fell back on the only reservation I had—of getting too carried away with my imagination.

"All aboard," came the last call.

With that, was I swept away with the rest of the crew to the gun line off the coast of Vietnam, to see our first real action.

MR. HART: *On or about what date did the Davidson arrive on the gun line?*
RESPONDENT: *October. No, September.*
MR. HART: *1967?*
RESPONDENT: *September, 1967.*

Having died to my self, as my faculties had suggested, in an effort to allay any doubts I had about returning to the world of the imagination, did I board the next train of images to pull out for parts unknown.

Looking ahead, I saw a physician who reminded me of Dr. Jekyll, though he looked a lot like Uncle Sam, standing over a young man whose battered body lay wrapped in a bloody sheet on the table before him. To the left of the young man's body, in the shadow of Uncle Sam, stood another nefarious surgeon general whom

I immediately recognized as Hyde, though he looked a lot like Ho Chi Minh. As they stood there bickering over the fate of the young man's life, I realized that neither of them could ever gain control, either in life or in death, of the spirit of the young man while it remained free.

Forced back into my body, I sat straight up on the table, looking a bit like the risen Christ, for I was not about to let these two thugs take control of my life. I had to take the helm if I didn't want to end up hanging from the cross of one or the other of these two thieves, who had already taken so much from the world in the name of their respective ism, there was little else left for them to take, but life itself. Since I was neither an unrepentant god nor an apologetic beast, I wanted no part in the killing of other human beings. Nor did I care to lose my life participating in such a dead-end affair. Although I sympathized with the plight of the apologetic beast, I knew that his way of life left as much to be desired as that of the moral right or unrepentant god. For hidden within the desire to destroy the terrible images they saw in each other, lay the hope of one day unearthing the missing link, a way of being that seeks to live out the best of both worlds rather than the worst.

Only, I could not imagine what the missing link looked like, much less how it would act in my situation. While I sincerely believed that Jesus would never have participated in the killing of another human being, I didn't know what to do about my own participation in such an act, now that I was in the position to take another's life. After all, I wasn't Christ; nor was I even Christlike. Yet, I knew the missing link was, despite its apelike appearance, more like Christ then I could ever hope to be, for this gentle humanoid was ultimately tied to its maker by the limits of its imagination, of which I was just now becoming aware.

"To you," stated my mentor, *"has been given the secret of the kingdom, but for those outside, everything comes in images."* Mk. 3:11.

"Only, I do not know this secret of which you speak," I insisted.

"When an animal looks," replied my mentor, "it does not perceive. Nor does it understand what it hears when it listens, for it lacks imagination. And so it is with all who have never learned to enter, a second time, the womb of the imagination, for I tell you, unless your shipmates become like children, they will never enter the kingdom. Bound by the images of Instinct, they will instead be left standing outside to wail and gnash their teeth like animals seeking entry to their master's house.

"Pay attention," admonished my mentor, "to what you hear rather than to what you see. *'For there is nothing hidden, except to be disclosed; nor is anything secret, except to come to light.'* Mk. 4:22.

"Now that you know," he concluded, "wherein the kingdom doeth lie—having seen the face of God there, with your own eyes—take care, lest you lose sight of this vital link to Who You Really Are."

"You see," explained Michael, "neither Jekyll nor Hyde would exist for very long without the other.

"Like a schizophrenic," he went on to say, "had the right hand of man lost touch with the left one when the right began to pay homage to those individuals whose central focus in life revolved entirely around the self and no one else. Having created a new god on Mount Olympus—within the psyche of man, that is—the right proceeded to amass for its self, so much of the power and wealth of the world, it left an incredibly huge vacuum. From this black hole, then arose the god of the left, or worship of the collective, to the complete denigration of the individual. In the rush to serve these gods, did the hands of men fabricate two titans, one to the east and the other to the west, to rule over themselves. In place of the one Lord Who had ruled over the hearts and minds of men since time immemorial, now stood the images of an old business tycoon and his nemesis, the bear. Since the world could ill afford to support one titan, much less two, there arose such a clamor between the two of them, for the souls of men, that many lives were needlessly lost in the struggle to find a military solution to the psychological problems of mankind—this schizophrenic split in man's collective psyche."

"To find healing for the terrible rift that divides you," proclaimed my soul, "you need only turn to me. Embrace me as of old, and I will show you the way to true happiness. Refuse me, and I will unleash upon you the madness that engulfed your fathers."

And so did the three of them disappear, leaving me alone atop my perch, to drift about aimlessly in a sea of conflicting emotions.

As my head spun round and round, faster and faster, I was caught up in a whirlwind of such magnitude it lifted the ship right out of the water, with me clinging onto it for dear life. While it dropped the ship somewhere off the coast of Vietnam, unharmed, I was carried aloft, into the clouds where sat the One Man whose words, though he spoke in tongues, did fall upon deaf ears.

Instantly, I realized He spoke in a language peculiar to all of humanity, and yet as different as every individual who has ever lived, for this babble was meant to confuse all but the one in whose tongue He spoke. To keep from losing touch with Who I Really Am, I had no choice but to listen to the One Voice as it painstakingly pointed out to me the way I must go. Otherwise, I would only find confusion.

"So few like what he has to say," proclaimed some strange ensemble from across the void.

"They might learn what He really wants them to do," I thought, "which may conflict with their own agendas. As out of touch as they are with their feelings—the original language of mankind—they are incapable of seeing through the great darkness that has descended upon us, and thrown our world into a tailspin."

A Real Tour de Force

As the clouds dispersed, I found my self dangling precariously in midair by no visible means of support, whatsoever.

"Fly," commanded Michael as I looked down, only to see my self standing upon the shoulders of my guardian angel.

"Very funny," I exclaimed. "But aren't you forgetting something?"

"What's that?" He innocently asked in reply.

"I don't have my wings yet," I shot back.

"O yes you do," he yelled out as he gave me the heave-ho. "Flap your arms and you shall see."

The instant I started flapping my arms, back and forth, I pulled out of free fall and took to the air like a seasoned angel. I couldn't believe it! I could really fly. Only, I got a little too carried away with this flight of fantasy when I looked heavenward, while trying to do the backstroke, and lost my balance. Plummeting to the earth, I landed in the bushes along a lane, unharmed by my fall from grace.

In the ensuing commotion, had my fellow countrymen wandered off without me.

"Where have they all gone?" I begged to know.

"To fulfill that great need of the body politic to preserve life as it is," replied my mentor.

"They have gone to soldiers, everyone," restated my shadow.

"When will they learn," admonished my soul, "to lose their lives for my sake, and mine alone, if they wish to preserve it."

"No man can serve two masters," pronounced my mentor. *"He will either hate one and love the other or be attentive to one and despise the other."* Mt. 6:24.

"In other words," reiterated my shadow, "you cannot give yourself to God and the military."

"To do so," warned my soul, "will only bring you ruin. Therefore, do not tarry here long, lest you lose the life you seek. Bring your self instead, to naught for me, to live on, forever, in the minds of men."

"You don't belong here," emphatically insisted all my faculties.

Had I heard them right? Or had I only heard what I wanted to hear? If that were true, I certainly would not have wanted to hear again, that I did not belong here, without some input from my faculties as to where to go from here. But alas, I never turned up anything more constructive than to resist what I am currently being forced to do, as if I have been doomed to a fate of always having to undo what I have just done out of complete ignorance of what I should be doing. For I had not a mother who knew any better, according to my faculties.

With that, did my soul take center stage where, with an Irish brogue, she started to sing the old Civil War song, "When Johnny Comes Marching Home." Only, she changed the words to the song as I remembered hearing it as a child.

"My darling dear, ye look so queer," she sang to her one-man audience. "Och! Johnny, I hardly knew ye."

And as my heart reverberated to the beat of the song she sang in a voice so shrill, I was pierced to the quick.

"With your guns 'n' drums and drums 'n' guns, hurroo, hurroo,
With your guns 'n' drums and drums 'n' guns, hurroo, hurroo,
With your guns 'n' drums and drums 'n' guns, the enemy nearly slew ye.
My darling dear, ye look so queer.
Och! Johnny, I hardly knew ye.

"I'm happy for to see ye home, hurroo, hurroo,
I'm happy for to see ye home, hurroo, hurroo,
I'm happy for to see ye home. O, but darling,
So pale and worn! So low in cheek, so high in bone!
Och! Johnny, I hardly knew ye.

"And where are your legs that used to run, hurroo, hurroo,
Where are your legs that used to run, hurroo, hurroo,
Where are your legs that used to run when ye went to carry a gun?
Indeed, your dancing days are done!
Och! Johnny, I hardly knew ye.

"And where are your eyes that were so mild, hurroo, hurroo,
Where are your eyes that were so mild, hurroo, hurroo,
Where are your eyes that were so mild when my heart ye beguiled?
Why did ye run from me and the child?
Och! Johnny, I hardly knew ye.

"They are rolling out the guns again, hurroo, hurroo,
They are rolling out the guns again, hurroo, hurroo,
They are rolling out the guns again but never will take our sons again.
No, they never will take our sons again.
Och! Johnny, I'm swearing to ye." [1]

With that, did my faculties break in, singing the refrain over and over until I couldn't stand it, for my mother hadn't known any better than to send me off to war.

And so was I left standing in the bushes beside the lane, staring down the end of a rifle, with a gook in my sights.

"Remember, my son, you are three persons in one," admonished my mentor as I stewed over whether to take his life or forfeit mine.

Squeezing the trigger, I stood and watched as round after round peeled away layer after layer of meat and bone from the side of his face, like a butcher's knife, before he slumped to the ground in slow motion. Seeing the others run for cover, I realized that not one of these poor peasant farmers was armed.

Looking down as I stood over the dead man's body, I watched in awe as his mutilated face transformed itself into mine, then yours, and back into mine, from whence it transfigured itself into a crucified Christ's before settling upon my dead brother's. Closing the eye that was left, after I had looked into it, I recalled a fight I'd had with my brother, many moons ago. Having been coaxed by my stepfather, into putting on the boxing gloves to settle an old score with Scott, whom I had overcome then, as easily as I had, a few moments ago, with a show of superior strength, I recalled a vow I had made as he lay on the floor, writhing in the pain of defeat. Upon realizing that all men are my brothers, I swore I would never fight again.

Until now, I had done remarkably well in keeping that vow. When, a year or so later, I was confronted by one of the neighborhood toughs on my own turf, I talked my way out of a fight and into a mutual respect for the other that lasted through high school. Having stood up to the real enemy, Brute Force, and overcome the beast, for months afterwards, I was looked down on, by the rest of my family, as a coward. Though, in the eyes of my soul, I was seen as the real hero, that day. And in spite of the hurt, I felt, over their response to my handling of the incident, I was encouraged by my soul to continue to pursue more peaceful solutions to the problems that confronted mankind.

Turning to the incident at hand, I broke down crying as I waited for the dead man's people to come back for him. Looking down at the uniform I was wearing, I cursed this bloody day and the man this naughty boy had become, for my face had, indeed, grown long with shame.

"Humpty Dumpty sat on a wall," proclaimed that eggheaded shadow of mine.

As the Davidson expended thousands of rounds of five-inch shells on enemy targets within range of its ghastly guns, in the days and nights that followed, I was fed a steady stream of radio messages, purporting the destruction of Viet-Cong-held positions, in a move calculated to bolster my morale rather than lower it as much as such news always did. With the uneventful transfer of my body back down to the shipfitters' shop, did I encounter some of the stiffest resistance I had ever experienced from my soul. While on the surface, I gave the appearance of doing very little, underneath this deception, I was just as guilty of murder, according to her, as the man on the ground squeezing off round after round from his M16. Instead of resorting to the more overtly crude methods of that grunt on the ground, Hyde, I was coerced into participating in the use of the more sanitized methodologies of his alter ego, that Jekyll in white, the common sailor.

When I saw some nasty yellow stuff dripping from the dead man's eye, I cried all the harder. I quit crying, though, when I realized with a snicker, that my soul had resorted to pulling down her knickers and behaving like some naughty little girl or madcap stripper, only to get my attention.

"*Humpty Dumpty had a great fall*," reminisced my shadow over the plight of this poor egg.

As I stood in this Asian garden, waiting for the sun to shine, I was forced, instead, to endure the scorching heat of the dragon, when the powers that be called upon the crew of our ship to provide continuous illumination fire for our troops on the ground. Apparently, a company of Viet Cong had ambushed them, I was told, near a village not too far away. While these phosphorescent lights hung high in the air like huge candles in the limbs of a gigantic tree, I stood by and watched, with a heavy heart, as we saturated the village in a firestorm of shells that left no one to return fire. In the ensuing silence, I spun around to leave and turned right smack dab into the pockmarked face of this big ole fat moon, a mere reflection of all that was left now, of this little bit of scorched earth.

While *all the king's arses and all the king's men* sat around the table in the war room, choking on their own smoke as they wrestled with the affairs of state, I thought I saw the Joker, Instinct, at the head of the table, laughing because *I couldn't put Humpty together again*.

O, how the heads of state did sneer with the facial contortions of the animals they had become.

Stung by such callousness, I was hurt even more deeply by the invocation of God that came over the ship's radio, from the fleet Chaplain's own mouth:

"O Lord our God, help us to tear their soldiers to bloody shreds with our shells; help us to cover their smiling fields with the pale forms of their patriot dead; help us to drown the thunder of their guns with the shrieks of their wounded, writhing in pain; help us to lay waste their humble homes with a hurricane of fire; help us to wring the hearts of their unoffending widows with unavailing grief; help us to turn them out roofless with their little children to wander unfriended the wastes of their desolated land in rags and hunger and thirst, sports of the sun flames of summer, broken in spirit, worn with travail, imploring Thee for the refuge of the grave and denied it—for our sakes who adore Thee, Lord, blast their hopes, blight their lives, protract their bitter pilgrimage, make heavy their steps, water their way with tears, stain their white sands with the blood of their wounded feet! We ask it, in the spirit of love, of Him Who is the Source of Love, and Who is the ever-faithful refuge and friend of all that are sore beset and seek His aid with humble and contrite hearts. Amen." [2]

"A-a-ah!" I screamed out in anguish. "What have I become?"

"A broken egg!" Replied my shadow in jest.

"Aw, shut up," I yelled out, in my anger over having received such a stupid response. "I ain't no goddamn egg."

"What you say is what you are," retorted my shadow, "because two negatives always make a positive."

"You're the egghead," I shouted back, "not me."

"You're the one who penetrated her womb and sowed the seeds of consciousness," he announced.

"What the hell are you talking about?" I demanded to know.

"What Michael is trying to tell you, if you would shut up and listen," exclaimed my soul, "is that I am with child."

"O, I get it now," I exclaimed. "What you're trying to tell me is that I, a mere mortal, got you, a spirit, pregnant. Yeah, right! Why don't you tell me another one of your goddamn lies."

"I do not lie," she strongly asserted, "for lying and deception belong not to me but rather to the evil magician."

Deep down, I knew she was telling the truth.

"You've been penetrating my womb for some time," she exclaimed, "with little regard for the outcome. Don't you see—it was bound to happen sooner or later."

"So what does this mean?" I asked out of my own bewilderment.

"It means that, in three or four months," replied my mentor, "you will be giving birth to some new aspect of yourself."

"Why must I wait so long?" I asked.

"It takes a long time for an idea to gain flesh," he responded. "And as you can see, there's a lot that needs to be done yet, in preparation for the birth of this work of art."

"Are we all eggmen?" I asked.

"Yes," replied my shadow, "just as I am you and you are me, you are Humpty Dumpty."

"*With your guns 'n' drums and drums 'n' guns, hurroo, hurroo,*" repeated my faculties, in a barely audible chant that quickly ground to a halt beside the dead man's body. "*With your guns 'n' drums and drums 'n' guns, hurroo, hurroo.*"

"*With your guns 'n' drums and drums 'n' guns,*" bemoaned my mentor, "*the enemy nearly slew ye.*"

Instantly, I knew that this part of the story would push the button of everyone who read it.

"Then keep it to yourself," scoffed an inharmonious voice from deep within me.

"*My darling dear, ye look so queer,*" moaned the dead man's spirit.

"Och! Johnny," began the right hand ere it was cut off by the left.

"I hardly knew ye," [3] completed the left hand, its ode to the dead.

"Knew who?" Asked a tremulous right hand.

"Who are you, anyway" entreated the left one.

"Dammit! Who are you?" Demanded the right hand, in an effort to ascertain what was going on here before the dead man's spirit slipped through my fingers, taking its awful secret with it.

With that, I realized I had finally destroyed the terrible image I had of my stepfather. He was the enemy I had shot and killed as I peeled away the lies that had hidden the truth from me for so long. With each round I had, figuratively speaking, fired into the face of this dark specter, I unveiled all the pain and suffering this miserable human being had inflicted upon me. No longer cursed to live out his fate, I was free now, to make my own choices. Or was I, for while the spirit was most willing, the flesh was still very weak.

Having internalized the war in Vietnam, I found my self getting less and less sleep after our guns had come on line. Forced to participate in an effort, so repugnant to me, I was consumed by my own misery when I couldn't find the time during the day to venture off into the world of the imagination. And so was I forced to lay awake at night, while I dealt with the incursions of my faculties upon my sleep. As I moved through the days like a zombie, I longed for the sleep denied me, stealing winks of it whenever I could. Why, I had even fallen asleep standing up, one night, when I was tossed back with the roll of the ship, and became wedged between the piping that ran up the starboard side, as I made my first round on the last sounding and security watch of the night. Relaxing my eyes, for just a moment, I slipped off into oblivion until the ship came round the other way and threw me up against the rail. Badly shaken by such a close encounter with death, I managed to stay awake until about dawn, when I slumped to the deck in a passageway back aft—completely exhausted—crawled up under a sheet of plywood leaning up against a bulkhead, and fell fast asleep. Having been given up for dead, I was later discovered lying there by Joe, as he came back to the shop to open up for the day.

"Git up, ya shiftless motherfucker," he demanded as he kicked away at the heels of my shoes. While I was getting up, he ordered me to turn the watch gear over to Aubrey, who had just walked up. "Git outta here," railed the pig in him as he turned to hightail his butt back to the mess decks, to get his share of slop before it was all gone.

"You really did it, this time," grunted the pig left standing there.

"I couldn't stay awake," bemoaned the missing link.

"You should've woke one of us up," exclaimed my relief as he turned and walked away, shaking his head.

A Real Tour de Force

For all the fear that took possession of me, like a demon, I was never put on report for having committed such a grievous offense in a war zone. As the horror of having to face a firing squad shot through my head, I thought for sure I was dead meat. Why Joe failed to write me up, I never understood until recently, when I realized that one was seldom, if ever, put on report for an animal transgression of the law, though he was sure to be written up for failing to fulfill the same law as a human being. As an incompetent animal was I relieved of ever having to stand another watch while I remained onboard the Davidson, a victory that suited me just fine, since it only served to further minimize my role in a drama of which I wanted no part.

Meanwhile, the Davidson had returned to the gun line for another round of harassment and interdiction to put an end to Viet Cong activity in the Rung Sat Zone of the Mekong Delta. In response to an emergency call, one night, from the Commander of Advisory Group 100, after he and his men had come under heavy attack from Viet-Cong-held machine guns, did we bomb the hell out of these enemy entrenchments, in a continuous barrage of five-inch shells—152 rounds to be exact. Stopping only to adjust our aim according to the directions continually being radioed back to us from the spotter plane that circled around above the battlefield, we eventually took out the Viet Cong bunker in a spectacular series of explosions that lit up the sky like a Fourth of July celebration.

"It's a direct hit!" Yelled the radioman as his words shot out of the loud speaker in our compartment, and smacked me upside the head like an insult to the soul.

As the rest of the ship's company jumped up to give themselves one of the wildest standing ovations I had ever seen, you would have thought it was the first Independence Day these guys had ever celebrated. To get a feel for what I am trying to say, you would have had to have been there to have seen the look I saw in their eyes, that night, for it was like unto no other than that of a predatory beast that has just tasted the blood of its first victim. As this drink went to their heads, you would have sworn they had been elevated to the level of a god, for had they not, in deed, taken life into their own hands? If you had been there, you would have seen the same defiant look of triumph over the God of Love, I saw in their eyes. You would have seen the very same illusion, they saw, that night, the death of man's immortal foe, that evil magician, Instinct. And you would have either laughed with the Joker or cried with me, depending upon whether you had sided with the forces of the animal kingdom or those of the kingdom of God. The only independence granted that night, if any, was to those poor souls fortunate enough to have made the grade as they left their bodies behind, upon the battlefield.

To make matters worse, I had a falling out with my soul when, later that night, she tried to seduce me in a dream.

"If only you would say no to the Great Gray Whore," had my soul whispered in my ear, "I would fulfill your desire for union with me. But you'd have to stop whoring around with her first," she insisted, "and run away with me to the Promised Land."

"If it were that simple," I explained, "believe me, I would be the first to take off with you, as in the days of old when I was younger and freer, and could run away with you at the drop of a hat. Only, I can't do that anymore. I'm tied down now, bound to this godforsaken can by a contract I made with the government of the United States, like a pact with the devil for two years of my life."

"Don't you see," she argued, "that it's a nonbinding contract."

"Like hell it is!" I exclaimed. "I can't just walk away from it. I would find my ass in the brig so goddamn fast, I wouldn't know what hit me."

"In the eyes of God," she retorted, "the only contract that is binding, is the one that bound you to me for life, in your mother's womb. Don't you remember the vows we made before you were born—how I promised to show you the way if only you would take me there—and how you promised, as you were leaving the womb, that you would come back one day, to take me with you, wherever we would decide to go. O, how I have longed for the day when we would be as one again!"

"You don't understand," I complained. "It would be insane for me to return with you to never-never land."

"No," she refuted. "It would be insane for you to go on as you are."

"There's nothing I can do about it," I insisted.

"You can always say no," she persisted.

"Yeah right," I contested. "And end up in the brig. What kind of deal is that?"

"Well," she conjectured.

"I'm afraid not," I exclaimed.

"I'm afraid so," she rebutted.

"What do you mean?" I asked.

"You're afraid to go to the brig," she replied.

"I am not," I insisted, even though I knew she was telling the truth.

"And you're afraid that's exactly what the Navy will do to you, too," she persisted, "if you start saying no to them."

"You're goddamn right!" I exclaimed.

"You just need to start dealing with your fear," she concluded.

"I'm not going to the brig," I insisted when, later on that morning, I resumed the conversation where she had left off, the night before.

"You would choose death over life?" She asked. "I don't understand."

"May I have your attention, please," interrupted the Captain, over the loudspeaker, as I glared into the mirror at my soul. "I would like to thank the Davidson for the efficient and professional manner in which she conducted her numerous..."

With that, I tuned out his gibberish, to pick up where my soul and I had left off, before he had so rudely interrupted us.

"Listen to him," she insisted.

"O, all right," I grumbled.

So did his words come drifting back into hearing range—"are a tribute to the professional ability and devotion to duty of every man onboard the Davidson. Having been a member of the Davidson crew during her first Seventh Fleet deployment, you are to be commended for your outstanding performance. Well done"—before dropping out of range again, at his own volition.

"Need I show you any more graphic examples of the havoc you have wreaked upon this people," she demanded to know.

"No," I pleaded with her. "I've lost enough sleep, as it is."

"You're so stubborn," she concluded.

"Look who's talking!" I exclaimed.

Laughing, she quickly changed the subject as she motioned for me to approach the mirror. "I want to show you something," she claimed, as she grabbed my hand, and pulled me through the looking glass that separated her world from mine.

"Welcome back," said she with much delight.

As I stood there, in the same meadow where I had first encountered the Lord, I squirmed at the thought of running into Him again.

"Don't worry," she assured me. "The Master has gone off to greet another soul, lest he slip through the narrow gate unnoticed."

"What is this narrow gate of which you speak?" I asked.

"It is the love one has for his soul," she replied, "which, if rejected, only brings him ruin, for there is no other opening in the fabric of life through which one may enter the womb, a second time, to create a new life for himself."

Just then, I spied the most beautiful white horse I'd ever seen, prancing back and forth across the meadow, as if it were uncertain of its destiny.

"This symbol of libidinal energy waits for its master's return," she informed me.

"Who is its master?" I asked.

"It is you who speak," she replied.

"I could never command such a magnificent beast!" I exclaimed.

"Alone—you're right—you could not," she responded. "But with my help, you would ride him as no other knight, in the history of the world, has ridden him—with unsurpassed excellence."

As I struggled with the appearance of the white knight, I grew extremely agitated. Having just had not only my horse, but my gal as well, stolen right out from underneath me by this villain, was I left standing in front of the mirror, looking at the image of a jackass instead.

"Until you say no to the Navy, in body," stated my mentor, "you will have neither the energy nor the will to go on as you have."

"O well," bemoaned the jackass as the last of his faculties abandoned him to his self.

"Good night and good luck," echoed the voices of my faculties from afar.

"That's the last straw!" Brayed a perturbed jackass as it chomped down on the words of its master, chewed them up, and spit the unpalatable cud onto the ground, to be trampled underfoot, pissed and shit upon by the beast.

And so was the donkey driven to play with its self, only on a much lower level than it had grown accustomed to, of late. Having pissed away another opportunity for union with soul, had the ass again banished itself to the barren reaches of its mind, to trudge through the endless sand in search of that oasis where the beast could unload itself of the burden of soul, with impunity. Like Jonah, had it only succeeded in further miring its self down into the belly of the whale.

"Let me out of here," screamed the horse's ass, to no avail.

As I stumbled through yet another depression in the space-time continuum, I wondered if I would not be better off closing my eyes to the outside world, as had my real father before me, for I was tired of always having to interpret and reinterpret the misunderstanding that surrounded me. Whether or not I became the person, I was meant to be, didn't matter anymore. As puny and insignificant as I was, I figured it'd all work out in the end, regardless of what I did or did not do.

"I must be losing my mind," I cried out, in response to the little musical charade that kept playing in my head. "I mean, one day I'm flying high, and the next, I'm wallowing around in my own shit, like some goddamn animal. I don't get it! Just once, I wish someone, outside my self, could see what I'm going through. Even then, I'm not so sure I would be any better off, for they would probably think I was nuts."

Until I have gotten my self into a heap of shit, or fallen flat on my face again, I never know if it's "me" who's getting in the way or not. In choosing to live out the dream instead of its meaning, I delude my self into thinking I know the way, when I do not. And even though I may disagree with my soul, I always wind up doing exactly what she wants me to do, for it seems she must be obeyed, one way or the other. Either I act upon the truth I find hidden within the dream; or I'm sucked down below the belt, to live out the dream like an animal. O, how I wished, I could live out the rest of my life in tune with my Self!

Having spurned my soul's suggestion to resist the Navy, was I confined to a body that, like any stubborn mule, refused to be pushed beyond the limits of its imagination. In my inability to drag my ass any further than the head or mess decks, I quickly found my self at odds again with the Navy when I failed to appear, one morning, at my appointed place of duty. Actually, I had gone by the head, to which

I'd been assigned, only to discover that I was out of scouring powder. Like a dumb ass, I made the mistake of leaving my station, without first having asked for permission to do so. And to make matters worse, I followed my ass right smack dab into a conversation with a fellow jackass down in the compartment, only to forget why I had gone down there in the first place. Having been assigned, as usual, to clean the head by myself, had I unwittingly responded to the greater need my brother, the ass, had for companionship. With no other explanation for my behavior than that, was I put on report. In the struggle to meet the demands of my being, thus did I learn the ins and outs of the art of passive resistance, that is, whom to resist and whom not to.

In a little musical charade that had captured my attention, did I hook up with my faculties again, as they went marching off to the beat of a different drummer. Where they were taking me, I knew not, until several days later, when it was announced that the Captain would be performing his first white glove inspection since we had left Pearl Harbor, back in April. Only this time, I didn't need brother ass to show me how much fun I could have with this inspection, for I was already in heaven, just thinking about it. Received, there, by a boisterous group of vaguely familiar faces, all done up in war paint, did I join my faculties as they danced and pranced around a huge bonfire, whooping and hollering like a bunch of wild Indians. For had I not been born into this world to resist a way of life, so inimical to the human condition, I really had no other choice but to be brave and stand up to it before it took away my humanity, and destroyed me in the process?

Having completed her mission in Vietnam, the Davidson had pulled out to sea where, on the day of the white glove inspection, she encountered some rough going. While I worked hard to make it look as if I had finished cleaning the head to which I'd been assigned, she tossed me back and forth with the shit she had belched up onto the deck, from the mouth of the toilet someone had forgotten to flush. As the shit broke down into little turds that rolled back and forth across the deck, like marbles, the great gray whale could not have helped me out any more than she did that day.

With the appearance of Chief Neely, I knew the Captain and the XO were not far behind.

"Dury," meowed this pussycat of a slothful chief as it peeped its head inside the door. "Is this compartment ready for inspection?"

"I suppose," mused the Cheshire cat in me, with a grin.

"Then get over here and present it for inspection," droned the slothful cat, "for you are keeping the Captain waiting."

Believing that this black sheep in disguise had rejoined the fold, the Captain stood outside the door staring down at his troublesome young ward, with the satisfied look of an old weasel upon his face.

"Ready, Sir," gleefully reported a very naughty little Cheshire cat.

"Mr. Drury, when you present a space to the Captain," sneered the primp little Victorian cat that usually accompanied the weasel on its excursions outside of officer's country, "you salute the Captain smartly, and present the space by its number, as being ready for inspection."

"I don't think this space has one," meowed the cat with a Cheshire grin.

As the primp little Victorian cat sprang back with the slothful one to look for the number that was obviously missing, the pompous old weasel, who had been standing silently by, flew into a rage. "Just present the space as a head, Mr. Drury," sizzled a simmering weasel, "and let us get on with the goddamn inspection."

"O Captain, my Captain," meowed the cat with a Cheshire grin, "thou mayest inspect thine own head, as suits thee, Sire." After a very disquieting salute—that started on the shores of this country, only to end up in Nazi Germany—did this most irreverent cat step aside, that the ole weasel might examine the contents of its head. Looking to catch a glimpse of its haughty self in the mirror, was the Cheshire cat taken aback instead, by the sudden appearance of the white knight. As the great white horse reared up on its hind legs in approval, the cat reckoned it had just seen its own transformation.

Having lost his marbles at a young age, the Captain grew irate at the sight of the shit he now found rolling around inside his head. Having lost them again, only this time, to the white knight, did he go out of his head, muttering obscenities to himself and the XO. Why, he was so beside himself, as he and the Victorian cat fled from the white knight, I am not sure, to this day, if he ever pulled himself together, long enough to complete his inspection of the ship.

"I can see now," hissed a not so docile pussy cat of a slothful chief as it exited the Captain's head, "that it was a mistake to think I could ever change you, Dury, for you're no diamond in the rough."

"No, Chief," I interjected, "I am the stone which you, the builders of this way of life, have rejected. And like any stumbling block, I have yet to take on my true form. When I do, I will dazzle even your eyes."

With that, did the slothful cat retreat down the passageway to lick its wounds.

Within moments, was I relieved of the duty of having to clean the head, and ordered below by Joe to pass out laundry. Finally, had I been relegated to the most innocuous position onboard the ship, which suited me just fine since I wanted little else to have to do for the Navy than clean the sleeping quarters of my fellow shipmates or pass out their laundry. Besides, I found it to be much more amenable to meeting the great need my soul seemed to have for fraternizing with the other members of the crew, around the real issues of the day, without the fear of being punished. Thus did I win my first real victory since going on the warpath again, against the Navy.

That night, as I approached the fire that burned within, to seek the counsel of my own faculties, I was handed a drinking gourd that contained the most refreshing liquid I had ever tasted.

"Whoever drinks the water I give him," proclaimed the old Indian, *"will never be thirsty; no, the water I give shall become a fountain within him, leaping up to provide eternal life."* Jn. 4:14.

"What is this water of which you speak?" I asked.

"It is the intuitive wisdom of the feminine side of your being," answered my mentor, "which must be followed if ever you wish to free your body from the clutches of the beast and the religious oppression of the white knight—the dichotomous result of not listening to her."

Appearing at a Captain's mast, several days later, charged with having failed to appear at my appointed place of duty on 3 October, I felt the full brunt of my mentor's words. And as I struggled to get out from underneath the stranglehold the Captain had on me, I feared what this Saul could do to the young David in me. Nor was I, as captain of my own ship, quite sure how to deal with this thorn in my side, till I stumbled on an opening into that twilit world between wakefulness and sleep, and fell headlong into a dream in which I had just been found guilty of the very same charge, by a mirror image of the Captain. Stunned by such a queer turn of events, I realized that on the day in question, I had committed the same offense on the spiritual plane that I had on the physical one, when as a jackass, I had wandered off to play with my self instead of making soul. As I was placed in irons down in the bilges of my imagination, by that captain in disguise, the white knight, I heard the real Captain restrict me to the ship for fourteen days, and give me forty-five days of extra duty, to boot.

Because I had looked forward to going ashore when we reached Hong Kong, I was beside myself. Having held onto these excursions for dear life, after my experiences in Subic Bay, I realized they were not nearly as important as those of the imaginary world. Had I never learned to take off on these flights of fantasy, nor met up with the likes of my own faculties, I would, long since, have buckled under the weight of the peer pressure that hung over my head like the Sword of Damocles. Nor had I inherited from my parents such a strong will to survive, in spite of the odds, I would never have found the strength to march to the beat of a different drummer. Luckily, I had learned, early on, to live out the young David in my mother rather than the old Saul in my stepfather who, like his counterpart in the Old Testament, was tormented by the demons of an old dying world order, because he refused to listen to the winds of change.

O, how it did please my soul to give form to life over death! Whenever my soul and I became as one again, I would be filled to overflowing with all the joy and satisfaction of the psychological equivalent of an orgasm. For I was being driven by a much deeper and more evolutionary aspect of the primitive urge to propagate the species—an insatiable desire to create a new life for my self, only one made in the image and likeness of the Original Being.

How often, though, did I succumb to the intransigent will of Saul. Forced to wrestle with Saul's demon and my old nemesis, Brute Force, whenever Saul tried to bully his way back into my life, I quickly learned to slam the door in his face, once I recognized him. Thus did I learn obedience by what I suffered at my own hand.

But I was still having a hard time dealing with the other two demons that remained at large, until the two showed up incognito, in a dream one night. While the one lay beside me on the bed, disguised as an extremely attractive, scantily clad, young female, the other passed himself off as an old James Dean look-alike with whom I'd gone to grade school. Apparently, she found the old classmate of mine, so desirable, she was prepared to have sex with him, right there in front of me. Convinced that I wanted nothing more than to see them reunited, did she finally con him into joining her on the bunk below, where I could overhear their crude intercourse. Aroused by their passion for unity, I awakened only to find my self entertaining another fallacy.

Boy, did I shrink from the demon that looked like Jimmy Dean when he hopped into bed with me, in response to the call that had gone out to him from the other member of my body. As he tried to convince me that he needed to have sex with me because he couldn't get it all out (meaning his seed) with the scantily clad, young succubus, I shoved the bugger out of my bed before he could cornhole me. Over and over, was I forced to replay this scene, as he repeatedly fought his way back up to my bunk, to mess with me.

Having jumped to the mezzanine in the next scene, with the hope of finding a more civilized way of dealing with this demonic urge, I was surprised to see the change that had come over him as he took on the form of his much larger, heterosexual counterpart. Here too, did I catch a glimpse of two men in black, hiding under the cover of dark, to observe the events about to unfold, from a more objective point of view. After I had shoved the urge aside with my foot, as he attempted to climb over the guardrail that stood between us, I wondered if I had hurt him. Looking over the side, to ease my conscience, I saw the cat land upright on his feet. Over and over was I forced to repeat this scene until I grabbed hold of a two-by-four, out of desperation, and whopped 'm upside the head. Having only succeeded in encouraging the cad to come up the stairs instead, did I resort to hurling cans of government peanut butter at him, to hold 'm at bay. As two other dark shadowy figures tried to enter the picture, I told them, in no uncertain terms, to stay out of this scene since it did not involve them—advice which, much to my surprise, they heeded.

Having reduced my opponent to some grunting and groaning, half-crazed animalistic urge, I found my self walking down a street with Michael and my mentor, dressed in black like the two observers, I had seen earlier in the dream. Just then, I spied my opponent walking toward us, in the form of some huge, dark, and menacing figure all dressed in black. Fearing what he might do to me despite the added protection I had taken on, I smiled nervously, and extended my hand in a gesture of reconciliation, it looked as if he were going to accept, until he pulled his hand back in contempt.

"Nah," he growled, "there's still too much bad blood between us to ever get along." With that, did he turn and disappear down the street.

"What does he mean?" I asked my mentor.

"It is difficult to say at this point, my son," replied my mentor, "without going back to the beginning of this encounter, and working our way through the seemingly incomprehensible maze of symbols. For practically speaking, it is the first real look into the nature of the demons, still plaguing you, that we have had since their exposure over a month ago. While this dream reveals very little about the one, other than the femaleness of the recessive side of your nature, it deals primarily with the dual aspect of the other, more dominant side of your animal nature which, of course, is every bit male."

"What I find most interesting," interjected my shadow, "is the passion with which your body responded to the other member of your dream."

"For the body desires nothing more," claimed my soul, "than union with who you really are."

"Don't you see," inquired my mentor, "how badly your body yearns to be reunited with the creative potential hidden within the banality of your own sexuality?"

"In learning to trust the body," advised my soul, "you must overcome your distaste for the language that she uses. Otherwise, you will miss what she is trying to tell you, in her own picturesque way."

"...And be left holding onto the other member of your body," added my shadow.

"Aroused by her passion for unity," expounded my mentor, "were you awakened to the nature of this demiurge when his genius sprang from the wild side of you to make a scene, you might comprehend once you saw it."

"As this daemon struggled to keep his anonymity," explained my shadow, "he used the cryptic language of the body to confuse you about a totally unrelated issue, namely that of your own sexual orientation."

"By getting you to reject him," acknowledged my soul, "on the basis of your fear of the homosexual factor hidden within the psyche of all mankind, he hoped to keep you from giving body to the more creative aspect of himself, imprisoned within this lie."

"Finding little satisfaction in his union with body on the metaphysical plane," continued my mentor, "he quickly turned his attention to you, when he realized you shared the same desire, albeit from a very different perspective. Unsure of your own perspective, you couldn't find it in your heart to accept the manner in which your creative daemon presented himself to you. Since you could only see him through the lens of your subjective bias, you played right into his hands whenever he tried to force himself upon you from this point of view. Thus were you forced, over and over, to seek union with the other member of your body."

"Having gotten nowhere with a gut level response," proffered my shadow, "you decided to take another look at him, only this time, from the perspective of my domain. Hoping to find a more reasonable way of dealing with the sexual aspect of this urge, you were just as disappointed by the more widely accepted heterosexual solution to the problem as you had been, earlier on, by the homosexual approach of this daimon in the rough. In the end, neither bias seemed to bring you any closer to the true nature of the demiurge."

"At that point," ascertained my mentor, "did you turn to the superior ability of your intuitive faculty, to examine the situation in view of some of the choices you had recently made. To kick the habit of giving into the urge, whenever it demanded union with the other member of your body, you realized that you would have to do more than just get tough with this part of yourself. No matter how hard you tried, in the past, to shove the urge aside, it always crept back into your life again, like a cat with more lives than you could count. In your desperation to find a more creative outlet for this urge, you latched onto the job of shipfitter with the hope, this time, of having hit it on the head. Encouraged by the response of this daemon, to take a more aggressive approach than passive resistance, you resorted to the same tactic the government uses, that old staple of throwing canned interpretations at a subject until one sticks. Confronted by your desires for willy-nilly sex, were you forced to put down this little rebellion which, much to your surprise, you succeeded, quite well, in doing."

"Having reduced the urge to its lowest common denominator—to an inordinate desire to spill your guts out," inferred my shadow, "did you step outside yourself, to look at it from a more objective point of view. Confronted by the truly awesome power of the urge, you wondered if we could even help you redirect it down a more appropriate avenue in life. Though you came close to getting a concession from the beastly side of nature, you ruined your chance when you showed your contempt for the other member of your body."

"Realizing that he still held the upper hand," reiterated my mentor, "he wasn't about to give into your prejudice against the racy workings of the lower echelons of your being."

"Accept your sexuality for what it is," broke in my shadow, "your sexual feelings for what they are, a reminder of your incompleteness."

"Don't you see, my son," exclaimed my mentor, "the triune nature of this urge—how you desire to be at one with your body and the creative potential hidden within it, as much as they desire unity with not only each other but you too, for you are their only means of expression. Until you find out what they want, you will be driven to fulfill their desires on an unconscious level."

"So don't be so hard on your self," reaffirmed my shadow, "for life has already given you enough hard knocks."

"Though you may feel as if an unfair burden has been placed upon you," admonished my soul, "in reality, you are being asked to do no more than what you would ask of the woman you will one day marry—to love the beast within you, with all her mind, all her heart, and all her soul, until it reveals to you, the secret it conceals."

"Until the desire for unity with your own creative potential is satisfied," concluded my shadow, "you will be forced to live out the autoerotism of your body."

"If you had been taken on this vision quest, around the time of your coming to sexual maturity," interrupted my mentor, "you would have been spared much of the anguish you are now suffering."

"What is this vision quest of which you speak?" I asked.

"It is the search for the insight, one needs, to find his way down the path intended for him alone," explained my mentor. "It is the chivalrous enterprise upon which any knight, worth his salt, must embark if ever he wishes to heal what ails him. It is the trek back to Paradise where lie hidden the contents of one's soul, the grail from which one must drink if ever he wishes to transform the beast that burdens him, into a gallant white steed."

"Where do I go from here?" Inquired I of my mentor.

"To Hong Kong," he replied.

"Hong Kong!" I exclaimed. "The way you were talking, I thought you were preparing me for another vision."

"Remember, my son," had my mentor reminded me, "Life comes from within and without. Obviously, She awaits you in Hong Kong; otherwise, She would not have asked you to meet her there."

With that, did he race off with my thoughts, leaving me behind, as usual, to wonder what lie ahead.

As we pulled into Hong Kong, that day, I was struck by the image of a child nestled snugly in the warmth and security of its mother's bosom, as she lay there on her side at the water's edge, contemplating its future, in view of the Red menace pressing at her backside for an end to their estrangement. Stranger bedfellows had

I never seen. Yet, I saw this child as a beacon of hope for their reconciliation, if only it could wean itself from its mother's side of the story, to investigate its father's version of their affair, for the Red Knight and Lady Liberty had once loved each other dearly, in that land before time, the psyche of mankind.

As the story goes, the trouble between them started sometime before the birth of Hope, when Lady Liberty jilted the Red Knight for Uncle Sam, without a word of warning. Destroyed by this sudden loss of soul, the Red Knight went off on the rest of the world, like some half-crazed animal, attacking everything for which she stood. Thus did he become known as the Red Menace.

Rankled by the shortcomings of Uncle Sam, she soon saw the folly in this choice too. After a brief honeymoon—in which he showed an unwillingness to defend her honor against the Red Knight, except in those instances when it suited his purposes—she took off for parts unknown with the only piece of the Red Knight left her. Before I could get a closer look at this wondrous little amalgam of her and the Red Knight, she disappeared again, with the child.

Frustrated because I could not go ashore to seek her out, I was informed by my soul, the following afternoon while performing extra duty, that the whole image was much too nascent to grasp yet.

"Who is she?" I asked as I slapped a coat of primer, called red lead because of its color, on the guardrail that stood between us, like a surrealistic painting of the barrier that normally protects one from such onslaughts by the denizens of the collective mind of mankind.

"She's but one of the many faces of the collective soul of mankind," replied my soul, "just as I am but the one face of your own soul, or that aspect of the collective soul which lives in you. While I am She and you are She as you are me and we are three persons in one, She's the mother of all the living, the Tree of Life, just as I am her daughter and you are my betrothed, the one who binds us altogether into one person."

Looking out across the water, I beheld a most wondrous sight, a vision from on high. Peering through a hole in the clouds that still enshrouded my mind in ignorance of heavenly matters, I saw the Virgin Mary standing triumphant over the serpent, atop the moon in her bare feet. With the passing of this image, I saw the Holy Spirit fluttering in midair above the bald head of a very rotund, oriental monk who sat atop some dark, indistinguishable force of evil, in the lotus position and without a stitch of clothing on his body. As this image faded, I saw Michael the Archangel standing over the dragon of ignorance, with his sword ever trained upon the belly of the beast, lest it belch out another lie and engulf him in a firestorm of misunderstanding. In the final scene, I watched as the swirling mass of confusion, contained within a gold ring, divided itself into two amorphous forms that rapidly evolved, right before my eyes, into the image and likeness of God, in a sped-up version of the creation or evolution of mankind.

Ecstatic, I asked my soul what this meant.

"You have just seen the Tree of Life in her true form—the triumph of Wisdom over Instinct—a pure, unadulterated reflection of the image of God," she explained. "You have seen how this Holy Spirit enlightens he who turns inward, to strip himself of all pretenses and quash the greatest of all evils, ignorance. And you have seen how vigilant you must be, in the struggle to keep your self from falling for the images that arise from the body to engage you on an unconscious level. Only, you have yet to see where you stand on the ladder of your own evolution towards full personhood, for both the masculine and feminine sides of your personality remain so underdeveloped, that you still demonize them."

"Hey, Dury!" Yelled out a particularly obnoxious third class boatswain's mate from across the fantail. "Quit your jabberin' and get back to work." For he had seen me talking to my self instead of working.

Getting back to the job at hand, I asked my soul why the collective aspect of herself had appeared as an adulteress in the fantasy I had seen prior to this one.

"That image," she responded, "reflects man's brief fling with these two opposites, and his loss of soul, for the way he must go lies hidden yet, somewhere between these two extremes."

"Your situation is no different," she added, "for you, too, must find a way to deal with the red menace, or animal passions this brief fling with Uncle Sam has stirred up in you. Now that you have seen the effects of this rampaging bull upon your body, hopefully, you see how much more of your being you have yet to expose to the light of day before this vicious cycle of abusing your self can be broken."

"What're you doin', Dury?" Growled my obnoxious overlord as he drew near.

"To tell you the truth," I replied, "I've been playing with my self."

"I thought so," he grunted. "Only I hope, for your sake, you haven't spilled any of that red lead down the side of the ship."

With the Chinese coolies, we had hired to paint the hull of the ship from the main deck down to the water line, having just completed their task, that afternoon, he didn't trust me enough to let my work pass without further scrutiny, especially since the wire-mesh rail, surrounding the fantail, leaned out from the deck at about the same angle, the hull took off for the water—an unfortunate oversight on my part.

"I don't understand," he sneered as he peered over the side, "how the hell you managed to spill that much goddamn paint down the side of the ship, unless you just don't give a fuck."

"I thought I had done a pretty good job," I responded, until I looked over the side and saw what a mess I'd made.

As the demon, Brute Force, rose up to take possession of his body, I stood there and watched with amazement, the transformation of this normally self-complacent Jekyll into the beastly Hyde. At the raising of the hair on the nape of my neck, I backed away, just in time for those who had gathered around, out of curiosity, to grab hold of him as the beast, he could no longer contain, lashed out at me.

"Lemme go," snarled the beast, as it struggled to break free of the last hold civilization had on him. "I'll kill the motherfucker."

Upon seeing just how hell-bent was the missing link, on spilling paint instead of blood, did my Neanderthal friend lash out at the more positive aspect of the Red Menace with all the fury of the negative side of this daimon in the rough. Having not yet evolved to the point of painting pictures on the interior side of his skull, whenever he saw red, was my caveman friend driven to live out the flipside of this urge to draw blood instead. Thus did he seek to destroy the only link he had to his own evolution.

Having raised quite a stink up topside, I was ordered below by the Officer of the Deck, in an attempt to defuse the situation before it really got out of hand. Spared the wrath of an angry lynch mob, I became a folk hero overnight.

"I don't know how you do it," exclaimed Marty. "This has got to be the best stunt you've ever pulled off. I mean you have every lifer on this ship steamin', Dury, while the rest of us are laughin' our asses off, at the crazy motherfuckers."

"That's what worries me," I responded. "This whole thing has gotten blown way out of proportion. It was an accident, pure and simple."

"Yeah, right," retorted a tittering Marty.

So did I teeter back and forth between conformity and outright revolt. If I veered from my destiny in the least bit, I would be filled with desire for unity with whichever side of my personality I had unwittingly abandoned. Until I walked again, in the penumbra of the Original Being—that space between the perfect shadow and the full light of the imagination—I found no peace of mind.

Looking back on the magic and the mystery of this tour de force, as the ship set sail for Pearl Harbor, I wondered what was to become of me. As I sat up topside, pondering over the matter, I watched the skies grow angrier and angrier, with the passage of our ship through the South China Sea. With the birth of Typhon, a tropical cyclone of such ferocity, I was forced below, like Jonah, to sleep on the matter.

There, I dreamed that the Lord of the skies had hurled such a great wind against the sea, she gave birth to a typhoon, so terrible, it threatened to break apart the ship. Abandoning the rest of the crew to their own fear, as they plea-bargained with their gods for a little more time in which to distance themselves from the sins of the past, I fell into a state of suspended animation until the Captain in my dream awakened me.

"What are you doing asleep?" He asked. *"Get up and call on your god! Perhaps he will spare us so that we do not perish."* Jon. 1:6.

When the crew cast lots to determine on whose account this calamity had befallen them, the lot fell to me.

"Tell us why this calamity has come upon us," they demanded of me. *"What is your occupation? Where do you come from? What is your country? And of what people are you?"* Jon. 1:8.

"I am a new breed of man called Homo sapiens," I replied, "the final act of a divine drama that has played itself out over millions of years, to help you get a better sense of the Original Being. Unlike previous species of man, I bring together the great wisdom of the body and the vast intelligence of that void, you call the mind, for within me are joined heaven and earth in one unique and harmonious whole. While heaven is my country, like an only begotten son do I strive to love the earth, from whence I have come, just as much as I do my father in heaven. Only I have yet to find she who is missing—the life I am meant to lead—my link to heaven in other words."

At that, they grew even more afraid. *"What is it you have done,"* (Jon. 1:10) they asked? For they knew that I had failed, as a sentinel for Uncle Sam, to warn them when I received word from the Lord concerning their condition or loss of soul.

"What shall we do," they asked, *"that the sea may quiet down?"* For the sea was growing more and more tempestuous. Jon. 1:11.

"Pick me up and throw me into the sea," I replied. *"Then the sea will quiet down for you, for I know it is because of me that this great storm has come upon you."* Jon. 1:12.

Instead, they tried to stabilize the ship, enough, so that she could be kept from capsizing and safely steered to calmer waters.

The sea only grew angrier with them.

In a last ditch effort to save themselves, they cried out, *"Please, O Lord, we pray, do not let us perish on account of this man's life. Do not make us guilty of innocent blood; for you, O Lord, have done as it pleased you."* Jon. 1: 14-15. And so did they throw me overboard.

Having gotten her man back, the sea ceased to rage.

Fearing the Lord even more, they sacrificed their animal natures to the Lord and vowed to live Neanderthal lives no more.

Swallowed up by a great gray whale, like a single spermatozoon by an egg, I was spared some semblance of a life. Forced to give body to one whale of an idea, did I struggle, for three days and three nights, to free my self from this notion before it absorbed me and spewed out upon dry land, a sentinel for the house of Uncle Sam.

"Get up," commanded the One Voice, "return to Honolulu and proclaim what I tell you."

Having just had one hell of a wet dream, did I awaken to my true calling in life.

The rest of the ship's company learned nothing from this close encounter with the gods. Having been inconvenienced by Typhon's temper tantrum, for three days and three nights, they simply looked upon the experience as just another bad dream. How often had they been forced, in the past, to live out this recurring dream on another level. For had they not, in deed, caved into the whims of this god back in Subic Bay when he pitched a storm for three days and three nights, demanding instant gratification. O, how they had missed the greatest act of love, ever, the creation of another bit of consciousness! To meet the demands of the body's passion for truth, had they behaved like animals instead.

As I went below to begin my father's work before it was time, I was pelted by the voices of my faculties singing some refrain about a street back home. And as my head filled with the sights and sounds of that all too familiar setting where Mary lived, I quickly found my self seated in the warm hold of her love and mine. Meanwhile—I just couldn't let go of her—not yet anyway, for I was still too attached to the sights and sounds of a physical love, the fruits of which I had yet to taste.

I am so worried—wrote Mary—*I don't even know how to begin this letter. Are you all right? If so, why haven't you answered my letters? Did you get the cake I sent you? In the last letter I received, you mentioned you were on your way back to Nam. I guess that's what has me so worried. O Butch, I wish you would write and tell me you're okay. I don't know if I'm being too pessimistic or what; but I keep thinking something terrible has happened to you. I've written four letters since I last heard from you. Have you received any of them? If so, why haven't you responded? If you have been busy, I understand; but at least let me know that. Please Butch! I am so worried.*

How much longer will it be before you get back to Hawaii? Are you still planning to come home around the first of the year, as you had written in your last letter? I hope so.

What've you been doing lately on the ship? Are you still out on deck or behind a desk now? I hope you are pushing a pencil instead, as that's a lot safer. How are you doing with the correspondence course? Or have you received it yet?

Please write, Butch, and let me know how you are doing. Even if it is just a few lines to let me know you are doing fine, I would be satisfied with that. Take care now.

Love,
Mary

While it certainly felt good to have heard from her, I wondered what had happened to the other letters she had written. Given her track record on keeping up with her correspondence to me, at first I did not know whether to believe her or not. Had she really written me as often as she had mentioned in her letter? Or had she only imagined she had written me after having been inspired to do so on four different occasions. Maybe she had forgotten to mail the letters or misplaced them. As my suspicions shifted from her to the Navy, I grew alarmed at the thought of anyone intentionally holding back my mail, for that smacked me as just the sort of thing the Communists would do. Did the Great Gray Whore see her, who had long ago captured the image of my soul, as the source of my rebellion? Or had this she-devil simply bungled again, and lost the letters? Or was this Fate's doing—an attempt by God to wean me from an unsuitable projection of my soul?

Having decided to sleep on the matter before I responded to her letter, I was rudely awakened the following morning by the call for reveille, an unusual sound for the only morning of the week upon which we got to sleep as late as we wanted. Confused, I got up amidst the moaning and groaning of the other members of the crew, only to discover that the ship had slipped through a time warp when it crossed the International Date Line during the wee hours of the morning. As I resigned my self to having to live this day all over again, I wondered just how many of the other days of my life had been repeat performances of the day before, and the day before that, and so on.

As word trickled down through the chain of command that we were to be given the day off, at the discretion of the commanding officer of each division, word of a very different kind—that the rank and file of First Division had gone on strike—spread like wildfire through the crew. Ordered to report up topside for work, like jackasses had they sat down on their haunches in the hangar bay, refusing to budge, no matter how hard their cruel taskmasters tugged at the reins of fear that bridled them. After learning that the members of every other division had been laid off for the day, except for those required to stand watch, of course, they grew irate with their superiors and demanded to know why they were being so mistreated.

Locked out by the officials of First Division, while they hammered out a face-saving agreement with those who had called this wildcat work stoppage, I stood in the passageway just outside the door to the hangar bay. There, I anxiously awaited any news of the outcome of this exciting new development in the feudal relationship of the rank and file to the officialdom of His Majesty's Navy. As the floodgates to my imagination burst open, I was inundated with the mutinous talk of a small coterie of disaffected seamen who had gathered up topside, late last spring, to revel in the myth that had gripped the imaginations of these would-be mutineers, like a vision out of the clear blue sky. Why, I was so captivated by my own thoughts of mutiny, I hardly noticed the XO as he whisked by, to rendezvous with the rabble in the hangar bay. In defiance, did I smile when he turned to glare at me in an accusatory manner, before closing the door, as if I had been the cause of this spontaneous event. As I saw it, I was no more responsible than he was, for the myth that had grabbed the imaginations of this mutinous lot was much larger than either one of us. Sure, I preyed upon the disaffection of my shipmates, but only as a point of contention, or means of getting back in touch with what I was really feeling, for I could not fathom what new life my soul would give birth to, in the coming months. And as the only breed of new man...

Just then, I heard the door open. Looking up, I saw the XO emerge with his head hung low. And as he scurried past me, with his tail between his legs, I knew that we had prevailed.

As I zeroed in on Greg, to get the scoop on what had gone down, I learned that they had been told to keep their mouths shut about what had happened, unless, of course, they wanted to be charged with mutiny when they all got back to Hawaii. Fearing that I had been misled by my perceptions of the XO as he emerged from the hangar bay, I asked Greg point-blank, if they had not won any concessions from him.

"You bet," he replied with an exuberance that touched me deeply. "We got the motherfucker to not only give us the day off, but also to guarantee us better treatment in the future, from our immediate superiors."

"See what can be done," I interjected, "when we ban together."

"Yeah," responded Greg. "We can all be hauled away for mutiny, court-martialed, and locked up, for the rest of our lives, in some godforsaken prison."

"Are we not now serving time for our rebellion against the Highest Authority in the world?" I asked.

"Maybe," he surmised. "At least I have the consolation of knowing that I'm going to get out of here, on good behavior, in about a year."

"Will the soul really be freed from its imprisonment in nature when one's self is released from this indentured servitude to embrace a life of unbridled greed?" I probed him more deeply. "I think not," I philosophically replied, "for such a life only further enslaves the soul to one's self. How does one free himself then, from the chains he has forged in this life with his own hands? Unless he embraces the life that is his soul, I daresay he can never escape the hell he has created for himself."

Having parted company with Greg, I wandered up topside where I was accosted by the voices of my faculties from somewhere across the void as I sat down at my usual perch, feeling a bit like one of the chosen people in the Old Testament.

While my life deconstructed itself, right before my eyes, I grasped hold of a whole new way of life, more beautiful than I had ever imagined. As I clung to her,

I was confronted by yet another image. For I was being given the choice now, to become Who I Really Am, if I so desired.

And as I danced onto a stage with her, in the performance of my life, I was left standing there alone in front of a huge stone arch, in the top of which was carved the figure of an angel who had just begun to break free of his imprisonment in the stone, like some prehistoric creature from a fossilized egg. Seeing how this arch represented the dome of my skull, or my own thickheadedness, I turned just in time to see a vapor sneak in through the back door to the mind of God, like a sigh of relief from His mouth. As this evacuation of the truth from the void animated my shadow, I watched it slowly raise its sultry self up from the ground of my being, like a phoenix from its own ashes, only to give rise to the haunting specter of the White Knight, towards whom I surprisingly enough showed no fear, this time. Not until he had removed his helmet did I recognize him as a mirror image of myself.

"Who am I?" I asked this image of me.

"You are a sentinel for the house of Uncle Sam," he replied.

"Tell me then," I begged to know, "am I to play the part of a sailor after all?"

"Nay," said he, "for the house of Uncle Sam is in need of a very different kind of sentinel, one who can interpret for him, correctly, the signs of the times or pull forth from this Trojan horse, the thoughts of God."

"How much deeper must I go before I find them?" Inquired I of the White Knight as this figure of speech put its arm around my shoulders, to welcome me back.

"Why, past your own egocentric view of the world," proclaimed the White Knight.

"How can I ever see that far?" I asked my host.

"Why, through the eyes of the sentinel who stands guard at the gate to the mind of God," replied he who dwelled there.

"How does it feel to be standing here?" Rang out the voice of he who had just stepped into my shoes.

"Darn good!" I belted out in unison with the voices of some heavenly chorus from somewhere deep within my being.

"As often as you have stood here, in the past, looking into your own puss, how could you have missed me?" he questioned my inability to see past its most prominent feature without his help.

"I saw nothing until you showed up, a few moments ago," I insisted on what I experientially knew to be true.

"In the end," he concluded, "will your wealth be measured in terms of the richness of the images you find buried here."

And O, how much richer are we, when someone takes the time to unearth this treasure trove of Wisdom, for all the world to see.

As we approached the coast of Oahu...

MR. HART: *When was that?*
RESPONDENT: *Late October, about the twenty-third I believe.*

...after having been gone for almost six months to the day, it felt good to be back home again. Having barely penetrated the magic and the mystery of my being, on this, my first tour of the interior world, I realized that I was not home free, just yet, in my quest for the vision into my life I still so sorely needed.

Though I was being led to believe that I could stand up to the Navy and prevail, I had some reservations as to whether or not I could ever beat the devil at his own game, since in the past, I had overcome Instinct on only the rarest of occasions. Why, I felt as if I were hopelessly locked into a body that was not mine, and into a whole way of life over which I had absolutely no control.

"You can do it," insisted the White Knight from out across the void, "but only if you step into my shoes."

"How can I do that in reality?" I asked my shadow.

"Love me," came back he in a way that almost verged on the unholy. "That is all you have to do."

"Would learning to love this aspect of my Self truly solve the problem of evil in my life?" I wondered to my self. "Or would it only exacerbate the problem? Don't I love my Self, as I ought to? And if not, how can I learn to love something about which I know so little?"

"You know," insisted my shadow as he loomed up over me, larger than life, to embrace the nothingness of the ego that now stood naked before him. "See, how easily I penetrate your facade."

And as I penetrated to the very core of my being, I ran smack dab into my soul.

"What child is this," burst in some heavenly chorus from deep within my being, *"who laid to rest, on* Jinny's *lap, is sleeping? Whom angels greet with anthems sweet, while shepherds watch are keeping?"*

"She loves me," interjected the White Knight, "above all else."

With that, did I realize how much more than anything else in the world I needed the love of my soul, for it was ultimately the only key to heaven I had.

10

Paradise Lost

Having avoided the big scramble to get ashore, I could not help noticing from my vantage point amidships, how different was the response of those who had betrayed their spouses' love, overseas, from that of the few who had remained faithful to the end. While those faithful few—fortunate enough to have found a familiar face waiting for them among the crowd that had gathered on the pier to welcome them home—smothered their loved ones with hugs and kisses, I watched as the mangy curs, who had messed around, came crawling back to mama and the pups with neither a kiss nor a hug for either one. In my inability to free those feelings still being held hostage by the beast within my own body, was I pricked with the pain of their plight. Thus did I continue to vacillate back and forth, between total abstinence and self-indulgence.

Aware that any solution, to the problems I was having with my self and the Navy, lay in remaining faithful to my soul, I tried my damnedest to accept the form in which she presented herself to me, only to fail, for in reality, I wanted her to be just like Mary. While she definitely was not Mary, I shuddered at the thought of what the differences between the two might mean to my relationship with the latter. For the life of me, I could not figure out what I saw in Mary, and held onto so tenaciously, other than the possibility of a sexual relationship. Yet, I truly loved Mary, or so I thought until I recalled what Jinny had told me awhile back—that it was she, as I saw her in Mary, whom I really loved.

"Why had I been singled out from all these people," I wondered as I descended the gangplank, "to see things as they really are?"

As I made my way through the crowd, I felt as if all eyes were upon me. Looking up, I noticed that was indeed the case. Just then, I thought I heard someone ask me, nonverbally, that is, what I had seen over there (meaning overseas). Feeling a little paranoid at first, I simply smiled, as if to say, it really wasn't anything that didn't show.

"Had I finally flipped my lid?" I wondered as I scooted down the pier. "Or had I really found something over there that showed forth from my being. If so, what was it that could make people stop and take notice?"

The more I thought about my situation, though, the more depressed I grew. I had so hoped it would all go away once I returned to Hawaii. That was not to be, I would soon learn.

"Why?" I shouted across the void, to no avail.

Left with no other recourse, I sat down, that evening, to write Mary a letter, for I felt as if God had abandoned me. Or had I abandoned God? Had *"not I"* shrunk from my new role as a sentinel for the house of Uncle Sam, I would never have succumbed to yet another depression. For was it *"not I"* who had to die? Yet, I could tell Mary only so much, for fear of losing her.

"O, where are you when I need you?" I screamed out in anguish, over the condition of my soul, again to no avail.

I soon realized that I had not abandoned God. I just didn't know myself well enough to get a handle on Who I Am from one moment to the next, much less from day to day or even from week to week. Apparently, it took a lot more energy, than I had ever imagined, for my faculties to raise these revelations to the surface—energy that was not always available to them, if I were being forced to do other things with my time that had little or no bearing upon my depression. While I found little to console me in these thoughts, I found even less in Mary's response to my impassioned plea for help.

Dear Butch,

What are you trying to do—give me a heart attack? I was so happy when I came home from work and found your letter waiting for me. When I learned you had pulled back into Pearl Harbor, I almost fainted. I had no idea you were due back in Hawaii so soon. I was so happy for you, I could have cried. It was all such a pleasant surprise.

Now to the next matter—please, Butch, don't get so depressed. Find something to occupy your mind so you won't get this way. If nothing else, roam the beaches for me, so that you can tell me all about Hawaii. You will find so much to write about (Hint! Hint!), you won't have time to get depressed.

I was quite upset when I learned you had not received the cake or my letters. I will make it up to you when you get home. Okay?

Thanks so much, Butch, for the great pictures of you, as they let me see a little more of who you really are.

Since you know how nervous I am, I hope you will at least let me know when you are coming home so that my heart won't fail me when I find you standing at my door. Really, Butch, I am dying to know when I will get to see you again. Please tell me. Okay?

Take care now, and get home soon.

Love,
Mary

While I wished that she could have met me when the ship pulled into Pearl Harbor, as did the wives of Greg and Harold, to share the splendor of this paradise with me in person rather than via the mail, I see now, just how disastrous that would have been. I would only have gotten lost in a relationship I was no more prepared to enter than I had been, the Navy. In my need to return to the womb of the Great Mother, to find out Who I Really Am, I wound up in the same boat as the other guys on the ship. As much as I wanted to physically penetrate the womb, I was forced instead, to make the return to the fertile womb of my own imagination where, as an inexperienced spelunker, I often got lost in the pit of despair when I couldn't find anything to paint. So there I was, stuck in dry dock with a skeleton crew, while the ship underwent some much needed repairs after her stormy affair in the South China Sea with Typhon, the father of unrealizable dreams.

That Sunday, while at mass, I stumbled on the same garden of olive trees, I had encountered during that other hellishly dry period of my life, back in the spring of the year. Only this time, I saw Abraham standing on the mount in front of a roughly hewed stone altar, offering an animal sacrifice to Yahweh as the priest elevated the host at the consecration. After the priest returned the host to the paten, I saw a pencil of light, much like a laser beam, shoot down from the heavens and into the host. Instantly, I knew that the bread had been transformed into the body of Christ—the visible likeness of the invisible image of God. And I saw the same pencil of light translate the animal sacrifice into an inscription on the face of the altar where Abraham had just laid it.

With that, I realized the mass is about the transformation of our animal natures into human nature—the image into the likeness of God.

Through the priest, do we offer our bodies up to God via the bread, so that we may literally be transformed into full human beings, the body of Christ. So too, do we imitate the priest (Abraham) whenever we sacrifice, on the roughly hewed altars of our daily lives, those animalistic tendencies which no longer befit us as human beings. Only when we see the handwriting on the altar, and embrace the holographic prescription etched there in place of the sin offering, can we truly give up such animalistic behavior.

Blinded by our materialistic myopia, we are unable to see Christ in the bread—the full human being within our bodies. Like some of our animal brethren, have we been endowed with a sixth sense, the ability to imagine—to see a mental image of something not present to the senses or never before wholly perceived in reality. Through the power of our imaginations, or symbolic perception, can we perceive the true nature of reality—the ultimate meaning of our existence.

For we have been called upon, by God, to wake up to our real fate—to drink from a cup that will not pass until we have sweat blood, or shed from our bodies, like crushed grapes, the wine of Dionysus. Ever driven by this intoxicating potion to behave like an animal instead of the human being we are slowly becoming, must we empty ourselves of this poison, and humbly drink from this bitter cup the antidote, human blood. As the wine, which has been transformed into His blood, goes to our heads and fills our hearts, we are momentarily elevated to human stature. In that one brief moment, do we taste the sweetness of our true destiny, the fullness of our humanity.

As the searing light of the Creator penetrates the unconsciousness of our animal natures, we become more aware of our true destiny. We must obey Him Who created us, no longer instinctively like an unconscious animal, but willingly as a conscious human being. Whether we like it or not, we have been created to do His will, not ours.

We have been born solely for the benefit of each other, for the purpose of raising every individual, or aspect of the body of mankind, from our animal roots, to create a new branch on the evolutionary tree of life. To create this new species of truly human beings, we must give ourselves completely, not only to each other, but also to every aspect of creation, like the leaves on a great tree. As we die to ourselves, year after year, we make the greatest contribution toward resurrecting the image of God still trapped in the wood of the tree.

Only, I saw my life in the Navy as a step back into the nightmarish prehistory of mankind, where the still invisible image of God lay hidden within unconscious life forms. Since these life forms bore little resemblance to the Creator, many of them were scrapped in a supreme effort to create a being made entirely in the image and likeness of the Original Being. With the evolution of our species, did God turn the task over to us, to complete. In our inability to let go of our animal heritage, we fell, instead, from the evolutionary tree to a level of existence that lay beneath our true dignity.

With the development of our capacity to think, were we freed from a purely instinctive response to the images of the imagination. Whereas our ancestors had been programmed to unconsciously mimic what they saw in the images that cropped up to guide them, we took the first truly conscious step in the creation of the image and likeness of God in the flesh. As the beneficiaries of millions of years of evolution, did we stumble upon the means to become aware of ourselves.

Out of the void that has occupied the head since time immemorial, did we catch wind, one day, of a whisper on the breath of a gentle breeze. As the wind spoke to us, we sensed that a momentous change was about to take place in our bodies. We had been reprogrammed. No longer were we to take the images of the imagination literally.

As Adam, was I overcome, one day, by an instinctive desire to penetrate the hole that had opened up before me. Sucked into the spiritual vacuum of the void that now stood between me and the truth, did I fall victim to a rapidly unfolding stream of images. There was I confronted by the unfathomable wisdom of my heart, in the guise of a naked woman. When the male member of my body overextended itself, like a serpent protruding from a tree, I lost my head—this newly won ability of mine to choose the real thing over its image. Out of ignorance, did I mistake the act of procreation for that of creating consciousness. I was bamboozled by Instinct into believing I would become all knowing, like the Creator, if I tasted the fruit of a close encounter with this image of God. Ignoring the admonition to avoid taking these images literally, did I cave into the gentle persuasion of the woman of my dreams. Thrusting my self into this fantasy, I gave my self up to her completely. As I came, I saw heaven penetrate the earth and sow the seeds for the creation of a new species of animal, one made in the image and likeness of God. On the Eve of my humanity, in the arms of the woman of my dreams, did I wake up to the truth of my own nakedness—that I had just participated in the conception of consciousness.

Confronted by the still invisible image of God, I realized my mistake. Immediately, I blamed the woman who laid the blame on Instinct, for he had filled our bodies with the desire to become as one again, like God. As half a man, had I lost my head over the very heart, she had just deferred to the wrongheaded views of Instinct. Thus did I learn that Instinct could no longer be trusted.

Born of Wisdom as She gave birth to Life, Instinct had enjoyed the highest position of any entity ever created, that of guide for all of creation. Until the day he was placed under the control of the heart that had been placed under the dominion of the head, he had carried out every command of the Creator as Wisdom had shown him via Her images. In his utter inability to see the likeness of the Creator and Her image, in the physicality of the man and the woman, Instinct rebelled against this new arrangement. He, who had reigned supreme over all of creation since time immemorial, could not see these two puny creatures as his Lord and Lady.

Fearing that this new drive for consciousness might lead to his own destruction, Instinct decided to seize it for himself, for he now longed to see the naked beauty of Wisdom with the all-seeing eye of the Creator. Since the man and the woman had just ripened to full sexual maturity, he filled their bodies with desire. As he conjured up the usual imagery for this rite of passage, he learned that they had received instructions, from higher up, not to indulge such fantasies. Using their one weakness, the separation of the head from the heart, he captured the heart and hid her from the head in a cloud of images. With the heart now, emotionally bound to an image out there in Nature, Instinct proceeded to capture the attention of the head with a plausible explanation of the events about to unfold. He convinced the head to encounter the image of this woman out there in Nature rather than within himself as God had instructed. With the fall of the head, Instinct easily took control of their bodies, the ultimate source of consciousness.

In his unwillingness to set Truth free from Her bondage to the images of the material world, Instinct unwittingly participated in the conception of consciousness. Fortunately, he never realized that Wisdom could be freed from Her imprisonment in Nature, whether we act upon Her images in body or in spirit. He failed to recognize the inexplicable bond between the head and the heart, that the head must not only penetrate the heart to free Wisdom, but also give himself up completely to Her, to free consciousness from the clutches of Instinct.

He took advantage of the heart's desire for unity with the head by filling the head with his own insatiable desire for unconscious unity with Wisdom. Having filled the head with images of the truth, he drove the head to make an unwise choice, one lacking feeling. After convincing the head he could have Wisdom if only he would penetrate Her image, Instinct tricked the heart into believing she could have Consciousness if only she would allow His image to fill her with what she thought she lacked, the seeds of consciousness. Thus did he drive the heart to make an unreasonable choice, one lacking thought. Instinct had played upon the head's desire for wisdom, and the heart's, for enlightenment, to keep them from conceiving consciousness. Only he failed.

With the conception of consciousness was Instinct fired from his post as guide supreme. For his transgression was he banished from Paradise to assume the lowest form of life in all creation, that of a serpent. Thus did he create hell on earth, enmity between himself and the heart.

As the heart now labored under the curse of pain, to give birth to the truth, Instinct grew fearful of her beloved's newly acquired ability to foster consciousness. In an attempt to turn the head against her, he poisoned the head with every image of instinctive desire he could conjure up. Having duped the head into being his stooge, did he begin his long reign of terror over her and her offspring, in a vain attempt to keep any more of the seeds of truth from being sown in the earth.

Under great duress was Consciousness born, again and again, always with the hope He would, one day, overthrow the evil reign of Instinct. Despite all the attempts on His life, down through the ages, Consciousness grew in strength under the nurturing care of the heart, for she knew this child alone was her only hope for salvation. Not until He came of age with the birth of Christ, did He attempt to take on this Goliath, face to face, in a fight to death.

During the early rounds of this god-awful fight, Consciousness had gained the upper hand over Instinct. Then, in a sudden blow to the head, He suffered a right cross that sent Him reeling. Stumbling over His own words, He fell to the earth where He died in the arms of His Mother.

Having apparently lost the fight with Instinct, was He laid to rest in a tomb within the earth. Unbeknownst to us, He had returned to the womb of His Mother so that we might understand the meaning of His words to Nicodemus—that one must be born of the Spirit to enter the Kingdom. While Wisdom labored for three dark days to give birth to a newborn Son, Consciousness finally realized His goal, the creation of the first human being ever made in His own likeness.

In spite of all the scrutiny of the history of Consciousness, which has taken place down through the ages, we have yet to see through the devilish trick Instinct played on us. Like Adam and Eve, we find it difficult to wake up from the Big Sleep—to walk through our dreams and visions, the very myths we live by, with the understanding and awareness of Consciousness. In our choice to sleepwalk through life, we remain oblivious to the myths that have driven us since time immemorial. Even when we are awakened to our dreams, we find ourselves incapable of penetrating Wisdom's images, to free the seeds of truth, which Consciousness deposited there, long ago, in safekeeping for us.

We see Consciousness as the enemy. As we enlist in the struggle to protect the life of our old mentor, turned traitor, we give up our lives for a mere shadow of what is. We seek the death of God instead of enlightenment. In our relentless persecution of the truth, we fool ourselves into believing that we have killed Consciousness, for in our blindness, we fail to see the death of Instinct in the crucifixion of Consciousness.

No longer free to pluck the truth from the images of Wisdom, like an apple from a tree, we have been cursed to toil by the sweat of our brows, to unearth the truth from the ground of our beings. From among thorns and thistles, the lies and misconceptions that surround the truth, must we now struggle to raise our level of consciousness. Like Nicodemus, must we learn to make the incestuous return to the womb of the mother of all images. So too must we learn to leave the body in spirit if, like Jesus, we want to enter the realm of the imagination to free the seeds of truth being held captive yet, by Instinct. Only, we must leave Instinct behind, to suffer and die on the cross, alone.

Despite all the enlightening fantasies I encountered in church that Sunday, I still could not see the invisible image of God within myself, the individual I was meant to become. Nor could I decipher the handwriting on the altar—the single most important clue to my identity, yet revealed—only because the prescription for what ailed me had been written in the language of my own confusing circumstances.

With that, did my soul grab hold of my hand, to lead me out of the pit of despair.

"Where have you been?" I chided her as I caught sight of her in the light at the end of the tunnel.

"I've been down in the dumps with you," she insisted, "scrounging around for clues to the nature of our being."

"Why haven't I seen you before now?" I persisted.

"You were so infatuated with Despair," she replied, "you could not take your eyes off her until my father started feeding you insight into some of the old myths that'd been relegated to the trash heap. That's why."

"We now know," interjected my mentor, "that your real identity lies just beyond our grasp, somewhere between the inner and outer circumstances of your life, waiting to reveal itself to you the instant these two seemingly irreconcilable realities come to the same realization. For it is written, my son, as the Word became flesh, so must the flesh become Word, and the two of them, one, before the identity of the Original Being is revealed. In other words, must you give flesh to your thoughts, and thought to your feelings, to gain insight into Who You Really Are."

No sooner had we sat down around the fire of my heart's desires, to contemplate my next move, than Michael suggested he and I go flying, of all things.

"I believe you and I are the ones who should take a hike," concluded my mentor, "so these two can spend some much needed time together, getting to know each other a little better."

"You're right," agreed Michael, as the two of them disappeared, leaving me alone with my soul, really, for the first time since I met her.

As I sat there poking around in the fire of my heart's desires, with a stick, I grew uncomfortable with the feelings I had stirred up. Fearful of letting the beast in me take over, I jabbed the stick, quickly, in and out of the coals before plunging it all the way into the fire and letting go of it. Immediately I climaxed without ejaculating.

O, how wonderful it was! Gone was the fire that burned between us. Gone, too, were the two of us, for in our place stood, for an instant, an invincible being of neither sex, before it returned to its former glory.

O, how she did radiate with the beauty of that little amalgam of her and me.

"What happened?" I asked with a grin.

"You have just experienced at-one-ment with me," she replied with that roguish little smile of hers.

Just then, the bubble burst. I knew I was in trouble again with the Navy.

"You're on report, Dury," shouted some PO as he disappeared up the ladder.

"For what?" I shouted back, to no avail, for I had absolutely no idea of why I had been written up again.

Expecting my soul to have already disappeared from the mirror, I was surprised, when I turned around, to find her standing there, glowing with the radiance of the new life taking shape within her womb. Instead of chiding her for having gotten me into trouble with the Navy again, I simply smiled at her, for it had just dawned on me how she was trying to help me get out of the Navy. Whenever she enticed me to cross the line between this world and the next, I literally left the Navy behind, as if it really didn't exist, to embrace the reality of Who I Am.

"I am Who Am," muttered I to my self, in my confusion over the true nature of this unnamed god.

"Yes," reaffirmed my soul, "and that is exactly who your shipmates and their kin saw walking among them on the pier, the day you returned to the isle of your Self."

"I wish I could've seen what they saw," I groaned.

"O, but you have," she exclaimed, "when you beheld the exquisite beauty of that unnamed aspect of your greater Self, that is, of you and me, I have been struggling so hard, over the past six months, to carry to full term for you in my womb."

"I'm sorry I haven't been more helpful," I confessed.

"When I realized how afraid you were, of assuming responsibility for the consequences of your own actions," interjected my soul, "I took the advice of my father and backed off for awhile, or at least until those times when your desire for unity with me overcame your fear."

Having been charged for failing to appear at my appointed place of duty, and for having been derelict in the performance of my duties, was I dragged before the Captain, several days later, with the added charge of having failed to shave that morning, for a real shotgun wedding of sorts. Finding my self surrounded, for the first time ever at a Captain's mast, by my soul, Michael, and her father, I stood there, before the High Priest and his entourage, dressed as the White Knight.

"Do you, Mr. Drury, take this woman to be your lawfully wedded wife?" Asked the High Priest.

"I do," I replied out of guilt.

"And do you, woman, take this man to be your lawfully wedded husband?" He asked my soul.

"I do," replied she out of her love for me.

"By the power vested in me, I now pronounce you man and wife," proclaimed the High Priest ere sending us on our way, with his blessings, to the Naval Station Brig at Pearl Harbor, for thirty days of correctional custody, and all for the paltry sum of half a month's pay.

Having been knocked off my high horse by my fear of going to jail, I found myself lying on the ground of my being, looking up the shaft of a lance at the darkest knight with whom I had ever jousted. Led off, a prisoner of my own fear, I heard Michael shout out, before he and the others disappeared into the wild blue yonder, on the back of my gallant white steed, "to stand tall against the blackest knight of all, Fear itself". As I approached the very citadel of Fear, I was confronted, just outside the main gate to the brig, by a red-haired, redneck marine sergeant who, upon sensing my fear, lit into me with the unredeemed side of his animal nature, like a drill instructor, a new boot.

"What's your name, puke," hissed the badgerer, as he rounded the corner of his desk to invade my space.

"Drury," I replied with the meekness of one who sincerely hoped that physical abuse was not a part of his repertoire of intimidation.

"Drury, sir," he screamed as he got right up in my face.

"I can't hear you," he snarled with a glare meant to maximize the effect he was obviously having on me.

"Drury, sir," I finally muttered, unwillingly.

"Are you a pussy, Dury?" He screamed into my face, after I had failed to respond to him with any balls.

Acting as if he had just seen my soul, did he turn and walk his puffed-up self to the front of his desk, to look at my confinement papers. "Well, what have we here," sneered the badger within him, "some pussy-ass fuckup?"

"What kind of pussy-ass name is Eodor," growled the beast within him, in an effort to live up to its namesake.

"Sir Eodor is my father's name," I replied with the pride of the eldest son and subsequent heir to the family coat of arms.

"I thought it was your mother's name," snarled some smart-ass corporal who had yet to earn his badge as a full-fledged badgerer.

"You think you're really somethin', don't ya Dury, better than the rest of us," yelled out the sergeant from across his desk, after having obviously been deeply disturbed by my tone of voice. "Well in my eyes, mister, you ain't nothin' but a god-damn puke. Ya got that, Dury."

Having failed to elicit any response from me, to get my goad in other words, he ordered me to empty out the contents of my pockets, which I did in all haste. Scarfing up what little money I had, he then placed it in a manila envelope and asked me to sign the damn thing, to verify that he had written down the correct amount on the outside of the envelope.

"Get this fuckin' puke outta my sight, before I get any sicker than I already am," he commanded.

Looking into the red beady eyes of this poor dumb brute, before I was taken to my new quarters, I caught a glimpse of his own suppressed humanity, hidden deep within his being, in some dark, dank and dirty cell. Immediately, I recognized his humanity as my own, and raced off to embrace it. In the compassion I felt, that day, for this poor wretched creature, was I liberated from my fear and taken aback by my humanity—or missing link—to a place in Paradise where lay the profane and the holy, side by side, like the lion and the lamb in Isaiah.

I had fully expected to be locked up behind bars in some loathsome cell, all by myself for thirty days. Instead, I was surprised when my charge, a fellow trustee, led me to a barracks-like room out in front and just to the right of the main gate to the interior of the brig—where resided those prisoners who had been confined to the brig at hard labor. As I stowed away, in the locker at the foot of my bunk, what little I had been allowed to bring with me, I was informed that I better not leave the brig without permission, unless I preferred to serve out the rest of my sentence behind bars—where any time served was considered lost time or time to be made up at the end of one's enlistment. With the appearance of my soul, I began to feel a little awkward, until my charge excused himself and disappeared out the door of our honeymoon suite.

"What're you doing?" I asked her as she bent down over my footlocker and began rummaging around through its contents as if she were looking for some long lost treasure of mine.

"I have come to help you sort through your feelings," she replied.

Instantly, I felt as if I had returned to Treasure Island, only this time, to seek out some hidden truth about myself.

"That's it!" She exclaimed. "You have been exiled here, on the isle of your Self, to begin living out your true vocation in life."

"What're you talking about?" I asked her.

"Don't you see," she exclaimed, "that you are being called by the Most High to serve out the rest of your enlistment, here, in the brig."

"Why, I can't do that," I insisted, even though deep down I felt more at home, here, than I had anywhere else since coming on active duty.

"Look!" She exclaimed as she held up the little treasure chest she had pulled from my locker. "Here is where your heart doeth lie. It is my gift to you, my beloved. From this moment on, you shall always know what you feel, for you now possess your own heart which belongs not to you, but rather to all those with whom you share its contents or infinite wisdom. It shall be the cause of all your pain and, at the same time, be the source of all your joy. It will allow you to search the depths of your being without the fear of being overcome by its contents, as was your father who in his weakness succumbed to the madness of trying to live out the vision of another rather than the vision with which he had been entrusted at birth. Use it wisely my beloved, and it will serve you well—unwisely, and it will become a Pandora's Box."

And so did my asking her, what she was doing, help me to see that I had been living out the vision of another instead of my own, when she had asked me, in the past, what I was doing.

Before she could hand me the box, it slipped from her hands and fell to the floor, causing the lid to fly open and release its contents. In a brilliant flash of light, did the Spirit of Love, boxed up within my chest, all these years, burst forth and shower down upon the badlands of my being, where still reigned the Prince of Beasts. As this wasteland began to bear fruit again, I struggled to accept that part of my nature whose appetite for sex I still held in contempt.

That night I dreamed, I had finally found the door to heaven, when the lid to Jinny's box flew open to reveal all the love Instinct had imprisoned within my chest. As I worked my way through the maze of feelings that had overtaken me as I penetrated this narrow gate, I concluded that sexual intercourse is a ruse, Nature uses to propel a facsimile of one's self deep into the womb of one's imagination, to give flesh to a new awareness or amalgam of self and soul. Simply put, I had no idea, before now, that I could ever have found heaven on earth, much less within the very thing, I feared most.

Overall, I must say that I rather enjoyed this little stint in the brig. Having survived the rigors of an initiation into the Navy's own version of a frat house, the International Brotherhood of Brig Brats, I was pretty much left alone. Sent out during the day to perform menial tasks about either the brig or the base, I rather enjoyed the companionship of my soul who, if she could not be with me in body, due to her present condition, would at least strive to be with me in spirit.

She had such a knack for turning the humblest of tasks into the holiest, that my time in the brig flew by, ever so quickly. A staunch believer in hard work, she made it all seem like play. In her ability to find the most extraordinary things in the humdrum realities of everyday life, she never ceased to amaze me.

Once, when I balked at having to clean a particularly dirty toilet bowl, she convinced me in her own magical way, with imagery, that is, to look at it as a fish bowl that could stand a little cleaning. Having conned me into jumping into the task, she then took me on an underwater tour of one of the most beautiful lagoons I had ever seen. There, in the womb of my being, did she give me my first glimpse of the new awareness that had been taking shape over the past seven months. As I scrubbed away at the sides of the bowl, in the service of my fellow countrymen, she conscientiously scoured the quarters of this objection of mine for any fecal matter that might get in the way of a healthy birth, somewhere down the road, of an awareness of the greater objection I had to military service.

"I see your conscience has not yet developed," she complained, "to the extent that you can distinguish service to your fellow man from military service, as the latter still so overshadows the former with its self-serving brand of selflessness. Indeed, I see your objections to meeting the real needs of your fellow man as very small, when compared to the objections I have raised to your service in the military of the rich and powerful elite that runs your country. For it does so, without any regard whatsoever, for the vast number of lives it has squandered away on the most ambitious effort, ever undertaken by man, to satisfy the insatiable appetite of the god, he has made out of his self."

Then God spoke these words (from deep within my being): *"I am the Lord your God; you shall have no other gods before me. You shall not make for yourself an idol, whether in the form of anything that is in heaven above, that is on the earth below, or that is in the water under the earth. You shall not bow down to them or worship them; for I the Lord am a jealous God, punishing children for the iniquity of their parents, to the third and fourth generation of those who reject me, but showing steadfast love to the thousandth generation of those who love me and keep my commandments."* Ex. 20:1-6.

"In other words," explained my soul, "you must become Who You Really Are, and no other person. You must never make anything more out of your self, whether in thought, word, or deed, than who you really are. And at all costs, you must never inflate another person's view of himself nor emulate such false images of one's true Self, for it takes many generations to work out the damage—the confusion and hurt—one inflicts upon himself and his offspring when he chooses not to live out Who He Really Is. Instead, you must stand out as a beacon to him who has yet to find his way back home to Who He Really Is."

Through her did I find greater joy in doing the little things in life that needed to be done. How quickly I learned that it made little difference whether I did these things for my Self or for another, because deep down inside ourselves, she informed me, we are all the same person, in spite of our differences.

"These differences have been created," she went on to say, "to give you some idea of the breadth and depth of the one who inhabits you. Only, it is the little things you do for each other that help to mend the terrible rifts these differences foster, for in your shortsightedness, you-all tend to dwell on the qualities of the lesser, more adversarial image of man than on those of the greater, more Christlike. Real differences, like real individuals, tend to promote a unity of purpose that is impossible to beat, only because the visions of those who bear these differences meld with the one vision for all.

"As Cain overshadowed Able, so does the lesser man, the greater. Stalked by his animalistic past, man really has no other choice but to take the high road," concluded my soul, "if ever he wishes to escape the terrible fate of his ancestors or the unparalleled mass extinction of his own species, a self-inflicted punishment worthy of the crime of having despoiled this paradise, you call earth.

"Come now," she added. "Let us not tarry here too long with matters which do not concern us, for the day is drawing near when you will be asked again, to choose between me and the Great Gray Whore."

While the Navy failed to accomplish its stated goal, the return to duty of a better motivated and disciplined sailor, it did help me overcome the greatest obstacle I had yet to face before I could assume responsibility for my actions. With this experience of the brig, I no longer feared being locked up in a cell with no one else to turn to but the denizens of my own interior.

Why I had been so afraid, in the past, to be alone, had as much to do with my fear of soul as it did, my fear of the creative daimon in me, for time spent with either would invariably stir up a lot of sexual feelings, I was not quite sure how to handle. While I never knew for certain, at this point, whether the object of my lust was he, she or it, I did at least find my soul, a bit more accommodating than the creative daimon with whom I wrestled. For no matter how hard I tried, I could never pin him down. If he pinned me, then was I forced to play with the other member of my body on a very low level, in deed.

Having failed to make any friends while I was in the brig only exacerbated the problem. For in the past, I had found that I could meet some of the demands of my creative daimon in either of two ways, through vigorous physical exercise or the intensity of a quality relationship. Due to a constantly changing brig population, with varying lengths of stay for each prisoner, and the availability of anything more taxing than the tedium of busy work, I had a difficult time meeting the need for a more challenging outlet than wrestling with the other member of my body.

Once, before I was released from the brig, I caught sight of my creative daimon as he wrestled with the demonic side of himself on the floor of some dark, dank and dirty cell, hidden deep within the bowels of my being. There I could see that he was not a demon, but rather a human being whose body had gotten so encrusted with the piss and shit in which he wallowed, that he had actually taken on the appearance of a demon. Horrified by the state of this poor wretched creature, I watched as he beat the hell out of his demon, to get it to spit out its secret. Unable to look on any longer, I pulled my self out of the fantasy, in disgust, for I was not quite ready yet, to see just how low I had stooped in the past.

By the time it dawned on me that I was dealing with two different aspects of myself, I realized the dark figure with whom I'd been forced to wrestle, of late, was none other than my old adversary, Instinct, trying his damnedest to keep me from seeing the true nature of my creative daimon. No matter how hard I tried to pick up where the previous fantasy had left me, I could not find the cell in which Instinct was holding my creative daimon prisoner. So there I was, stuck in limbo—with one foot in heaven, the other in hell—after I had blown the only chance, I'd had, to reconcile soul with my creative daimon since returning to Oahu.

In my struggle to work through the confusion and hurt, I had left behind when I entered the brig, I received a letter from Mary, I found very reassuring.

"Remember," she wrote, *"this is Operation: Keep Butch Occupied So That He Won't Get Depressed."*

Only, I couldn't tell her the truth, that I had found heaven in such an obscure place as the brig. I couldn't bear the thought of being rejected for Who I Really Am. Besides, I had not come up with anything more conclusive than some ragtag bag of fantasies that were leading me in a direction contrary to conventional wisdom. In truth, I could only tell her what I thought she wanted to hear, that Peter Pan had elected to live out the Big Lie, the visions of others rather than his own.

While all was still not right in Paradise, I wooed the day my sexuality drove me from the slumber of never-never land, to penetrate the wall of illusion that enshrouds the truth of the Father in the images of the Mother, to create the tension needed to prod one into waking up to Who He Really Is. Only, I hated the pain that the tension to create a new life caused me. If I was not being driven to reunite my self with the Creator, then I was being forced to live out some semblance of the truth like any other beast. Because I did not care to live like an animal, I was hurt when I would be forced to do so in lieu of the ever-elusive truth of my being.

Through my dreams did I learn to distinguish one object of lust from another. If the Creator was after me to lend him a hand at putting His thoughts down on paper, I would find my self struggling in a dream, to fight off the sexual advances of my normally straight but very creative brother, Scott. If, on the other hand, I were being wooed to penetrate an image of the Great Mother to share Her gems of wisdom with another, then I would dream of having intercourse with some unknown woman. If, as was so often the case, I was being driven to release the tension that had built up along the fault line between the yin and yang aspects of my being, as the one slipped into the other to create consciousness, I would dream of ejaculating over and over, like a volcano, until the unknown content had been expressed. Thus did I come to the realization that this triune demiurge was driving me to give it some form of expression in the physical realm.

As I struggled with the tendency to take these images literally, I found my self playing more and more with the imaginal rather than the anatomical intrusions into my life. But I still could not see where these images were leading me. Having been forced by my own folly to wed the source of my fantasies, had I finally succeeded in turning my life over to a higher power than my self—to one of the holiest spirits I had ever met. For I just knew she was the only one who could help me free the more sapient man, tucked away somewhere in the back pages of my mind, within some long forgotten image of the first Homo erectus.

Awakened, one night shortly thereafter, by the sound of my own laughter, I watched that raw instinctive part of me, known as Homo erectus, chase down one nymph after another, only to have her evaporate right before his eyes and leave him holding onto his own lust. With that, I realized that I had been taking those images, which bore little resemblance to the true nature of my soul, far too seriously. To regain control of my senses, I had abandoned Homo erectus to begin the long trek northward, when I stumbled upon a clearing deep within the wood of my being where sat my soul wrapped, like a queen, in the flaming orange light of the very fire of life itself. As a small entourage of nymphs waited on her, hand and foot, I recognized, in the faces of these flickering flames, the face of every beauty into whose eyes I had ever looked, in my lust for a life of my own. Somewhere in the struggle to wriggle my self free of every flame who had tickled my gonads, I found my self rolling around on the ground of my being, tickled pink to have received such a spectacular insight into my life. From that day on, I knew, beyond the shadow of a doubt, that she was my life, whether I liked it or not, until death did part us from this modus vivendi.

"Psst," I heard her whisper in my ear as I dozed off to sleep.

"Come on, ya sleepyhead," she insisted. "Let's go play."

"In the middle of the night!" I exclaimed.

"There's a full moon tonight," she whispered spookily.

"I knew it," I proclaimed, from the moment I laid eyes on her, it was that time of the month when, beaming with the light of my interior, she was the most fertile, and I felt the strongest urge to penetrate the womb of my imagination.

"Come now," she insisted. "We haven't much time before you must rise and shine and give God your glory."

"Where are we going?" I asked.

"Deep into the wood of your being," she replied.

Instantly, I found my self struggling to keep up with her as she made her way through a thicket of dickweed to a tree that jutted from this little oasis like a gigantic palm tree. Following her lead, I grabbed hold of a vine, and began the difficult ascent into the small but dense, mushroom-shaped canopy of this great tree. Having reached the crown in record time, I paused to catch my breath, for there wasn't a thing I couldn't see from up here. Grabbing hold of her hand, I stopped her long enough to ask what tree this was.

"It's the Tree of the Knowledge of Good and Evil," she exclaimed ere plunging us both into the black hole in the crown of the tree.

"Touch me," she moaned as we fell into the dark wood of the tree.

As I embraced her, in a climactic turnaround were we hurled from the trunk of this great tree, at breakneck speed, towards the pudendum-like canopy of an even greater tree, the Tree of Life.

Looking down from the dizzying heights of this great tree, I saw myriads of people gathering round, from the farthest corners of the earth, to pay Life the respect due her.

"Choice is but a hollow tree," resounded the voice of this great tree, "to him who denies me. To him who embraces me, however, she is life everlasting. While *'he who has brought himself to naught for me discovers Who He Really Is'* (Mt. 10:39), she brings ruin to him who seeks his own self—denying the soul the right to life.

"Nourish each other, then, like the leaves on a great tree, and deprive no branch the right to a life of its own. Woe to you," she warned, "if a single leaf should fall from grace because of you. For you shall be, likewise, dropped from this tree to relive the cycle of life—to which you have condemned your brother—over and over, until your sin is purged from the tree of man. As Cain killed Able, so must you die to Instinct, the lesser man or self within you.

"Is not the I That Can See," she continued, "but he who can stand with one foot in heaven, the other in hell, and fall for neither image? Is not your task to free yourself from the schizophrenic split or tyranny of the opposites, that you might one day return to Paradise where lay the lion and the lamb side by side? And is not your goal, to seek out the one truth common to both images? Is not that the I Who Really Is?

"Yet you continue to rely on the blind eye of Instinct to get yourselves out of the mess you have made of me. You, who so pride yourselves on your ability to manipulate the images of the material world, cannot free the simplest truths about yourselves, from their imprisonment in Nature. In your passion for the truth, are you driven instead, with an eye for the instinctive, to seek satisfaction out there in Nature. Again and again do you turn to the same images of Nature, always with the underlying hope that you might one day look at her with the I that can see.

"To release the shaman trapped in the wood of this tree," she concluded, "the activities of the right hand must correspond with those of the left as well as with those from above and below the plane of existence. It is a very difficult task to accomplish, but worthy of him who would deign to bear such a primitive coat of arms as the cross of Christ."

Thus did I awaken, the following morning, to the realization that I was about to be expelled from Paradise for my transgressions against the nature of my being. As

I left the brig, after my release later that morning, I turned to see Michael assume his position as the invincible guardian over the Gates of Eden.

"See you in a few months," he said rather nonchalantly, as the vision vanished within the twinkling of his eye.

With that, did I trudge back to the ship on the heels of the master-at-arms who kept barking at me to hurry up.

"As far as I can see," complained the master-at-arms, "you haven't changed a lick, Dury, in the thirty days you've been gone."

"If only he knew what had transpired in the brig," I thought to myself, "he would not have given his self such a bad rap. Alas, he cannot see with the I That Can. He cannot see that the fault, bedeviling him, lies within himself rather than with me, for he has not changed a bit since I last saw him.

"Ah, but I am the great scapegoat," proclaimed I to the world from the depths of my being. "I am all that is wrong with every lifer onboard this ship, only because I reflect what is truly wrong with this way of life. As the devil's advocate, I am, in reality, the mirror into which they are forced to look upon their own ugly reflections."

"For the I That Can See is just as transparent as the looking glass through which it sees," claimed my mentor, once when we were seated around the fire of my heart's desires.

In his unwavering fondness for the I That Can See, Marty was the only one on the ship who had not emotionally distanced himself from what I stood for, while I was in the brig. A welcome sight, he knew, in his own uncanny way, just how much the I That Can See needed the acceptance of another human being, for no other reason than to verify that I did indeed stand for something very real.

Feeling the need to consult my faculties, that night I sought out the counsel of my old mentor as we sat around the fire of my heart's desires at the mouth of the tunnel of vision where, according to him, my forefathers have met with him since the beginning of time.

"Having made all of the arrangements for your wedding and subsequent honeymoon in the Naval Station Brig at Pearl Harbor," admitted my mentor as I sat there staring into the fire that burned within, "I was quite pleased with your response to my attempt to get you going again, in the right direction with your life. However, I would like to share a few insights you overlooked while you were in heaven, under the tutelage of my daughter, your soul.

"Keep in mind, my son," continued my mentor, "that it is the nature of the beast to look for soul, as long as she remains unknown, within the faces of those flames which ignite, in you, the desire for unity with her. In her desperation for union with you, is she forced to rely upon the sexual appeal of Beauty, to get your attention. Until you learn to differentiate your soul from the pack, you will be driven to seek those aspects of her, of which you are still unaware, in the faces of those who embody what you find so attractive. Regardless of how you feel, you must never give body to the attraction itself, as it will prove fatal to your well-being. If you must, you may only give body to the woman who embodies your soul—the one, in other words, whom you take from the real world to be your wife until in death you do part. At all costs, my son, must you avoid the pitfall of so many of the men of your age, into a fatal attraction.

"Where, then, is one to find a life of his own but on the cutting edge of man's advancement toward the goal of finding out Who He Really Is, for is not the life of a tree found only in the new growth?

"And what is death, but the laying down of one's life, or the shedding of one's former selves for this new growth, like the dead wood or vainglorious leaves of a deciduous tree.

"Is not she, whom you seek, the sum of all the truths—rather than of the objects themselves—hidden within the material things of the world? Why, then, do you fall for such fatal attractions? Is not that which you truly seek the growth of the Spirit instead of the gross national product? Are not the material things of this world and those who seek them, the dead wood of the tree that must give way to this new growth? Why, then, do you continue to shed your life, year after year, for the dead wood of this tree? Seek ye instead, that which will endure forever. Give body to the truth of your being, to Who You Really Are.

"Within the wood of your family tree lies hidden a cross that has weighed heavily upon your forefathers, as it waited for he who would arise from the dead wood of the tree to bear, once again, the full weight of this coat of arms. Having succumbed to the bent of the elder members of your family tree, after it had lost its left arm and head board to atrophy, had this cross fallen upon your father, crushing him in the process. Limited to the overextended growth of its right arm into the world of the intellect, had the root of this tree firmly planted itself in the ground of your being, giving rise to an offshoot that is destined to bear the full weight of the cross. Thus did the lot fall upon the shoulders of a young sapling like you, to develop a healthier relationship to this insightful old coot, his bleeding-heart daughter and her guardian—the shadow of your senses.

"Until you learn the truth about the shadow of your senses," concluded my mentor, "you will remain forever at the mercy of Instinct. For you have yet to unearth the foot of this cross from the ground of your being, so that you may function, once again, as a whole tree instead of one that has been cut off from its roots."

With the flickering out of the last flame of the fire, he disappeared, leaving behind a few smoldering embers to enkindle the fire of my unquenchable thirst for knowledge, the next time we should meet.

With the twenty-fifth day of December looming upon the horizon, I was invited to Greg's place to celebrate not so much the birth of Christ as our return from the edge of the Great Abyss, with our humanity still intact. Unlike the other members of this small coterie of Cro-Magnon men, I was the only one who had turned to his imagination without using drugs. Having stumbled on Peter Pan's secret, I had only to become like a little child again, to enter the Kingdom. Through these flights of fantasy, had I learned to use the power of my Peter, or creative self, to penetrate Pan's nightmarish world without having to act like an animal, one day, and a god, the next.

After a sumptuous meal, consisting of booty taken from the officer's pantry back onboard the ship, by those who had access, I watched the others drift off, on the smoke rings of their minds, in search of what they knew not. Whether these chemically induced encounters produced anything more than an orgasmic high, I never knew for certain, as they were reluctant to share their experiences with a nonuser like me. Although they seemed to have stumbled upon the chemical equivalent of the right touch that releases one from the inhibitions, which prevent one from experiencing such orgasmic encounters, I nonetheless felt their pain. Only, I suffered not their fate, the anguish of an uninvited guest who knows not when he will be tossed out on his ear with nothing more than the memory of what might have been, had he listened to the admonition of the father of the bride, to dress for the occasion.

Before he got stoned out of his mind Sleepy approached me that evening, with the troubling news he had received earlier, in a letter from the prostitute, he had fucked while our ship was docked in Subic Bay.

"She's pregnant with my kid," he soberly stated, for he obviously had some feelings for the young lady other than her just having been another good fuck.

"How do you know if it's your child?" I asked.

"She told me, in the letter, that I was the only one she had fucked since her last period," he replied.

"How do you know if she's telling you the truth?" I inquired further.

"She'd never lie to me," he informed me with the utmost certainty.

With raised eyebrows, I scratched my head. "Well then, what are you going to do?" I asked.

"I'll probably send her some money," he responded.

"Do you love her, Sleepy?" I inquired.

"I like her, but not enough to marry her," he said of his affair.

While I had to give him credit for giving the plight of this poor prostitute any consideration at all, I wondered how many other women who, like her, had gotten pregnant after whoring around with a GI. I wondered, too, how many of the other guys on the ship had been made aware of the consequences of their actions, and had been driven, like Sleepy, to assume some responsibility for the child they had foolishly fathered. As I wondered how many other kids were being born of these illicit unions, I realized that many of them would be branded as outcasts and treated as half-breeds, when Sleepy commented about how funny his kid would look if it only inherited his freckles and flaming red hair, and took the rest of its features from its mother.

Driven by Nature to recreate the one truth that would end all of the division and separation the opposites have brought us, we reject the outcome of such unions, in our inability to let go of the half-truths that we embody. For we have been told, again and again from the bully pulpit, that Christ's *"mission is to spread, not peace, but division"*. Mt. 10:34.

"Do not suppose that my mission on earth is to spread peace," He tells us, *"for I have come to set a man at odds with his father, a daughter with her mother, a daughter-in-law with her mother-in-law: in short, to make a man's enemies those of his own household."* Mt. 10:34-36.

"In other words," proclaimed my mentor from somewhere across the void, "he who will not deal with the problem of good and evil within himself, and seek its solution in consciousness, is not worthy of eternal life. Whoever loves the half-truths, his father or mother, son or daughter embody, is not worthy of the truth that encompasses them all, for Consciousness has come to set a man at odds with the attitudes of his father, a daughter, with those of her mother: in short, to make a man's enemies, the very attitudes within his own head. And while he who responds like a beast brings ruin upon himself, he who seeks Consciousness discovers Who He Really Is—that he is much more than the summation of all the attitudes that he has acquired from those who have had a hand in his formation."

"Well, *God said to Abraham, 'Kill me a son',"* rang out this raspy, nasally sounding voice from the recorder playing in the next room.
"Abe said, 'Man, you must be puttin' me on.'
God said, 'No.'
Abe said, 'What!'
God said, 'You can do what you want.'
Abe fucked up.
'Next time you see me comin', you better run.'
'Well,' Abe said, 'where you want this killin' done?'
God said, 'Out on Highway 61.'" [1]

"How readily do the fathers of your land sacrifice the lives of their sons for the half-truths they embody," mused my mentor.

"Because your countrymen have withheld their sons from Me," rang out the voice of the Lord Most High, "I will take from among their sons not one life less than the number they have denied Me. I will inflict upon those left behind, a wound that shall not heal. I will split *'father against son and son against father, mother against daughter and daughter against mother'* (Lk. 12:53), brother against brother and sister against sister, and a man against his own soul and his soul against himself, until the truth about this war shall be known."

"Don't you see, my son," continued my mentor, "that it is the nature of Consciousness to polarize you-all around the truth, like iron filings in a magnetic field. Because mankind uses his left hand to pick the fruit that upsets the apple cart or status quo, Consciousness causes the left to look like the bad guy, and the right or moral majority, the good guy. Whenever the left exercises this freedom, Consciousness quickly brings it to loggerheads with the might of the right, its law and order—that vast warehouse of what the moral majority has established over time as right. In their repulsion for each other's point of view, Consciousness drives them apart until, behaviorwise, you cannot tell them apart. At that point, Consciousness outflanks the rank and file entrenched behind the Maginot Line of their extremist points of view. As more of the unentrenched are repelled by the extremism of either camp, Consciousness draws upon the disaffected, and in a flip-flop, reunites the two sides, like the opposite poles of a magnet, behind a broader view of the truth, consisting of some form of both points of view. In other words, Consciousness maintains one's right to choose so long as such a choice denies not the soul the right to life.

"Don't you see, my son," concluded my mentor, "why you and your shipmates are being driven to reunite your selves with the very souls or ways of life, the military machine—that has overtaken your country—has denied you. It is the choice to become a card carrying Martian for those who have capitalized on the invasion of this alien god, that has denied the soul a life of her own and sent you on the warpath against your brothers to the west, as if they were the culprit. Until East meets West, and the two become as one again, so shall this rift fester in the psyche of mankind, and afflict him with the scourges of the Four Horsemen of the Apocalypse—war, famine, pestilence, and death."

"*I ain't gonna work* for the Great Gray Whore *no more*," pelted out the poet in that same raspy, ole nasally, singsong tone of voice from somewhere across the void. "*No, I ain't gonna work* for the Great Gray Whore *no more*.

"Well, I wake up in the mornin', hold my hands, and pray for rain. I got a head full of ideas that are drivin' me insane. It's a shame the way she makes me scrub the floor.

"Aw, *I ain't gonna work* for the Great Gray Whore *no more*."

Having been stimulated by the insights of my mentor and the words of the poet, to begin thinking for myself, was I left standing alone, outside, wrapped in the mantle of a starlit sky. Like some great wizard who has just released the thoughts of heaven from their imprisonment in nature, had I stumbled upon the magic of free association. Having been encouraged by them to express everything I knew about a certain content of consciousness, without censorship or control, did I finally acquire an awareness of the innate ability of man to gain access to the processes of his own unconscious nature, by reporting the first thought that comes to mind in response to the stimulus initially given.

"I ain't gonna work for the Great Gray Whore *no more,"* interjected the poet again, in that same monotonous tone of voice. *"I ain't gonna work* for the Great Gray Whore *no more.*
"Well, I try my best, to be just like I Am. But everybody wants you, to be just like them. They say sing while you save; and I just get bored.
"Aw, I ain't gonna work* for the Great Gray Whore *no more."* [2]

Because I had not yet found the truth that could emotionally rather than sexually stimulate me to act, I felt like half a man. Though the feminine side of my nature—that triumvirate of emotions, feelings and values which comprise the soul—had suffered under the tyranny of my stepfather, I had not let the ogre so completely destroy my image of her that I could ever have taken the life of another human being, simply because I had lost my own. Having learned from my mentor, that he who has found his way has no need to take the life of another, since he already possesses life eternal, I now understood why so many of my contemporaries were killing each other off, at such an alarming rate. Clearly, I saw the haves as the ogre responsible for this carnage. If the haves, in their relentless pursuit of a life beyond their wildest expectations, had not taken from the have-nots the life one needs to transform the beastly side of one's nature, the have-nots would never have followed their example to prey upon each other—the remains of life at the bottom of this cruel pyramid scheme—like little ogres. Having seen this ogre as the negative pole around which every other hate and prejudice gravitated, had I gotten into the habit of destroying the monster and its cronies whenever they showed up in my house with their ugly faces. Only, I still had not penetrated the ogre's defenses surrounding my own masculine identity and its relationship to the feminine pole of my being—those parts of my nature which could ultimately free me from having to act like an animal, one day, and a god, the next.
Whenever I retreated within, at the beck and call of the poet—or rode off, like some *cowboy angel*, on my great white steed to resolve yet another thorny con-

flict—I encountered a truth I have found nowhere else, *except when neath the trees of Eden*. Urged to obey only those truths that connect one to the ground of his being, from which all truth springs to life—through the chinks in one's armor—like a newborn babe, without censorship or control, I now understood why, for him who believed that *no sound ever comes from the Gates of Eden*, so much of its eloquent poetry fell upon deaf ears. Only, I pitied the poor bloke who, in his savage pursuit of heaven on earth, has never learned to communicate with his soul in any other manner than sexual intercourse, or who, like some misguided Aladdin, has never turned to the lamp of his imagination for anything more lasting than the promise of paradise to which material possessions only allude. Rather than wait, like a condemned man, for those whom we have empowered with our lives to decide my fate, had I opted to bring my life into harmony with the One Voice that continued to pour its heart out to me—from behind the Gates of Eden—with such passion and authority, as I had never before experienced. Having overstepped the bounds of conventional wisdom with my marriage to Jinny, had I caused the lesser man within us all to cry foul *to wicked birds of prey* waiting in the background to pick up on these *breadcrumb sins* of mine, even though I had done nothing wrong in the eyes of God. As I watched these paupers waste their lives, *the kingdoms of experience and the precious winds* that bring them to us, on exchanging possessions—*each one wishing for what the other has got*—I discovered, later on, in a discussion with my soul around what is real and what is not, that *it doesn't matter inside the Gates of Eden,* where what is not real, simply does not exist. Forced to watch my friends as they tried to escape their fates and leave themselves *wholly totally free to do anything they wished to do but die* to the instinctive eye that forever squints upon a way of life that was never theirs, I longed for life behind the Gates of Eden where *there are no trials*. As they got lost in their dreams, *with no attempts to shovel a glimpse into the ditch of what each one means,* I wondered, with the poet, if there were any *words but these to tell what's true—and there are no truths outside the Gates of Eden.* [3]

"In other words," interjected the Old Indian, "there are no truths outside the myths of the imagination, to which mankind can turn when he has strayed too far from the ground of his being—where little distinction is made between the images of She Who Must Be Obeyed and the poetry of He Who Really Is. For is it not in terms of the visible, or this poetry in motion, that mankind comes to understand the invisible?

"Toward this task," continued my mentor, "has modern man only succeeded in bringing down the gods from Mt. Olympus, to idolize in those whom he has raised to such stature. Like the Greeks of antiquity, has he fashioned these gods out of incomplete images of himself. In his inability to see what truly makes a man great in the eyes of the One Who Really Is, has he made these individuals—the lesser man rather than the greater—the center of his universe. Thus far has man failed to recognize Who He Really Is whenever this God manifests Himself in those who elect to expend their lives on the greater man or community of mankind rather than on themselves. Instead, has he taken on the image of a lesser god, with its limited sense of right and wrong, as a more attainable goal than becoming Who He Really Is. Like any true red-blooded Olympian, he has found it far easier to take the life of another than to give up his own, in the struggle to meet the American dream's absurd goal of providing an Olympian way of life for all when, in reality, the earth can barely sustain those who have already attained this perversion of immortality.

"Since Nature must be obeyed, one way or the other, as an unconscious animal or as a conscious human being, man goes wild whenever he chooses to live out the concrete realities of his dreams rather than their meaning. When those who have attained immortality in this life—who have reached the summit of Mt. Olympus or apex of the pyramid—are driven wild by their insatiable hunger for the truth, these predatory beast-gods go after everything with unbridled greed. In their lust for the truth still imprisoned within the objective world, these rich and unscrupulous demi-gods either turn on their own people and feed off the less fortunate via insider trading and leveraged buyouts, or they create another war and go after easier prey. Driven by their addiction for more of what will never satisfy their need to possess the truth, these velociraptors breed rapidly, once they have freed themselves from the conventional restraints of their own civilized veneer, setting off an epidemic of wilding—the taking of what does not belong to them. How quickly does it infect the mass of mortal men at the bottom of the pyramid who, after having been robbed of the means to simply live, are then forced to either prey upon the neighbor next door or abroad, or physically and psychologically starve to death.

"The greater the crime of the gods—or disparity between their *grandiose materialist dreams* and the opportunities afforded those at the bottom of the pyramid—the wilder will that generation of men, and those who succeed it, grow. For wild beasts, whether mortal or immortal, only beget wilder beasts as they infect the social fabric of their society, like a virus. As *one dangerous person can make a community wild, by bringing on aggression, violence and a fortress mentality, so can a particularly competitive salesperson or executive turn a whole office into a jungle, since those who do not follow suit and sharpen their own swords may be left sundered in the dust. As neighborhoods and families erode under the weight of extreme economic hardship, kids who lack the security to care about anyone but themselves disrupt schools and workplaces, and create even more unstable families of their own. Thus do wilders weaken economic institutions and communities* which, *in turn, only produce new wilders*, in a *vicious and self-perpetuating cycle.*

"To stop and root out this epidemic," concluded my mentor, *"requires a vision and a passion for change that can arise only by coming fully to terms with the specter that haunts [4] you."*

With the setting of the I That Can See, was I left standing in an open field beneath the instinctive eye of a full moon, one that can shed light on the darkest nights of the soul, so long as the instinct being investigated does not cloud its vision. Overcome by my own instinct to survive, was I transformed into the haunting specter of a wolfman who could think of nothing, at that point, but himself and his own survival.

"Me, me, me," hollered the demons that dwelt therein.

"Look after number one," echoed the voices from on high.

With that, I understood why I was driven, on occasion, to behave like half a man. In the past, I had only to act as some egocentric canine or self-conscious humanoid, devoid of any feeling, to satisfy my broken nature. Now, I was being asked to act like both man and wolf, only I did not know how, just yet.

However, I did understand why we are driven to our excesses, for that is where Instinct still holds prisoner Who We Really Are.

"Until you and your countrymen," interjected my mentor, "recognize the pursuit of wealth, beyond the means one needs to live simply, as an insidiously evil way of life, to be pursued by no man, you will continue to condemn a number of your brethren to a hellishly mean existence, as a result of your stinginess. In your failure to use your talents to help pull them from the depths of the hell to which you have condemned them, you will continue to condemn yourselves to the same hellish fate in the hereafter—to an eternity of living like the animal, you have become.

"While you are certainly a god, in every sense of the word," concluded my mentor, "you are also an animal. If you neglect to live out the truths hidden within your own animalistic tendencies, like Sisyphus, will you be thwarted every time you try to mount the summit of your being, or claim mastery over yourself in the guise of any other god than Who You Really Are. In the age yet to come, shall you be remembered as the Prometheus of your time, as the one who stole the truth right out from underneath the gods who sit on it in an effort to maintain their inhumane hold on mankind. So too, shall you become known as the lone wolf who resisted the pressure of the pack to indulge in the animal side of its nature, that it could, instead, lead you up the mountain of evolution towards the truth and immortality of your being."

Thus did I come to see the animal side of my nature as both a help and a hindrance to my own personal growth. While I often took pride in this newly won ability of mine to pursue another course of action than the instinctive inclinations of an animal, I quickly realized that the freedom to choose rested entirely upon my willingness to seek and live out the truth inherent to that animal behavior, the god within me sought to overcome. A casualty of the internecine warfare between the gods of Mt. Olympus and the beasts that inhabited my body, I had assumed, like any good trooper who had fought for the gods in those days, that my body was the enemy when, all along, it was the gods, with their condescending attitudes toward the body, who were my worst enemy. Even though I had risen above some of the savagery of my animal past, I still had a long way to go before I could ever lay claim to my own immortality. Having learned the hard way that I was neither a god nor an animal, but rather an equal measure of both, I quickly realized I had better start making friends with the lower half of my nature if ever I wished to bring peace and harmony back to this humble abode of mine. Unwillingly, at first, did I come to befriend the wolf within me.

Because the wolf was all white, like the White Knight, I tended to associate him with Michael, for like my shadow, he had an uncanny way of sniffing out the truth whenever I got lost in the wood of my being—or in those areas of my life to which I had never given any thought. In his never-ending search for the truth that would satisfy his appetite, the wolf could pick up the scent of a distant prey or vague notion, and in a series of rapid associations, as he assessed and reassessed the flood of data streaming toward him, hone in on his quarry in no time flat. On other occasions, he might not catch up with his prey for some time, especially if the data was scant and led him off in the wrong direction. Or he might even lose the trail of his quarry, and have to start all over again, or at least let off hunting for the truth in this area for lack of anything remotely true foraging around in the vicinity of his last hunch. Though he might have to wait awhile before anything more nourishing than a rodent of an idea came along, if he was patient, he would eventually find what I had been looking for. No longer was the wolf within me at odds with the Man That I Am, the White Knight that embodied my own immortal thoughts, for we were all three one again, wolf-man-god.

Now I understood why I was so driven, at times, to think only of my self, my own survival or immortality, as that is how I arrived at the truth of my being. For I was being encouraged to rub the lamp of my imagination—rather than the other member of my body—to enlist the aid of the genie contained therein, or Who I Really Am, to arouse my self from the Big Sleep or evil reign of Instinct over my soul. To free this genie from its imprisonment in Nature, I had only to wish that I could live my life in the name of the Father, and of the Son and of the Holy Spirit, or in other words, in the name of the god, and of the man and of the very soul or spirit of the beast I am. I had only to seek and live out Who I Really Am rather than some puffed up image so far removed from the ground of my being that I am forever driven to act like the beast I have rejected in my haste to embrace the immortality of the gods on Mt. Olympus.

"Is not the essence or soul of the beast the very map you seek, to help you locate the treasure of your own immortality?" Asked my mentor. "Seek then to understand the symbols on the map, lest you be led astray by its images—a language that had been given to mankind long before Instinct had run amok of the Creator's plans to awaken man from the Big Sleep, via the experiences of the imaginal realm rather than of the instinctive world."

Having taken me twenty years to come to a fuller understanding of the language of my body, I shuddered at the thought of the cataclysmic events in my life that had precipitated my return to the isle of my Self, for the healing I needed. Had I not been hardened by the constant threat of a volcanic eruption along the fault between the upper and lower echelons of my being, I would never have withstood the shake-up that finally broke the backbone of my resistance to the new way of life the Creator and his beloved Holy Spirit had created for me. Once I got my life back in order though, I sincerely hoped, like Job, I would be healed of any affliction or impairment I had suffered in the physical realm as a result of the years of wear and tear such an inappropriate life'd had upon my body.

Alas, the rightful heir, or God-man, had not yet assumed the throne upon which Instinct still sat in his evil reign over the kingdom that was once his, for too much of Who I Really Am still remained hidden from me, in the outback of my being.

O, how I did long for the King's return—the return of Order, Consciousness and Love to this humble abode of mine.

"Well by this time," observed the poet from his own point of view, *"I was fed up at tryin' to make a stab at bringin' back any help for my friends and Captain Ahab. I decided to flip a coin about either heads or tails—would let me know if I should go back to ship or back to jail. So I hocked my sailor suit and I got a coin to flip. It came up tails, reminded me of sails, so I made it back to the ship."* [5]

Having grown weary of trying to free my faculties and this recalcitrant self of mine from their imprisonment in nature, I flipped a coin and decided to go back to ship instead of jail when it came up tails and reminded me of sails. For this association, with the instinctive way of life that still held my true persona in hock, was the only one that made any sense to me, at the time.

With Marty having pulled duty and Greg and the others indulging in the ever-increasing use of marijuana, I found my self wandering alone down Waikiki Beach on New Year's Eve, 1967. And as I trudged through the sand with the weight of the world on my shoulders—the sound of the surf pounding in one ear, and auld lang syne, in the other—I freaked out when I heard the roar of a wave that could drown the whole world. Grabbing hold of my ears, to drown out the din of death as I ran down the beach, deserted now, by even the sun, I screamed out in my anguish over the darkness that had befallen me. Blinded by my own salty tears, I lost my footing in the loose sand and tumbled over onto my back, where I lay until I cried my self to sleep.

Awakened shortly thereafter, by the sweet caresses of my soul, I knew of no other who could ease the pain of a shipwrecked sailor, marooned on the isle of his Self, than she who, like Penelope, had awaited the return of her other half from his twenty-year odyssey. Had I known then, what I do now, that this sweet dove was she whom I really sought, I would never have turned my attention back to the home of my youth and the flame that burned there brightly, in the likes of Mary—to a paradise lost, in other words. For I could not let go of her long enough to see that she was but the doorway to a deeper reality, that life is but a journey up a mountain of images that must be washed to the sea before one can safely rest behind the Gates of Eden. Nonetheless, I wanted to go back home where, oddly enough, lay the key to the long sought-after answer to the question of why I wanted out of the Navy so badly.

With the passing of one of the most horrendously difficult and yet incredibly wonderful years of my life, I flipped that imaginary coin in my head, which came up tails again. Reminding me of sails, I made it back to the ship.

Having completed most of the first year of my enlistment, under anything but ideal conditions, I was granted permission to take thirty days leave on 6 January, just one month to the day shy of my anniversary date. I felt torn when I learned my soul could not accompany me back to the mainland, due to the possibility of her going into labor any day now. Having bade Marty and the gang back on the ship farewell, I nonetheless made my way over to Hickham Air Force Base with her at my side, or in other words, with much apprehension.

"What if something would happen while I am gone!" I declared. "I could never forgive my self for having left you here alone."

"I'll be fine," she insisted, "whether you are here or not, for you have a much more important task to perform, that ultimately concerns the survival of both me and the child if you fail to find the key to the Gates of Eden, or your own happiness, before we fade away."

"What do you mean?" I shot back.

"I mean this," she went on to say, "that we will not be here when you return, if you fail to make the connection between your world and ours, or give us the reality we so desperately need to survive."

"I still don't understand," I insisted.

"Unless you give us the means," she reiterated, "or body to live out Who You Really Are, we will be driven underground by Instinct, to operate through unconscious channels from the animal side of your nature, until conditions in your life become more conducive to our gaining the strength we would need to rise again, into conscious view. We can no longer allow you to sit idly by while we entertain you with fantasies. Though you have made great strides in participating more fully in your fantasies, we feel it is about time you make the same concerted effort to live them out, one way or the other, in real life.

"The choice is yours," she concluded. "Either you work with us willingly or unwillingly. If you fail to unearth the vital link with reality, we so desperately need to survive, upon your return, you will simply find that neither the child nor I have survived the birth."

With that did she disappear, leaving me in a real stew.

"What a wonderful way to begin a vacation," I thought to my self as I embarked upon the single most important archaeological dig of my life.

11

Paradise Regained

Forced by a lack of sufficient funds to rely on the mercy of the military to get me back to the mainland, I managed, after a brief wait—in military parlance—of several hours, to land a seat for next to nothing, on an old turboprop destined for San Bernardino, California. There I hoped to catch, without any further delay, another flight out, at military standby, for my hometown of St. Louis, Missouri. As slowly as this thing took to the air, I was prompted to make a slight readjustment in my expectations of getting back to the mainland any sooner than I had originally anticipated. With nothing in the walls of this airship, but skin and bones to protect me from the cooler temperatures outside its body, or insulate me from the incessant screaming of this pterodactyl's engines, I found my flight from paradise to be anything but ideal. Having been left with no other choice but an aisle seat, I flopped down beside the only person towards whom I had felt any affinity, a young corporal named John Doe. As this mighty old bird swung up and around, toward the mainland, in a laborious effort to gain the altitude it would need to make the journey, I caught my last glimpse of paradise through the porthole beside which he sat.

Having managed to survive the killing fields of Vietnam without physical injury to himself, had he nonetheless incurred the deeper wounds of a house divided against itself. Tormented by his participation in the blood bath that war is, he suffered the same inability to leave behind the memories of the past year as they welled up in the tears that burst forth like the long-awaited thundershower that can no longer hold back from clearing the air of the dirt around which its droplets have formed. Sequestered from the other passengers, by the sheer noise of its engines, did my friend open up to me like a repentant sinner in a confessional.

"Forgive me, Father, for I have sinned," I thought I heard him say as he began to unload the memories that haunt those who have been forced, against the better judgment of their souls, to murder their fellow man, in the name of the god and country or warlord back home in whose service they have enlisted.

"I don't know how you felt," he confessed, "when you got back from Nam. I was so goddamn glad to have gotten my ass outta there in one piece, that no sooner had I hit land than I fell down on my hands and knees, and kissed the earth as if she were my own mother. And I would've hugged her too, had I been able to get my arms around her. For I felt as if I had freed myself of the monster I'd created over in Nam, until this Frankenstein came creepin' back to haunt me.

"For almost a year," he went on to say between fits of sobbing and outrage, "have I been forced to live like an animal, slitherin' about the jungles of Southeast Asia on its belly, never knowin', from one moment to the next, whether or not it'd survive the hunt. As both the hunter and the hunted, I played the deadliest game of all, the survival of the fittest, killin' other human beings—even women and children— before they killed me. Like a beast, I trusted no one but the members of my pack and the gods back home, for whom I fought, that they might retain their dominion over the monsters they'd made outta me and my cohorts in crime.

"Havin' made a pact with the devil, early on, I traded lives with the other members of my pack, that I too might live as long as the gods back home. For unlike the Audie Murphys and John Waynes, I held back to let the daredevils take the fall. As the face of my squad changed, with the death of one after another of these poor fools, I imagined I was next in line to die. I must've died a thousand deaths before I was released from this firestorm of bullets, for every time I watched one of these unsung heroes die, oddly enough, I saw a part of myself die..."

[Having succumbed to the sudden swell of a ringing sound in my ears, I found my self standing outside my body, looking a bit like the Lilliputian who first discovered Gulliver's ponderous body lying shipwrecked on the isle of his Self. As I stood back to take in the full magnitude of my body, I thought I spied the earth instead, from which I saw a great body of land rise up, like a spirit from its own grave. As this formless mass took on the mantle that normally cloaked the earth, I beheld a great and holy spirit, a woman of magnificent beauty.

"Who're you?" I asked as I bent down on my knee and bowed my head in response to some inner urging to pay my respects to the remains of this aspect of the Original Being.

"I am She Who Must Be Obeyed, the Great and Holy Spirit you seek—the Eve of your manhood," She unabashedly proclaimed.

"How might I best serve thee, O Wisdom?" I begged to know.

"You must put an end to this abuse of my body by you and your fellow countrymen," She demanded.

"And what abuse is that?" I asked, as if I didn't already know.

"Look!" She commanded as She opened Her mantle to reveal the most hideous scenes of man's perversion of paradise, I had ever seen.

Passing out, I came to, back on the airship, just in time to pick up where I had left my companion amidst the more sordid details of his life.]

"...Seein' 'em get their hands and feet, or arms and legs, blown to smithereens after havin' touched off a booby trap or land mine, I'd crawl up to their sides to comfort them as any mother would, an injured child. As I washed their faces clean with my own tears, I'd watch the life, I held onto so dearly, ebb with the blood that flowed from their broken bodies to mingle, once again, with the mother of us all. O, how often did I hear them cry out to their mothers as I hugged and rocked their tremblin' bodies back to sleep, only this time, forever.

"O, how often did I, like the king's men of old, labor in vain to put these poor eggs back together—to stuff their bloody guts back into their bodies before they ceased to exist as men and assumed some lower or higher form of life dependin' on how they had lived out this one..."

[As I honed in on the shrill sound of a woman in labor, screaming out to me from across the void, I recognized the woman's voice as that of my soul. At the crowning moment, I lost sight of the birth of this little objection of mine to military service, as our plane hit a pocket of turbulence and dropped me from the vision.]

"...Angered at the loss of yet another member of my platoon," continued the corporal, "I'd go wild with hate, killin' as many gooks as I could to avenge this death and assuage my fear of dyin' if I didn't start kickin' ass before Charlie kicked mine. Until I saw a pregnant gook, I had mowed down in one of my rages, get shot in the head by another member of my squad, *'to put the fuckin' bitch out of her misery'* as she lay there on the ground beggin' me, with an outstretched hand, to help her, I never realized what a beast I had become. From that day on, I hated the beast within me.

"But I never got a good look at the true nature of the beast until some time later when, in the heat of a skirmish with Viet Cong guerrillas, this massive gook pops up out of nowhere with an AK-47 in both hands, and starts mowin' us all down like flies. Pinned down by the fire of both friend and foe, I lay there under the cover of a thicket of tall grass like a dead man, waitin' for the big ape to come chargin' by, so that I might rise up with a fixed bayonet and drop the fucker before the motherfucker kicked our sorry asses. Havin' expended my last clip, I could do no more than play possum and hope like hell the son of a bitch would fall for it. As the last few guys in my squad riddled the fucker with round after round, I couldn't imagine what was keepin' the motherfucker goin', till I looked up and saw that shit-eatin' grin on the fucker's face, at which point the asshole toppled over on me and died. Drenched in blood, I struggled to get out from underneath the son of a bitch so I could see what manner of man or beast this was. Confronted by that same shit-eatin' grin when I rolled the fucker over, I knew this was no mere mortal lyin' here, but rather the very beast that inhabited my own body. As I realized that too many people have died at the hands of the motherfucker, I grew to hate the beast even more..."

[At that point, I found my self standing beneath the cross of Christ as the soldier thrust his lance into Jesus' side. Drenched in blood and water, I saw the final act in the annihilation of the body of mankind, as we know it today. And I realized that man was to have a hand in bringing about an end to his own earthly existence. What manner of man was to come afterwards I hardly recognized, at first, since this new man looked so different than the Neanderthals who had previously stalked the earth and ruled over her with such an iron hand.

"Now the whole group" of this new race of men *"was of one heart and soul, and no one claimed private ownership of any possessions, for everything they owned was held in common. With great power"* did those, who had become Who They Really Are, give testimony to the rise and fall of the first born of this new species of man, *"and great grace was upon them. There was not a needy person amongst them, for as many as owned lands or houses sold them, brought the proceeds of what was sold, and laid it at the feet"* of the first born of this new species, from whence *"it was distributed to each as any had need."* Acts 4:32-35.]

"...Havin' regained my senses," he added, "I realized I was gonna survive this hellhole, for no other reason than to tell my story. From then on, I shot at imaginary enemies. For I would much rather have died than take the life of yet another human being..."

[As he recalled an incident in which one of his buddies was blown to kingdom come while trying to rescue a baby that'd been booby-trapped by its own family, which now lay dead, all around it, inside a hut his companions were preparing to torch, I heard a woman scream out from somewhere across the void, as she labored to give birth.

Then, I saw two eyes pierce the darkness that envelops the mind. Through them I could see that all I had to offer this troubled troubadour were the insights they had given me, to help ease the pain the incomprehensible causes one to experience in its prodding of the ignorant to become conscious of themselves.

With that, I turned just in time to see a fountain of lava burst forth from a fissure in the ground swell that had created this little bump in the road. Having regurgitated the half-digested body of a red and white frog—or about half the story of the struggle between the upper and lower echelons of my being—I witnessed the birth of something far greater than I could ever have imagined, a work of art of indescribable beauty.]

"...That's when I saw her," proclaimed the corporal.

"Saw who?" I blurted out as I was pulled back into his world at the mere mention of her.

"As I held 'm close," claimed the corporal before his buddy died, "I was taken aback when he reached out to his mother instead. Looking up, I saw this woman standin' there, all decked out in the magnificence of the earth's mantle. As the spirit of my friend left his body, I saw her pick up a little boy who'd fallen while playing soldiers with the other boys in the neighborhood. Dumbfounded, I watched the little boy grow younger and younger, until he was but a mere babe in her arms. With that, she disappeared, I was made to believe, to deposit this new life in the womb of a mother close by, where it'd be given another chance to break the endless cycle of livin' 'n' dyin' like an animal, only this time, from a very different point of view."

"So that's what purgatory looks like," I exclaimed.

"Hell is what I've been through," he assured me.

"And more," I proclaimed, "for it is the life of an animal which lives in total darkness, oblivious of anything but its own burning desire to survive at all costs, and if it can't, to at least die fighting."

"Then, what is heaven?" He asked.

"Why, it's the living out of Who We Really Are," I replied, "the only life that frees the soul from having to make the eternal return to this purgatory, we call life on earth, to purge itself of any lingering attachments to its own animalistic past.

"Who're our children," I went on to say, "but little reincarnations of those aspects of ourselves that have yet to be born or given form. They are the result of our drivenness to give body to soul, that she might give flesh to the unknown. How often are they bred merely to propagate the Neanderthal within us, or worse yet, some throwback to the age of the dinosaurs, like Hitler or Mussolini.

"In our failure to live out Who We Really Are," I concluded, "we rob the soul of life eternal, forcing her to return, again and again, to the physical realm, that we might one day free her from the chains of Instinct or strings of failed attempts—or past lives—to attain immortality without her. If we are to build a vehicle capable of transporting us from this world before Instinct has destroyed it, which he most surely will, just as he did the body of Christ, we will have to live up to our fullest potential.

"And by vehicle, I refer not to some technological tour de force by man, but rather to a psychological mode of transcending the meanness of our animalistic materialism, for the void that separates us from Who We Really Are is no deeper than the inner space to which the outer reality alludes. To overcome the immensity of this illusion, I need only walk backstage, to see who's pulling the strings. Only, I see us going nowhere, unless we start giving the contents of our imaginations the reality they so deserve, for no one may leave this purgatory until he has died to his animal past, been born again or evolved into his own full humanity."

[Just then, I caught a glimpse of this newborn child of mine, from somewhere across the great void that separated me from my soul, as she held it up before my eyes via something the corporal had said.]

"If I had it all to do over again," proclaimed my young friend, "I, who never once thought I'd choose jail over tails—or the wail of my soul over the tales of a good fight—would refuse to go. For am I not now a prisoner of my past? How long will I have to endure this punishment before I am freed from the chains I have forged with my own hands?"

"Until you forgive yourself," I replied, "you shall carry the past with you, like a great millstone around your neck."

"How can I ever forgive my self?" He begged to know.

"Can't you see the good that's come out of telling me these tales?" I asked.

"No!" He asserted.

"Don't you see how you have helped me make up my mind to never go back to Nam again?" I questioned him further. "Don't you see how many other souls you might save from the same terrible fate, by telling them your story? Don't you see this as the penance you must accept if you wish to find forgiveness?"

"How the hell will that help me forget the fuckin' nightmare?" He asked, out of his frustration with himself for ever having gotten involved in the goddamn war.

"It will only take away the sting of guilt or torment of the nightmare," I replied. "The images will stay behind as a reminder to share these grisly tales with others that they might avoid the same cruel fate. For *'whatever you declare bound on earth shall be bound in heaven; and whatever you declare loosed on earth shall be loosed in heaven.'"* Mt. 16:19.

"I don't understand," he exclaimed.

"In other words," I explained, "man is bound by the laws of Nature to live out the images of his imagination in one of two ways, by either mimicking them like an animal, or giving body to the meaning of them, like the conscious human being he is slowly becoming. In choosing to live like an animal, he binds the truths of his imagination to the images of the earth, until he can free them from their imprisonment in both the real and the imaginary—the latter being but a mirror image of the former."

"How can I do that?" Questioned he, the power of the imagination.

"There is only one way I know, to free the truth from Nature," I assured him, "and that is by returning to the womb of the imagination."

"You speak of the imagination," he interrupted, "as if it were some place I could walk to, like the back of this plane."

"Indeed I do," I exclaimed, "for it is that space between wakefulness and sleep—known as the dream state—we so easily slip into, whenever we relax the mind long enough to quell its fear of fantasy—a fear we normally overcome by racing off, like Pan, after every fleeting nymph or thought that pops into our heads."

"I don't dream," he insisted.

"You are dreaming constantly," I added, "even now as I speak. Only, you're not aware of your dreams because you are listening to mine."

"How can I become more aware of my dreams?" He asked.

"By listening to the other within you," I replied, "just as you have listened to me."

"I can't do that," he insisted.

"Only because you're afraid you'll hear your Self speak to you," I added. "Didn't you see the Great Soul of Mankind as the life of your friend left his body, tearing a hole in the very fabric of life—allowing you to see beyond the here and now?"

"That was a different situation, triggered by the death of my friend," he insisted.

"It was triggered by something you had seen but could not comprehend. Isn't that right?" I asked.

"Yeah, but only because the son of a bitch had gone off and left me when I needed him most," he confessed.

"Then forgive him," I insisted.

"I already have," he reluctantly admitted.

"Have you forgiven those who have taken his life and the lives of all your other buddies as well?" I inquired further.

"No, goddamn it, I haven't!" He shouted back.

"If you wish to find forgiveness for yourself," I persisted, "you must first forgive your enemies."

"How can I ever forgive them for what they have done?" He asked.

"Haven't you committed the same crimes they have?" I fired back.

Finding it hard to admit that he had, he turned to look out the porthole where, in a flash of light that had just pierced the clouds, he found the true meaning of forgiveness.

"Forgive us our trespasses as we forgive those who have trespassed against us," he muttered under his breath.

"I understand," he blurted out as he turned from the porthole, beaming with delight. "To find forgiveness, I had only to find it in my heart to forgive those who had wronged me in the same way I had wronged them. When I did, I found it there, just as you had said I would."

"How can I ever repay you?" He begged to know.

"You already have," I replied, "more than you will ever know."

"O thank you, Father," I thought I heard him say, "thank you for forgiving me of my sins."

"Go now," I thought I heard the Father say, "and commit these crimes against humanity, no more."

Along with its concomitant truth in the imagination was another small part of humanity freed from its fetters to an earthly existence. And so were soul and spirit reunited—for one brief moment of ecstasy—in the body or only place where one can experience such encounters.

While an animal encounters no one, not even its own self, we humans are more fortunate, or unfortunate, depending upon how you view the matter, in that we can encounter our Selves on four different levels. In encounters of the first kind, we gain some small sense as a child that "I" exist, though not as an island entirely unto itself. Not until we reach the age of puberty are we awakened to the strong feelings we hold for that nebulous other, out there in nature, in encounters of the second kind. But it isn't until we start thinking for ourselves, or erroneously assuming who we are, that we experience the other in encounters of the third kind, which seem so alien to us, we actually believe they take place outside the body, only because we are still so unaware of Who We Really Are. As we gain further insight into ourselves, we begin to see the experiences for what they are, in reality, encounters of the fourth or soul kind, and to discover Who We Really Are, men with souls whose selves can see all three aspects of our greater Self—the Father, Son, and Holy Spirit—with the four faces of our faculties—our own sensations, thoughts, feelings, and intuitions.

Just because these experiences take place within the realm of the imaginable doesn't mean they are any less real than those of the material world. They appear less real only because the truth transcends all dualities such as inner and outer or real and imaginary. In the end, they are no more absurd than our own perceptions of reality, to which they only allude. In that sense, they are much closer to the truth than we realize, for is not the goal of the experiences of both worlds, to assist us in finding the imaginable hidden within the real, and vice versa, the real hidden within the imaginable?

While we could certainly use the help of our imaginations, we continue to turn almost exclusively to the outside world to satisfy our hunger for what only the imagination has to offer. Why we continue to use her, like some cheap-ass old whore, baffles the mind until one looks at the matter from her perspective—that what we really desire is the truth, which remains hidden from us, within the objective world. For we see only what we want to see, what will benefit us most in the here and now, never once realizing that it is the life of the hereafter we seek and want so badly to live out in the here and now.

Bamboozled by the wonders of our technological wizardry, we sincerely hope to one day find the key to everlasting life when, in reality, the key already exists. In choosing the way of the soul, we find heaven's door, waiting for us—within our very beings—to knock, that it may be opened. In our failure to see death as just another one of Instinct's masks for the reality of birth, are we born, again and again, into the purgatory we call life. Convinced that we will live on forever in our progeny, our spirits wait in limbo for them to fulfill an old myth whose ultimate goal in life is self-destruction, or destruction of the self, that we may one day give birth to a way of life, which is truly eternal.

Exhausted by the events of the first day that I'd taken leave of my senses, I fell fast asleep.

As the plane dropped from the sky over San Bernardino, the following morning, I wrestled these words from the poet before I woke up:

"I was riding on the Mayflower when I thought I spied some land.
I yelled for Captain Ahab, I'll have you understand,
Who came running to the deck, sayin', 'Boys forget the whale;
We're goin' over yonder, cause the Injuns changed the sails.'
All along the bowline, we sang that melody,
Like all tough sailors do when they're far away at sea.
'I think I caught America,' I said as we hit land..." [1]

"What did you say?" Asked the corporal.

"I dreamt I was riding on a phantom ship as an indentured pilgrim," I replied, "when I thought I spied the Promised Land. To get a better handle on what exactly I had seen, I yelled out to the Captain who, in his ruthless pursuit of the truth of the beastly side of his nature, came running up on deck, only to tell me that this was one whale of a problem I would do well to forget. It was then that I saw, in the simple lives of the indigenous peoples of this land, what life lived in harmony with Nature really looked like. As we hit land, I caught sight of just how far we, their conquerors, had strayed from the wisdom of our bodies.

"Having strayed from the simple truths of their natures, had the early settlers of this country set sail, in search of the lost side of themselves, only to come into conflict with it when it confronted the instinctive tyrant that'd overtaken them in their failure to live out Who They Really Were. Guided by brute force instead of love, they set out to fulfill the words of their sacred scriptures—or manifest destiny—by systematically subduing the land and taking dominion over everything, in the name of the god and country to which they owed allegiance. Like Cain, did they kill off their brother, the Indian, and build up for themselves a whole way of life, unpleasing to the Lord.

"Under the guise of the advancement of civilization, did the more primitive man take over. And to this day, does Hyde rule over the land in the guise of Uncle Sam. So does the darker side of Uncle Sam continue to take, from the Mother of us all, more of what will never satisfy his deepest longings for life everlasting, his own soul, Lady Liberty, and the pursuit of Who He Really Is.

"Returning home after having gone off to the Far East on some crazy ole crusade against the Red Knight, he now finds it in total disarray—the members of his household terribly divided over his latest fiasco in Southeast Asia. Even now, as the forces of Nature rise up against him in the form of his fraternal twin, Ho Chi Minh, and soul mate, Lady Liberty—who at this very moment rides like the wind across the land, to stir the conscience of this country from its slumber—does he sit on his ass up in Washington. Surrounded by his cronies, he pretends that he has the full support of this side of the family, in his ongoing feud with the other side—a feud, which started some years ago when he got greedy and tried to take more than his share of what we have all inherited from Mother Nature, in equal measure. Boy, is he ever in for a rude awakening, cause he's going to lose this one, big-time, and pay dearly for his folly, as his soul's just not in it.

"Then, I'm not so sure she ever went along with any of his quixotic little crusades, for she never was one to tolerate his addiction to material things, or his sudden outbursts of violence when he didn't get his way. In the end, I believe that is why she divorced him—for these indiscretions. Only, I don't know how to tell the incorrigible old fool that he has lost his way, other than refusing to go along with his bizarre schemes."

"You know, you are really somethin'," commented a leery young corporal. "The way you see things is so uncanny that, if I didn't know any better, I'd swear you were an alien in disguise."

"All I know for sure," I replied laughingly, "is that I embody the next great step man must take if ever he is to evolve into Who He Really Is. And at times, I feel like an alien that has been marooned on some godforsaken planet, to coax its inhabitants to don the right masks, or play the parts assigned them in the greatest show on earth. For the second act, or coming of our humanity, is unfolding so fast that many will be left behind to wail and gnash their teeth before they realize, their only chance to have escaped the hell that they have created for themselves, has already come and gone.

"In the past," I said as we hit land, "I got caught up with all the glitter and the glitz of the American dream, the images rather than the truth. Now, thanks to you, I see the real nightmare behind it all. And I realize how far I have yet to go before I find the real Promised Land."

On that note, we parted company, never to see each other again.

"Had he been an angel in disguise?" I wondered as I turned to get his address, only to find that he seemed to have vanished. "O, he had been real enough, all right, for I had shaken his hand before we parted. Or was he just another freak of Nature, like myself, alienated from the rest of the culture because he dared to use his imagination to rise above the meanness of his own animal past?"

Having been forced to take a bus up to Los Angeles, to catch a commercial flight for St. Louis, I finally found myself onboard a real plane. As I collapsed into my seat from sheer exhaustion, and fell back to sleep, I ran into my mentor somewhere along the way.

"*I still have much to tell you,*" set he my heart on fire, "*which you cannot bear now.* Jn. 16:12. *When a woman's in labor, she has pain, because her hour has come. But when her child is born, she no longer remembers the anguish because of the joy of having brought another human being into the world. So you have pain now; but I will see you again, and your heart will rejoice, and no one will take your joy from you.*" Jn. 16:20-22.

"*I have said these things to you in figures of speech,*" revealed He, His real identity. "*The hour is coming when I will no longer speak to you in figures, but will tell you plainly of the Father.* Jn. 16:25.

"*In the world,*" proclaimed the Lord, "*you will face persecution. But take courage; for I have conquered the world!*" Jn. 16:33.

"*I have given them your word,*" concluded the Master, "*and the world has hated them because they do not belong to the world, as I do not belong to the world. I am not asking You to take them out of the world, but I ask You to protect them from the evil one* (Jn. 17:14-15), *that they may be one. As You, Father, are in Me and I am in You, may they also be in Us* (Jn. 17:21) *so that they may be one, as We are one.*" Jn. 17:22-23.

Turning to leave, I ran smack-dab into the monk standing behind me. Looking into the eyes of this mirror image of myself, I caught sight of the fullness of my humanity, the image and likeness of God all in one, before the whole vision vanished. Having been awakened from the Big Sleep, for one brief moment, I fell asleep again, unaware of the full import of what I had just seen.

Drawn inexorably back to that black hole in the great wall of our civilized veneer, I was sucked down into its deepest depths where dwell those aspects of mankind—of which he remains so unaware—that bedevil him like fallen angels, that he might one day wake up to Who He Really Is. There, I found my self running scared with the spirits of the dead—those who had fallen in battle but did not yet realize they were in limbo. Ostracized by them because life still clung to me, did I race about the battlefield trying to convince the living of the insanity of war, only to be confronted by the Great Magician, as he stood at the center of this great vortex laughing at me.

"Ya fool, they can't hear you," he yelled out mockingly, "as my legions have already taken possession of their bodies."

"That's not true," countered another voice from somewhere on high, for there was a very different battle going on here, than normally meets the eye, for the ultimate control of man's soul.

"Michael," I shouted as I turned in recognition of his voice.

"Look over yonder!" He commanded as he pointed his sword in the direction in which he wished me to look.

Just then, I spied the young corporal and his friend standing outside a hut, surrounded by those spirits of the dead who had lost their way in the land of the living, and now sought the door to heaven. As these spirits stood there arguing amongst themselves—the more conscientious with the more instinctive—I heard one of them yell at the top of his lungs, for his buddy to go in and save the baby crying inside, before the other members of his squad torched the hut. With that, he rushed in, only to be sent reeling from an explosion that landed him back outside at the feet of the young corporal, at death's door. As the same lance, that had pierced the side of our Lord, pricked the heart of the young corporal with the departure of a dear friend from this world, I saw heaven's door open to admit three more spirits into its realm, for each, in his own way, had found the very soul he sought.

"The battle for her is not over yet," yelled the Great Magician.

Looking down, I saw legions of demons spinning out of the vortex of this black hole to take possession of the souls that had filled the ranks of the armies of the world, as he spun madly out of control, laughing all the while, at how easily we are deceived by our fantasies.

"The battle is over, Luther," countered Michael. "The Son of Man overcame you two thousand years ago."

"Tell them that," laughed the Joker as he spun ever more wildly in upon his self, till he had dissipated into the nothing he really is.

"Who will win the skirmish for your soul," concluded my mentor from somewhere across the great void that separated his world from mine, "is up to you now, my son. May the force of truth be with you on the final leg of your journey home."

As the plane came in for a landing at Lambert-St. Louis International Airport, I found myself slipping from yet another flight of fantasy. Looking back, I saw eternal life as much more than coming to an awareness of one's true personhood, for I had yet to live out what I had found there, within my own fantasies. I saw too, how one could step out of this world, the world of fantasy, that is, and into the next when he chooses to live out Who He Really Is—the truth of his fantasies rather than the fantasies themselves. Having stepped off the plane and planted my feet firmly on the ground, I concluded this was not the real world after all, since the real world still eluded my grasp.

It was then, that I saw modern civilization as a barrier to the evolution of mankind—one so constructed as to protect himself from the terror of his own imagination and the fear of those who, like me, would one day free the truth hidden there long ago, from the uncomprehending mind. When this facade would finally give way to the rising tide of truth that gushed forth from the chinks in its armor, like the blood and water from the gaping wound in Christ's side, I knew not. Although the signs of the wilder society, which normally precede such momentous changes, had risen up on the horizon, I knew only that many would die in the wake of the Four Horsemen as they rode across the sky, at the beck and call of Nature, to surgically remove the last vestiges of Neanderthal from her face.

"I have to find the truth of my being," I muttered to myself as I wandered through the terminal in search of a phone to call my folks—to let them know I was back in town and in need of a ride home.

"Hi, Mom," I said as she answered the phone. "It's me, Butch."

"Hi! How are you?" She genuinely inquired.

"Not bad, for an old salt," I jokingly replied. "How about you?"

"Not bad, for an old lady," she rejoined as she laughed at her soon-to-be-forty self.

Even though I had detected a slight twinge of pain in her voice, with regard to the life that had slipped through her fingers unlived, it felt good to hear her voice and her laughter again.

"Where are you?" She asked after a brief pause in which we'd had a good laugh at the pain that we shared.

"I'm at the airport," I responded out of my inability to tell her I was really stuck in limbo, waiting for the next flight of fantasy out.

"How's Pat and Little Joe?" I asked her instead.

"Your brother's already in bed, asleep," she replied. "Your sister's out for the evening, with some of her friends, and will probably be late. Both are doing as well as can be expected, under the circumstances."

"And the ole man?" I asked with fear and trepidation.

"Joe is Joe," she replied in such a way as to make a bad situation sound better than it really is. "What else can I say?" She philosophically inquired.

Moving onto the more pressing matter, did I ask my Mom for a ride home.

"What about a cab?" She countered, to avoid having to ask anything of my stepfather who, by now, was already half-soused.

"If I had the money, Mom," I replied, "I wouldn't have asked you for a lift. As it is, I have so little, that I hate to waste it on cab fare from here to South County."

"I guess I'll have to call your father at the malt shop," she snipped.

As far as I could see—and that wasn't very far without the eyes of my mentor—things hadn't changed much at home, other than to have gotten worse, since that's the only choice left those who refuse to go with the flow of the truth of their beings. While it didn't appear that much had changed for me, inside, things were changing so rapidly, I could hardly keep up with my own transformation.

Having arranged with my mother, to meet my stepfather in front of the main terminal, I was surprised to see him arrive so uncharacteristically soon after I had talked with her. Hoping against hope as I flew over to greet him, I came crashing down to the ground with this brief fantasy of mine—of finding a changed man inside the car—when I opened the door and saw how much more he had deteriorated since I had last seen him, eleven months ago. Unable to elicit even a simple hello from him, I sat down in the front seat of the car, only to find the man so goddamn drunk, he could not have responded to me if he had wanted to. Smiling nervously, I braced myself for the long quiet ride home, broken only by the sound of his incessant wheezing, coughing and spitting.

It was then, as we headed south on Lindbergh Boulevard, that I was confronted by one of the most startling aspects of my being, ever presented to me in the guise of another human being. Glancing at my stepfather, as he drove down the highway in complete control of the car, in spite of his inebriated condition, I saw the most hideously grotesque figure, sitting there in the driver's seat, upon which I had ever laid eyes. As I looked into the face of a creature with all of the features of a human being, except for those of his head and left hand, which were unmistakably fly-like, I grasped the fourth face of the pyramid that now comprised all of my abilities as a human being to perceive Who I Really Am. While I had already familiarized myself with that triumvirate of perceptive abilities most accessible to me, that is, first and foremost, my innate ability to intuit, then those which had led me to feel and think for myself, I had encountered each of these abilities within myself, through the figures of my mentor, his daughter and her protector, respectively. Now, I sat staring at a projection of the one that I could never completely free from its roots in the animal kingdom, my ability to sense the slightest ripple or movement of the God that stirred beneath the surface of my imagination, like a babe in the womb, waiting to be borne into conscious awareness of its Self. And as we both took a long, hard look at each other, for the first time in my life, I realized that it was this same innate ability in my stepfather upon which he relied to get him home when he had drunk too much.

With the disappearance of my shadowy new friend, as we pulled up to the house, safe and sound, I wondered if I would ever see him again, or more importantly, if I would ever come to a fuller understanding of the language that he used—that of my own bodily sensations.

As my mother opened the door to greet me, and the human being in whose shadow I had once walked, I turned to help my old man, the fly, up the steps and into the house. Instead, I was shoved aside, for the fly obviously did not need me. Nor did I, from that point on, need the image of the fly for anything more than what I had already gleaned from it.

"Welcome home," proclaimed my mother, as my old man, the fly, made their way to the couch where they collapsed until morning.

Confronted by my own unwillingness to change, had I resorted to wallowing around inside myself, as of old, until I let go of my self, long enough to give my mother the ear she seemed so intent on bending. I had simply to admit to the existence of this pesky little fly, or annoying little truth, and resolve to be more open to change in my life, to rid myself of these noisome emotions. Having encountered a truth that, at first, seemed so alien to me, I had only to imbibe it before it swallowed me up and went to war with whomever I found to be a suitable projection for what I could not accept about myself. Thus was I freed from my own pressing need to be heard, so that I could listen more attentively to my mother, whose emotional needs were great indeed, in view of the fractured mirror into which she had to look for insight.

In his utter failure to live out those aspects of himself, he saw in my mother when he married her, did he deprive her of the masculine mirror into which she needed to gaze for insight into herself. Having passed the same sad legacy onto me, had he left me with the very difficult task of bridging the gap between the masculine and feminine poles of my being without a road map of any kind. Thus did he leave us both with a puzzlingly fragmented picture of ourselves.

Unfortunately, my mother was no more open to change than I was, for like me, she feared what harm it might bring her. Confronted by a tyrant of no less stature than the one I faced, she cowered in fear, almost to the point of immobility, protesting in little ways only, her indenture to the beast that had swallowed her up. Now she was looking to her son, just as Nature had some two thousand years ago, to save her.

Only, I was looking to the King of Hearts Who appeared in our midst—unbeknownst to my mother, who was blind in her intuitive eye—as He said He would when two or more gathered for Consciousness' sake.

"What profit does a man show," asked He, *"who gains the whole world and destroys himself? What can he offer in exchange for his life? Mk. 8:36-37. For is not the kingdom of heaven like unto a merchant's search for fine pearls? When he found one really valuable pearl, he went back and sold all that he had, and bought it." Mt. 13:45-46.*

With that, He handed me a pearl about the size of a large grapefruit and disappeared, leaving me with the truth of my being, for whatever it was worth.

"O where have you been my blue-eyed son? And where have you been my darling young one?" Sang out my mother in the voice of the poet within us all.

"Having stumbled onto Who I Really Am," I replied, "like the apostles, I have either walked upright as the human being I Am, or crawled on my belly like a snake, after overstepping the bounds of my humanity into the various realms of the Seven Deadly Sins: pride, envy, avarice, anger, lust, gluttony and sloth. If I tried one, I must have tried a dozen different ways to get out of living Who I Really Am, whereupon I was thrust into one of the deepest depressions I'd ever encountered, a black hole in which even death seemed more desirable than life."

"And it's a hard, it's a hard, it's a hard, and it's a hard, it's a hard rain's a-gonna fall," warned the poet within me.

"O what did you see my blue-eyed son? And what did you see my darling young one?" Inquired she who longed to see what I had seen overseas.

"From amidst the animal kingdom," I answered, "I saw the birth of my humanity or Second Coming. I saw the narrow path which few ever take. And much to my dismay, I saw whole branches of mankind—after they had been cut off from life, liberty, and the pursuit of happiness—revert to animals to get back the inheritance that had been taken from them by those who had devised this economic disaster, we call capitalism. From the side lines, did I watch the banksters struggle in vain, to attain immortality at the expense of the mass of mortal men at the bottom, whom these false gods have kept divided over the issue of what is or is not rightfully theirs."

"And it's a hard, it's a hard, it's a hard, and it's a hard, it's a hard rain's a-gonna fall," repeated the poet within me.

"And what did you hear my blue-eyed son? And what did you hear my darling young one?" Asked she who did so long to hear what I had heard overseas.

"Like Jonah," I reluctantly responded, "I heeded not Nature's call to serve as a spokesperson for her in the struggle to get man to evolve into the human being he inherently is, until I found my self drowning in my own animality and was swallowed up by a great gray whale. As I listened to the death knoll of modern man, in his reckless pursuit of a dinosaur's way of life, I heard many people speak of the need for change, in their failure to act upon their own words. While the others laughed and scoffed at me, in my struggle to satisfy that insatiable appetite of ours for the truth, I suffered an ignominious death and did weep over every blind alley that foolish clown or lesser self of mine had taken."

"And it's a hard, it's a hard, it's a hard, and it's a hard, it's a hard rain's a-gonna fall," reiterated that nerve-racking poet within me.

"O what did you meet my blue-eyed son? And who did you meet my darling young one?" Queried she who did so long to experience what I had, overseas.

"Besides a dead way of life," I began, "I met a young girl, the soul of my youth, who introduced me to he who had sired her, my spiritual father—an insightful old seer native to my being. Shortly thereafter, I met her guardian and mine, a white knight who dared to walk amid the dark shadows of my mind, to liberate the truth still being held captive there by the beast in me. There too, within the burning desires of my own flesh, did I find union with my soul, but only after I had dealt sufficiently with the wounds that had been inflicted upon me, both in love and in hatred."

"And it's a hard, it's a hard, it's a hard, and it's a hard, it's a hard rain's a-gonna fall," prophesied the poet within me.

"And what'll you do now my blue-eyed son? And what'll you do now my darling young one?" Asked she who feared doing what I would do to set her free.

"I'm goin' back in before the rains a-come," I declared, "to penetrate the dark side of nature where misconceptions still abound—where one moment I find my self feeling at home with my body, the next, imprisoned within her, in her stubborn refusal to yield the truth for which I so hunger on these dark, soulless nights. When I find the truth, like the poet *I'll tell it and speak it, and think it and breathe it*. I'll reflect it in a way that all souls may see it. And I'll stand up to their disbelief until I'm drowned out by their dissonance, for like the poet, *I shall know my song well, before I start singin'*."

"And it's a hard, it's a hard, it's a hard, and it's a hard, it's a hard rain's a-gonna fall," [2] concluded the poet within me.

"You only have a year to go," interjected my mother, as if she had not heard a word of what I'd shared with her. "Why not serve out the rest of your enlistment, honorably, take advantage of the GI Bill when you get out, and go back to school."

"What more could I say," I wondered, "to get her to see things from my perspective? How many years would it take her to hear my sad complaint? And how many deaths would it take before she realized that too many people have died?"

"The answer, my friend, is blowin' in the wind," replied the unrelenting poet within us all, *"the answer is blowin' in the wind."* [3]

On that note, I bade her good night.

While it felt queer to be back in my old bed again, I must have dreamed a thousand dreams that night, of which only one really stands out. As I stand there in my dream, I am handed this great pearl, first by an Oriental monk, and then by a

Catholic priest. Thus was I made aware of what I had been feeling the night before, as I lay down to sleep—that the inner and outer truths of my being were rapidly coming together, just as my mentor had said.

Only, I never did wake up until my last day at home. Having purchased an old '54 Chevy automatic, I showed up at heaven's door, a day or so later, much to Mary's surprise. There I stayed till it was time to go back to Hawaii. So deeply did I sleep the Big Sleep that, to this day, I cannot remember what transpired.

Great was the pain I felt, the day I had to leave this paradise, as heaven slammed its door in my face, just as it had back in Tokyo.

Feeling blue, I went back home to prepare for the trip back to hell. There, on a table in the living room, I stumbled upon the key to the question of why I wanted out of the Navy. Having had my interest piqued by an article in the February issue of the Atlantic Monthly, entitled "Leo Tolstoy's Advice to a Draftee," as I thumbed through the magazine to wile away the time, I read with great relish, the following:

"Tolstoy's letter," read the intro, "was addressed to a young Hessian named Ernst Schramm, whose earlier correspondence with the writer has been lost; Schramm evidently wrote a second time in an effort to evade Tolstoy's argument that he refuse conscription. The letter printed here is Tolstoy's response to Schramm's second letter, and seems to have terminated the exchange. In reading Tolstoy's words against killing, one should bear in mind that both parties understood that the Hessian army in 1899 was a peacetime army, but that the penalty for evading conscription was death. Tolstoy addressed the letter to Schramm in Darmstadt, and the Hessian post office forwarded it to Aschaffenburg in Bavaria, leaving us to infer that Schramm decided not to join up but to change countries instead."

"In my last letter," began Tolstoy, "I answered your question as well as I could. It is not only Christians but all just people who must refuse to become soldiers—that is, to be ready on another's command (for this is what a soldier's duty actually consists of) to kill all those one is ordered to kill. The question as you state it—which is more useful, to become a good teacher or to suffer for rejecting conscription?—is falsely stated. The question is falsely stated because it is wrong for us to determine our actions according to their result, to view actions merely as useful or destructive. In the choice of our actions, we can be led by their advantages or disadvantages only when the actions themselves are not opposed to the demands of morality.

"We can stay home or go abroad or concern ourselves with farming or science according to what we find useful; for neither in domestic life, foreign travel, farming, nor science is there anything immoral. But under no circumstance can we inflict violence on people, torture or kill them because we think such acts could be

of use to us or to others. We cannot and may not do such things, because we can never be sure of the results of our actions. Often actions, which seem the most advantageous, turn out to be destructive; the reverse is also true.

"The question should not be stated: which is more useful, to be a good teacher or to go to jail for refusing conscription? but rather: what should a man do who has been called upon for military service—that is, called upon to kill or to prepare himself to kill?

"To this question, for he who understands the true meaning of military service, and wants to be moral, there is only one clear and incontrovertible answer: such a person must refuse to take part in military service no matter the consequences. It may seem to us that this refusal could be futile or even harmful, that it would be a far more useful thing, after serving one's time, to become a good village teacher. But in the same way, Christ could have judged it more useful for himself to be a good carpenter and submit to all the principles of the Pharisees than to die in obscurity, repudiated and forgotten by everyone.

"Moral acts are distinguished from all other acts by the fact that they operate independently of any predictable advantage to ourselves or to others. No matter how dangerous the situation may be of a man who finds himself in the power of robbers who demand that he take part in plundering, murder, and rape, a moral person cannot take part. Is not military service the same thing? Is one not required to agree to the deaths of all those one is commanded to kill?

"But how can one refuse to do what everyone does or finds unavoidable and necessary? Or must he do what no one does, what everyone considers unnecessary, stupid and bad? No matter how strange it sounds, this is the main argument offered against those moral acts that face every person called up for military service. But this argument is even more incorrect than the one that would make a moral action dependent upon considerations of advantage.

"If I, finding myself in a crowd of people, run with them without knowing where, it is obvious I have given myself up to mass hysteria; but if I should push my way to the front, be gifted with sharper sight, or receive information this crowd was racing to attack human beings, towards its own corruption, would I not stop and tell the people what might rescue them? Would I go on running and do things I knew to be bad and corrupt? This is the situation of every individual called up for military service, if he knows what military service means.

"I can well understand that you, a young man full of life, loving and loved by your mother, friends, perhaps a young woman, think with a natural terror about what awaits you if you should refuse conscription; perhaps you will not feel strong enough to bear the consequences of refusal, and knowing your weakness, will submit and become a soldier. I understand completely, and I do not for a moment *blame you, knowing very well that in your place I might perhaps do the same thing. Only do not say you did it because it was useful or because everyone does it. If you did it, know that you did wrong.*

"In every person's life there are moments when he can know himself, tell himself who he is, whether he is a man who values his human dignity above his life or a weak creature who does not know his dignity and is concerned merely with being useful (chiefly to himself). This is the situation of a man who goes out to defend his honor in a duel or a soldier who goes into battle (although here the concepts of life are wrong). It is the situation of a doctor or a priest called to someone sick with plague, of a man in a burning house or sinking ship who must decide whether to let the weaker go first or shove them aside and save himself. It is the situation of a man in poverty who accepts or rejects a bribe. And in our times, it is the situation of a man called to military service. For a man who knows its significance, the call to the army is perhaps the only opportunity for him to behave as a morally free creature and fulfill the highest requirement of his life—or else to keep his advantage in sight like an animal and remain slavishly submissive and servile until humanity becomes degraded and stupid.

"For these reasons I answered your question whether one has to refuse to do military service with a categorical 'yes'—if you understand the meaning of military service (and if you did not understand it then, you do now) and want to behave as a moral person living in our times must.

"Please excuse me if the words are harsh. The subject is so important that one cannot be careful enough in expressing oneself so as to avoid false interpretation."

April 7, 1899   Leo Tolstoy

In an experience of déjà vu, I found my self standing on the precipice of utter darkness where, in a brilliant flash of light, I see, for the first time, my own cross. Confronted by one of those moments in which a person comes to know Who He Really Is, I knew, beyond the shadow of a doubt, that I, like the young Hessian, must refuse further service in the military since I now understood the true meaning of such service. As I shrank from this cross in terror of what awaited me should I refuse to serve out the rest of my enlistment, I saw my self weaken and submit to the Great Gray Whore. With that, I knew I had done wrong.

Having failed to seize the opportunity to behave as a morally free creature and fulfill the highest requirement of my life, did I return to the Davidson on 5 February 1968, with that key issue of the Atlantic Monthly in hand. I was determined, as hell, to do something that I had never done before—to reprint and circulate Tolstoy's letter about the ship—with the hope of opening the door, I did not know existed until now. Wracked by the pain of separation from my soul, did I drag my tail end up the gangplank to let the officer of the deck know that this thorn in their side had returned to the good ship Nineveh, to show her crew the true meaning of military service. For I knew, in my heart of hearts, I could not continue doing what everyone else did or found unavoidably necessary, no matter what the consequences of this resistance might be. Only, I was not ready to take on the Pharisees and outright refuse to cooperate with them in any way, just yet, or at least until I had gotten a better understanding of who they said I was or was not, as I prepared to go public with my message, for the first time since last spring.

"Hey, Dury!" Shouted Marty as he came galloping over, like a riderless horse, to greet the only person, he had ever met, who could rein him in to the truth of his being, whether he liked it or not. "If you aren't a sight for sore eyes," he went on to say as he honed in on the one friend he had, who would listen to the old nag in him and its shortsighted view of the world. "How was your leave?" He asked as I wished in vain, I could remove the blinders from his eyes, as Jesus had, the scales from the blind man's eyes.

"Too short," I reminiscently replied. "Why, I can't even remember what the hell I did for thirty days—it went by so fast."

"It seems like you've been gone longer than that," he rebutted, "for I haven't had a good conversation with anyone since you left."

"I believe it," declared the enlightened man within me. "For it's hard enough to awaken oneself from the Big Sleep, much less another."

"Aw, the ignorant motherfuckers," bemoaned Marty, "just want to live like animals, that's all."

"How much easier it is for a man to live like an animal than to embrace the humanity, Nature has forced upon him," proclaimed the White Knight in me. "Until he returns to the womb of his imagination, to seek out the soul meaning of his fantasies, he will be forced to continue living like an animal, which can only mimic what it sees. Nor can he forestall the Second Coming, or coming of our humanity, as there are many, like me, who have accepted the challenge to evolve. Even though we may look like strangers in a strange land, he is the one who, like the dinosaurs of the latter days of the Cretaceous Period, will become an anachronism.

"I want to show you something," I concluded as I opened the door between epochs to show him the future of mankind as it had been revealed to me in that fateful February issue of the Atlantic Monthly.

"Whoa!" Yelled out the rider from somewhere deep within himself, as it caught sight of a ghost of the truth and pulled back on the reins, causing the horse's ass to rare up and take notice.

How much of the truth he saw that day, I would never know for certain. That he saw it is indisputable, for when he was done reading the article, he looked as if he had just seen a ghost. Instead, he opted for the old nag he was so used to riding, as she began to fill his head with all those nagging doubts about what he had just seen.

"I don't know," he conceded as he backed off from the truth and the magic spell it had cast upon him. Having momentarily been transformed into the White Knight, he found the white horse, or truth of his libidinal energy, too much to handle. He had grown so used to seeing the world through the eyes of the old nag, that he could not allow himself, for even a moment, to see things from a different perspective.

"All right!" Exclaimed the more insightful old fool within him. "I can see by the grin on your face, you have somethin' in mind. What is it?"

"I'm thinking about asking Harold to run off a hundred or so copies on the ship's copier, so I can leaflet the ship," I proclaimed.

"Do you think I can get the old buck to do that for me?" I asked the Marty who, I knew all too well, could leave behind the old nag when he wanted to, and venture out on the limb for the only cause worth fighting for—the evolution of mankind.

"Boy, are they gonna shit when they see this!" He exclaimed.

Delighted by our boldness, did we race off to confront the old buck with our newest harebrained scheme. So were the old nag and the missing link transformed—for just one brief moment—by the truth, into that gallant white steed and its rider, the White Knight.

As the old buck perused the article, he hopped around inside his cage, wrestling with his feelings before he finally bolted for freedom and embraced our latest harebrained scheme, with the zest of a man who has just found the pearl of great price. With that, did the old buck hightail it up to the ship's office to do his part for the cause ere he got cold feet and retreated to the confines of his cage. Only, he disappointed us when he came hopping back to tell us he had been thwarted by one of the other yeomen who had burst in on him—before he'd even had a chance to get started—to type up some stuff for the XO.

Since we could ill afford to jeopardize our only access to a free press, by compromising Harold's position as a yeoman on the ship, in the interest of the evolution-revolution, we decided to postpone our first move until Sunday, when our detractors would be gone for the day. For what seemed like an eternity, did we keep our latest harebrained scheme to ourselves. O, how alive we did feel, as we had back in the days when we had first talked of mutiny.

In the end, we pulled it off without a hitch. While Harold worked to bring the whole thing to fruition before word leaked out about our newest brainchild, Marty stood guard outside the ship's office to ward off any attempts to abort it. Like an expectant father, I paced the floor down in the compartment. With the emergence of the old buck from the delivery room, it wasn't long before word of the birth of some communist conspiracy, to poison the minds of this country's finest, filtered back down to us via the mouths of the pit vipers that slithered about the ship, to spread such venomous lies.

The reaction of our command was swift; for immediately after quarters the following morning, was I taken up to see the Captain rather than any of his go-betweens.

"You wish to see me, Sire," I stated as I entered the Captain's stateroom at his behest.

"Do you know anything about this, Mr. Drury?" Demanded the Old Weasel, as he flung one of the leaflets up into my face, under false pretenses, though, for he was much more afraid of it than he was angry.

"Why, that looks like one of the pamphlets I had printed up and circulated about the ship," replied the White Knight in me, in a supreme effort to override the fears of the missing link before they got out of hand.

"Where did you get this crap?" Demanded the Old Weasel, as if he were on the verge of uncovering the tip of some huge conspiracy to undermine the military from within its own ranks.

"Why, I got it from this month's issue of the Atlantic Monthly," I answered with the smugness of one who had finally found out what he stood for, which only seemed to further aggravate the Old Weasel.

"Why did you reprint this shit and pass it around my ship?" Inquired a more subdued Old Weasel, after having had the wind taken out of his sails in his pursuit of that ever-elusive white whale of a plot to undermine the American dream with some red shadow of the truth.

"I wanted to expose the men onboard to the true meaning of military service," came the reply of one who is so far above the reach of the law, he is literally untouchable.

"And what do you perceive to be the true meaning of military service?" Inquired this Hook of Pan, Peter Pan, that is.

"Why, I find it hard to believe," I began, "that after all these years in the Navy, you still have not grasped the true meaning of military service as an excuse used by mankind, in his shortsightedness, to abort the fifth commandment and make it legal to kill whomever he wishes, and all for some ill-gotten gain."

"You ungrateful bastard!" Bellowed this shadow of my old man. "If it were not for the likes of me, you would not be standing here today."

"You're right," I concurred, "I would be doing something far more constructive than standing here with an anachronism, arguing about who has control of my life, he or God."

"Don't get smart with me," commanded the Old Weasel, "or I'll..."

"...Fine me and throw me in jail," I interjected. "Do you really think that will change the way I feel?"

"I may not change the way you feel," replied the surly Old Weasel, "but by golly I'll change your behavior or break you in the process."

"Then let the tournament begin," boasted the errant knight in me. "And may the best man win."

Having been unseated from his high horse by the White Knight in me, in the first round of jousting, he quickly pulled himself together, long enough to ask me what I meant by that last verbal thrust of mine.

"I mean to expose the men to the truth," I remarked as I teasingly waved its double-edged blade in his face.

"You will do nothing of the sort," he commanded. "I forbid you to pass out any crap like this on my ship again."

"Like some two-bit dictator," I rebutted, "have you taken it upon yourself to deny me the very rights for which we're supposed to be fighting. How ironic!"

"Son," he concluded with a sore buffet to my head, "you gave up any rights you had under the Constitution, the day you joined the Navy. You have no right to do anything on this ship but what I tell you. You got that, mister?"

"When I joined this outfit, I relinquished none of my rights under the Constitution," proclaimed the White Knight in me, loud and clear, as he struggled to maintain his stance after such a glancing blow, "least of all, my right to spread the truth by any means I see fit."

"Get out of here," yelled the Captain, "before I..."

"...*Tear ya limb from limb*," voiced the right side of the poet from afar.

"*Ya know they refused Jesus too*," I sang in unison with the left side of the poet.

"You're not him," yelled the Captain, from the poet's other side. "*Get out of here before I break your bones. I ain't your pop.*"

Like the poet then, *I decided to have him arrested and went lookin' for a cop*. [4]

Only, I really had nowhere else to turn but my imagination.

For flagrantly flaunting the illegal authority this Saul held over the head of the young David in me, like the Sword of Damocles, was I banished, once again, to the scullery, to watch the storm clouds gather on the horizons of my imagination. Until my psyche would release the energy building up within the current and extremely limited atmosphere for expression, I had no clue of what she was brewing in her cauldron. And as I slaved away in the sweltering heat of yet another tropical depression, I found my self dragging my ass up to the scullery, each day, with less and less energy available for the task at hand.

I had a slight reprieve when, a day or so later, I was sent back to the dispensary for yet another psychiatric evaluation. There, I underwent a preliminary interview by a young, likable intern named Reisman, to obtain a brief history from me before being fed to the real doctor, a medicine man whom the Navy had resurrected from the dead, named Lazaroff. This quack wasted no time in chewing me up and spitting me out or diagnosing me as an emotionally unstable personality, passive-aggressive type #000-X465, according to the Navy's own manuals, as manifested by chronic conflicts with authority, impulsivity and poor judgment. In reality, I was being seen because I had scared the shit out of my command after having circulated material among the ship's crew, capable of undermining their morale.

It has never ceased to amaze me how such fools, guided by their own fear of enlightenment, ever gain the respected title of psychiatrist or doctor of the soul. As they stumble through the tangled growth in the garden of one's soul, they invariably gravitate to its darkest depths. Like some prehistoric bird of prey, do they pick up on one's breadcrumb sins rather than the truth hidden within the sin, in their relentless search for that ever-elusive trauma in one's past upon which they can squarely lay the blame for one's current difficulties. Never once do these learned fools ever give it a second thought that one's problems may ultimately be due to the preponderance of their own ignorance of the soul, which breeds in the mindless vacuum of their heads, like some highly contagious virus, to infect the fertile minds of all those with whom these Typhoid Marys come into contact. And so do they continually sucker the blameless into believing that they can do what's never been done—point the way to nirvana—when, in reality, the fucking Pharisees never lift a finger to lighten one's burden.

"There's something wrong with you, so terribly wrong," they write in your chart—they dare not share the name of the demon, lest you be cured of what ails them too. To keep the demon alive, they label you instead, for one has no control over an unnamed demon.

"No shit," you wrongly reply. "Why, I've known for some time now, there's something wrong with me. At least I've had the gumption to admit that what is wrong with me is also what's wrong with you—for it is ultimately you and this whole way of life that are wrong for me.

"Having been wronged at home, admittedly I got off on the wrong foot. Wronged again, I am told that something is wrong with me, while the real wrong gets off the hook with having apparently done nothing wrong. I believe that's wrong, that it's you and the Navy who are wrong—that military service, or the killing of other human beings, is wrong for me. And I believe, Dr. Wrong, that after you have examined the facts, you will find what's wrong with me is you and this whole goddamn fleet of fools, who keep shoving the wrong way of life down my throat, only to have it thrown back up into your faces because I don't have the stomach for it."

"Why don't you apply for discharge from the Navy as a conscientious objector?" Finally asks the right side of Dr. Wrong.

"I didn't know... Er, I mean... What's a conscientious objector?" Asks the dumb brute in me, after sensing he may have just stumbled upon the biggest find of his life, the much-coveted pearl of great price.

"Huh?" Belches out the dumb brute in its inability to hear the response of Dr. Wrong above the hue and cry of all the feelings that have risen up, like the dead, to seek reunion with their body.

Having been handed a dictionary by the right side of Dr. Wrong, I clawed my way through its pages, like a madman through the last layers of earth that stood between him and the treasure, he had every reason to believe, lay hidden beneath her cloak. As the hairy fingers of Hyde slid up beneath the last article of clothing that stood between him and his prize, the forbidden fruit of paradise, I scanned the page with the piercing eyes of the good Dr. Jekyll, ever in search of the diagnosis that would set him free from the beastly side of his nature. The instant I laid eyes upon the words my fingers had instinctively underscored, I felt the god and beast within me come together, as never before, into one harmonious whole, known only, up until then, as the missing link. For the first time in my life, I knew who I was—that I was not some poor conscientious soul trapped in an objectionable body. I was an amalgam of the two, a conscientious objector, or one who refuses to serve in the armed forces or bear arms on the grounds of moral or religious principles, as defined by Mr. Webster. From out of the pages of the dictionary, was I finally handed this newest born aspect of my Self by my soul—neither of whom I had seen since returning to Hawaii.

"Boy, am I glad to see you two," I said as tears welled up in my eyes. "I was beginning to wonder if I'd ever see you and your mother again, you little squirt."

Sensing he could pry no more out of me than this simple truth, the good Dr. Wrong terminated my second parole hearing with the Navy, and sent me back to purgatory to serve out the rest of my sentence.

"Drury is an immature young man," he wrote, *"who is chronically rebelling against society and who has no insight into his provocativeness. He tends to provoke the environment into retaliating against him, which explains to him, his depression. Of course, his depression has deeper roots than his current problems but his behavior helps him to look on current problems as an explanation for his difficulties rather than to look into himself and his past. At this time, he has little capacity for insight and improvement although any guidance rendered to him by his officers could possibly be of help to him. He has had continued difficulty in the service and it is recommended that he be given a trial of duty and if there is any further difficulty, administrative discharge be considered for reasons of unsuitability."*

So did the judgment, of the powers that be, come crashing down upon me as I raced from the shipyard dispensary, laughing and crying like some madman, to embrace my soul and the first fruits of the womb of my imagination to be corroborated by someone outside myself.

MR. HART: *When did you first learn of the existence of the term "conscientious objector"?*
RESPONDENT: *About the 20th of February.*
MR. HART: *1968?*
RESPONDENT: *Yes, 1968.*
MR. HART: *Had you ever heard the term "conscientious objector" used at any other time during your first year of active duty?*
RESPONDENT: *No, I had not.*
MR. HART: *Did you even know that such a classification existed for those in the military?*
RESPONDENT: *No, I did not.*
MR. HART: *Before this incident, had you ever been informed there was a way in which you could have claimed status as a CO?*
RESPONDENT: *No, I had not.*
MR. HART: *Go ahead then.*

Finally, had I stumbled upon the reason why I wanted out of the Navy so badly—one of its best-kept secrets—that pearl of great price, my own conscientious objection to the killing of other human beings for God and my country. Through these experiences, did I enter, for a second time, our mother's womb to be born again. With that, did I step into the light, that my deeds would be seen as having been done in God.

Only, I still could not say no to the Navy. As the storm clouds of an angry God built up in my imagination, with the release of a bolt of lightning, was I jolted free of the inertia that had me in its grip, and sent reeling from the scullery. With pots and pans flying everywhere, had I whipped through the mess decks like a tornado throwing up everything in its path. Winding down as I hit the compartment, I finally fizzled out on my rack where the coarse and ugly Hyde within me—in harmony with the wishes of the good Dr. Jekyll—flat out refused the orders of my immediate superior and my division officer to go back up to the scullery to clean up my mess. Left alone, like a drunken man, did I exalt in my newly won freedom. No longer was I the monster or its creator but rather a morally free creature, I call the missing link. Having had about enough of their telling me what I was or was not going to do, I had finally got up enough nerve to tell them no.

Having been forced from the quasi-paradise of my home to go on active duty in the Navy, like an egg which had been dropped from the fallopian tubes of Nature, had I collided with one meteoric insight, late last spring. As this new life took shape within the womb of my imagination, over the next nine months, I struggled mightily with this unwanted pregnancy, until it was born of its own accord on 5 January 1968. Like a newborn then, had I thrown my first real fit to get the recognition the conscientious objector in me so badly needed.

About all this Moses received from his Pharaoh was a Captain's mast, the following morning. Hauled before the obstinate Old Weasel, I was charged with two counts of disobeying the lawful order of a superior officer, one count of showing disrespect in language and deportment to a superior officer, and one count of willfully destroying government property. Like a condemned man, did I stand before this Pilate, oblivious to everything but the pounding of horse's hooves in my head. Looking out across the barren reaches of my imagination, I saw a cloud of dust racing towards me. With the approach of this unknown quantum of libidinal energy, I recognized this beast as the white horse of my dreams. As the wind began to howl, I saw three riders—all shouting something the pounding of hooves had drowned out. As the burden of responsibility for my own feelings, thoughts and insights came crashing down upon me, I was sentenced to twenty days of confinement at hard labor in the Naval Station Brig at Pearl Harbor. In unison with the voices of my soul, her protector and my mentor, I yelled out to the Captain, before he disappeared, that I wished to be processed as a conscientious objector. Left standing there in such rarely unified form, did I learn to speak, that day, with the voice of the monk I had encountered earlier in this chapter of my life.

As I stood there, so far above the reach of the law that I remained untouchable, I felt the Old Man's sword tap my shoulder. "I dub thee, Sir Eodor, Knight Exemplar," I heard Him say before I was pulled back down to the banal realities of an earthly existence.

> MR. HART: *Now when was that?*
> RESPONDENT: *That was about the tenth of March.*
> MR. HART: *March of '68?*
> RESPONDENT: *Yes, March of '68.*
> MR. HART: *And this was during the course of a mast?*
> RESPONDENT: *Yes, a Captain's mast.*
> MR. HART: *All right. And at this mast on the tenth of March 1968, was it there that you first made any kind of a formal request of the Captain, that you be processed as a conscientious objector?*
> RESPONDENT: *Yes.*

MR. HART: *What happened after that?*

RESPONDENT: *He looked at me as if I were the very demon he had failed to exorcise from the ship, closed his little black book and walked out without saying a word.*

MR. HART: *And I believe you stated there were others present?*

RESPONDENT: *Yes, there were about a half dozen other members of the crew present, like my division officer and the XO.*

MR. HART: *What happened after that?*

RESPONDENT: *I spoke to the XO, before I was led away, who assured me that he would personally see that my request to declare myself as a conscientious objector would be handled in a timely fashion.*

MR. HART: *All right, go ahead.*

SENIOR MEMBER: *I would like, at this point, to take a short break for lunch, if that's all right with counsel, and afterwards, to pick up with Mr. Drury's testimony where we have left it.*

MR. HART: *Counsel concurs.*

SENIOR MEMBER: *All right then, this board shall recess until 1330 hours, at which time it shall be expected that all here present will have returned to this courtroom.*

Left standing alone with Brook, I asked him how I was doing.

"You are doing fine," he replied, putting his arm around my shoulders as any father would a son in whom he is well pleased.

"Just fine," echoed my spiritual father in heaven as the full weight of Brook's hand came crashing down upon my shoulder.

"How do you think they will judge me?" I asked my Self.

"Does it really matter?" Inquired my spiritual father in heaven.

"I guess not," I said to my Self as I walked through the doors of the courtroom, just as I had some twenty years ago, a free man.

Notes

Chapter Nine

A Real Tour de Force

[1] *"Johnny, I Hardly Knew Ye"* (Trad) Schlamme (voc); Tanya Gould (p). Rec. 1954. Vanguard VRS-9019.

[2] Mark Twain, *The War Prayer*; n.d. (A St. Crispin Press Book published in association with Harper & Row). Please note that the words in regular text are my own.

[3] Ibid. *"Johnny, I Hardly Knew Ye."*

Chapter Ten

Paradise Lost

[1] The poet's words (except for those in regular print) were taken from Bob Dylan's 1965 recording of *"Highway 61 Revisited," Highway 61 Revisited*. Columbia Rec. CK 9189.

[2] The poet's words (except for those in regular print) were taken from Bob Dylan's 1965 recording of *"Maggie's Farm," Bringing It All Back Home*. Columbia Rec. CK 9128.

[3] The italicized words in this paragraph were taken from Bob Dylan's 1965 recording of *"Gates of Eden," Bringing It All Back Home*. Columbia Rec. CK 9128.

[4] Charles Derber, *The Wilding of America: Money, Mayhem, and the New American Dream (4th Ed.)*, Worth Publishers, 2007.

[5] The poet's words were taken from the 1965 recording of *"Bob Dylan's 115th Dream," Bringing It All Back Home*. Columbia Rec. CK 9128.

Chapter Eleven

Paradise Regained

[1] "Bob Dylan's 115th Dream," *Bringing It All Back Home*. 1965 Columbia Rec. CK 9128.
[2] "A Hard Rain's A-gonna Fall," *The Freewheelin' Bob Dylan*. 1962 Columbia Rec. CK 8786.
[3] "Blowin' in the Wind," *The Freewheelin' Bob Dylan*. 1962 Columbia Rec. CK 8786.
[4] Ibid. *"Bob Dylan's 115th Dream."*

Images

Chapter Four
— From *Hecate* by William Blake

Chapter Five
— *The Calling of Samuel* by Joshua Reynolds

Chapter Six
— *Captain Hook and Peter Pan* by F. D. Bedford

Chapter Seven
— *The Coronation of the Virgin* by El Greco

Chapter Eight
— From the *Transfiguration of Christ* by Giovanni Bellini

Chapter Nine
— From *Alice and the White Knight* by Sir John Tenniel

Chapter Ten
— From *Adam and Eve* by Albrecht Durer

Chapter Eleven
— *The Crucified Snake* by Nicolas Flamel

Index

A

abilities, perceptive
  triumvirate of 250
Abraham 209, 227
acceptance
  need for 224
act, striptease 173
actions, own
  consequences
    assuming responsibility
      fear of 215
    become aware of 227
active duty 25, 33
active imagination 112, 122
Adam 157, 211
Adam and Eve
  pain of 4, 254
adrenaline 67, 166
adultery 163
adultress
  collective aspect 199
adversary
  Instinct 220
Adversary, the 123. *See also* Great Magician
Advisory Group 100 187
affair, Sleepy's 226
alive
  feel 80, 258
altar, stone
  handwriting 214
  inscription 209
American dream 61
  absurd claim 231
  glitter and glitz 247
ancestors, animal 150, 210
angel
  guardian 156
  in disguise 175
animal
  cycle of living and dying like 241
  to live like 190, 242
    hurt 221
    right 109
animalistic tendencies
  truths hidden within 232

animals
  bring out humanity of 166
  revert to 164, 252
animal kingdom 187
  belly of 190
animal nature
  dominant side
    dual aspect 195-196
  transformation 209
Ann King, the 27-29
antidote 135, 159, 177
  human blood 210
apology
  inner mother's 142
archaeological dig 236
article. *See* Draftee: Tolstoy's advice
associations
  loosened 78
  rapid 233
at-one-ment 214
Atlantic Monthly
  February issue 254, 259
Aubrey 100, 186
authority 71, 119, 230
  chronic conflicts 11, 261
autoerotism 197
awareness
  fleeting 134

B

baby, booby-trapped 240, 248
bad guy
  the left 154, 228. *See also* left, the
barren desert 66, 190
bathhouse 131
beacon to all 120, 175, 219
beast
  apologetic. *See* Ho Chi Minh
  collective 149
    war 141
  predatory 187, 231
beast, the 77, 120, 165
  defined 140
  indenture to 251
  slaying 116

soul of 233
transformation 58, 197
true nature 239-240
within 131, 167, 200, 224
Beauty 225
beauty, magnificent
   woman of 238
Bechtol 58
behavior modification 55, 106
being
   first fully human 157
   ground of 52, 119, 205
   invincible 214
   unexpressed truths 253
betrothed 198
Big Lie, the 50, 221
Big Sleep, the 33, 148, 170, 254
   defined 233
   to wake up from 213, 247, 257
birth 236
   giving 185, 204
      vision of soul 239
   reason for 191, 210
bitch, the 239
blackest knight of all 216
blackout 27, 32, 50
   emotional 53
black hole 65, 123, 128, 248
   depression 252
blind obedience 63
blood
   spilling 158
      spilling paint vs 200
   sweat 66, 210
   taste of first victim's 187
boatswain's mate, first class. *See* petty officer: first class
body
   instinctive brother 128
   out of 41, 238
   wisdom of 54, 195, 245
body of mankind
   annihilation of 240
   urge to stand out 120
boilerman, third class 131-132, 134-135
born again. *See* full humanity
born from above 147, 263
box, Jinny's 218
bread
   to see Christ in 209, 210
breakdowns, mental
   defined 131
brig

fear of 188, 216
   liberation from 217
first stint 216-224
   honeymoon 224
   Paradise 224
brothers 17
   Little Joe 18, 249
   Scott 1, 18, 25, 221
      fight with 183
brother ass. *See* jackass
brush fire 125
Brute Force 144, 165, 170, 183, 200
Buddha, the 152, 157, 176
bunker, VC 187
BUPERS manual, the
   Article C-10310 93
bush, the 28
   reverting back 79
butcher knife. *See* knife: butcher

C

cabby 150-153, 155
Cain & Able 220, 223
cannon, old Spanish 161
capitalism 154, 252
   sins 61
Captain 51-52, 85, 132, 188
   caricatures
      Hook 259
      Old Weasel 191, 259
      Saul 193, 260
Captain's Mast 11, 85
   fifth 264
   first 91
   fourth 215
   second 117
   third 193
categorical imperative 23
cause worth fighting for, only 258
cave man 52
chain reaction 141
change 26, 111, 193, 232, 252
   fear of 251
   resist 162
chant, the 143, 146
Chao Phraya River 148, 152
Chaplain
   fleet 184
   ship's 72-73
charade 9, 51, 117, 150
   musical 178, 190, 191
cheek, other 166

Chief Sheriff. *See* Neely, Chief
Cheshire cat 192
chicken
  game of. *See* Russian ship
child 106
  foolishly fathered 227
  soul's 185, 235, 242, 262
children
  become like 179, 226
chivalry, Marty's 167
choice 42, 141, 180, 205, 236
  asinine 133
  irreversible 69
  real vs imaginary 211
  right 24, 86
Christ. See also Jesus
  the crucified 183
  the risen 179
  transfiguration 134
circular thinking 62, 114
civil rights 27-28
close encounters 92, 129, 135, 202
  chemically induced 226
  kinds 244
cloud of the unknown 135
clue, single most important 214
coat of arms
  cross of Christ 223
  family 216
cold war, the 22
collective, the
  individual vs 61
  insanity of 98
  worship of 180
collective soul 198
combat
  defined 42
commitment
  soul's demand 104
commodities 172
Communism 54, 61, 154
communist conspiracy 259
companionship 191
conscience 169, 219
  defined 58
conscientious objection 8, 12, 81. *See also* pearl of great price
conscientious objector 9
  defined 262
  request to be processed 264
Consciousness 161, 251
  conception 211-213
  crucifixion. *See* Instinct: death of
  goal 227
  history 213
  seeds of 115, 130, 185
    urge to sow 120
consciousness 179
  creating 133, 158, 202, 211, 221
  energy for 135, 208
  images
    island 7, 76
    light 1, 125
    pure thought 39, 48
    voice 2, 73
  level of 63, 213
  source 212
  spectrum of 148
    visible band 151
  truths that defy 133, 140
consciousness & material world 114
conscious human being
  unconscious animal vs 141, 210, 231
contempt 195, 196, 218
contract, nonbinding 188
control 69, 179, 212, 259
  lack of 75, 119, 206
  losing 141, 155
    fear of 113
  out of 125, 146, 248
corporal on plane 237-247
Corpsman, the 67-68, 73
Council, the 135, 140
Counsel. *See* MR. HART
counsel 37, 132
counselor, high school 1, 19, 32, 84
crack 22, 126. *See also* soul: images
creative daemon
  approach
    heterosexual vs homosexual 196
creative daimon
  fear of 220
creative self 226
Creator, the 210, 221
creature
  morally free 256
    missing link 263. *See also* missing link
  wretched 217, 220
crime
  real vs obvious 9
  unnameable 53
critical mass 141
Cro-Magnon men 115, 226
cross
  family 225
  personal 12, 256

crusades, quixotic 246
cue to misbehave 94
cup that will not pass 66, 210
cyclone 200-201

D

daimon in the rough 200
damnation
  fear of 22
Dantices, the 30
darkness, forces of 7, 141
dark night of soul 90, 95, 114, 232
dark side, the 1
  images
    gray twilit world 132
    human ignorance 8
    Hyde 11, 50, 116, 131, 175. *See also* Hyde
daydream. *See* dreams: type
deadliest game of all 238
dead man, the 183-185
death 170, 238
  defined 225, 245
demiurge
  nature of 195-196
  triune 197, 221
demon
  destruction of 144
  failure to exorcise 194, 264
  protect life of 167, 261
demonize 199
demons
  defined 140, 142
  personal 129, 194
    expose 135, 139
    voices of 232
depression
  depths of 190
  feelings of 12, 262
  Mary's response 208
  tropical 164, 168, 260
deprivation 72, 130
desire 70
  fire of 26, 125
  Nature's 50
  one's every
    to fulfill 116, 169, 187
  truly 135, 245
desires
  heart's
    fire of 214, 224
  Instinct's

    object of 45
  sexual 75, 89, 129
Despair 214
desperation 31, 194
  quiet 18, 155
  soul's 225
devil, the 116
  beat 206
  pact with 188, 238
dialogue 156
diamond in the rough 192
differences 161, 207
  pain of 169
  reason for 219
Dionysus
  wine of 210
direct order 118
  disobeying 70, 103
discharge 5
  endorsed 73
  types 14
    administrative 37
      for conscientious objection 262
      reasons of unsuitability 93, 262
dissociation 38, 52
Dlubec, Ed 27, 29
Dr. Jekyll 131, 200. *See also* persona
  Uncle Sam 178
Dr. Jekyll/Mr. Hyde 22. *See also* Jekyll/Hyde dilemma
  union 262
Dr. Wrong 262
doldrums, the 105, 107, 158
domestication 111
down in the dumps 214
Draftee
  Tolstoy's advice 254
dragon 149, 184, 198
dreams
  become aware of 243
  grandiose materialist 231
  type
    auditory 2
    daydream 52, 84, 125, 149
    fantasy. *See* fantasy
    nightmare 18. *See also* nightmare
    recurring 202
    vision 117, 198, 224, 239, 247
    waking 2-3, 112-115, 122-130
dreamworld 130, 148, 224
dream state 243
dream symbols
  truth hidden within 190

duty
    appointed place of
        failure to appear 190, 215
        leaving 103, 118
    performance of
        derelict 85, 91, 215
        sacred 104
        soldier's 254

E

ecstasy 113, 130, 147, 244
Eden 62
    Gates 230, 235
eggmen 185
ego 161
    alter 145, 158, 183
    images
        me 124, 127, 190, 232
        recalcitrant self 6, 234
        self 45, 114. See also puppet dictator
    will 39, 120, 194
    nothingness of 206
ego control 155
El Cid 161
emotions
    defined 38
enemies
    attitudes 227
    images of
        destroy 144
    imaginary 42, 240
    to forgive 243
enemy
    Consciousness 213
    our own worst 62, 233
    the real 156, 162, 177, 183, 186
enlightenment 146, 157
    fear of 40
evaluations, psychological 11
    first 77-78
    second 260
Eve 157, 211, 238
evil 95, 101
    problem of 227
    solution 206
evildoer
    resist not 166
evils
    greatest of all 199
evil one, the 247. See also Adversary
evolution 199
    emotional 15, 81, 111, 162
    great barrier to 249
evolution-revolution 258
evolutionary link 52. See also missing link
evolve
    challenge to 252, 257
    refusal to 161
exchange, the 163-165
existence
    instinctive 76, 86, 140
    ultimate meaning 210
experience 98, 113, 142, 154, 170
    near death 23, 147
experiences 193, 234, 244. See also close encounters
extinction 154, 220
extraordinary. See ordinary, the
extra duty 119, 193, 199-200
eye
    instinctive 223, 230, 232
    intuitive 251
    neighbor's
        speck in 141, 147
    one's own
        beam in 135, 154, 156
eye for an eye 146, 166. See also hatred: chain of
Ezekiel 128

F

facade 58, 101, 124, 206, 249
faculties
    counsel of 150, 193, 224
    four faces 244
    voices of 178, 190, 202, 204
fall, the 210-211
fantasies 77, 104
    enlightening 213
    giving body to 102
    soul meaning 257
    source 163, 222
    to live out 111, 236
    wisdom within 78
fantasy 7, 53, 61, 66, 124
    fear of 243
    flight of 148, 181, 248
fantasy life 135
Farris 102, 105, 118
fast, the 66-73
fatal attractions 225
Fate 53, 80, 102, 126, 203
    She Who Must Be Obeyed 83
fate 17, 37, 181, 210, 242

father
  ancestral 54
  real 21, 77, 170, 217
  soul's 125, 149, 214, 215
  spiritual 253, 265
Father, the
  live in 233
  see 244
Fat Man, the 143-144, 240
fear 32, 76, 186, 217
  Captain's 259
  reigns of 203
feeling
  sudden swell 133
feelings 118, 244
  affirmation from 114, 157
  getting back in touch with 47, 106, 132, 175, 204, 262
  light of 92
  sexual
    accepting 48
  soul's 45
feelings and emotions
  difference 38
feminine entity 41, 63
feminine side 114, 157, 170
feminine trinity 198, 229
fire that burns between 214
fire that burns within 19, 125, 193, 224
First Division
  transfer out 99
flashbacks 5, 16
flirt 126
folk hero 200
forbidden fruit 262
force
  brute 154, 161, 246
    urge to use 166
  paradoxical nature 147
forgiveness 97
  true meaning 90, 243
Four Horsemen of the Apocalypse 228, 249
Frankenstein 141, 238
fraternal twin
  Magician's 128
fraternizing 118, 192
  decrees 103
free association 229, 234
free love 134
free will 45
friendship
  courtship vs 30, 65
  sex vs 89

frog, red and white 2, 241
fulfillment. *See* self-fulfillment
full humanity 242
full moon 198, 232
  effect 222

G

garden, the 66, 209
gate 123, 175
  narrow 146, 170
    defined 189
    Jinny's box 218
    shadow 144
general quarters 52
genie 233
  God 48
  Great Prostitute 116
  soul 98
Gleason. *See* RECORDER
God
  call 3, 73, 160, 210
  death of 213
  encounters 113, 170, 219
  face 124, 179
  feminine side 114
  first experience 51
  image and likeness 80, 136, 157, 210, 247
god
  female genitalia 109
  take life of 145
gods, the 230, 233, 238, 252
  crime 231
  food of 145
  live like 116, 123, 176
god and beast
  union 262
God and the military 181
god of the left 180
good guy
  the right 154, 228
gook 182
  massive 239
gook tycoon 108
gorgon 174
Gospel quotes
  John 114, 147, 175, 193, 247
  Luke 96, 228
  Mark 179, 252
  Matthew 156, 166, 176, 181, 242
grace
  fall from 4, 181, 223

grail, the 197
greatest obstacle 220
greatest show on earth 246
great abyss
   defined 132
   edge of 45, 77, 226
   to bridge 115
Great Gray Bitch 49, 102
Great Gray Mother 37
great gray whale 201
   USS Davidson 191
   US Navy 33
Great Gray Whore 75, 106, 174
   Navy 86, 187, 203, 228, 256
   soul vs 220
Great Magician 248. *See also* Adversary, the; *See also* Instinct
Great Mother 221
   images
      Mary (Mother of Jesus) 241
      Mother Earth 238
      Mother Nature. *See* Mother Nature
      She Who Must Be Obeyed 234
      Tree of Life. *See* Tree of Life
      Wisdom. *See* Wisdom
   witch 133, 142, 145
Great Necromancer 126. *See also* Great Magician
Great Prostitute. *See* Great Gray Whore
Great Separation. *See* Original Being
Great Soul of Mankind 243
Great Spirit 91. *See also* Holy Spirit
great void, the 107, 242, 248, 260. *See also* void, the
greed 61, 204, 231
Greg 95, 121, 149-153, 171-175, 204
   caricatures
      tortoise 164
      turtle 80
guide supreme
   Instinct 212
guilt 18, 77, 147, 215
   take away sting of 50, 242
gun line, the 53, 178, 187

H

half-breeds 227
happiness, true 54, 180, 235
Harold 86, 95, 121
   caricatures
      caged rabbit 81
      hare 164
   old buck 258
Hart, Brook 8. *See also* MR. HART
hatred
   chain of 90. *See also* eye for an eye
haves and have-nots 61, 229
Hawaii 40
   return to 207, 256
head
   author's
      price on 110
   Captain's 192
   pounding sound 264
   screaming in 47, 48, 53, 77
   voices in 122-124
healing 30, 135, 180
heart 68, 174, 217
   ache inside 41, 48, 104
   door to 115, 123
   lead of 3
   speaking from 69
   thoughts from 38, 63, 75
heartstrings 136
heart of hearts 24, 39, 51, 90, 257
heaven 79, 113, 159, 191
   brig 221
   defined 224, 241
   key to 206
   secrets of 176, 179
heaven's door 89, 254, 218, 245
hell 232
   Davidson 89, 254
   defined 108, 140, 212, 241
   Great Separation 115
   only chance to escape 246
hellhole
   home 29
   Nam 240
hermaphroditic 157
hero, the real 126, 183
heterosexual counterpart 194
Hewhay 149. *See also* mentor
higher power 37, 222
Highest Authority
   call of 144
   rebellion against 204
High Priest
   Captain 215
   LCDR Kihune 117
Holy Spirit, the 158, 233
   blasphemes of 15
   to see 198, 238, 244
Holy Trinity
   dwelling place 113

Index

homosexual factor 196
Homo Erectus 222
Homo Sapiens 201
honeymoon suite 217
host, the
  consecration of 209
house divided 237, 246
Ho Chi Minh 246. *See also* shadow: Uncle Sam's
hut, the 240, 248
Hyde 58, 180, 263. *See also* dark side, the:
  images
    creation of 144
    grunt on the ground 183
    rule of 246
    stepfather 146
    transformation of Jekyll 200
hyperthyroidism, Mary's 64, 160, 208

I

I Am Who Am 114
  images
    being of neither sex 214
    Old Man 3
    unnamed god 215
identity, true 129, 157
ignorance 125
  to pierce darkness of 63, 175
illicit unions
  Asian-Americans born of 227
images 69, 129
  killing real vs imaginary 141
  meaning of
    giving body to 242
  play with 115
  train of 178
imaginable, the
  real hidden within 244
imagination
  accessing (without using drugs) 226
  entrance
    black hole 130, 135
    getting carried away by 114
    illuminating light 129
  images of
    looking-glass world 7
    never-never land 139. *See also* never-never land
    realm of God 4
  lamp of 130, 230, 233
  limits 179, 190
  myths 230

  powers of 243
  reality vs 178
  to stretch 124, 135
immortality
  nature of 134
  perversion of 231
incestuous return 133, 176, 213
individual, the 8, 141, 214
  collective vs 61
  to worship 180
inmost being
  secret of 197
inner world
  trash heap of 214
insanity
  brink of 77
insight 63, 135, 178, 244, 262
instability 12, 78, 261
instant gratification
  need for 115, 137
Instinct. *See also* Great Magician; *See also* Joker, the
  clutches of
    to free soul from 170
  death of 187, 213
  evil reign 212, 233
  fantasies of 163, 212
  loss of trust in 211
  prisoner of 221, 232
  to be driven underground by 235
  to die to 223
instinct 45
  asinine 54, 112, 113
  free truth from 159
  to investigate 232
  tyranny of 39
intercourse
  physical vs spiritual 136
International Brotherhood of Brig Brats 218
intuit
  innate ability to 250
iron curtain 61, 62
Isaiah 111, 176, 217
I That Can See
  defined 223
  inability to accept 224
  setting of 232

J

jackass 54, 189-191. *See also* mule
Jacob 95
James Dean look-alike 194

Jekyll/Hyde dilemma. *See also* mind/body split
   solution 111, 126
Jeremiah 114
Jesus 71, 73, 157. *See also* Christ
   vision of 176
Jinny 149, 156, 180, 207. *See also* soul
Joe. *See* stepfather
   first class PO 101, 186, 192
John Doe. *See* corporal on plane
Joker, the 184, 187, 248. *See also* Instinct
Jonah 33, 140, 190, 200-201, 252
joy
   source 23, 106, 194, 217
judgment 15
Jun 88-89
   Mary's thoughts about 106
Jurassic period 155

K

Kahoolawe 53
kamikaze sampans 96, 158
key, the. *See* Navy: why author wanted out
Kihune, LCDR 117-119, 204, 265
   caricature
      Victorian cat 192
kill 42, 146, 177
   to make legal 259
killing 54, 179, 261. *See also* images: killing real vs imaginary
   intoxication with 145
   Tolstoy's words against 254-256
killing fields, the 155, 237. *See also* Vietnam
King of Hearts 251
knife, butcher 143-147, 183
Knight Exemplar 3, 264
Kraft 108-111, 115

L

Lady Liberty 5, 198
   divorce from Uncle Sam 246
language of the body 38, 116, 150, 162, 195
law
   evolution of 154
   levels 8
   reach of
      to move beyond 119, 259, 264
laws of nature 39, 45, 53, 141, 242
law and order 153, 228
   clarified 228

leap in faith 76, 98
learned response 38
leave 235, 245, 254, 257
left, the 153, 155
   conscience 154
left hand, the 185, 228
letting go 63, 90, 97, 125, 135
libidinal energy
   misuse 141
   quantum of 264
   symbol 189
   truth of 258
lies 123, 129, 186, 213, 259
lies we live by 61, 108
Life 150, 197, 211, 223
life 235
   dead way of 161
   eternal 227, 245
      clarified 248
      to possess 229
      to rob the soul of 241
   everlasting 223
      key to 245
      pursuit of 246
   failure to adjust 12, 21
   gray area 98, 119
   highest requirement 256
   image that acquires own 141
   new way 204
      struggle to give birth to 77
   Olympian way 231
   real 28, 137
   sleepwalk through 213
   take another's 23, 141-147, 179, 187
   triune nature 233
   unsuitable way 113
      whore 76, 104, 160
   wrong way 169, 224, 261
lifers 49-50, 56, 81, 116, 160
light
   blade of 143
   flash 218, 243, 256
   pencil 145, 209
limbo 124, 245, 248
   stuck in 221, 249
lion and the lamb 217, 223
listen
   learn how to 57, 150
literal interpretations 79
Little Joe. *See* brothers
living simple 62
looking glass, the 53, 130, 135, 189, 221
   transparency of 224

loosed on earth 90, 242
Lord, the 3, 176, 189. *See also* Christ
loss of soul 45, 49, 201
   mankind's 199
   Red Knight's 198
love 125, 129, 189, 197
   immature 65
   real 207
   spiritual 59
      physical vs 136
   ultimate act 130, 202
lust. *See* instant gratification: need for
   object of 220, 221

M

madness 180, 217
Magician's mask 18, 124, 127, 133
   examples 142, 245
Magician, the 125, 140, 163. *See also* Instinct
   Ho Chi Minh 126
   shadow of 129
magic lamp 130
man
   free 265
   Jurassic image 155
   lesser
      greater vs 219, 230
      to die to 223
   modern
      death knoll 252
   new species 116, 201, 204
      first born 240
   next great step 246
manhood 18, 49
   robbed of 141
manifest destiny 246
mankind
   future 257
   prehistory 210
   psychological problems 180, 183
marijuana
   use of 80, 101, 122, 234
marine sergeant 216-217
Marty 81, 103-105, 107-111, 161-168, 224
   caricatures
      gallant white steed 258
      old nag 257
      talking horse 164
Mary. *See* O'Daniels, Mary
   mother of Jesus 157-158

mass, the
   meaning of 209
mass hysteria 61, 255
master 91, 189
   mentor 190
   monk 4
masters
   difficulty serving two 86, 181
mate 130
   eyes of
      to look for insight in 251
materialism 62
   meanness of 242
materialistic myopia 210
material progress
   delusion of 61
material things 153, 225
   Uncle Sam's addiction 246
meat
   piece(s) of 71, 158, 172
Mekong Delta 158, 187
memories that haunt 18, 237
mentor 144-148, 156-158, 179-181, 195-197, 224-234. *See also* father: soul's; *See also* old Indian, the
Merwin, LCDR 71, 91-92, 93
mess decks
   stints
      first 56
      second 102
      third 260
   transfer off 66
Michael. *See* white shadow
Michael the Archangel 198, 224, 248
middle, the 116
military service 58
   conspiracy to undermine 259
   soul's objection to 219, 239
   true meaning 255, 261
      to understand 256
mind
   feeling of losing 31, 190
   Navy's affect 56
mind/body split 18. *See also* Jekyll/Hyde dilemma
mind and body
   infinite love for each other 175
mirror 105, 224
   fractured 251
   Ho Chi Minh 128
   image of soul 130, 188, 215
   image of white knight 5
   no reflection 53

missing link 164, 175, 179, 186, 200
  defined 81
  fears 259
  soul as 201
  transformation 258, 262
mission from God 108
MR. HART 9-10, 77, 94, 178, 263-266. *See also* Hart, Brook
Mr. Hyde. *See* Hyde
mistress
  She Who Must Be Obeyed 76
  Wisdom 158
monk within 2, 4-6, 16, 247, 264
morale
  lower 183
  undermining 102, 261
moral acts 255
Moss 44-45, 49, 58
mother
  author's 16-18, 22, 47-48, 86, 249-253
    devouring image 142, 145
mothers
  cry out for 239
  virgin 172
Mother Nature 148-149. *See also* Nature
  alter ego 145
Mt. Olympus 180
  gods of 230
Mouse 108. *See also* Kraft
mule 54-55, 66, 112, 117. *See also* jackass
multitude of voices 128, 150
murder 183
  take part in 255
mutiny 102, 111, 204
myth
  defined 80

N

Nam 40, 238. *See also* Vietnam
Nature
  dark side 140. *See also* dark side
  exquisite beauty 114
  freak of 247
  Wisdom's imprisonment 158, 212
nature
  beastly side. *See also* beast, the
    communicating with 38
    concession 196
    to transform 131
      life one needs 229
    truth hidden within 141, 245
  soul's imprisonment 204

Nature's call 23, 119, 252
Naval Station Brig at Pearl Harbor. *See also* brig
  sentence to 216, 264
Navy
  dislike for 52, 57, 80, 104
  enlistment 25
  how soul helped author get out 215
  saying no to 189
  why author wanted out 12, 73, 263
    the key to 235, 254
Neanderthals 8, 52, 115, 241
Neanderthal friend 162, 200
Neanderthal lives 201
Neanderthal man
  to remove last vestiges 249
need to be heard 57, 251
Neely, Chief 99, 191
never-never land 188, 221
Nichols, Cheri 20-21, 26-27
Nicodemus 4, 147, 213
nightmare 54, 61, 242, 247
nirvana 176, 261
noncooperation 11, 56, 83
nymphs 161, 173, 222

O

O'Daniels, Mary 30
  letters
    addressing leave 208-209
    dissatisfaction with Navy 58
    Dear John 64-65
    fickle friend/jealous lover 106-107
    plea to behave 137-138
    plea to write 210
    regarding ring 159-160
    author's depression 221
oasis 19, 23, 51, 66, 190
old Indian, the 124-125, 128, 132, 134, 193. *See also* mentor
old seer 253. *See* mentor
Old Weasel. *See* Captain: caricatures
Olongapo 169, 171-175
one
  become 63, 194, 211, 228, 254
  three persons in 182, 198
  to be as 188, 247
One Voice, the 143, 146, 180, 202, 230
on report 85, 103, 105, 191, 215
opiate of the masses 153
opposites, the 199, 227
  tyranny of 223

orange peeling incident 84
ordinary, the
   extraordinary within 134, 218
orgasm
   psychological equivalent 194
Original Being 157-158, 160, 201, 238
   feminine side. *See* feminine side
   Great Separation 33, 115, 126
   identification with 170
   identity 214
   image and likeness 194, 210
original language of mankind 180, 234
others
   inability to relate with 20, 30, 39, 48
other within 47
   listening to 243

P

pain 53, 70, 106, 109, 142
   cause 59, 217, 221
   Greg's 80
   incomprehensible causes 240
   Mother Nature's 149
   personal 20, 22, 186, 235
      responsibility for 50
   Sleepy's 101
   soul's 47
   stepfather's 17, 18
   uninvited guest's 226
Pan 160, 226, 243
Pandora's box 30, 218
paradise 108, 197
   despoiling
      crime of 220
   expulsion from 136, 212, 221
   fleeting glimpses 130, 170, 176
   man's perversion of 239
paradise lost 235
parental image
   annihilation 171
passive aggressive 12, 13
passive resistance 23, 119, 191
   failure of 203
Pat. *See* sister, author's
peace 227
   inner 12, 24, 63, 233
peace of mind 54, 105, 130, 171, 200
Pearl Harbor 208
pearl of great price 92, 123, 252
   conscientious objection 262, 263
peer pressure 42, 193
penance, corporal's 242

persona
   Dr. Jekyll 146
   masculine 160
Peter Pan 139, 160, 221, 259
petty officer
   first class 43, 98, 101
phallus
   fallacy 161
Pharisees 257, 261
   submit to principles of 255
pimp
   Kraft 109
   Uncle Sam 161
pit of despair 209
play, imaginative 156
poet, the 228-230, 234, 245, 252-253
poetry in motion 230
point of view
   monk's 16
   objective 194, 196
   soul's 41, 47, 130
polarize 228
possession 102, 126, 133, 200, 248
potential 137
   creative 1, 32, 152, 197, 234
      unity with 195
precipice of utter darkness 1, 256
predator, the 165-166
pregnancy
   unwanted 37, 106, 264
prejudice 197
   to confront 28, 229
prescription, holographic 209, 214
primordial soup 131
Prince of Beasts 171, 218. *See also* Instinct
projections, own
   go to war with 128, 142, 251
Promised Land, the 245, 247, 188
propagate
   urge to
      evolutionary aspect 194
property, government
   destruction of 71, 264
prostitute 50, 75, 172
psyche, collective
   schizophrenic split 180, 228
puberty 21, 69, 146, 171
   age of 4, 141, 244
   onset 18, 126
puppet dictator
   self 126
Pure Thought. *See* soul: guardian
purgatory 245, 241, 262

pyramid 229
  faces of 135, 250
pyramid schemes
  American dream 104
  modern capitalism 154

Q

quarrel
  inclination to 166

R

rage 90, 192, 201
rapture 155
reality 23, 148, 242
  deeper
    doorway to 235
  kaleidoscopic picture 130
  true nature 19, 210
  two sides of 47
  vital link with 236
real and imaginary
  need for others 129
real individuals 219
rebellion
  source 13, 203
rebelliousness
  spread of 110
rebellious spirit 26, 27, 31, 76
rebel without a cause 102
rebel with a cause 116
RECORDER 11, 13, 16, 20, 44
Red Knight 198
red lead
  spilling of 200
red menace 199
Red scare 61
red shadow 259
reflect
  instinct to 112, 114
reflection 53, 102
reign of terror
  Instinct's 212, 234
reincarnation 241
rejection
  fear of 221
relationship 38
  need for 89
  only consistent 64
  sexual 207
remorse 69, 142, 145
reservists 80, 115

resistance 128, 183, 234, 257
RESPONDENT 16, 37, 77, 94, 263-265
reveille 43, 171, 203
revenge
  cycle of 146. *See also* eye for an eye
rich man and the thief 153
rift 22, 228
right, the 153-154, 180
rights 118, 260
right to life
  deny soul 223
  right to choose vs 228
ring, the 151, 159
riverboat 27, 30
roots
  animal 168
  cut off from 225
rowboat 85
  daydream as 84
Rulli 43, 57, 82-83
Russian ship
  game of chicken 82
R & R 116, 176

S

St. Paul 23, 92
St. Peter 23, 28
St. Thomas 76
sanity
  path to 98
Sasebo, Japan 121
  bathhouses 131-132
Saul. *See* Captain: caricatures
scapegoat 18
  images
    author 224
    Scott 25
schizoid personality 12, 77, 78
schizophrenia
  real father's 21-22
schizophrenic 41, 53, 79, 99, 155
Scott. *See* brothers
scullery 260
  refusal to go back up to 263
sea snakes 158
second birth 4-5
Second Coming 177, 252, 257
secret
  dead man's 186
  dirty little 70, 220
  Navy's best kept 263
  Peter Pan's 226

Index

Self 190, 206, 262, 265
   aspects 244
   beating off advances 144
   become mindful 151
   false images 219
   fragmented picture 251
   isle of 217, 235, 238, 245
      return to 215, 234
self. See also ego: images
   die to 178, 210
   forgive 90, 242
   hear Self speak to 243
   play with 86, 114, 190, 193
self-centeredness 137, 180
self-control 136
self-destruction 245
self-esteem 27, 30, 146
self-fulfillment 69, 119
self-knowledge 59, 111
SENIOR MEMBER 8, 20, 44, 78, 265
sensations 135, 244, 251
senses
   insight into 63
   material from 140
   shadow of 225
sentinel. See Uncle Sam: house of
separation
   pain of 21, 30, 257
serpent, the 198, 211
service 3
   human vs military 219
sex
   appetite for 75, 174, 218
   extramarital 49
   need to have 194
sexuality 21, 77, 197, 221
   dark side 171
sexual appeal 225
sexual intercourse
   well-orchestrated ruse 218
sexual orientation 195
shadow 117-118, 139-142, 144-146, 195-197, 206
   angelic aspect 153. See also white shadow
   defined 139
   integrate 140
   stepfather 143, 251
   to no longer cast 113
   Uncle Sam's 128, 178-179
She Who Must Be Obeyed 120
   loosely defined 133, 163, 238
   search for 82

serve 75, 106
   shadow of 76
ship-over spiel, Kraft's 107-109
shipwrecked sailor 53, 64, 235
shortsightedness 100, 219
Shorty 92-93, 100-101
sin
   truth hidden within 261
   unpardonable 18
sinking feeling 28, 123
Siren 77, 95, 99, 169
Sir Eodor 3, 216, 264
sister, author's 17, 18, 25, 30, 249
sixth sense 210
slaughterhouse, Southeast Asian 67, 108. See also war in Vietnam
Sleepy 101, 226
Smyth, Lt. 68-71
snake 176
society
   infect 231
   rebelling against 12, 262
   wilder
      signs of 249
soldiers 184
   playing 241
   refuse to become 254
solitude
   need for 112
Son, the 213, 233, 244
soul 145
   betrayed 105
   companionship 218
   compulsion for 49
   discipline 58
   doctors 13, 261
   encounters with 142, 222, 262
      brig appearance 217
      falling out 187-189
      father's skits 123-130
      form painted 97
      life saved 84
      love revealed 135-136
      vision of Trinity 112-113
   father. See father: soul's
   give body to 241
   guardian of 176
      Pure Thought 132-133
      shadow 225
   images
      childhood playmate 86
      crack 122, 129
      dove 112

feeling 41
lady of the house 2, 5
little girl 19, 84
Mary 42, 203
mother 49
rebellious spirit 26
Spirit 129
sprite 85, 99
the way 97
unknown woman 53
woman screaming 46
insult to 187
love of 215
  need for 206
lust for 123, 135
pregnant 185
screams 77, 95
separation from 107
to reconcile creative daimon with 221
transgressions of 15
triune nature 198, 229
union with 253
  fear of 157
  lost opportunity 190
unsuitable projection 203
warnings 51, 79, 96, 181
way of 50, 163, 245
wedding 215
speaking up
  fear of 69, 117
spell 147
  enchantress' 174
  instinct's 76
  Magician's 127
  myth's 135
  witch's 133
spirit 103
  in the form of 4, 176
    leave the body 213, 238
  love/hate relationship 59
  to beat off advances of 28, 133
spirits of alcohol 48, 116
stand tall 51, 86, 117
  urge to 120
stepfather 16, 78, 128, 142
  further deterioration 250
  help finding work 27, 31
  inability of 20, 48
  letter from 24
  ogre within 229
  old Saul 193
  shadow of 259
  terrible image of 186

strike
  First Division 203-204
strike a chord 41, 115, 124, 138
Subic Bay 177, 202
suffering
  learn obedience 39, 194
  source of 37, 92 177, 186
survival of the fittest 238
survive
  instinct to 145, 166, 232, 241
  reality soul needs 235, 236
sword 144
  double-edged 149
  handle of 143
  meaning 145
  Michael's 153, 198
  Old Man's 3, 264
  pen 4
symbolic perception 210

T

T. Rex 154-155
talking horse. *See* Marty: caricatures
tears 175
  to wash clean with 142, 239
  welled up 106, 127, 142, 237, 262
teeth
  gold 17
  wail and gnash 179, 246
temple, Buddhist 151
tension 59
  buildup 22, 50
  to create consciousness 133, 221
  to create new life 131, 158, 177, 221
terror 255, 256
Theory of Relativity 19
thieves, two 179
thinking vs feeling 63
thorn in side 19, 92, 141, 193, 257
thoughts 244
  give flesh to 214
  immortal 233
  meaningless 39
thought form 139, 142
threshold of consciousness
  images. *See also* precipice of utter darkness
    barrier 23, 79, 80, 123, 198
    Berlin Wall 22
    birth canal 147
    edge of the Great Abyss 132, 226
    mirror 53. *See also* mirror
    semipermeable wall 131

Index

thundershower 90, 237
titans 180
Tokyo 87-89
Tolstoy, Leo. *See* Draftee: Tolstoy's advice
tongues
   speak in 180
torpedo
   incident around 84-86, 91-92, 96
tough
   neighborhood 18, 183
   Philippine 172
treasure chest 217
Treasure Island 33, 40-41
Tree of Knowledge 223
Tree of Life 223
   daughter 198-199
trial by fire 125, 128, 131-132
trick, Instinct's 213
Trickster, the. *See* Adversary, the
true calling 202, 217
truth
   birth of 106, 147
   body's passion 202, 223
   fear of 13, 47, 96, 105
   flow
      refuse to go with 250
   force of 71, 147, 161
   ghost 257
   give body to 225
   insatiable appetite 154, 231, 252
   nature of 134
   persecution 213
   point of 38, 135
   right to spread 260
   search for 233, 245
   shadow of 147
tunnel of vision 152, 170, 224
   defined 134
twilight zone 105, 112, 122, 143, 174
Typhon 200
tyrant
   instinctive 245
   stepfather 17, 251

U

Uncle Sam 127, 161, 198
   darker side 246
   house of
      sentinel for 201, 205
unconscious
   symbols
      irrational side 38

netherworld 23
underworld 120
unthinkable side 123
underground resistance 42, 54, 102, 120
unity 197, 212
   all-encompassing 113
untouchable 259, 264
USS Davidson 4, 40, 191
   first morning aboard 42-46
US Naval Academy 23-25, 78
   appointment 21
   daydream 57
   release 25

V

Van Slagle, Elrie 38, 40-41, 57, 168
veil of matter 62. *See also* wall of illusion
Vietnam 54
   coast 95, 96, 158
Viet Cong 187, 239
violence 255
   cycle of 144
   Uncle Sam's outbursts 246
Virgin Mary 198. *See also* Mary: mother of Jesus
vision for all 219
vision of others 217
vision quest 197, 206
voice. *See also* consciousness: images
   one 128, 138. *See also* One Voice, the
voices. *See* demons: personal. *See* faculties. *See* head. *See* multitude of voices
void, the 52, 139, 151, 201, 242. *See also* great void, the
vows, solemn 188

W

wakefulness and sleep
   place between 193, 243. *See also* twilight zone
walk on water 86, 97
wall of illusion 124, 221. *See also* veil of matter
war 182
   cause 141-142, 228, 251
   personal vs transpersonal 140
   the real 61, 62, 177
   within 41
war games 52, 82
war in Vietnam
   disaffection 98, 116, 170, 186

resistance to 11, 12, 103, 131
War Prayer, The 184
wave, the 121, 138, 234
way, the 65, 76, 188
   find 63, 158
   images that light 140
way of life 109
   evil
      insidiously 232
      necessary 61
   illusory 124
   inimical 191
West Pac cruise 53, 108, 169
whale
   belly of 121
whale of an idea 201
whale of a plot 259
whale of a problem 245
When Johnny Comes Marching Home 181
white glove inspection 191-193
white horse 2-3, 189, 264
White Knight 205-207, 215, 233, 257-260
   soul's love for 206
white knight 75, 116-117, 253
   fear of 3
   meaning 76
   religious oppression of 193
white lie 54, 61, 108
white shadow. *See also* shadow
   Michael 149, 156-157, 185-186, 215
whore. *See also* life: unsuitable way
   the one 108
   war 127
whorehouse, biggest little 160, 172
whores, Thai 149
Who He Really Is
   to live out 249
   wake up to 247, 256
Who I Really Am
   commune with 151
   stumble upon 252
   to become 205
Who We Really Are
   failure to live out 241, 245
   where Instinct holds prisoner 232
wife, lawfully wedded 215, 225
wilding
   epidemic 231
wild side 164, 195
will, God's 66, 210
wind, the 96, 170, 211, 264
wine, the
   transformed 210

Wisdom 114
   abuse of 238
   incarnation 158
   treasure trove 205
   triumph 199
   union with 134
   who must be obeyed 156
wisdom
   conventional 221, 230
   defined 114
   intuitive 193
   true 156, 168
wishes, three 233
witch, the. *See* Great Mother: images
wolf 166-167
   great gray 142, 145
   white 233-234
wolfman 232
wolf-man-god 233
woman, voluptuous 163, 173
womb
   Consciousness' return 213
   desire to penetrate 209
   mother's 188
      enter a second time 263
womb of imagination
   first fruits 263
   to penetrate
      time of strongest urgings 222
Word, the
   His nemesis 150
   in the flesh 214
word of God 69-70, 163, 172
work of art
   birth 185, 241
world
   Instinct's destruction of 241
   Pan's
      to penetrate 226
   real 249
world order, old
   demons of 193
wound that never heals 17, 39, 127, 146, 228-239
wraiths 60
Wraiths of the State 123, 125
wrong 256
   the real 261
Wulf, Signalman 60-64

X

XO. *See* Kihune, LCDR *See* Merwin, LCDR

Index

Y

Yankee Station 96
Yokosuka, Japan 86-87
  psychic storm 90

Z

zoo 109
  escape 164

www.ingramcontent.com/pod-product-compliance
Lightning Source LLC
Chambersburg PA
CBHW081210230426
43666CB00015B/2701